May, 1984

Dear Mike -
        Special fond wishes come
to you on your birthday.
                Much Love
                Mother

THE ITALIANS

Texts by

KARL CHRIST

BRYAN WARD-PERKINS

J. R. HALE

ERIC COCHRANE

FRANCIS HASKELL

FRANCO ANDREUCCI

THE ITALIANS

HISTORY, ART,
AND THE GENIUS OF
A PEOPLE

EDITED BY
JOHN JULIUS NORWICH

HARRY N. ABRAMS, INC., PUBLISHERS,
NEW YORK

*Editor and publisher wish to acknowledge the generous advice given by all the authors
on the selection of the illustrations and the wording of the captions; it must
be made clear, however, that final responsibility for the picture
sections remains entirely with the publisher.*

Endpapers: Mosaic pavement from St Mark's, Venice.
15th century

Library of Congress Cataloging in Publication Data
Main entry under title:

The Italians.

  Bibliography: p.
  Includes index.
  Contents: Rome and the empire, prehistory to AD 500 /
Karl Christ—The medieval centuries, 500–1300 /
Bryan Ward-Perkins—Humanism and Renaissance,
1300–1527 / John Hale—[etc.]
  1. Italy—Civilization—Addresses, essays, lectures.
I. Norwich, John Julius, 1929–
DG441.I86   1983   945   83–2490
ISBN 0–8109–1108–6

© 1983 Thames and Hudson Limited, London

Filmset in Great Britain by Keyspools Ltd, Golborne, Lancs.
Monochrome origination in Great Britain by D.S. Colour International Ltd, London
Color origination in Switzerland by Cliché Lux, SA, La Chaux-de-Fonds
Text and illustrations printed in the Netherlands by Royal Smeets Offset, Weert
Bound in the Netherlands by Van Rijmenam, B.V., The Hague

CONTENTS

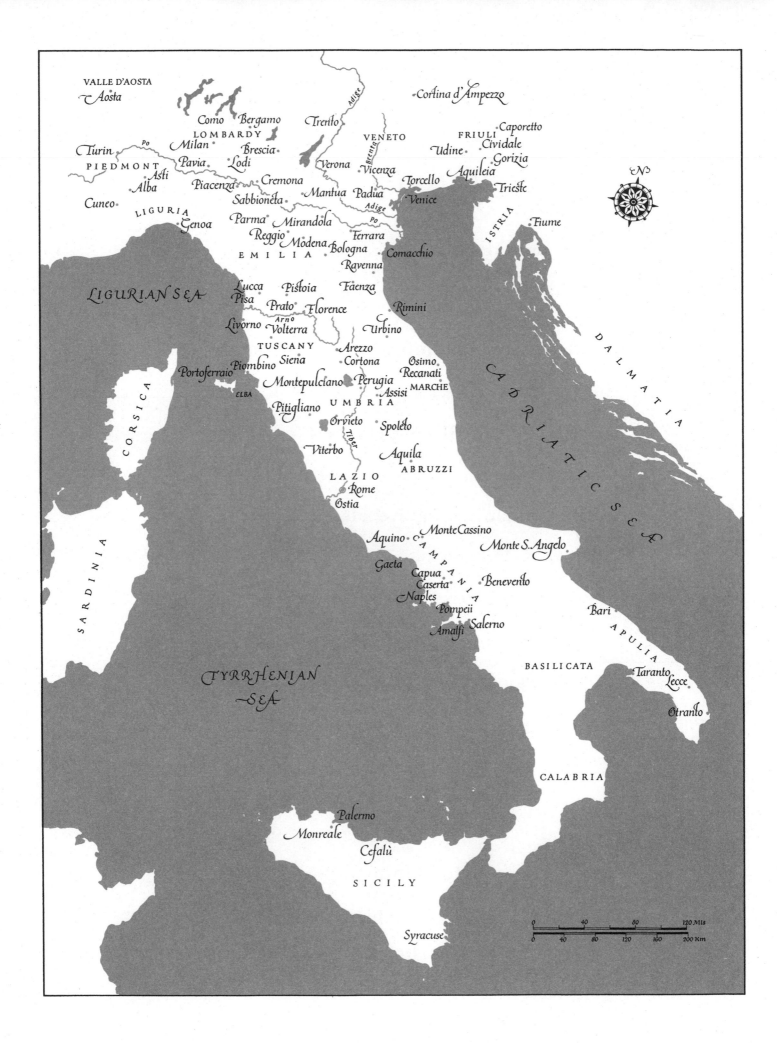

INTRODUCTION

A TRAVELLER
IN ITALY

THERE ARE TWO ITALYS – the one that Italians themselves live in and the one that foreigners see. Both are made up of the same elements, but seen from different angles they can seem almost two different countries. In the succeeding chapters of this book the viewpoint will be consistently Italian, presenting the history and people of Italy in their own terms and through their own works. In this opening section we approach them from outside and ask: what draws people from all over the world to Italy? What do they go to see? What *do* they see?

From the Renaissance to the 18th century foreigners went to Italy primarily for the sake of its classical remains. This was natural enough at a time when education was itself primarily classical, when Roman history was more familiar to most European gentlemen than the history of their own country and when surviving Roman buildings were the models for architects from Russia to America. From the mid-18th century and throughout the 19th this classical interest remained paramount, but visitors also expected to study and admire the splendours of Renaissance art and to learn something of Italian literature and music. In the 20th century that interest has expanded: today's tourist is ready to appreciate everthing from the Roman Forum to Milan Railway Station.

But while dutifully absorbing the artistic achievements of Italy, the Northern visitor increasingly found himself succumbing to another charm – that of the Italian way of life itself. Here he found many of the qualities that captivated him in Italian culture – an apparently innate sense of style; a warmth of emotion spilling over from the family circle and expressed directly and without inhibition; an instinct for display, for the large gesture in life as in art; and underneath it all, the feeling of a community rooted in the past with intense local loyalties. All these go to form a picture of Italy which perhaps only the outsider can see, but which is nevertheless as real as that offered by the historian, the economist and the social scientist.

The first sight of Italy
to greet travellers on the express rushing out of the Simplon tunnel is the sun-lit lakes and plains of Lombardy: this 1906 Italian railway poster advertising holidays on Lake Maggiore captures the thrill of arrival and expectation of delight that have been experienced by visitors to Italy for centuries. (1)

AL LAGO MAGGIORE

PARIS–MILAN

SIMPLON

ORARIO 15 MARZO 1906.

STAZIONI	CORSE	STAZIONI	CORSE

SERVIZIO DI RISTORANTE A BORDO

Cultural pilgrims

Italy's unique importance lies in the fact that at two
crucial periods it determined the character of Western
civilization: at the time of the Roman Empire and at the
Renaissance. Every European and North American
knows, therefore, that in going to Italy he is going to a
major source of his own culture.

From the cold north painters, poets and connoisseurs have
flocked to Italy to learn and to be nourished. *Above*: a self-
portrait of the Flemish artist Maerten van Heemskerck, who
also shows himself sketching the Colosseum in the
background, 1553. *Above right*: Goethe, whose Italian
journey of 1786–88 had a decisive influence on his mind,
and through him on subsequent German literature. *Below*: a
detail from Zoffany's great collective portrait of 18th-
century English *cognoscenti* at the Uffizi in Florence, here
admiring two antique statues. *Right*: Danish artists in a café
in Rome, 1837; the sculptor Thorwaldsen is on the extreme
right. (2–5)

The tourist, once a member of an educated élite (*above*: the American Mrs William Page, wife of the artist, in 1868) may now belong to any class or background. *Below*: today's crowds in the Uffizi – are they drawn by love of art or only by the desire to see what is world famous? (6, 7)

Triumphant pageantry

The Italian genius for spectacle and display is reflected in the tradition of the triumph – originally a public parade celebrating a successful soldier or statesman. The motif of the triumph has also been adapted to express other ideas, from moral allegory to commercial prestige.

A Roman spectacle: the consul, Junius Bassus, at the circus. Behind his chariot are bare-back riders wearing the colours of the circus factions, the blues and the greens. This picture in coloured marble was executed between AD 330 and 350 for Junius Bassus' basilica in Rome. (9)

The triumph of love: this Florentine *desco da parto* (a dish presented to a woman who had given birth) is one of a series illustrating poems by Petrarch. Cupid is carried forward in victory, surrounded by examples of sensuality conquering the intellect: Samson lies with his head in Delilah's lap and Aristotle carries the prostitute Phyllis on his back. (8)

The triumph of the church: Pius VIII (pope 1829–30) is carried in a procession which acts as a celebration of the spiritual might of the church and a reminder of its wealth and secular influence. (10)

The triumph of Caesar: Mantegna's famous series of nine canvases was painted between 1486 and 1492 for the Gonzaga court at Mantua, and is now at Hampton Court. It played an important part in the festivities celebrating the ruling family: in 1501 it formed the backdrop to a theatrical spectacle. This section, the climax of the series, shows Caesar himself holding the palm of victory and being crowned with a laurel wreath. (11)

The triumph of industry: an advertisement for Fiat equates trucks carrying troops (to Abyssinia?) with the march of ancient Roman soldiers. (12)

Images of woman

Women have never been ignored in Italy, but they have been obliged to conform to a limited number of male stereotypes: the pure virgin, the desired mistress, the beloved mother – all in a sense objects of devotion but none free to be themselves.

Art has crystallized many of these attitudes by producing images that haunt the memory. *Right*: Cossa's Renaissance personification of Autumn and (*far right*) a Tuscan vineyard worker at the end of the last century. (13, 14)

Where does artifice end and truth begin? *Above*: first, the classic prototype of a woman carrying a basket on her head, from a cassone by Pesellino; then a real woman, but carefully posed in a photographer's studio, *c.* 1900; finally a real woman and real life – laden with shopping while the men stand by doing nothing. (15–17)

Woman created by clothes (*right*), in 15th-century Milan and 20th-century Rome. Both pictures, incidentally, tell us something about the Italian gift for that indefinable quality, style. (18, 19)

Talent was and is the great liberator.
Left: Eleonora Duse, the great tragic
actress of the years around 1900.
Above: Oriana Fallaci, whose post-war
writings have carried political
journalism to a new level; her
interviews with powerful world
leaders are as startling for their
fearlessness as for their probing
intelligence. (20, 21)

Economic freedom came when
women could earn their own living
(*above*). Now the fight is for freedom
involving moral responsibility, such as
abortion (*right*): even the overalls
symbolize rejection of the male-
dominated image. (22, 23)

15

City and symbol

The Italian's devotion to his native place finds expression in a whole range of colourful local festivals which both mark important anniversaries in the life of the community and provide an excuse for an exuberant holiday. The traditions behind them often go further back than history can trace.

Siena has for centuries held festivals in the Campo, the semi-circular main piazza of the city. The twice-yearly horse race, the *Palio*, is the most famous, but it was by no means unique. In this painting of *c.* 1600 bull- and bear-baiting are being watched by an appreciative audience; also in evidence are several fearsome 'dragons' worked by teams of men hidden inside them. (24)

Rome's festivals were more cosmopolitan than parochial, but the strange practice of flooding the Piazza Navona in the 18th century is an exception. The only reason for it seems to have been the pleasure of driving through the water in one's carriage. (25)

Gubbio's Festa dei Ceri (Feast of Candles) is a race between three guilds to carry 'candles' – large wooden structures bearing a saint's statue – up to the hill-top church of the city's patron, S. Ubaldo. Held every 15 May, it may have begun as a pagan spring festival. (26)

The dynastic theme

The Italian family unit has been (and to some extent still is) the basis of political as well as social life, creating hidden networks of power, influence – and violent rivalry.

In ancient Rome the cult of the family included reverence for ancestors. In this statue of about the time of Christ a patrician walks in a funerary procession carrying two busts from his domestic shrine. (27)

The princes and popes of Renaissance Italy commissioned numerous works to celebrate their dynasties. In a detail (*below left*) from Mantegna's frescoes in the Camera degli Sposi, Mantua, completed in 1474, Ludovico Gonzaga greets his son, Cardinal Francesco, watched by three of his grandchildren. Mantegna's festive warmth contrasts sharply with Titian's cold analysis in his portrait of Paul III with his grandsons Alexander and Ottavio Farnese (1546). (28, 29)

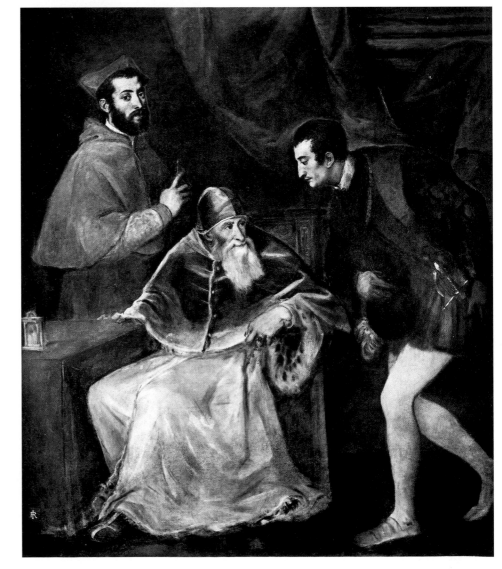

Even after death family loyalties are kept alive by elaborate tombs: this sculpture of 1872 in a Genoese cemetery shows the Raggio family gathered around a death bed. The 19th-century cults of death and of the family are combined in a scene of operatic pathos. (30)

A modern family, in their grocery shop on the outskirts of Rome, resembles families in the Italian communities of many foreign cities – New York and London for instance. Wherever they have emigrated, the Italians have, by maintaining their family loyalties, preserved their national character. (31)

Water – the essential luxury

Italy is a hot and a dry land, but in the mountains a plentiful water supply is never far away. From Roman times onwards it has been a prominent aspect of community life and relaxation; in fountains and gardens it becomes an opportunity for the national love of festive display.

With its line of sparkling cascades and gleaming pools hung like pearls on a necklace, the great watercourse in the gardens of the Villa Medici at Pratolino, laid out in 1569 for the grand duke of Tuscany, Francesco I, demonstrates how the designer of Renaissance gardens used water to spectacular effect. Pratolino was only one of a number of such amazing creations. Alas, it was redesigned during the vogue for landscape gardens and the watercourse destroyed. (32)

The world's most famous fountain, the Fontana di Trevi in Rome, fills a tiny square with a theatrical display of water and sculpture. Designed by Niccolò Salvi it was built in 1732–62 on the orders of Clement XII; the water is carried from springs at Salone, 14 miles away, by a Roman aqueduct. The central figure of Neptune driving his chariot is by Pietro Bracci. (34)

The bath had been one of the centres of Roman social life and some of its features survived into medieval times in the form of medicinal spas. This 13th-century miniature of the baths at Baia, near Naples, is from a poem in their praise dedicated to Frederick II, who had visited them for a cure. (33)

Hand signals

Italians have evolved a flamboyant language of gesture – to such a point that they seem able to convey virtually any shade of meaning without words. Many of these gestures are strongly ritualized and were embodied in the commedia dell'arte and the conventional poses of the theatre. But all attempts to compile a 'dictionary' of gesture have failed because so much depends on spontaneity and individual expression.

A musical point: producer Franco Zeffirelli (*below*) expounds his ideas to the singer Geraint Evans. In the larger-than-life world of opera such movements are an essential part of the performer's technique, but they are no more than exaggerated versions of ordinary mannerisms. (35–37)

Plenty to say . . . nothing to say: two Neapolitan studies (*right*), the man earnestly enlisting interest, the woman almost contemptuously rejecting it. In both it is the combination of hand-gesture and eye-contact that makes the effect. (40, 41)

Fascist, Communist: the two wings of Italian politics, expressively symbolized in Arturo Michelini, of the Italian Social Movement, and Enrico Berlinguer, secretary of the Communist Party. (38, 39)

Grief and joy: the priest is at Balvano, a Southern Italian village devastated by earthquake. The farmer has just discovered an exceptionally large white truffle. (42, 43)

Introduction: A Traveller in Italy

JOHN JULIUS NORWICH

MY FIRST INTRODUCTION to Italy was not of the best. It was in 1937; I was seven years old and had been taken off to Sestriere by my mother on my first skiing holiday. Early on a bitter January morning our sleeping-car pulled into the railway station of Turin and I read – or tried to read – my first Italian sentence, inscribed in huge stark letters on the wall: MUSSOLINI HA SEMPRE RAGIONE ('Mussolini is always right'). Of the four words, I could understand only the first; I had heard my parents talk of him and he was the subject of a hilarious imitation by one of the older boys at school. My mother translated the rest, adding a few characteristically trenchant remarks on the iniquity, and more particularly the idiocy, of Fascism. She pointed out, furthermore, that the pope also claimed to be always right and that, since he and the *Duce* were frequently – if discreetly – at loggerheads, one of them at least must be wrong. I pondered this syllogism all the way to the hotel but came, so far as I remember, to no significant conclusion.

It was a decade before I saw Italy again. Conditions could hardly have been more different. The month was August, our destination a small cypress-fringed hotel at S. Vigilio on the shores of Lake Garda, which my parents had discovered in 1926 and to which they had returned every year until the war. We drove among vines and olives, through walled towns more beautiful than any I had ever seen, threading our way at sunset through many an evening *passeggiata*, when everyone comes out to walk, to see and to be seen, and, in the outskirts, through clouds of bicycles pedalled by laughing boys, their girl-friends side-saddle on the crossbar. It was dark when we arrived at the hotel. We had dinner – of fish straight out of the lake – outdoors on the terrace, with the old house's tiny chapel opposite us and the unseen water lapping at the walls beneath our feet. Then we slept, on those rock-hard Italian beds of

Tutta l'Italia. A postcard stall in Palermo is a panorama of the most popular themes in Italian life – demonstrating, incidentally, that they spring from the Italians themselves and are not just part of the foreigner's projected image. There are babies, pop-stars, sunsets, scenery, religion, young love, flowers, racing-cars, footballs, art, motherhood . . . Sentimental and superficial, perhaps; but these are just the features on which a serious analysis of contemporary Italy would have to be based.

the kind I have since come to know so well, and I woke up in the morning to find my room flooded with red-gold light reflected off the sail of a fishing-boat that was just slipping into the minute harbour outside my window. In those days there were no hordes of tourists – half the hotel's dozen rooms were empty – no speed-boats, no water-skiers: 'no sound', as my mother subsequently wrote to a friend, 'but the sound of peace, and a girl rinsing her hair'.

It was that summer, too, that I discovered Venice; staying there, on that first occasion, only for the inside of a day but falling in love with the city on the spot – a thrill I still feel, with the same exquisite sharpness, every time I return. I have described elsewhere how my father, who loved it almost as much as I do, walked me through the length and breadth of it on foot – the only way that any city can be properly appreciated – talking as we went not so much of its architecture (which I could see for myself) but of its origins and its history, its traditions and its institutions, all of which set it apart from the rest of Italy – and indeed Europe – just as decisively as did the waters of its lagoon. He taught me, too, the other sublime truth about Venice: that the whole is even greater than the sum of the parts and that, however brilliant the basilica or sumptuous the *palazzi*, however opulent the churches or dazzling the pictures, it is the city itself that constitutes the greatest miracle of all.

Later, we headed south into Tuscany, stopping for a few days in Siena – another *coup de foudre* – where, on a memorable blazing afternoon, from a high window above a restaurant, we watched the *Palio*. To this day it is the only horse-race I have ever witnessed, and I am content that it should remain so: any other would be an anti-climax. And yet, strangely enough, my clearest memory from those days in Siena is of something else: it was there, for the first time in my seventeen years (for I was an unprecocious child), standing in front of Simone Martini's glorious fresco of Guidoriccio da Fogliano on his way to battle, that Italian painting suddenly came to life.

Florence followed – and was, frankly, a disappointment. Perhaps I had expected too much; perhaps I had cultural indigestion, which would not have been surprising; perhaps, too, the weather had something to do with it, for the radiant summer was gone and I saw the city through a grey drizzle. Sadly, and despite frequent return visits, that first impression has never entirely left me. I have tried, again and again, to love Florence. I have seen it in all weathers and at all times of the year. I love much that it contains – how could one not be moved by Benozzo Gozzoli's frescoes in the chapel of Palazzo Medici-Riccardi, or by the sheer joyfulness of Fra Angelico at S. Marco? – yet I cannot love the city itself, which has always struck me as somehow grim and austere and strangely devoid of sparkle. It seems ungrateful, I know: the debt that I owe, that we all owe, to Florence is one that can never be computed, far less repaid. But there is nothing to be done. The fault is entirely mine; mine, too, is the loss.

Such was my first real experience of Italy. It was not, the reader will agree, in any way a remarkable one. Nor was it at all comprehensive. I was not to see Rome for another ten years; Naples, the *Mezzogiorno* and Sicily for even longer. By this time I had joined the Foreign Service; my duties – and, it must be admitted, my inclinations – took me elsewhere. But the seeds had been sown. In the early 1960s my life turned in a new direction, towards Italy; and over the last twenty years I have written four books about it, while contributing to several more. The rewards have been great.

My task as General Editor of this volume has not been an easy one, since I am – if anything – a historian, and this work is concerned not with the history of Italy but with her civilization: her art and architecture, her literature and music, her philosophy and ideas. In the early stages of planning, the publishers and I considered several different ways of tackling the subject, and it was only after first trying and then rejecting every other method that we finally decided on a straightforward chronological approach. Even this leaves many problems unsolved, since, as more than one of our contributors points out, the intellectual and artistic development of a people does not lend itself to tidy divisions into periods – least of all when that people is as talented, and at the same time as heterogeneous, as the Italians. Thus, although 1350 may be notionally as good a date as any other for the dawn of the Renaissance, the latter's true beginnings must be sought with Dante and Giotto – both of whom had by then been for several years in their graves – or even before. And this, it should be emphasized, holds good only for Florence. Venice, for example, which was always oddly unadventurous in cultural matters, was to resist Renaissance ideas for the best part of another century: the earliest surviving manifestation of them is probably Andrea del Castagno's decoration of the apex of the Chapel of S. Tarasio in S. Zaccaria, which dates from 1442, and is anyway the work of a Florentine. Architecturally we have to wait another eighteen years, until Antonio Gambello completed, in 1460, the main front of the Arsenal.

Moreover, the Renaissance itself was an essentially North Italian phenomenon, never spreading significantly beyond Rome. In the South and in Sicily, where artistic and intellectual influences, coming principally, as they did, from outside – Byzantine, Arab, Lombard, Norman, German, Angevin, Spanish – were utterly dissimilar and far more varied, there is quite another story to tell. Dealing as we are with Italy as a whole, we are thus faced with a cultural pattern of formidable complexity. Had we attempted to reflect this in the planning of our survey, the reader would have become inextricably lost in the labyrinth. We have therefore concluded, with some relief, that the simplest method of approach is also, for all its shortcomings, the best.

The more one reflects upon this complexity, and particularly when one considers also the nightmare quality of much of Italian history, the more miraculous it appears that Italy should have developed any unified civilization at all, let alone two of the most remarkable ever seen in the Western world. That history was, for well over a thousand years, a relentless succession of foreign invasions and foreign dominations, punctuated by seemingly endless – if ultimately inconclusive – bouts of internecine warfare. Goths and Huns, Greeks and Lombards, Frenchmen and Germans, Normans and Spaniards, even Arabs and Turks, all at one time or another swept across Italy's frontiers or landed along her coasts, fighting not only Italians but each other as well. And when there were no foreigners to fight, Guelf could march against Ghibelline, Verona against Venice, Florence against Milan. For most of that millennium *Italianità* was nevertheless a watchword, and a unified Italy a perennial dream; and yet, as late as 1849, Metternich could still write: '*Italien ist ein geographischer Begriff*' – 'Italy is a geographical expression'.

But unity came at last, within the memory of the grandfathers – and even the occasional father – of Italians still alive today; and now, not much more than a century later, there is little to suggest to the superficial eye that it was not always a reality. You do not, however, have to live in Italy very long to see just how decentralized the country still is: not so much politically – there are, for example, except in Sicily, no regional parliaments – but socially and culturally. The Italians have no national daily newspaper. Only to politicians is Rome the capital; the average cultivated and well-to-do Milanese, Venetian, Florentine or Palermitan sees no reason to forsake his home city for the dubious delights of the so-called metropolis. His house – it may even be a family palace – is probably just as grand and sophisticated as those of his Roman counterparts; his opera house is larger, better or more beautiful; his social life a little more restricted, perhaps, but still anything but provincial. He is happy where he is and knows that that is where he belongs. A greater contrast with English attitudes – still less with French – could scarcely be imagined.

And yet, however fierce his loyalty to his native city – or town, for what is true of the great cities might apply equally well to Mantua or Modena, Lucca or Verona –

he also feels deeply and devoutly Italian; and it is pertinent to inquire in just what this Italianness consists. The oldest bond, and therefore perhaps the strongest, is, I would suggest, the consciousness of former greatness, of being heir to ancient Rome. Attempts to revive that greatness, whether by Cola di Rienzo in the 14th century or by Benito Mussolini in the 20th, have always – not surprisingly – proved unsuccessful; yet the glorious memory remains, quickened by the baths and aqueducts, the temples and triumphal arches that the Romans left behind them: a source both of pride in the past, and hope and encouragement for the future.

And then there is the language – among the most beautiful ever created by man, polished and perfected by one of the sublime poets of the world, Dante Alighieri. In a way, perhaps, Dante was almost too great. Not only did he impose his native Tuscan upon Italy, making it thenceforth the literary language of the entire peninsula; he also gave it an extraordinary permanence, rendering it almost impervious to morphological change. The French of the *Roman de la Rose* (dating, for the most part, from some ten years before the *Divina Commedia*) or the English of the *Canterbury Tales* (begun some sixty years after it) are full of problems and pitfalls for the untutored reader; Dante's Italian, by comparison, might have been written yesterday. This makes him accessible to his present-day compatriots in a way that Jean de Meung and Chaucer can never be to theirs; and his tremendous poem, still after six and a half centuries the supreme work of Italian literature, remains – after the legacy of ancient Rome – the grandest single element in the Italian heritage.

Italy, however, like all countries, means to its native sons something very different to what it represents to outsiders. The inhabitants of Northern Europe have been willingly or unwillingly attracted to it for at least two thousand years; but the reasons for that attraction have varied. In the days of the Roman Empire men made the long and perilous journey simply because they knew that at the end of it they would reach the hub of the universe – where, with courage, hard work and a modicum of good fortune, their highest ambitions might be achieved. In the Middle Ages they came more humbly, as pilgrims, for Rome was, after Jerusalem, the most sacred shrine in all Christendom. Many of them, indeed, having prostrated themselves in St Peter's, travelled on to the Holy Land – normally by way of Bari or Brindisi, a route which enabled them to pause also at the peninsula's second holiest place: Monte S. Angelo in Apulia where, in 493, in a cave sunk deep into the mountainside, the Archangel Michael had appeared to a local herdsman. (It was, incidentally, in this cave in 1016 that a number of Norman pilgrims were invited, with as many of their compatriots as they could muster, to help liberate South Italy from the Byzantines: an invitation that ultimately led to the Norman conquest

Palladio's 'Four Books of Architecture', once in the library of every gentleman in Europe, is a statement of the principles of classical architecture that was accepted as a strict rule-book by most of its readers although not always followed by its author in practice.

of the entire peninsula south of Rome and the foundation of the Kingdom of Sicily, thus changing the whole course of history in the *Mezzogiorno*.)

By the 15th century, though the pilgrim trade continued to flourish, two new classes of traveller had begun to appear in far greater numbers than before on the roads leading to Italy. There were the rich merchants and, still more significant, the representatives or messengers of foreign powers; for the age of diplomacy had begun, and although the first professional diplomatists were Italian, their very existence soon made it necessary for the various princes of Northern Europe to follow the example that Italy had set. These distinguished government servants were increasingly accompanied, or followed at a discreet distance, by others – humbler than they, yet performing tasks which might often be of equal importance and even greater delicacy: the spies and agents of those far-reaching intelligence services that, from about 1500 onwards, no conscientious European ruler could afford to be without.

Thus, in those days, foreign travel was normally undertaken by those seeking either political or financial gain in this world or salvation in the next. No one, save for a few adventurous artists and scholars, travelled to improve his mind, still less in search of pleasure. Only towards the end of the 17th century do we find the earliest precursors of a new and peculiar breed, the forefathers of the tourists of today. By the second quarter of the 18th, however, that initial trickle had become a flood. For the young English milord, and – to an only slightly lesser degree – for his counterparts in France, Germany and Austria, the Grand Tour was an essential element in a gentleman's education, furnishing his mind with ideas, experience and taste just as elegantly as the treasures which he brought back – the imperial busts, the biblical or mythological scenes of Guido Reni or Guercino, the views of Venice by Canaletto or Guardi, the portrait of himself by Rosalba Carriera or Pompeo Batoni, the cabinets in *pietra dura* or Palladio's *Four Books of Architecture* – furnished his closet, saloon and library.

And yet, for most of the century at any rate, his mind remained obstinately closed to much of what he saw. Goethe, who for all his genius remained the archetypal Grand Tourist when he got to Italy, passed straight through Assisi in 1786 'turning away in distaste' from the church of S. Franceso with its fresco cycle by Giotto. In his account of the Royal Palace in Palermo he makes no mention of the Cappella Palatina, and he apparently managed to visit Monreale without setting foot inside the Cathedral. For him and his contemporaries, Byzantine mosaics were barbarous; as for paintings, the primitives were precisely that, those of the early Renaissance very little better. The history of Italy was a history of steady decline since classical times, and it was above all the ruins of ancient Rome that claimed the attention of persons of culture and sensibility – particularly after the discoveries of Herculaneum (1709) and Pompeii (1748) and the elevation of archaeology, largely through the writings of Winckelmann, to the status of a humane science. The Roman Forum was worth a dozen baptisteries in Florence or Pisa, and any number of mosaics in Venice or Ravenna.

It was only towards the close of the century that foreign visitors began to understand the richness of the Italian experience – not only in works of art but in natural beauties as well. Any confrontation with nature in the raw – thunderstorms amid the Alpine passes, for example, or any of those scenes beloved of Salvator Rosa and his followers – would have aroused, in the heart of a fastidious *dilettante* of the 1730s or '40s, only feelings of horror and revulsion. But now with the first whiff of Romanticism in the air, men reacted differently. The lakes of Como and Garda, the Bay of Naples, the distant Apennines blue against the sky – such

visions now evoked universal gasps of ecstasy and pages of fulsome description. Hand in hand with this came a new appreciation of medieval Gothic and Renaissance art, and also of Italian music – above all of opera, which Italy had invented and in which she incontestably led the world.

From this time forward, the taste of the average visitor to Italy – if such a person can be said to exist at all – seems to have grown steadily more catholic. Only one powerful 19th-century voice was raised in an attempt to stem this surging tide of tolerance: that of John Ruskin, whose diatribes against the classicizing architecture of the Renaissance are a characteristic combination of brilliant invective and sublime wrong-headedness:

The whole mass of the architecture founded on Greek and Roman models, which we have been in the habit of building for the last three centuries, is utterly devoid of all life, virtue, honourableness, or power of doing good. It is base, unnatural, unfruitful, unenjoyable, and impious. Pagan in its origin, proud and unholy in its revival, paralysed in its old age ... an architecture invented, as it seems, to make plagiarists of its architects, slaves of its workmen, and sybarites of its inhabitants; an architecture in which intellect is idle, invention impossible, but in which all luxury is gratified, and all insolence fortified; – the first thing we have to do is to cast it out, and shake the dust of it from our feet for ever.

(*The Stones of Venice*, III, iv, 35.)

Ruskin probably influenced the ways in which Englishmen thought about Italy – and even to some extent the views of Frenchmen and Germans too – more than anyone else of his time; but on this occasion his attacks went unheeded. Now, more than eighty years after his death, we have learnt that there are no good and bad styles, only good and bad architecture within them. And our capacity for the enjoyment of all that Italy has to offer has increased in proportion.

But Italy is something more than just her cultural heritage. There are also the Italians themselves; and in the first group of illustrations in this book, after a brief glance at some of the 'cultural pilgrims' who have been drawn to the peninsula over the past five centuries or so, we have tried to explore some significant themes which seem to characterize not so much the country as its talented and mercurial people. The first is their passion for spectacle and pageantry. The Italians are extroverts, and acutely conscious of what others think of them. To make a *bella figura* is, and always has been since the days of ancient Rome, of primary importance; a *brutta figura*, by contrast, is to be avoided at all costs. This, it need hardly be said, is nothing to do with popularity; the essential is not to be liked, but to be admired. And what better way is there of compelling admiration than to dress in fine clothes and parade through the streets? Such parades must of course have a purpose, whether religious, military or stemming from some misty tradition of popular folklore; there must, in short, be something to celebrate. And if that something should be a victory or a triumph – if, in other words, one is celebrating one's proven superiority over others – then that is the best reason of all.

This same instinct for the *bella figura* lies, I suspect, at the root of another particular characteristic of the Italians: their sense of style. Whether in cars, clothes or coffee-machines, whether in architecture or in advertising, that one quality is ever-present and unmistakable. The eye must be beguiled, admiration wrung from the most unwilling. Whatever the strains, however great the anguish behind and below, the surface must shine, the show must go on. Another manifestation, alas, is noise; it is important to establish beyond contradiction that one's car, voice or radio is more powerful than anyone else's. It may be hard to convince oneself that the youth racing his motorcycle engine under one's window at 2 a.m. to impress his girl-friend is in fact demonstrating precisely the same characteristics that inspired the great princes of the Renaissance; but he is.

And so we come to women. Few peoples in the world, I suspect, raise womankind on so high a pedestal as do the Italians; and few peoples, in the Western world at least, have proved so determined to keep them there. The pedestal, of course, can be of several kinds. First and foremost comes the image of purity, eternally symbolized by the Virgin Mary. Next comes the young mother, later the middle-aged matron – paradigms that date back to Roman days – who eventually turns into that all-important figure in Italian family life, the grandmother – *la nonna*. Lower pedestals, but pedestals none the less, are those reserved for the beloved mistress – in whom, whatever the relationship with her lover, there is always an element of Dante's Beatrice or Petrarch's Laura – and for the sex symbol, who in more puritanical centuries was invariably associated with evil (Messalina perhaps, or Lucrezia Borgia) but who can nowadays be worshipped with a clear – or almost clear – conscience. The problems arise only when, as happens increasingly often, the lady grows tired of her pedestal and wants to get off.

For any woman to attempt to live and compete on her own terms in what was still very much a man's world was, until the Second World War, almost impossible in Italy. Only the artists – great singers like Tetrazzini or Galli-Curci or famous *tragédiennes* like Eleonora Duse – were able to break their shackles with any degree of impunity. It is less than twenty years since Italian law has been amended to allow divorce; legal abortion is still in the future. And among the peasants, particularly in the South, standards are in many places much the same as they were a century ago. And yet, even there, the old order is beginning to change. In the villages of Sicily, for example, one way for a young man to obtain the hand of a girl against the wishes of her father has always been to kidnap and then to deflower her – a step which in the past has always effectively destroyed her chances of marriage to anyone else. Some

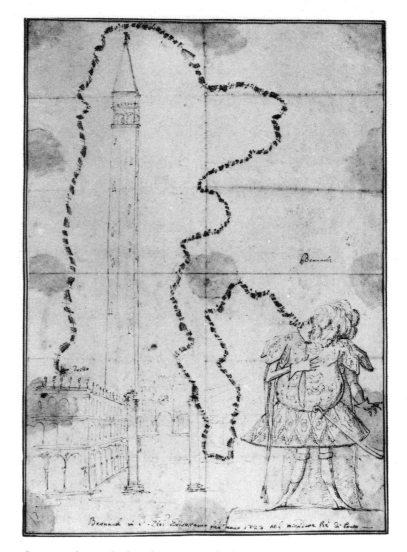

Opera was born in Italy and for centuries Italian composers and singers were the leaders of the art. This caricature of 1723 shows the male contralto Antonio Bernacchi (1685–1756) in Venice; the range of his voice is indicated by the notes soaring over the campanile – their meandering path, ending in a trill, perhaps indicates a lavish use of ornament. Bernacchi was famous for his Handel roles, which he performed both in Italy and in England.

fifteen years ago, however, a girl who had suffered this fate refused point-blank to marry her abductor, in defiance of her family's orders. Her case, being unprecedented, made the headlines in the national press; but instead of being disgraced she found herself hailed as a heroine. Letters of congratulation flowed in from all over the country and she was inundated with proposals of marriage.

Our fourth spread of pictures we have called 'City and Symbol'. Once again it is concerned with ceremonies and celebrations; this time, however, they are not imaginary or allegorical but real, historic festivities, pecular to – or at least distinctively characteristic of – the cities in which they are held. I have already remarked, earlier in this essay, on the fierceness of an Italian's loyalty to his native city or town. What we see here are, in a way, external manifestations of that loyalty. The causes for its existence, together with the reasons why life in Italy became so firmly centred on these cities and towns at such an early stage – for the process was already well on the way by AD 1000 if not even before – are outside the scope of this essay; they will be discussed, by more learned pens than mine, in the pages that follow.

And yet in the heart of any Italian, there is one other commitment more binding still; that which holds him to his family. The quality and depth of Italian family feeling can seldom be truly understood by foreigners; those wishing to do so are advised to study Luigi Barzini's book *The Italians*, where for the first time, so far as I know, the subject is thoroughly – and brilliantly – analysed. Barzini's thesis is, briefly, that life as viewed by his compatriots has always been unpredictable and is often dangerous. To remain on top demands a continuous struggle. One's rulers are cynical and callous; the Church has to look after itself; who, then, can one trust, apart from one's family? We tend to shake our heads today over the blatant nepotism practised by the Renaissance popes; but we have to remember that in their day they were the only autocrats in Europe whose throne was not, at least effectively, hereditary. All their fellow-princes openly favoured their families and it was considered perfectly right that they should. Can we really blame the Borgia, Farnese, Medici and the rest for following suit?

We end this first series of illustrations by looking at two other Italian characteristics that strike first-time visitors to Italy: delight in the flow of water and virtuosity in the art of gesture. Italy is fortunate in that it is hot and dry enough for water not to be taken for granted, yet well enough supplied with it to be able, at most times and in most areas, to use it relatively freely. The result has been a superbly Italian performance – the creation, over the past four centuries or so, of literally thousands of works of art which happen to use water as their principal medium. This is not to say that artificial fountains did not exist in Roman times; but their golden age really began, as one might have expected, with the Renaissance – at Pratolino and Tivoli, the Villa Farnese at Caprarola and the Villa Lante at Bagnaia. It reached its apogee, equally predictably, with the Roman Baroque masterpieces of Bernini in Piazza Navona and the ultimate *tour de force* of the Trevi – both of which, to me at least, fulfil one of the vital requirements made of all great works of art: that, every time one sees them, they should prove to be just that little bit better than one remembered.

But, you may ask, is not all this just another symptom of what we were discussing before, the old Italian *penchant* for the spectacular, the display of wealth for its own sake as a sign of prestige and power? Certainly it is. Ignoble motives of this kind – if they *are* ignoble – have been responsible for many of the great monuments of the world since the days of the Pyramids. The fact that such a mentality should be particularly well-developed among the Italians simply means that they have produced appreciably more major works of art than any other country of their size; it does not mean that the quality of the works themselves is diminished.

As every foreign visitor to Italy discovers during his first half-hour, Italians speak two languages simultaneously: that which is called by their name and another, equally typical of their country and race, which is no less expressive for being articulated by hands and arms rather than the tongue. This language of gesture has always provoked amusement among the less demonstrative peoples of the North, not always without good cause; anyone who has ever watched an exasperated Italian in a telephone box will know what I mean. Nevertheless, when practised by an expert, it remains a joy to behold; and there can be no doubt that it adds a new dimension to conversation, allowing for a wealth of nuance – not to say innuendo – which, without it, would be impossible. It is, of course, the old Italian theatricality coming out again, but used this time as a means rather than an end. However wild and seemingly exaggerated the gestures may be, they are not – usually – intended as a performance; for most Italians, few actions are less self-conscious. They serve admirably, however, to clarify an opinion or to drive home an argument; and if that opinion is not altogether sincerely held or the argument not entirely watertight – then they are more essential still. It is no coincidence that the Italians have always been spell-binding orators, from Cicero through Cola di Rienzo and Savonarola to D'Annunzio and Mussolini in our own day; nor that they possess the oldest law schools in the world.

'There is', wrote Sir Thomas Browne more than three hundred years ago, 'another offence unto Charity ... and that's the reproach, not of whole professions, mysteries and conditions, but of whole Nations, wherein by approbrious Epithets we miscall each other, and by an uncharitable Logick, from a disposition in a few, conclude a habit in all ... It is as bloody a thought in one way, as Nero's was in another, for by a word we wound a thousand, and at one blow assassine the honour of a Nation.' Generalizations are indeed dangerous things, and I am only too aware of how many I have made in this essay. All I can say in my defence is that I believe them to be as true as any such generalizations can ever be; and that it seemed desirable to preface the detailed and scholarly chapters that follow, bound as each one is within fairly strict chronological limits, with these few admittedly superficial and subjective reflections on the Italian character which could be said to apply, in greater or lesser degree, all through history. For that character, though certain of its facets may have glowed more brilliantly at some moments than at others, has never really changed; and, when we consider the sheer splendour of the Italian cultural achievement as summarized in this volume, we can only pray that it never will.

·I·

ROME
AND THE EMPIRE

PREHISTORY TO
AD 500

THE ROMANS were not the first Italians, but they were the first citizens of a nation that we can call Italy.

Italy was the first European country to become an organized state. The Greeks, the Carthaginians, the Etruscans all achieved a high degree of civilization, but it was left to the small city-state of Rome first to conceive and then to carry out a process of political unification that subordinated local to national loyalties. Once this had been achieved, with the resources of the whole peninsula behind her, Rome was by far the greatest power in Europe, a position which she kept for half a millennium. This fact, remote as it is, still gives Italy a certain pre-eminence. No part of Western Europe except Scandinavia can forget that it began its civilized history under Italian tutelage. And for Italy itself, as we shall see throughout this book, ancient Rome has acted as a standard against which all later ages have measured themselves. It was present in Mussolini's mind as vividly as in Cola di Rienzo's.

What was the secret of Roman success? Historians point to a number of factors – the forging of the army into an invincible fighting force; the integration of the army into a balanced social structure; the creation of a body of law that gave stability to that structure; the formation of an efficient civil service to administer the law; and the construction of the physical apparatus to make administration possible (from roads and bridges to law courts and public baths). All these were necessary and perhaps sufficient. The Romans themselves would probably have given a simpler answer – that the gods were on their side. It is easy to overlook Roman state religion, since by the end of the empire it was little more than a token observance of set rituals. But during the early centuries it gave purpose, motivation and reassurance. Rome was great because Roman virtues ensured divine protection.

This belief produced a 'myth' of Roman history which for long took the place of reality. It permeates such works as Livy's *History*. It underlies Roman official art, which offers an image of dignity, probity and high-minded devotion to ideals. It hypnotized later ages, from the Renaissance onwards, producing resonances between art forms (classical architecture for instance) and moral values which have not faded even today.

The essential Roman
was the civil servant. Even when leadership at the top faltered, the bureaucracy continued to function relatively smoothly. An unusually vivid source for research into this subject is a body of documents once belonging to a late Roman official and known as the *Notitia Dignitatum*. The original is lost. A Carolingian copy was at one time in the cathedral of Speyer. This too is lost, but while it existed it was copied, in 1436, for Petrus Donatus, bishop of Padua, and this version survives. It includes a series of naive drawings representing the insignia of officials, symbols of the various provinces they governed, and representations of other aspects of Roman life. On the page opposite we reproduce seven of them. At the top, the emperor himself, *Divus Augustus Pater*, a black eagle standing on a globe. In the central row: a panel showing Roman coins; a frame showing books and scrolls, with heads representing *Virtus* (virtue), *Scientia rei militaris* (military science), *Auctoritas* (authority), *Felicitas* (good fortune), and others; and the insignia of a *Comes largitionum*, an official of the treasury. In the bottom row: the province of Campania; the insignia of a Quaestor; and that of the *Vicarii septem provinciarum*, with personifications of seventeen provinces. (1–7)

COMMODAE AVCTORITATIS VARIAE PRISCOR MONETAE

AEREI

LVTEI

DECORIO

DE INHIBENDA LARGITATE.

Bellicam laudem æ cham mactaris imperatoris reprima
triumphos: utilitas semper tur non amplius bellu: flore
imitatur gratu: ne profusa bit improbitas: sed collatio po
largitio semina magis excire tius defecta subsidia recreant
pretios: Que si prudentia Qd si largitio immoderata

DIVVS AVGVSTVS PATER

S C

Sub dispositione uiri illus
tris questoris:

Leges dictande.
preces.
Officium non habet sed
adiutores de scriniis ques
uoluerit

Insignia uiri illustris
Comitis Largitionum.

Largitiones

VIRTVS   SCIENTIA rei militaris

AVCTORITAS   FELICITAS

CONSVLARIS CAMPANIAE.

CAMPANIA

VICARII SEPTEM PROVINCIARVM.

INSIGNIA VIRI ILLVSTRIS QVESTORIS.

LEGES
SALV
BRES.

Sub dispositione uiri illustris questoris
Leges dictande. preces.
Habet subaudientis Adiutores memoriales de scriniis diuersis

At the top was the emperor, head of state, commander of the army and high priest. In this 2nd-century AD relief Marcus Aurelius is shown in his priestly role (head covered), presiding at a sacrifice. Art of this kind had an important propaganda function. All over the empire statues and reliefs of the emperor, with inscriptions listing his titles and dignities, reinforced the structure of power. The official deification of the emperor after his death was merely a symbolic way of affirming divine approval of the Roman state. (8)

Men and rank

Roman society was ordered and hierarchical, with the privileges and duties of each class embodied in law. But it was not a rigid caste system and one's position in it depended as much on money and ability as on birth.

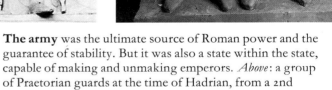

The Senate represented a survival from the Roman Republic, when senators actually initiated laws. Throughout the imperial period they still commanded respect and on occasion wielded influence. As a source of patronage they were important socially if not politically. (9)

The army was the ultimate source of Roman power and the guarantee of stability. But it was also a state within the state, capable of making and unmaking emperors. *Above*: a group of Praetorian guards at the time of Hadrian, from a 2nd century AD relief, now in the Louvre. (10)

The people in whose name and that of the Senate imperial edicts continued to be issued, was a vast and heterogeneous group, dependent economically and often legally upon their social superiors. They were part, however, of an Italian way of life that was to last in many respects unchanged into the

Middle Ages and beyond. *Above*: a relief from the tomb of a smith, showing his shop with its display of knives, hooks and sickles, and a farmer returning from the fields carrying a basket of fruit and driving his ox, laden with sheep, before him. (11,12)

35

Painting: the accidental heritage

Roman painting, of which only a tiny fraction has chanced to survive, mostly from Pompeii and Herculaneum, shows us a Rome very different from that seen by the Neoclassical generation, which had to rely on sculpture and architecture. Instead of a chaste, monochrome and silent world we see one that is full of light and colour.

Girl gathering flowers: one of the most enchanting of Roman paintings so far discovered, the visual embodiment of a pastoral poem by Propertius; from Stabiae, near Naples, 1st century AD. (13)

The architectural vistas (*opposite*) that became a feature of Pompeiian wall decoration owe something to fantasy, but they evoke, as no actual ruins can do, the look of a Roman town in the 1st century AD. A comparison of this painting with similar examples from later periods (pp. 68–9), strikingly confirms the continuity of the Italian urban tradition. (15)

A musician prepares for a recital: another painting from Stabiae (*below*). He sits on a cloth-covered bench tuning his cithara, a stringed instrument, the ancestor of the zither. (14)

The relics of greatness

To later ages the Roman Empire left not only the memory of a great civilization that was past but material remains that were overwhelmingly part of the present. It is not surprising that the theme of revival is one of the recurrent motifs of Italian history.

The vast scale that impressed Roman engineering upon posterity rested largely on the principle of the arch. The Colosseum (seen *above* in a dramatic bird's-eye view by Piranesi) is basically nothing but a series of concentric arcades arranged in tiers. It was the largest of hundreds of arenas built all over the empire to serve the apparently insatiable Roman appetite for bloodshed. *Below*: the Milvian Bridge in Rome, dating from the 2nd century AD and many times repaired; and a length of aqueduct in the Campagna, bringing water to the fountains of Rome. (16, 17, 18)

To the business of living the Romans brought the same ruthless efficiency as they applied to military campaigns and civil administration. Public baths (*thermae*) were among the most dominant buildings in every city. Those of Caracalla and Diocletian towered over medieval and Renaissance Rome; the central hall of the latter (*above*) was adapted as a Christian church, S. Maria degli Angeli, by Michelangelo and Vanvitelli. *Below left*: the Cloaca Maxima, the main sewer of Rome, which possibly dates back to Etruscan times. *Below right*: the House of the Vettii, Pompeii. (19–21)

The triumphal arch which Constantine built to celebrate his victory over Maxentius in 312 AD was, like all Roman triumphal arches, a symbolic monument. Seen in the perspective of history it is even richer in meanings, for it looks two ways – to the past and to the future, to the classical era and to Christianity. In its forms it is classical – indeed a museum of classical art, since much of the sculpture on it was assembled from pre-existing monuments of Trajan, Hadrian and Marcus Aurelius. The roundels above the side arches, for instance, showing scenes of hunting and sacrifice, date from the time of Hadrian. The long reliefs underneath them, however, are Constantinian and depict the victories that brought him to the throne.

These victories spelled the triumph of Christianity. Constantine first removed the restrictions on Christianity and then made it the privileged religion of the empire. It was the ideal of a Christian empire, combining all that was greatest in both civilizations, that appealed so strongly to the Renaissance, and which we shall find taken up by artists like Botticelli in a later chapter. (22)

I

Rome and the Empire: Prehistory to A D 500

KARL CHRIST

'IT MAY BE SAID that all ancient history flows into that of Rome, as into a river, flowing out into the sea; and that all modern history stems from the Roman. I will even go so far as to say that, had the Romans not existed, there would be no history to speak of.'

So wrote the 19th-century historian Leopold von Ranke, and it is a view that is still often accepted today. Ancient Italy is seen as essentially Roman Italy. Yet the two were by no means the same thing. Between Rome and the rest of Italy there was a continuous two-way interaction. Rome's greatest achievement was to bring all the forces of the Apennine peninsula into political unity, but we must not be misled by the Romans' own conception of their development into taking that conception as objective fact. Modern research is uncovering much that was previously unknown about the pre-Roman communities of Italy, and showing how these local and regional centres continued to exert their influence upon subsequent history.

ITALY BEFORE THE ROMANS
The first Italians

Italian prehistory has to be reconstructed from a series of individual finds and cultures extending over whole millennia. During this long period life became settled; men learned to cultivate the land, to control fire and to domesticate animals; the craft of pottery emerged and later the ability to work metals. The first traces of human presence so far discovered are hand-axes dating from the early Palaeolithic age. From the late Palaeolithic (i.e. as early as the 6th millennium BC) we have some female statuettes, cave carvings and decorated objects. The Neolithic provides evidence for solidly constructed homes and defended settlements, and amounts of pottery large enough to be grouped regionally according to shape and decoration.

Subsequent cultures can often be related to particular areas. Thus Chalcolithic remains are most numerous in Apulia, with its great megalithic tombs. Bronze Age finds are prominent in North Italy (the Polada culture), though characteristic weapons have been found from the Alps right down to the South. The islands of Lipari, Sardinia and Sicily seem to have evolved self-contained cultures of their own.

Towards the end of the prehistoric period came the 'Apennine' culture (14th-12th century BC) and the 'Protovillanovan' (from about 1200 BC), with its distinctive cremation cemeteries. By the early Iron Age – certainly by the 9th century BC – the different types of social organization had come together to form a single civilization, with large town-size settlements and a basic population structure that was to persist into historic times.

That structure was probably the result of successive moves of Indo-Germanic settlers imposing themselves upon a stratum of 'old Mediterranean' inhabitants. In some places these indigenous inhabitants were wiped out. In others, e.g. Liguria, Picenum, parts of Apulia, Campania (the Opici), Calabria, Lucania, Sicily (the Sikani) and Sardinia (the Sards), substantial pockets of them survived. Of the invaders, linguistic analysis shows that they probably arrived in two waves, the first in the early 2nd millennium, the second between 1000 and 800 BC. Generically known as the 'Italic' races, they are thought to have had their original home in the central Danube and Balkan regions.

They were farmers and graziers, probably with a strongly patriarchal family system; the very loose tribal alliances found cohesion above all through common religious cults – of which one of a sky-father (Jupiter) and one of an earth-mother (Tellus, Ceres) are traceable from an early stage. The earliest social and political institutions above the family were an association of all able-bodied men, a council of elders, and a military kingship. While this tribal structure and way of life was able to continue with only slight variation over a long period, strong winds of change were blowing from outside.

The Phoenicians and the Greeks

Early Phoenician contact with Italy was limited and had no far-reaching political effects. The Phoenicians were essentially traders, exchanging oriental wares for Spanish silver or African gold. For this purpose they set up trading posts all over the southern Mediterranean. One of these was Carthage, which soon after its foundation in 814 BC was making its presence felt in Sicily and Corsica.

The first Greek ventures to Italy go back to about 1400 BC. By the 8th century, trade was being supplemented by colonization. The first colony was Cumae, founded c. 750 BC by settlers from Chalcis, on the island of Euboea. Cumae later acquired consid-

Greek civilization was firmly established in Southern Italy before Rome began her career of conquest, and Greek qualities of life contrived to flourish there throughout the Roman period. This drawing, showing a mourning woman, is from a recently discovered tomb in the Greek colony of Paestum.

erable importance, for it was from this town that the Chalcidian alphabet spread throughout Italy; the equally important influence of Greek religion was diffused by way of the Sibyl of Cumae. Other bases in Sicily and Southern Italy quickly followed, the whole area becoming known as *Magna Graecia*. Naturally, however, the remarkable success of this process of colonization would not have been possible without the solid foundation of pre-colonial commercial contacts.

The Greek colonies were almost always situated on coastal vantage points, usually facing out to sea. The relatively restricted area of Greek influence in Sicily and Southern Italy should not lead to the wrong conclusions: isolated cities dotted along the coast were the norm; the Greeks had no vision of extensive territorial dominion. By the spread of their mode of life and their sense of values, of their religion and their art, however, the Greeks influenced the development of Italy to a degree that can hardly be exaggerated. For centuries they were to be the Romans' most formative mentors, both in their concept of urban civilization and – far more – in their supremacy in virtually every sphere of cultural and intellectual life.

The Etruscans

The dominant feature of Etruscan civilization was its division into discrete geographical blocks. First emerging in what is now Tuscany in about the 8th century BC, it soon expanded to the Po valley and Campania. Its main towns lay along the coast, on the Tiber and the Arno, and in the Chiana valley; and despite all that they had in common, they always retained their individual identity. This polycentric structure meant that they could offer no united resistance to outside threats – first the Celts and finally the Romans.

The same lack of unity is also reflected in what remains of their monuments – in the great necropolises such as Caere (Cerveteri), in the cruciform domed tombs at Volterra, or in the frescoed burial chambers of Tarquinii. In each case we seem to be confronted by a preoccupation with death, but this clearly did not inhibit an intense refinement of life. The Etruscans evidently enjoyed feasts and games, dancing and music, and they loved jewellery and the decorative arts, producing impressive works of clay sculpture and metalwork, both large and small. The 'Apollo of Veii' is as typical an example of their creative legacy as the 'Chimera of Arezzo', or their toilet caskets, mirrors, and other exquisite artefacts for feminine use. Women were clearly held in respect by the Etruscans, who have been claimed by some archaeologists as a model matriarchal society.

The question of the Etruscans' religion still poses many problems. What is certain is that it was a religion of revelation, at the centre of which was continuous exploration of the will of the gods, by means of a highly sophisticated system of observation of the skies, reading of entrails, and interpretation of portents. The brightness of the living shone far down into the underworld, but, curiously, made all the keener a sense of the passage of time in this world. In Volsinii, for instance, the passing of time was marked by the yearly hammering of a nail into a temple wall; and it was the Etruscans who conceived the temporal unit of the *saeculum* (roughly a century), which Rome was later to adopt.

Rome – at a far more modest level of civilization to begin with – adopted much of the Etruscans' culture and intellectual understanding. This included their concept of town planning, numerous religious and aesthetic criteria, the magistrature (*sella curulis*), the rod-bound axe (*fasces*), the triumph, gladiatoral games and much else besides.

THE ROMAN REPUBLIC
The origins of Rome

Rome's origins were already lost in the mists of obscurity by the time the city began to produce its own historians, and for very many years its genesis was more a matter of conjecture than systematic investigation. The site that was to become Rome had no real importance during the period of the Indo-Germanic settlement of Central Italy. The early Roman archaeological finds – potsherds, urns in the shape of houses, simple pieces of jewellery, small human figurines, and the remains of tiny huts – have led to the modern theory that the Palatine was at first a centre for several small settlements on the hills of Rome – which, some time between 625 and 575 BC, formed themselves into a loose alliance ('*Septimontium*'). This somewhat crude unity then became more soundly organized as a town *c.* 575 BC, following Etruscan example. This evolution to town status entailed the creation of a paved marketplace (the Forum), the construction of monumental temples and a citadel (the Capitol), the laying down of new streets, and the gradual change from thatched huts to houses with tiled roofs.

Of course these modern findings sharply contradict the various traditional legends – the connections with Troy and Aeneas, Rhea Silvia, and Romulus and Remus, the lineage of Roman kings down to the expulsion of Tarquinius Superbus, the rape of the Sabine women, and the dishonouring and suicide of Lucretia. Such stories have been shown to have parallels in other cultures. But even if they are not historically true, it would be hard to exaggerate their importance to the Romans themselves. In 27 BC Octavian represented himself as another Romulus, in order to be recognized as a new founder of the city. Even St Augustine felt it necessary to combat the powerful Romulus myth. And the legendary, though admittedly perverted, picture of the Roman kings as hateful tyrants meant that republican Rome had an in-built anti-monarchic attitude.

Social structure

The family was always the most vital social unit of Roman civilization. An essentially peasant 'community' for procreation, work, and home comfort, the family was strictly patriarchal. The male head of the family (*pater familias*) at first enjoyed almost unlimited authority over all the other members of the family; children were as slaves: he owned them, both economically and legally, and his ownership was sanctioned by religion. Such authority could indeed only continue as long as it was backed up by religion. In Rome, the all-embracing recognition of the basically religious ties of *pietas* applied equally to gods and parents.

A second fundamental element of Roman society was the institution of clientage. Originally, no doubt, this arose through pressure of necessity and through the circumstances of early agrarian economy, where one man is dependent on another for land and the means by which to exploit it (seed, draught animals, etc.), as well as other forms of support, as occurs in any small subsistence economy. Later on, legal protection came to play a more important role, with the influential, informed, and experienced aristocrat having to help those less well off than himself to maintain their rights. The *cliens* would still continue to acknowledge his dependence on his *patronus*, and this produced a relationship of loyalties by which both sides were strongly bound. The patron now accepted a total commitment to help and protect his client; the client for his part was duty-bound to offer service, both as part of his patron's public retinue, and in the form of certain material goods. With the establishing of such a relationship, different families became linked together in a way that passed down unchanged for generations and had a profound influence on Roman political life

(for example, on the way votes were cast). The ratio of members of a patrician family to their respective clients often reached 1:10. This increased later, when, with the expansion of Rome, whole villages, towns, and districts became clients of the Roman aristocracy. These 'foreign *clientelae*', as they have been called, were to become a fundamental feature of the structure of the Roman ruling class.

The social and political order of Rome thus rested primarily on the conscious recognition of obligation and authority. This authority, though, was based on past and present aid; there was no question of arbitrary exploitation. It was accepted on the one hand because it was rooted in religion, and on the other because it furthered the interest of all concerned. Furthermore, it had continually to prove itself anew. On the whole the Roman *pater familias* was not a despot. When decisions were to be made, the other members of the family would generally be consulted, just as a Roman magistrate would take counsel with his advisors in the *consilium*, a body of legal experts. Any patron who abused his authority was socially condemned. This deeply traditional understanding of authority extended first to the more narrowly political ruling body, the Senate, and later also to the *princeps* (emperor). The *auctoritas senatus* and the *auctoritas principis* hence constituted the foundations of all political, military, and even judicial policy-making.

Roman religion and 'declining morals'

Authority also, at the same time, resided in rules and patterns of behaviour inherited from the past through the canon of the 'Roman virtues', and accounts of ancient decisions and judgments. Blue-blooded Romans justified their claim to leadership – with considerable subtlety from the very first – by reference to the services their family (*gens*) had rendered the community, the *res publica*, in the past. Over and over again, the holding of unpaid high state office, membership of the magistrature, administrative and military service, the bringing in of booty or the conquest of some territory were vaunted as proof of personal suitability and competence, in order to maintain present social standing.

The effect of this constant harking on the past was to idealize, and so render abstract, certain specific qualities. The striving after manly *virtus* and *gloria* was equated with the ancestral principles of the old Roman ruling class – toughness and persistence, discipline and obedience, loyalty and probity, openness and at the same time discretion; the defence of dependents, friends, and allies; commitment to the *res publica*. Only later (around the start of the 2nd century BC) were intellectual and artistic interests and achievements accepted on the same level, and honourably earned material advancement accorded the same respect. Interestingly enough, however, this was accompanied by a general belief that the Romans were experiencing a decline of moral standards; the enlightening radiance of the past was becoming clouded by the decadent, corrupt present. Politicians, orators, poets and historians never tired of pointing out and lamenting this phenomenon. Rarely did they take into account the fact that the conditions under which those old standards had evolved had radically changed. Rome had become a metropolis, controlling a vast empire; the horizons and skills of an ancient agricultural community were no longer adequate.

It is no coincidence that this apparent decline of standards was most strikingly evident in the religious sphere. The Romans of the republic had felt dependent on the gods in a very literal-minded way. The regulating principle of both individual and state identity, and political conduct, was to divine the will of the gods and to act accordingly. The constant, fearful search to discover the gods' wishes was conducted largely along Etruscan lines: examining entrails and observing lightning, interpreting the flight of birds, finding significance in deformed births, both animal and human, or seeing warning portents in natural catastrophes. Sacrifice, thanksgiving, prayers and worship, on the other hand, proceeded according to the simplest of patterns, not directly at first, but through a 'mediator'. For the family, the *pater familias* was the mediator of all religious experience; for the *res publica*, the aristocratic *pontifices* performed the same function.

The sense of always living and acting in accordance with the wishes of the gods gave the Romans an extraordinary self-confidence in all spheres of life, including their political resolutions. It was to this *sequi deos* that they attributed their success; for the Romans themselves, it was their religion that ultimately accounted for the 'grandeur that was Rome', rather than their sound grasp of political and social order, principles of government, military superiority, or any other such secular aspects of Roman might. Indeed they were certain too that they owed their supremacy, their *imperium*, to the favour of the gods – which they deserved because they were the most religious of all peoples.

Economic structure

Roman economy was at first almost exclusively agricultural; crafts and trade were at first of very little importance. For a long time farming was on a very small scale – tiny properties of between 2 and 10 *jugera* (1 *jugerum* equals a quarter of a hectare or 2,990 square yards), able to produce little in excess of what the owners themselves needed. The various tools, utensils and textiles that each family required were made at home. In this subsistence economy, the small private farmers were able to make headway only because they were also entitled, within limits, to make use of common land, the *ager publicus*. Additional manpower was rarely needed, and so at first slaves were only very occasionally employed.

Obviously, from the outset, there were enormous differences in terms of material possessions between the aristocratic landowners and the great number of small freeholders. Yet even among the patrician ruling class, properties were in the first instance run by members of the owning family, rather than by hordes of slaves. At a later stage they were aided by their humble peasant clients, and later still also by day labourers and freeholders who had dropped, through debt, to serf status. From the repeated protests of the Roman *plebs* against debtor-serfdom and usury, it is apparent that it was this aspect of the system that caused the most distress. Such abuses worsened throughout the transition period from the 'natural' economy to a money economy, in the 4th century BC. For instance, the *lex Poetelia* of 326 BC, though it abolished the guaranteeing of debts by the actual person of the debtor, made expropriation of small farmers easier.

Roman agrarian history always lies behind the wider social and political evolution of the Roman Republic; even in Caesar's first consulate (59 BC) a law concerning fields had a decisive impact. The economy and ownership system which we have just briefly described will explain why the Roman yeoman farmers were prepared, for decade after decade, to support the expansionist policies of the republic. For, while the ruling class always profited far more than the masses of small farmers from the booty and potential for exploitation of conquered lands, the parcelling out of these lands, the increase in the *ager publicus*, and the establishment of colonies afforded them their only real chance of being able to provide their children with modest freeholdings such as they themselves owned. (Until the great building fever of the 2nd century BC the city of Rome, unlike many other large towns around the Mediterranean, was not an 'industrial' centre – and hence the younger sons of the small farmers did not have the option of entering workshops.)

The Roman body politic

The Greek Polybius lived in Rome for some time in the 2nd century BC, and was thus able to gain an insight into the workings of Roman politics. Applying traditional Greek political criteria, he saw the Roman state at that time as the ideal 'mixed constitution'. In the Roman consuls he detected a monarchical element, in the Senate an aristocratic element, and in the people a democratic element – all working constructively, organically together as a perfect combination. Polybius's view may well be thought rather theoretical, especially in his identification of the monarchical element; yet there can be no doubt that his recognition of the successful co-operation of these different constitutional bodies was quite correct in the era of the classical republic. At first sight this seems surprising, given the ceaseless 'class struggle' between patricians and plebeians during the early centuries of the republic. However, in the course of this long, bitter power-contest, certain compromises were reached and a common consensus achieved. The patrician ruling class did indeed have the upper hand in this consensus, but it had none the less made important concessions: the people could play a part in drawing up laws (the Twelve Tables, 451/0 BC), and the more affluent were able to occupy high state positions: the first plebeian consul held office as early as 366 BC. The *plebs* also managed to assert its right to elect magistrates, and to have a say in questions of war and peace, the adoption of new laws, and criminal procedure for political offences. In 300 BC every free Roman citizen was granted the right to appeal to the people if condemned to death by a magistrate; this, for the individual plebeian, was no less important than the official state recognition (by the *lex Hortensia* of 287 BC) of the decisions of the people's assembly, the plebiscite.

A basic feature of the Roman 'class struggle' was this gradual recognition of bodies set up by the plebeians. One of the most striking examples was the people's tribunes, whose function it was to protect members of the *plebs* from the arbitrary, loaded judgments of patrician magistrates. In order that they could operate effectively, the people declared them to be unimpeachable; it was to this *sacrosanctitas* that the institution always owed its special status.

The most important body in the Roman Republic was the Senate. Originally this was the assembly of the heads of the various patrician families (*patres*). Later it took its members from among those of the Roman ruling class who occupied high offices of state (the magistrature). It was the Senate that dictated virtually all home and foreign policy – consistently, that is, with the prerogatives of the people's assembly. At any rate, the greatest political, administrative, and military authority in Rome was concentrated in the Senate. The three hundred or so senators enjoyed the highest social and political esteem.

The will of the ruling class was executed by the magistrates, who were holders of short-term, unpaid posts, endowed with comprehensive official powers (*potestas*) wherewith to perform their state duties. They were always extraordinarily few in number, and for long periods in Rome's history, given the ever greater importance of the state, were therefore completely inadequate. Yet the Roman aristocracy opposed the creation of a permanent bureaucracy as tenaciously as it opposed any form of long-term personal rule. Loyalty among colleagues and the principle of yearly change were thus the golden rules of the Roman magistrature. The magistrature was usually shared between two men at least, and the term of office was generally a year. Any exceptions to this norm – six months in the case of the dictator, one and a half years in the case of the censors – were due to special duties or conditions of jurisdiction. A further characteristic of the Roman magistrature was that there was no split between civil and military, administrative and executive spheres.

Thus the consuls, the highest officers in the Roman state hierarchy, were the most important representatives of the executive, the heads of the overall administration, and at the same time also the commanders-in-chief of all current military operations. (The term *imperium* was used at first to define the overall competence of the highest magistrates, *provincia* to refer to their more specific responsibilities. Both terms later took on a geographical connotation, *imperium* signifying the whole territory ruled by Rome, *provincia* one portion of that territory, e.g. Africa, Asia, Cisalpine Gaul, and so on.) The praetors, originally the most high-ranking of the magistrates, later came to be specifically legal officers in charge of the courts of justice. However, they could also command armies and govern provinces. The aediles were responsible for the market police and for the extremely costly business of games and feasts. Finally, the quaestors, the lowest magistrates, were predominantly concerned with administration, especially of finance. These four categories of magistrate all had a one-year mandate.

The census – normally held every five years, conducted by the censors – was a comprehensive registration, examination and assessment of the entire population. But the censor also had a vital influence on the formation of Roman society and the ordering of its morals. Not only could he diminish a man's social standing by an official reprimand; he could also dismiss discredited men from the Senate. He also exercised strict control over state assets – the issuing of large state grants to aid production – and kept a close eye on building work, fiscal policy and taxation, which were all part of the censor's brief.

In times of unrest, when the regular magistrates failed to cope with domestic or foreign crises, the classic solution of the republic was a dictatorship. After a debate in the Senate, the dictator was appointed by one of the consuls. He was then authorized himself to choose his own cavalry commander, so that there should be no dissension within the leadership. In its initially militaristic form, dictatorship was resorted to chiefly in the 4th and 3rd centuries BC. Sulla and Caesar later invoked the principle, in a much tauter form, as a constitutional basis for their restructuring of the state.

Another sign of aristocratic bias within the social order and constitution of the Roman Republic was that the democratic principle of equality as we understand it now – *égalité* – was never once aspired to. Such an idea would have flown in the face of the fundamental assumptions underlying family, cliental, and religious relationships. As it was, since more wealth and possessions meant proportionately greater and more public commitment to the common good of all free citizens, the inherited structures of state and society were not questioned. Once the richer plebeians – who served in the legions, and who could afford to hold the unsalaried and sometimes even financially draining office of magistrate – were able to stand for the highest positions of state, then a new upper class began to emerge: a *noblesse de robe* distinguished by virtue of office and achievement rather than nobility of birth (though the latter distinction remained the grander).

Another aspect of public political life in Rome appears in the structure and composition of the centuriate assemblies. These assemblies carried considerable political weight, and thus the magistrates and other members of the ruling class found themselves constantly obliged to argue, to the satisfaction of the citizens of Rome, the real merits of their political decisions and personal recommendations, thereby ensuring a broadly based consensus.

The army

In few of the great civilizations of antiquity was the army so closely identified with the common citizenry as in the Roman Republic. The armies of Carthage and the Hellenistic monarchies, Rome's great rivals from the 3rd century BC onwards, had long been made up of specialized mercenary forces; yet Rome continued, year

Map showing the political complexion of Italy before Rome's great expansion in the 4th century BC. The Etruscans and Greeks were conquered piecemeal, the Carthaginians beaten in three bitter wars.

after year, to fight its campaigns with armies of ordinary citizens and farmers – who were of course fighting for their own interests. The use of heavily armed legions, which had superseded the old military conception of groups of aristocrats with their retainers (first evolved in Greece, and hence closely tied up with the rise of the *polis*), had, like so much else, been borrowed from the Etruscans. These formidably unified legions were able to crush all their opponents. Even the weaker citizens were borne along by the impetus of the common assault, their courage fired by the emotion of the common cause.

The only wars in which more flexible tactics were required (with a need for rapidly changing points of main effort) were those against the central Italic mountain tribes, notably the Samnites (343–290 BC). To meet this need, the legions were subdivided into the *hastati*, the *principes*, and the *triarii*, each of these sections comprising 10 maniples of roughly 100–120 men. These maniples were disposed in chessboard fashion, grouped according to small orientation points around the field. All battles started with a hail of javelins hurled at the enemy; the maniples would then charge, and engage in man-to-man combat with their short Roman swords. Such tactics – which were to become increasingly common – were of course highly demanding and had to be handled with great care. The fact that they worked was due to the absolute reliability of the individual legionaries and the long experience of the subordinate officers gained over many years of active service on different campaigns.

Of course, the rights and actual political leverage of individual citizens existed only within the limits of the social structure, the distribution of power, and the Roman tradition as they were in harsh reality. Nevertheless, in no other state of the ancient world was the abuse of official power so severely hampered, or the rights and personal liberty of the individual so comprehensively protected. This in itself filled every Roman citizen with a lively sense of republican freedom and encouraged him to identify himself with the state. The whole tradition of republicanism in Europe, as indeed also that of the Founding Fathers of the United States, originated in the Roman system.

Consolidation and expansion

Since the geographical heart of the Roman Republic, despite the effects of Greek and Etruscan influences and attacks by the central Italic mountain tribes and the Celts, was never under foreign domination for any length of time, Rome was able to embark on a policy of expansion with singular thoroughness and dogged continuity. In the space of about two and a half centuries, the town on the Tiber had extended its power over the whole of Central and Southern Italy. In the process it had naturally experienced crises and setbacks. Rome's most dangerous Etruscan rival, Veii, was only taken and destroyed in 396 BC, after years of fighting.

Nine years later, however, the Romans were themselves routed on the Allia by the Celts, who seized and sacked their city. Ruin stared them in the face also with the revolt of the Latins (340–338 BC), the Samnite wars (343–290 BC), and finally the bloody campaign in Southern Italy, against King Pyrrhus of Epirus, who had been called in by Tarentum (Taranto): 280–275 BC.

Initially, Rome was content merely to share in Latin colonization; then increasingly she began to subordinate the Latin colonies to her own interests; and finally, around the middle of the 4th century BC, she began establishing large numbers of colonies of her own citizens. The earliest of these colonies were clearly set up for coastal defence, at a time when Rome had no war fleet to speak of. However, the defence functions of the later settlements were rather more complex: there were now roads, passes, and river crossings to guard, and ports and borderlands to protect, in order to confirm and consolidate Roman rule in the various areas of Italy.

Unlike most of the other Latin colonies, those of Rome were at first very small. They usually had no more than about 300 colonists, who each received a tiny plot of land of a couple of *jugera* (about half a hectare, or 6,000 square yards), as well as their entitlement to use the *ager publicus* (for comparison, the Latin colony of Venusia, founded in 291 BC, numbered some 20,000 colonists). Their responsibilities as colonists were continually urged upon them, for on them depended the success or failure of the colonies. On them Rome now quite deliberately set the hopes of her small farmers for their sons' futures. They appeased the hunger for land, serving as a safety valve within society, and for a long time also helping to postpone the evil day of an unemployed proletariat. Overlordship proved an eminently successful socio-political tool.

The major difference between Roman and Greek forms of colonization was that the Roman colonies never grew independent. The more powerful the city became, the more Roman citizenship came to be worth. The free Roman citizens in the colonies thus never dreamed of giving up the privileges of Roman citizenship, although in many ways they were unable to use their practical political rights. A further important difference was that Greek colonization was confined to the Mediterranean coastline, while the Roman penetrated ever further into the hinterland. The map of the Roman colonies in Italy was simultaneously that of the republic's zone of influence and security.

Citizenship policy

The process of colonization eventually produced a new approach to citizenship. The groups with the most privileges were the Roman inhabitants of the city of Rome, those in the colonies and the various districts of the *ager Romanus*, and those in scattered, far-flung settlements, who, as far as possible, were regarded as a single organizational entity. On a lower level were the *cives sine suffragio*, who in effect had full Roman citizenship in all areas of private and civil law, especially those concerning marriage and trade, but who had inferior political status, and so were excluded from the popular assemblies. Districts that came under this category, the *civitates sine suffragio*, lost both their military sovereignty and their right to conduct their own foreign policy, but were nevertheless allowed to retain local autonomy. The Etruscan town of Caere was the first community to hold this legal status (342 BC).

More closely associated with Rome at first were all those enjoying Latin rights, Rome's old Latin allies. In fact, if people from these towns went to settle permanently in Rome they were even, to begin with, granted full Roman citizenship. After the great Latin rebellion (340–338 BC), when Rome systematically smashed the Latin League, the special privileges accorded through membership of the Latin race were abolished. But by the 2nd century BC, full Roman citizenship was automatically granted to all former officials of towns under Latin law: thus the governing class among the Italic middle classes became closely integrated with Rome. In this way, Latin citizenship became a sort of stepping-stone to Roman citizenship. This whole episode provides a good illustration of how cleverly Rome manipulated the privilege of citizenship to guarantee and extend her power. No other ancient city state managed so successsfully to use her citizenship as a method of political integration on her own terms. Under the late republic especially, Roman (and indeed also Latin) citizenship was increasingly conferred on individuals who had furthered the cause of the republic; and it was not long before it was being granted also to entire military units of allies, and then corporatively to even larger numbers of people.

The Roman confederation

The third feature of Roman rule was the immensely wide-ranging and yet rigorously systematic structure of Roman alliances in Italy. As Rome expanded, she formed treaties of alliance (*foedera*) with states of vastly different constitution and degrees of civilization, by the terms of which the new partner became one of Rome's *socii*. One after another, Latin, Etruscan, and Greek towns joined this group – together with communities and tribes of all sizes throughout Central and Southern Italy. As a rule they always retained their local autonomy and their own right of jurisdiction. However, Rome insisted on alone determining the relations between different states, and, most importantly, she mobilized the military potential of her allies to further her own interests. According to size of population, they each had to raise a certain number of troops in the event of war; these troops would be commanded by one of their own officers, but he himself would be under orders from Rome. These alliances were permanent and irrevocable. They also contained a so-called 'majesty clause' of Roman sovereignty, by

47

which the ally was obliged to show loyal respect for the *maiestas* of the Roman people.

As the *socii* gradually came to include the whole of Italy, the ratio of Roman citizens to allies became ever smaller: in 265 BC the Roman population numbered probably some 900,000, while their allies came to around 2·1 million. In that same year Rome herself occupied some 24,000 square kilometres (about 9,300 square miles); the total area occupied by her allies came to about 106,000 square kilometres (about 41,000 square miles). Yet far from being crushed by her allies, Rome managed for centuries to employ their tremendous combined strength to her own ends. By the 3rd century BC allies exceeded Romans in the armies of the republic: among the infantry they were in some cases actually twice as numerous, while among the cavalry they could be anything up to three times as many. This remarkable, long-continuing commitment of forces to the Roman cause can, presumably, only mean that Rome's allies had no doubt that their political interests were identical. During the campaign against Pyrrhus and the Second Punic War the Roman confederation stood firm even under the severest strains. In later periods, admittedly, there was to all intents and purposes no alternative to Roman rule.

Building an empire

The first large-scale Roman construction works were functional rather than ostentatious: the paving of streets and squares, the draining of marshy meadowland, the provision of sewage systems (including that early masterpiece, the *cloaca maxima*), the building of bridges and roads and the construction of paved long-distance main highways and impressive aqueducts. Appius Claudius, who was censor in the year 312 BC, lives on in memory today in the Via Appia (Appian Way) and the Aqua Appia.

Rome was the first great European power to lay down a systematic grid of highways throughout its area of control. These roads not only rendered troop movements easier and improved communications, they also encouraged all kinds of exchange between the different regions of Italy and, later, the other provinces. Such a road network was by no means useful exclusively to its builders; as with Rome's other improvements in local 'basic amenities', bridges, ports, and canals, it did much to justify her dominion.

With the victory over Pyrrhus (275 BC) and the consolidation of Roman control over Southern Italy, the might of Rome seemed to have reached its natural limits. However, intervention in a local war in the Sicilian city of Messana (now Messina) in 264 BC sparked off a whole chain of political and military consequences which led ultimately not only to the fall of Carthage (146 BC), but also to the paralysing of the entire Hellenistic state system and, after long periods of indirect domination, to the establishing of Roman provinces throughout the Mediterranean area. At first

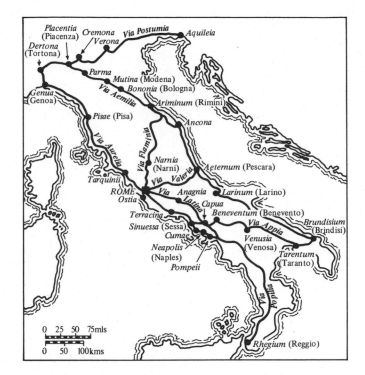

The network of Roman roads in Italy, with the chief cities that they served.

glance this development might appear as a realization of a deliberate plan to conquer the whole of the Mediterranean world. Yet in fact no such plan ever existed. On the contrary, Rome for a long time resisted taking political responsibility for endless new regions, which the crude machinery of government of the republic could not have successfully handled. Hence the modern concept of 'imperialism' is inappropriate, since neither the desire for new sources of raw materials and market outlets, nor any other economic or strategic principles – not even the slave trade – satisfactorily accounts for Rome's expansion.

Neither can it be interpreted solely in terms of the interests of Roman self-defence, although it is quite correct that, one after the other, Rome destroyed the various politico-military power centres by which she felt threatened. This was so of Carthage, just as of the Macedonian and Seleucid monarchies. It is true that Rome often considered her own safety an absolute priority; true too that she would sometimes be motivated by obligations towards allies, yet in their own eyes, the true justification for the Romans' claim to supremacy lay in their religious convictions. Certain of the approval of the gods, they had long since ceased to worry about whether their power needed any further moral sanction.

However, it was not only the Romans, but all the Italic races who profited by this power. They were equally at the privileged receiving end of the *imperium romanum* and as traders, merchants, entrepreneurs, and bankers, they too seized the opportunities offered by the spread of the Roman sphere of influence. Throughout the known world, Greeks from Southern Italy and

Rome's various Italic allies travelled, traded and prospered – in Asia Minor (where they numbered some ten thousand in 88 BC), on the island of Delos (which, thanks to Roman interference in the Mediterranean trade network, had become a major trading point), in North Africa and in Gaul (where commercial enterprise was often far in advance of political and military activity).

Social and economic change

Other effects of Roman expansion were less beneficial. The continuous influx of slaves (many of them prisoners of war, but some also the victims of pirates, as well as others captured and enslaved from all around the Mediterranean), which began in the 3rd century BC, led to a fundamental shift in the demographic and economic structure of Italy. Modern scholars calculate that at the time of Augustus the total Italian population of seven and a half million must have included at least some three million slaves. Given the relatively large numbers who were freed, a fair proportion of these slaves must have made their way up the hierarchy of Roman citizenship. Owing to the devastating war against Hannibal and the unremitting demands of active service during the 2nd century BC, many of the small freehold farmers had lost their livelihoods, while the Roman ruling class had, thanks to the introduction of a fully evolved money economy and to the material gains accruing from Roman expansion, acquired vast amounts of capital. All these factors combined to produce far-reaching changes in all areas of the economy.

In agriculture, farmers over large parts of Southern and Central Italy had to rely on pasturing, but in the country as a whole a new system of cultivation was becoming popular, the so-called 'villa economy' based on very highly organized medium-size properties producing mostly oil and wine (though fruit and vegetable growing, and fish farming were also developed) and situated near suitable markets and other outlets. As we know from Cato's *De Agricultura*, each villa would be worked by up to two dozen slaves, under an overseer. It was quite common for more affluent senators to own several such villas in various places throughout Italy; farming in large-scale units, *latifundia*, did not develop until later.

Manufacturing and service industries also saw changes, and the gap was widening between them and the professions. More energy was expended on the satisfaction of upper-class demand for luxury and prestige. On the whole the market remained one of small businesses – in other words, one in which free producers, working with just a few assistants and one or two slaves, themselves sold their products. Larger concerns, employing some dozens of workers and specialist teams (as in the pottery business), were exceptional; and systematic production for export was even rarer. What did improve dramatically at this time, in all spheres – though most notably in building and fine craftsmanship – was sheer quality, the result of contact with the highly skilled, technically sophisticated workshops of the Hellenistic East.

In the great town establishments of the patricians it was perfectly normal to find slaves in every imaginable position of specialist service. Alongside the janitors and gate-keepers, the chefs, bakers, cellar-masters, and servants of all types, were also artists, musicians, dancers, and actors; intellectuals (teachers, doctors, librarians); and experts in all the most vital branches of business and administration (commercial experts, office heads, secretaries, accountants, and highly responsible financial managers). Besides these there would also be nurses, messengers, grooms, stenographers, and others, often bringing the total number of domestics in such establishments – both slaves and freedmen – to many score. Such servants would often be entrusted with very considerable powers of discretion.

These various economic and social developments, closely interlinked as they were, caused the traditional structures to fall apart. In certain peripheral areas the subsistence economy of the small farmers survived, thanks to generally favourable conditions; but the thousands who had lost their livelihoods now flooded into Rome, soon forming a huge, impoverished *plebs urbana*. And the only way of appeasing this new class, for whom there were often no jobs, was 'bread and circuses'. At the same time there emerged, from the ranks of the *equites* ('knights'), who were slowly forming a new social level, from among the ruling class of the Italic cities, and from the unseen hosts of the freedmen, the commercially flourishing contractors and entrepreneurs (the *publicani*), who supplied the armaments, transport, provisions, construction services, and tax and excise collection which the Roman Republic was now unable to provide itself. These enterprises operated in grand style, making vast profits.

Measuring corn: a scene from the merchants' quarter at Ostia, where a series of floor mosaics illustrates various trades.

The death throes of the Roman Republic

The extremes of wealth and poverty, the compartmentalization of society, and the ever increasing materialism of Roman life, all led to a complex interlocking of political and economic power, such as would have been inconceivable earlier; this in turn created social tensions, and finally led to profound internal conflict. The old ruling class became corrupted through its exploitation of the provinces, its unscrupulous abuse of military authority, its monopolization of the *ager publicus* and its excessive demands on its allies. Nevertheless, even in the midst of these critical developments, Rome revealed that she was still capable of reform: in the area of farming, in the treatment of slaves and in dealing with allies, for example.

Despite bitter opposition from the patrician oligarchy, the Gracchan reforms (from 133 BC) gained the small farmers at least a modicum of security. Following the great slave revolts in Sicily (136 – 132, 104–100 BC) and Asia Minor (133–129 BC), and after the quelling of the rebellion of Spartacus (73–71 BC), which shook the whole of Italy, more reasonable methods of pacifying slaves were found. And after the fearsome losses of a war (91–88 BC), in which once again most of Rome's Italian allies – especially the Samnites and the Marsi – provoked by a long series of snubs and prejudicial discriminations – had revolted and declared their own independent state, they finally achieved full legal and political parity. The end result of this hard-won concession was an extensive levelling off of Roman domination right up to the Po.

In the long term, however, the most significant changes proved to be those that had occurred in the composition of the army and in the structure of society. Given the virtually continuous state of war during the 2nd century BC and the protracted overseas expeditions involved, the legionaries were unable to return regularly to their civilian professions, and hence the traditional militia system of the Roman army was no longer viable. The minimum level of property ownership permitting entry into the army had to be repeatedly lowered, until eventually the recruiting authorities were having to fall back on those who had no property at all. For such motley troops as these, the officers in command found themselves obliged to guarantee suitable conditions and rewards. The usual solution was to offer small plots of land after so many years' service, thus providing the soldiers with some sort of security. In this way new social – and so also political – ties were forged, with the army assuming a position of 'client' to the commander, replacing the time-honoured cliental relationship of patricians and plebeians.

The Roman aristocracy, owing to the immense military and political problems involved in running the republic's world empire, was meanwhile obliged to abandon its traditional principles of annual tenure and collegiality for the magistrature, investing leading politicians with special plenary powers, and senior army officers and organizers with great armies under their command. This resulted in hitherto unheard-of concentration of military and political power. The rise of the *colossi* of the late Roman Republic – Marius and Sulla, Pompey and Caesar, Antony and Octavian – was made possible by this process. On the other hand, the entire strength of Italy and the provinces was poured into the great Roman civil wars of the 1st century BC, and the internal struggles of the city of Rome were fought out on the broader stage of the whole Mediterranean area.

In the various battles – between optimates and populares; between the supporters of Sulla and the Marians under Cinna; between the defenders of the traditional patrician republic (Pompey, Cato, Brutus and Cassius) on the one hand and the adherents of Caesar and the triumvirate of Antony, Octavian and Lepidus on the other – tens of thousands of Italians lost both property and life. The progressive disintegration within society and the brutality of political extremism, which reached its nadir with the proscriptions of Sulla and the triumvirate, affected them just as much as the actual inhabitants of Rome. The death agony of the Roman republic determined what would succeed it.

Intellectual, artistic, and religious developments

Roman literature in the 3rd century BC consisted of direct borrowings from Greek models. In many ways it was a literature of pure transmission and receptiveness. This was true especially of early drama, even the work of Plautus and Terence. It is significant that the first works of Roman history were actually written in Greek, in order to convey the Roman standpoint to the Greek world. The gradual expansion, in the 2nd century BC, of the cultural and intellectual notions of *humanitas* – both in literature and art, and in philosophy – shows that the Romans were able to learn the value of foreign achievements in these spheres.

Greek and Hellenistic influences made themselves felt above all – and ever increasingly – in the sphere of religion. Thus we have the cult of Hercules among the merchants and traders of the Ara Maxima; that of Aesculapius, practised as from 293 BC on an island in the Tiber; the acquisition of the cult symbol of Cybele, the *Magna Mater,* from Pessinus in 205 BC; and the spread of the orgiastic forms of the cult of Dionysus – which resulted, in 186 BC, in official action against the 'sacrilege of the Bacchanalia'. In all kinds of ways these and other cults streamed into Rome and Italy, becoming so readily accepted largely because the traditional forms of worship of the old state religion no longer satisfied men's needs. People now longed for direct, individual worship of the gods; meanwhile, simultaneously, wider and wider portions of the population were being influenced by cults of fatalism and astrology, as well as by Hellenistic enlightenment.

If one had to sum up in a single word the main emphasis of the spiritual developments of this period, 'individualism' would perhaps be the most appropriate. Amid all the great political crises that we have described, the most remarkable works were appearing in varied intellectual and artistic fields, all of which in some way reflect this trend of individualism. The satires of Lucilius stress the importance of personal values just as strongly as the great poetic expression of the Epicurean system in Lucretius's *De Rerum Natura* (*On the Nature of Things*) or the passionate love poems of Catullus. Two other aspects of the same concern can be seen in the development of the portrait – in both painting and sculpture and in the new literary genre of autobiography which was coming into vogue at the same time. And if any individual Roman ever erected his person into a veritable monument, it was surely the dictator Julius Caesar, who bequeathed to posterity his own, highly selective, version of his character in statues, busts and – most persuasive of all – his accounts of his political and military achievements.

IMPERIUM ROMANUM
The principate of Augustus

Notwithstanding the chaotic civil wars of the late republic, Roman expansion continued, first with Pompey, and later with Antony, affirming Roman rule in the Near East, then with Julius Caesar conquering Gaul, and finally with Octavian consolidating the Illyrian regions and annexing Egypt. But Rome's territorial bases around the edge of the Mediterranean were still in effect merely bridgeheads, the administrative and defence structures of the empire were still far from satisfactory, and there was a general lack of cohesion. Augustus was the first to set about remedying this in a comprehensive way.

The fact that he, unlike the dictators Sulla and Caesar, did not establish an obvious, provocative autocracy is indicative of the continuing power of Roman tradition. It is also significant that he did not try to introduce all his changes at once. Indeed, a remarkable feature of Augustus's innovations was the retention of republican ideas – or at least the outward form of those ideas. His *imperium* was still limited to a set period, and life-appointments (such as Caesar's *dictator perpetuo*) were avoided. Effective absolutism was, however, legalized in subtle stages: different groups were integrated into the new political system, and public opinion was continually being manipulated. Thus the Roman Republic under Augustus was quickly transformed, through skilful power manoeuvring, into a principate.

For all Augustus's insistence on his constitutional authority (*auctoritas*), his actual personal power was vast and very active. His power of patronage grew larger and larger, and both citizens and senators did as he wished. Any opposition to the new system was effectively quashed. Most important, he had sole control over the armed forces: the legions, the navy and the auxiliary troops were all either directly or indirectly under him. In material terms, he became so rich after the defeat of Antony and the conquest of Egypt that he – alone of all his rivals – was able to subsidize state activities. His influence among both the judiciary and the administration became ever greater, and it was not long before he was being worshipped as a god. The guarantor of peace, the *pax Augusta*, and the figurehead of official law and order, he everywhere received public recognition and acclaim – in the East, in the manner of the Hellenistic cult of the divine ruler; in the provinces, in the twin cult of Roma and Augustus; and even, among the urban poor, in that devoted to the *lares* presiding over cross-roads.

The Senate and the popular assemblies could no longer initiate independent practical policies under the new system, and were therefore reduced to mere ciphers. But apart from this 'de-politicizing' of the traditional Roman decision-making bodies, Augustus did not fundamentally alter the social and economic structures of the empire. Rather, he refined them and adjusted them to suit his own political method. His principate disappointed many Roman hopes in the military sphere, as he failed to fulfil expectations of major offensives (such as Caesar had launched) in Parthia, Germany, Dacia, or Britain. Politically and administratively, his achievements were undeniable. The new system was reaffirmed and rendered stable, as was shown by the title *Divus Augustus Pater*, conferred on him after his death and deification.

The social structure of the Roman Empire

We have already indicated certain refinements in the social structure of the empire which were made during the principate. The main development, however, was a shift from the traditional 'vertical' structures to 'horizontal' patterns of advancement, and a continual upsurge of new social groups. Society was now led by an imperial ruling class which held the reins of government over the entire empire. All political, military, administrative and legislative decisions were taken by the members of that class; only in economic areas were they seldom directly concerned. This imperial ruling class did not just consist of the *princeps* alone, nor exclusively of the members of his family (although from the first they managed to acquire enormous influence – only strong *principes* were able to dominate them). It also included the consulars (i.e. any senator who had been a consul), prefects belonging to the knightly class (*equites*) and the prefect of the guard (the *praefectus praetorio*), governors, and members of the *consilium principis* (usually tried and reliable military and administrative officials, lawyers, and friends who advised the *princeps*). Under certain rulers, such as

Claudius, Nero, and Domitian, freedmen enjoying the special confidence of the *princeps*, or holding central administrative positions, would also be included.

The imperial upper class, as distinct from the ruling class, did not play any active governing role. Its privileges came through birth, wealth and possessions, through membership of the Senate or the *equites*, through personal achievements, and – last but not least – through the favour of the *princeps*. Its enormous social prestige was recognized not only at local and regional levels, but also at that of the empire as a whole. It was made up above all of those senators and *equites* who had no state duties, and the small, highly qualified officer group of the senior centurions.

Distinct from this imperial upper class were the local and regional upper classes, whose sphere of influence was confined to their respective areas, and who for instance sat on the town councils or were priests of the individual provinces. This important social group also enjoyed considerable privileges – through local traditions, property, and private means – although its members admittedly often worked very hard. It included a certain number of *equites* in its ranks, but above all it consisted of the municipal aristocracies of large and medium-size cities, rich citizens, and the occasional intellectual, specialist, or friend of the *princeps*.

The middle class of the imperial period was far more diverse. The deciding factors here were determined less by family and class than by wealth, ability, and influence. Its membership rested essentially on independent work, private means, military service, and specially qualified skills. It was to this class that the majority of free Roman citizens belonged, as long as they had not fallen into poverty. With them were the municipal aristocracy of the smaller towns, the centurions, junior officers and rank and file of the legions, the praetorians and members of the Roman special units, and the privileged veterans. One should also include well-to-do ex-slaves (freedmen) who had either been in the service of the *princeps*, and so enjoyed a certain reflected influence, or had amassed wealth and possessions greater than those of many free citizens. Even certain actual slaves of the *familia Caesaris* could be counted as middle class.

The vast lower class of the empire was totally heterogeneous. It was differentiated only by the endless forms of dependence by which its members' lives were conditioned. Some were employed in trade or industry or as servants, some received state support, some private aid, some – as clients – contributions from patrons. It was to this class that the bulk of the Roman *plebs urbana* and *plebs rustica* belonged, together with the provincial poor, soldiers, sailors and auxiliaries, the poorer freedmen, and finally the vast mass of slaves, who themselves could be divided into many different categories and who led very different kinds of life according to their employment and qualifications.

It should be remembered, meanwhile, that at its most extensive, at the beginning of the 3rd century AD, the Roman Empire covered (according to admittedly disputed modern estimates) some three and a half million square kilometres (about one and a third million square miles) with a total population of about eighty million. An idea of the ratio of legally privileged Roman citizens to the total population of the empire can be hazarded from the results of a census taken around the middle of the 1st century AD (a period in which an inner levelling-off of legal categories had just started), when the number of Roman citizens was 5·9 million. But at the same time the overall trend was towards the polarization of social differences and the wide-ranging abolition of old legal categories, so that mere citizenship came to mean very little. The *Constitutio Antoniniana* of Caracalla (AD 212) conferred Roman citizenship on virtually all inhabitants of the empire.

Economic structures and evolution

In its early years the Roman Empire was by no means a single coherent entity economically. It was just a conglomerate of extremely varied forms and styles of economy, and for long the most diverse economic systems worked together on a free-market, free-competition basis. Under the empire the central authorities had no more effective means of acquiring direct control of the economy than they had under the republic. Thus the prosperity of the empire was above all the result of a consolidation and improvement of the general conditions under which it operated, aided by such factors as the creation of a currency system (both a relatively stable imperial currency and a continuing system of local coinages in the Near East, especially Asia Minor), an improvement of amenities of all sorts throughout the Mediterranean area and the inland provinces, greater security of ownership and more efficient protection of the shipping lanes. This last factor was particularly vital because sea transport was far cheaper, and so more profitable, than road. Thus, as M. I. Finley has shown, it was less expensive to ship corn from one end of the Mediterranean to the other than to carry it even 120 kilometres (about 75 miles) by cart overland.

Of great economic importance was the concentration of the legions and auxiliary troops around the frontier areas. The new markets attracted producers, increased demand led to the systematic exploitation of mineral resources, and both river and land communication links were improved. Moreover, in the North African and Arabian frontier zones and elsewhere considerable progress was made in irrigation.

Large quantities of Sicilian corn, North African oil, Spanish fish sauce, and luxury articles of all sorts now came onto the Roman and Italian markets, and the foreign trade network spread throughout Central, Northern, and Eastern Europe, the shores of the Black

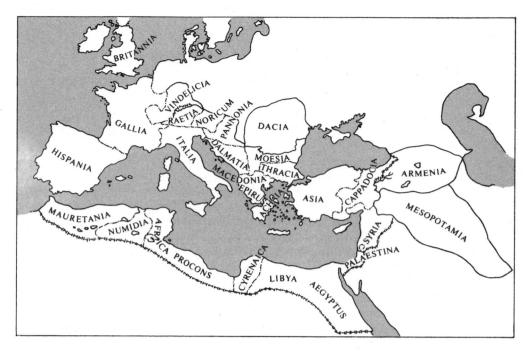

The Roman Empire at its greatest extent, showing the provinces into which it was divided for administrative purposes.

Sea, and even as far as India (the finds consist mostly of pottery, glass, metal ware and coins). In the long run, the producers and merchants in the provinces benefited more from all this than the natives of the Italian peninsula. Here – as indeed throughout the empire – the dominant economy was agrarian, showing a clear trend towards larger-scale farming. And although Pliny the Elder's terse remark that the *latifundia* (large landed properties) were ruining Italy should not be applied too generally, it was true to the extent that large estates farmed by small leaseholders (the *colonatus* system) were becoming increasingly common. This development was further encouraged by Trajan's insistence that senators, even those originally from the provinces, invest at least a third of their fortunes in land in Italy. At the same time the richer members of the ruling class – most notably the *princeps* himself – acquired ever more properties in outlying provinces of the empire.

Urbanization and Romanization

The well-tried republican traditions of consolidation of rule, colonization, and the granting of citizenship as a political reward were deliberately retained and intensified under the principate. By contrast, the system of federation based on treaties had become anachronistic, still serving a purpose only in relationships with certain specific cliental states. Roman colonization had been revitalized under Caesar and Augustus. Caesar had set up numerous new colonies in the Narbonensis, Spain, Greece, North Africa and the north-western part of Asia Minor; Augustus had done the same in Sicily, Dalmatia, Galatia and Pisidia. Other areas of intensive Roman colonization were the Danube region, where Trajan was particularly active, Spain and North Africa. In Asia Minor and the Near East there were notably fewer new foundations because a fair density of towns in these areas already existed before the advent of Roman rule.

In the early principate these colonies were still in effect no more than settlements of Roman citizens with a borough constitution authorized from Rome. From the time of Claudius, however, it became increasingly common to bestow the status of colony on already existing towns. The official status of *municipium* (municipality), on the other hand, was mostly reserved for settlements organized as towns, and already inhabited largely by Roman citizens. As with the formalities of citizenship, the degrees of legal status for towns in the empire were at first very distinct: first came the category of colonies and municipalities of Roman citizens; below these were colonies and municipalities under Latin law; and below these again the vastly more numerous category of the free and allied towns subject to taxes.

Towns constituted an absolutely vital element of the *imperium Romanum*, representing its most important political, administrative, social, and economic units. Indeed, the Roman Empire under the principate was essentially a network of towns. Roman civilization was first and foremost urban, and had already assumed its characteristic form by the time that towns had reached the level of ten to fifteen thousand inhabitants. It went on to pervade and inform every aspect of imperial life, and is given concrete expression everywhere in the Roman world in amphitheatres, temples, theatres, porticos, gymnasia, market buildings, granaries, underground storehouses, squares with dozens of commemorative statues, arches, and columns, baths, and other monuments. The Greek sophist Aelius Aristides observed that the whole civilized world had now become a single city.

The Roman Empire only really functioned properly because the various municipal authorities were able to take on certain vital aspects of state government – administration, taxation, minor cases of law enforcement and financial business, religious worship and games. In all these areas, as in urban building projects, the local ruling hierarchy of the municipal aristocracy was crucially involved. On their sense of social responsibility and willingness to commit themselves the whole system either stood or fell. It was when they became over-stretched, and when the towns became saddled with excessive financial burdens at the end of the 2nd century AD, that the crisis of the empire began.

Citizenship policy under the empire, like colonization, depended very much on individual rulers. Claudius and Nero, for example, were particularly generous in granting Roman citizenship to Greeks, though such an attitude had earlier been exceptional. The traditionally restrictive policies were now rendered somewhat nonsensical, however, by the fact that each year thousands of slaves were freed, and that large groups of people were becoming eligible for full citizenship as a reward for service in the army auxiliary forces. Twenty-five years' service in the infantry or cavalry, the cohorts and *alae*, would earn the auxiliaries – with their wives and children – the right to full Roman citizenship.

Town life under the emperors

The principate guaranteed peace and security, though admittedly at the cost of extensive 'de-politicization' of both Senate and people. In every town and city of the empire, however, the scramble for prestige and professional success continued, and the rat-race of social advancement reached its climax. Yet contemporary writers more and more warmly extolled the modest happiness of life in the country, contrasting this with the fickleness of princely favour, the hordes of people from all parts of the empire swamping the capital, and the hollowness and vanity of the social whirl in the metropolis.

The enormous diversity of Roman and Italian buildings of this period is in itself an indication of cultural breadth. Rome was old in sophistication. With its countless monumental buildings, it had become a city of marble. The great imperial palaces, such as the 'Golden House' of Nero or Domitian's palace on the Palatine, outdid each other with their showy grandeur. At the same time, however, the imperial country villas, decorated with the most exquisite Greek works of art – that of Tiberius on Capri, Sperlonga in the bay of Gaeta, or the unique architectural complex of Hadrian's Tivoli – also set the fashion for the upper classes generally, although they were never really able to compete in terms of sheer luxury.

Typical of more ordinary habitations are the many urban residential complexes such as have been found in great numbers at Pompeii, Herculaneum, and Rome itself; and the numerous tall blocks of rented accommodation, such as those in Rome and most especially the economically flourishing region of Ostia. The town houses in Pompeii – mostly of *atrium* design (i.e. laid out around a central hall) – and their

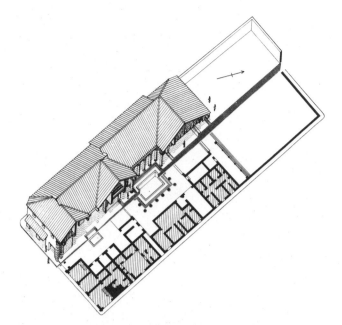

The house of Pansa, Pompeii: plan and section as reconstructed from the extant remains. Like all wealthy Pompeian houses, it occupied a whole city block (insula) but parts of it, shaded on the plan, were let out as shops. Entering by the door at the left end one passed through two courtyards, both with pools in the centre; the second was surrounded by a colonnade. There was a garden at the back.

impressive gardens often covered an area of several hundred square metres. The narrow tenement blocks (*insulae*), on the other hand, rose five or six storeys high, affording their occupants on the whole extremely restricted and totally unhygienic living conditions.

A major feature of this period throughout Italy was the central role of the games and baths in public life. The vast *Circus Maximus*, which could seat over 150,000 spectators, was kept mostly for horse races, chariot races, and athletic competitions; the Flavian amphitheatre – the Colosseum – holding some 45,000 spectators, was principally used for animal fights and gladiatorial contests. The slaughter of ever more exotic animals soon reached staggering proportions: in the 26 animal fights sponsored by Augustus a total of 3,500 African animals were killed. In the games organized by Trajan in AD 107, the butchery extended to no fewer than 11,000 animals, from all over the known world.

Gladiatorial games were even more barbaric. Their original religious purpose (the spilt blood was initially an act of *pietas* towards some dead person) was quickly forgotten as the numbers of specially trained, highly specialized gladiators, using all kinds of weapon increased dramatically. Under Trajan, between AD 106 and 114, some 23,000 men fought to the death in veritable orgies of sadism and perversion. Certainly there were sporadic attempts to stylize these battles and disguise them as history – as in the case of the great naval battles sponsored by Claudius and Domitian. But such artistic *naumachiae* were exceptions to the everyday

A surprising amount of ancient Rome survives, and much of the rest can be reconstructed from excavation, contemporary written accounts and a few graphic sources, of which the most valuable is the so-called Marble Plan, inscribed during the reign of Septimius Severus. Only fragments survive (above), and are kept at the Museo Capitolano. But they enabled the Renaissance architect Pirro Ligorio to construct his own elaborate version (detail right), in which any gaps in knowledge were filled in by imagination. We are looking east. The Mausoleum of Augustus is at the bottom, the Column of Marcus Aurelius (Antonini) on the right, and at the back the rising ground now occupied by the Spanish Steps.

norm of blood frenzy and mass hysteria. Emotions and passions were now expended there, rather than in political debate in the forum. Indeed the games can be seen as, in a sense, the tribute paid by the *principes* to the effectively disfranchised public.

A second form of tribute was the large public baths. New public bath complexes sprang up in Rome one after another from the time of Augustus until the Constantinian era. These complexes included various special areas, squares and park enclosures, and occasionally also libraries and museums. All types of bath (air, sun, steam, and water at every temperature) were combined into a single highly refined system. The gigantic baths of Caracalla and Diocletian, substantial parts of which still remain, occupied 11 and 13 hectares respectively (approximately 27 and 32 acres).

Arts and sciences

Under the late republic, Latin prose achieved its first masterpieces. Earliest in time, and closest to Greek models, are the plays of Plautus and Terence, which are adaptations from Menander, with real character traits surfacing only rarely from stock comedy types. However, the individualization of society soon found itself mirrored and re-created in art. Cicero's legal and political speeches, cherished for their literary quality, together with his voluminous correspondence and above all his numerous writings on rhetoric, politics and philosophy, struck a universal chord, surviving down the centuries to form a corner-stone of humanist thought. In poetry, the most notable name before the empire is that of Catullus, who died probably in 54 BC. His is a complex personality, revealing intense and

55

AR MAVIRUMUVE
CANOTROIAE

The opening words of the Aeneid were found painted on a wall in Pompeii – an indication of Virgil's popular fame: ARMA VIRUMQUE CANO TROIAE, 'Arms and the man I sing (who from the shores) of Troy . . .'

ambivalent emotions in verse that is as subtle and highly wrought as that of his successor, Horace. Lucretius's great philosophical exegesis in verse, *De Rerum Natura*, has an importance that is more than merely literary. It is a passionately felt description of the world, human beings and the human mind in purely material terms, unsubject to gods, demons and supernatural powers.

Sallust, chronicler of the war against Jugurtha in Africa and of the conspiracy of Catiline, is the great (though not impartial) historian of the crisis of the Roman Republic, while Livy, who created almost single-handed the 'official' version of Roman history, stands as the finest representative of the Augustan era, an era of incisive renewal and recovery of vigour, if also at the same time of a stylization of tradition. This basic process of integration of tradition, knowledge and interpretative understanding is similarly reflected in other Augustan writers: Varro's works on antiquity, literature and agriculture; Vitruvius's *De Architectura*, which was to have an enduring influence on European architecture and engineering, Palladio being his most outstanding heir and disciple; the Latin world-history of Pompeius Trogus; Agrippa's map of the world; Strabo's painstaking Greek-language geography; and the *World History* of Diodorus.

In the self-conscious, constructive adoption and exploration of Greek models, it was the Augustan age that produced the universal classical masterpieces of Latin poetry. Refinement of language, mastery of form, flexibility and precision of vocabulary, and force of imagination together with a subtle sense of imagery – all these were of course general preconditions for such a flowering; yet no less a precondition was the individuality of each writer. Perhaps the supreme representative of the mood and spirit of this age is Virgil, with the shepherd poems of his *Eclogues*, the consummate educative poetry of the *Georgics* (on the subject of agriculture) and the great historical epic of the *Aeneid*, in which Roman origins are linked with the Homeric past. It is a poem rich in mythological associations, in sensitivity to nature and in psychological depth (especially in the tragic story of Dido), all permeated with a sense of Rome's destiny and looking forward prophetically to its ultimate fulfilment in the rule of Augustus. Horace is a more personal writer but his

cultivation of literary form gives his poems something of the same universality and timelessness. In his *Odes, Epistles* and *Satires* he paints a portrait of his own existence, living quietly on his country estate (though he was in many ways a typical townsman), cultivating the pleasures of the mind and the senses. Other Latin poets outstanding for their lyrical quality are Tibullus, Propertius and Ovid. The first two confine themselves to elegies and pastorals on the Greek model. Ovid's natural temperament seems to have been sunny; he excelled with his treatment of love, light-hearted and witty in the *Amores* and *Ars Amatoria*. Banishment to the dreary shores of the Black Sea, over a scandal possibly connected with Augustus's profligate granddaughter Julia, sobered both his outlook and his style. The *Metamorphoses* (charming versions of the myths, by now frankly enjoyed as fiction) and especially the *Fasti* (a calendar of seasonal festivals) have an autumnal quality that he had not shown hitherto.

The universality and long-term effects of Augustan literature cannot even be sketched here. No writer of epic could escape the long shadow of Virgil, from Dante in the 14th century through Ariosto, Tasso and Milton to Klopstock in the 18th. Horace has been the model for countless imitators – as valid, it seems, for the severest classicist as for the most unrestrained romantic; while his *Art of Poetry* is perhaps the most widely read work of literary criticism ever produced. Ovid was a quarry from which practically every Renaissance poet (not excluding Shakespeare) carried something away, and his decisive influence on the history of European eroticism is as apparent in the visual arts as in literature.

Only in a few instances did post-Augustan literature attain the same mastery. Among prose writers, the younger Seneca is a major figure, especially in his letters and dialogues (in which elements of Stoic morality are imparted, thus earning him the posthumous approval of the Church Fathers). Another major figure is Petronius Arbiter, with his satirical novel *Satyricon*, from which the episode of 'Trimalchio's feast' (in which the rich but totally boorish Trimalchio touches dizzy heights of vulgarity) has always been exceptionally popular. In more specialized fields other writers can also be included: Pliny the Elder, with his great encyclopaedic work *Naturalis Historia*; Quintilian, who wrote an influential handbook on rhetoric, *Institutio oratoria*; Frontinus, with his pioneering treatise on water-works, *De aquis urbis Romae*. Of the many historians of the period, Tacitus is the most outstanding. In language pared down to its most incisive and unyielding, this brilliant stylist used the traditional Roman form of annal-writing to explore – critically and without any illusions – the real world of the principate. (His astute sense of political realities struck Napoleon I as so dangerous that he forbade him to be read in French schools.) This annalistic conception of history was, however, not typical of the imperial age; the biographical approach of Suetonius, in his *De vita*

Caesarum, was much more so. And this latter approach (without Suetonius's often frankly sensational excesses) had considerable success over the years: Marius Maximus, the late antique *Scriptores Historiae Augustae*, and the writers of the *Lives* of philosophers and saints continued the genre of the Hellenistic and Roman biography, while numerous medieval *Lives* of emperors, most notably Einhard's *Life of Charlemagne*, followed in the same line.

A plethora of works (mostly now based on earlier Latin models rather than Greek) testifies to the developments in the field of poetry. Persius produced further masterpieces of satire, while Lucan wrote remarkable (if occasionally gruesome and bombastic) epic verse on the subject of *Pharsalia*, and Martial and Juvenal cut and polished the art of the epigram, giving it a formal perfection that often outlives its particular critical point. At the same time there developed a not inconsiderable school of panegyric and of court poetry by such writers as Statius. Pliny the Younger is now chiefly read for his elegantly written *Letters*, revealing accounts of the everyday life of a cultivated Roman gentleman, but his panegyric of Trajan established a form that was to achieve great prominence in late antiquity.

A dominant aspect of Rome's artistic creativity was, from early on, her architecture and urban planning. Roman surveying skills and ability to create successful areas of open space, on both a large and a small scale, were due to the co-ordinated manner in which land was registered, divided up, ordered, and exploited. The layout of an imperial forum (of which that of Trajan, designed by Apollodorus of Damascus, was the supreme example) was just as carefully conceived in terms of regularity of line, orientation, and axial symmetry as the legionary camps or town plans. Mortar and poured-concrete building techniques, barrel- and groin-vaults and domes made ever more daring buildings possible. As Jacob Burckhardt observed, the Romans were a people who endeavoured to set the seal of immortality on all that they did.

Much Roman art originated in a religious context, and religion was indeed as determinant an influence as all the Greek, Hellenistic, and (later) Oriental models. Under the principate, however, it tended to become secular and even overtly political. This is most clearly evident in the design of the forum of Augustus and the official Augustan altar of peace, the *ara pacis Augustae*, the Primaporta statue of Augustus and the equestrian statues of Roman rulers, the sculpture on the numerous triumphal arches, the portraits of the *princeps* and his family, and finally of course the long spiral reliefs that wind round the imperial columns. Art of this type was not restricted to Rome itself: commemorative structures, triumphal arches, victory monuments, and statues of emperors were erected in towns all over the empire.

Roman art also excelled in portraiture, historical

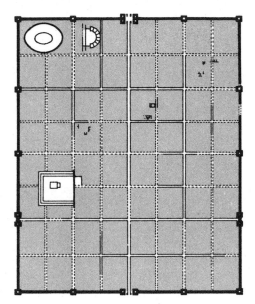

Plan of Roman Aosta. The basic grid still survives in the modern city; the monumental gate at the top is still standing, together with remains of the theatre and amphitheatre, top left.

reliefs, sarcophagus carvings, and mosaics (which had started to spread throughout Italy in the 2nd century BC). Of Roman painting only fragments have come down to us. Whole genres – such as portraiture and historical painting – have been almost completely lost, though the full-face portraits of the 2nd and 3rd centuries found at Fayum in Egypt are an astonishing colonial product. The discovery of the murals in Pompeii was a revelation; their illusionistic effects, mythological episodes, garden and architectural perspectives, still-lifes and theatrical scenes fascinated later artists and critics, from Goethe to Art Nouveau.

No less remarkable was the artistry of Roman craftsmen and artists in the minor arts. The same representational awareness penetrated to all categories of Roman society – silverware, Arretine red-glazed pottery (and indeed all forms of ceramics), the thousands upon thousands of small objects, statuettes, candlesticks, glassware, gems, cameos, and of course medallions and coins. These small objects have contributed as much as the enduring monumental works to the cultural resonance of Roman art down the ages – to which, in ways, we still respond today.

In the sciences and engineering functional considerations were of even greater importance than in architecture. The Romans were not interested in pure theory. It was in the field of construction that their innovations were specially concentrated. Surveying and levelling instruments, small-format calculating boards, hoists and pulleys, cranes, and presses of all kinds were brought to a fine degree of sophistication. In various sectors – 'hydraulic cement' (which hardened under water), the use of highly fired tiles for hypocaust heating systems, the development of the screw, and techniques of glass-firing – impressive progress was made.

Law

In no other field, however, was Roman influence to be so profound as in law. Roman law initially was not an abstract systematic code; it was an agglomeration of different, heterogeneous elements taken from different historical sources. The authority of precedent, of old rights, was as fundamental to Roman legal thinking as the ever-open possibility of modification and new legislation, through the *praetor* or the *princeps*. The striving after justice (*aequitas*) and the formula '*summum ius summa iniuria*' ('right taken to extremes makes the greatest wrong') together encapsulate its character. It was typical that as little as possible, rather than as much as possible, should be enshrined in written legislation. And even there one finds extensive and comprehensive recognition of reciprocal ties which cut across the rules.

For a long time the fabric of Roman law combined elements of the Twelve Tables and of the *ius civile*; laws and Senate decisions co-existed with pronouncements by the magistrature and the later edicts and constitutions of the *principes*. At first Roman law applied only to Roman citizens, but from quite early on legal dealings with foreigners were settled by special institution of the *praetor peregrinus*. As, from the start, legal protection and arbitration were patronal duties, the technical evolution of the law proceeded in the hands of the aristocracy. Jurisprudence therefore enjoyed the highest social status. As the *principes*, following on from the magistrates, became ever more involved in juridical problems, the influence of jurists became greater.

One of the first milestones came with Hadrian (AD 117–138), when the old laws of office became systematized in the *edictum perpetuum*, and the famous jurists Juventius Celsus and Salvius Julianus published their great *Digests* of legal rulings. Even in the 3rd century AD the law still carried sufficient prestige for jurists such as Papinian, Paulus, and Ulpian to rise to the eminent rank of praetorian prefect. It is to Ulpian that we owe the celebrated definition of law and jurisprudence: 'Justice is the firm, unshakable will to render to all that which is rightfully theirs (*suum cuique*). The commandments of the law are as follows: to live honourably, not to harm one's fellow men, and to render to all that which is rightfully theirs. Jurisprudence is knowledge of divine and human things, knowledge of what is right and what is wrong.' (*Digests* I, I, 10). The substance and forms of Roman law were widely diffused through the governors' courts, Roman schools of law such as that at Berytus (modern Beirut), and above all the jurisdiction of the *princeps*. Yet the various pre-Roman systems already existing in the different provinces were not abolished. The 'people's rights' of the Hellenistic East remained valid until the late imperial age, and all personal legal ties with non-Roman legal communities were fully acknowledged. It was not until the general levelling process in the fields of politics and citizenship, in the 3rd century AD, that this situation changed.

A whole range of mystery cults competed with the official religion during the late empire. This relief shows a priest of Cybele and Attis carrying symbolic objects (pomegranate, dish of fruit, pine-cone) and flanked by liturgical instruments (rattle, drum, flute, cymbals and whip).

The codification of Roman law was essentially undertaken in late antiquity, in great part thanks to the already 'classicist' mentality of the early Byzantine Empire and the personal ideals of Theodosius II and Justinian. In this form it then enjoyed a new lease of life in Europe, after the rediscovery of the *Corpus Juris* in about 1100, and with the work of the Bologna jurists of the 12th century. With each new intellectual and scientific current it gained fresh impetus – through, for instance, the 'elegant jurisprudence' of Hugo Donellus (1527–91), as much as through the fusion of classical and Romantic elements in the school of Friedrich Carl von Savigny (1779–1861). Only with the creation of modern national legal codes did Roman law in practice become superseded.

Religion

A far-reaching revival of the official Roman religion had been inaugurated under Augustus; under subsequent emperors, worship of the traditional state gods was, with differing emphases, officially encouraged. With the refurbishing of many old temples, the building of many new, and the systematic reorganization of the various priestly bodies and cults, Roman religion now (at least judging from purely external appearances) experienced its greatest flowering. This was due in no small measure to the fact that in many instances the worship of certain divinities was closely tied up with emperor-worship, so that sacrifices to the Roman state gods were often demonstrations of political loyalty.

Worship of Roman divinities was made easier for those newly integrated into the empire by the Romans' own conviction that their gods were the same as those worshipped by other peoples under different names. The result therefore, was the *interpretatio Romana*, a reconciliation of many different conceptions of the gods, and a powerful, many-sided syncretism, in every respect typical of the way religious life developed in the empire under the Caesars. For example, the great Egyptian goddess Isis became assimilated with numerous divinities, especially Venus or Aphrodite, and was soon being widely venerated in Italy although her cult was repressed in Rome under Tiberius.

From the very outset, indeed alongside the (in part politically motivated) reinstatement of the traditional official gods, there was also a willingness to accept foreign cults, as long as they could more or less be reconciled with the Romans' basic polytheistic assumptions, and as long as they did not threaten the security of the state, public morals or law. Consequently, as Tacitus describes, all the most fearsome and abominable religious practices in the world were to be found in Rome. (*Annals* 15, 44). This unusual degree of toleration, which for a long time was similarly shown towards the exclusivist monotheism of the Jews, also facilitated the spread of Hellenistic mystery religions – undoubtedly the most vital of the new cults.

For it would be a mistake to assume, from the great number and wide distribution of temples and statues of gods, or from the highly formalized mass ceremonials of the old cults, that there was a corresponding intensity of deep belief. The success of the mystery religions – especially the cults of Mithras, Cybele, and other Eastern divinities – suggests that large elements of the population no longer drew any spiritual solace from traditional religion. By contrast, these mystery religions offered small groups of believers vivid religious experiences, through secret dedication rituals and liturgies. They were able to awaken primal emotions and convey a sense of deep purification. To weak, suffering human beings they gave a sort of inner cleansing, and above all affirmed salvation and a life after death. Compared with such dramatic ceremonies as *taurobolium* (whereby the believer underwent ritual purification with the blood of a freshly slaughtered bull), found in the cults of Cybele, Atargatis, and Mithras, the mechanical cult worship of the Capitoline Triad (Jupiter, Juno and Minerva) must have seemed completely sterile. The Mithraic cult, with its rigorous dualism, its emphasis on action and the manly virtues of courage and loyalty, was deeply enhancing of human life, and it is not surprising that it quickly spread not only in cosmopolitan centres such as Ostia or Rome itself, but also – indeed predominantly – among the legions in the frontier garrison towns, until it became the most serious rival to early Christianity.

Along with the Eastern religions and Judaism, Christianity was also quick to appear in Rome. Jewish Christians were already being openly expelled from Rome under Claudius, but the first great Christian persecutions occurred in connection with the burning of Rome in AD 64. Tacitus wrote that many Christians (whose religion he dismisses as 'impious superstition') were condemned not because of the fire itself, but because of their 'hatred of humankind' (*odium generis humani*). As many other witnesses testify, the early Christians were suspect at first because they withdrew far away from the public gaze, to practise, in secret, among small bands of believers, a kind of worship that was misunderstood both in its liturgy and in the faith it professed. What made the open avowal of Christian belief a capital offence, however, was their refusal to sacrifice to the gods, which in Roman eyes was tantamount to a refusal to recognize the authority of the state. Even so, action against Christians was on the whole half-hearted and sporadic. Trajan restrained active investigation by the state, and both he and his successors always insisted on legal correctness in procedures against Christians. Such procedures were fairly common, as Christians were continually being blamed by deliberately incited mobs for every disaster that occurred. Yet in the end, as Tertullian expressed it, the blood of the martyrs was the seed of Christianity.

The crisis of the empire

Under the principate extensive political disfranchisement was the price of inner stability. The price of prosperity for the provinces and the consolidation of the frontier areas was the relative decline of Rome – and indeed Italy – as the centre of power. Hadrian's peripatetic style of government had already affected the status of Rome; from the end of the 2nd century, the emperors spent longer and longer periods of time at the threatened borders of the empire. The empire was increasingly being forced onto the defensive, and under Marcus Aurelius (AD 161–180), with the wars against the Parthians, the irruptions of the Marcomanni and other Germanic tribes, and the consequences of plagues, inflation, and other serious problems, the old order began to totter.

Out of this deep-seated, far-reaching crisis arose the Severan dynasty (AD 193–235), under which the army became unequivocally the dominant political force. New sections of the population acquired influence, notably the professional soldiers and their dependents from Illyria, Pannonia, North Africa, and the regions of Syria and Arabia. The sequel was the undisguised military monarchy of the soldier emperors (AD 235–284) – an era of extreme external pressures, with the attacks of the Sassanids, the Germans, and the Arab and North African nomads, usurpations, and the gradual loss of particular areas, such as Gaul, Britain and Palmyra.

The military Caesars sought to mobilize the last powers of the empire by a maximum of state control and regulation (leading to an authoritarian state), wholesale regimentation of life and beliefs (even to the extent of supervised participation in sacrifices, which inevitably resulted in the systematic persecution of Christians) and change of political and economic autonomy to rigid forms of obligatory service and responsibilities. Yet none of these measures was enough. One after another, crushed under the increasingly heavy demands made on them by their own rulers and the remorseless pressures from outside, the ranks of the social hierarchy collapsed – the old municipal ruling classes just as much as the tradesmen, craftsmen, and free farmers. Where previously settlements had been open, lying in exposed agricultural land, guarded only around the edges, now all large settlements were heavily fortified. The Aurelian walls around Rome are the most sombrely impressive testimony to the altered situation. Even the ancient capital of the empire was once again in danger.

From this crisis the empire managed to construct a totally new system, that of the tetrarchy of Diocletian and the empire of late antiquity. At the head of this empire, egregiously over-inflated both ceremonially and ideologically, was the person of the emperor himself. Milan, Trier, Serdica (Sofia), and Nicomedia served as temporary capitals, until the construction of Constantinople in 330 – a 'second Rome' deliberately planned as a counterpart to the first. It was at this time that the bureaucracy of the administration reached its peak. Under Diocletian the empire was divided into 12 dioceses and 101 provinces, the civil and military spheres were systematically separated, the frontier garrisons differentiated from the mobile field army with its great cavalry units, and the entire army was newly equipped, armed, and trained to cope with the new situation. The number of 'barbarian' units in the Roman army was constantly increasing, however, and whole army groups were now under the command of Germanic officers. New regulations held town councillors permanently to their positions and dignities, while ship-owners, merchants, skilled craftsmen, and even humble tradesmen such as bakers were obliged to remain in their professions. The same was also true for the small farmers (*colons*) on their land. Diocletian attempted, with his *edictum de pretiis* in the year 301, to regulate all prices and wages throughout the empire, making any infringement a capital offence. The attempt was a total failure. Under the stifling weight of state bureaucracy, and battered by repeated waves of invasion, the towns experienced a marked decline. Only the large estates remained viable, evolving into economically self-sufficient entities. After the final split in 395 the Western Roman Empire died a death of slow attrition. The main imperial centre of gravity lay clearly in the East, in the Byzantine Empire, which the 'new Romans' were to maintain until 1453. In the West, the catastrophe of Adrianople in 378, the fall of Rome to Alaric the Goth in 410, and finally the deposition of the last Western Roman emperor, Romulus Augustulus, in

476, were simply milestones in an inexorable progress of decline. Neither Germanic ambitions to revive the empire on Roman territory nor Byzantine efforts at restoration, however much of the old Roman tradition they tried to retain, could substantially affect this process.

Late antiquity: culture and self-awareness

Life under the shadow of the invasions and under the legislation of the authoritarian government of late antiquity – which, from the 3rd century onwards, aimed at controlling people's minds as well as their bodies – meant that new human priorities, modes of behaviour, and cultural horizons had to take the place of the old. At the risk of over-simplification, it could be said that the ancient civilization, for all its religious bonding, was nevertheless imbued with belief in the autonomy of the rationally thinking and acting individual; whereas late antiquity took refuge in belief in a divine world order – in other words, it was theocratic rather than 'man-directed'. As a result, the unreserved commitment to this world, the frank affirmation of a vital life in the here-and-now (which, it is true, also discouraged the search for transcendent harmony) gave way to an uninhibited acceptance of 'the other world'. Men now thought of themselves as part of an 'other-wordly' order which was to be fulfilled only in the hereafter. St Augustine's *De Civitate Dei* is, in this respect, the most characteristic work of this age.

The great divorce of Christianity from the old religions and the formulation of Christian faith amid violent theological controversy coincided with an increasing concern on the part of the Roman state with questions of personal belief. In consequence, the internal politics of the empire in late antiquity revolved largely around religious matters. The last revival of the old faith in the aristocratic circles around Symmachus (a distinguished consul of the late 4th century, who led the party opposed to the introduction of Christianity) springs from the same background as that in which Ambrose in Milan forced penance from Theodosius. Withdrawal from both state and society could now claim a new legitimation. Just as the earlier pagan ruling class had retreated into quiet, refined scholarship and cultured isolation on their great estates (which were becoming increasingly independent of state controls), so now the new Christians retreated into the first monasteries, which represented a complete rejection of both state and society in general.

Monasteries also represented Christians' most emphatic protest at the 'secularization' of the Christian Church itself; for ever since it had been declared the official state religion by Constantine the Great this Church had increasingly come to resemble a social institution. Vast sums of money were required for the construction and decoration of the basilicas, the upkeep of the martyrs' graves and Christian cemeteries, the maintenance of the clergy, and above all the care of the sick and needy, for which the church was increasingly responsible. Gifts from the imperial house were insufficient to cover all these outgoings. Only as a rich institution could the Church fulfil its functions, although such a secularized Church found it ever harder to satisfy the more ascetic among its members.

The sounder the Church's secular standing became, the more powerful were her bishops. In the Western Empire, Athanasius and Ambrose certainly affected political developments very strongly. It was the bishops of Rome, however, who remained the most influential of all. Whether Peter and Paul were actually martyred in Rome may well be disputed by modern historians, but for the early Christians there was no doubt about it, and occupancy of the Apostolic See, as successors of Peter, gave the Roman bishops immense authority. Figures like Damasus (366–384) and Leo the Great (440–461) enhanced this prestige by their own exceptional personalities. The evolution of the papacy into the centre of the new Roman Church was also furthered by repeated claims to the highest spiritual jurisdiction in the entire empire, by the deliberately authoritative nature of the decretals (the circular epistles dispatched by the bishops of Rome), and by the Council of Constantinople's recognition in 381 of Rome's primacy in the church hierarchy.

The essential spirit of late antiquity comes across above all through its art. Aesthetic ideals were no longer conceived in terms of natural form, classical harmony, and artistic composition. Physical beauty was neglected in favour of that of the soul. Of course there were still classical elements, both under Gallienus and under the Constantinian dynasty. But such elements were secondary. The dominant features of the art of this era were a tendency towards abstraction and full-frontal representation, compositional arrangement in regular rows, and the subordination of figures to their significant aspect or attribute. Monumental stylized representations of both Christ and the emperors were also very common.

Neither the tetrarchy nor the Christianity of the late Roman Empire could have existed as they did without vast and spectacular 'staging'. This is exemplified by the vast palace built by Diocletian for his old age in Split – both a military fortress and a grand, ostentatious seat of power – by the massive Basilica of Maxentius in Rome (finished by Constantine), and by the similar edifices in Trier and Salonika. With the retreat of the Emperor Honorius in 402 from his still dangerously threatened capital of Milan to Ravenna (which was easier to defend, and which also had better links with Constantinople), a new imperial residence came into existence, albeit in the midst of the empire's ultimate decline. And the buildings and churches of this latest capital – especially their mosaics – are masterpieces of late antiquity.

The main works of architecture after the time of Constantine were churches. The Lateran Basilica in Rome, built in 313, incorporating elements of law courts and official public buildings so as to create an appropriate style for a community church, became a standard model. Throughout the empire, the architectural needs of the Church (chapels in memory of martyrs, mausoleums, baptisteries, etc.) provided the building trade with constant employment. In Rome itself ever larger and more magnificent churches were constructed – S. Sabina on the Aventine with its aisled nave, the double-aisled basilica of SS. Peter and Paul, and finally S. Maria Maggiore, the city's most ancient church of the Virgin.

Empire and Church often seem to be trying to outdo each other. Thus we find monumental statues of the emperors (for example, the giant head of Constantine the Great in the Palazzo dei Conservatori, or the so-called 'Colossus of Barletta' in Apulia, a bronze statue probably of the Emperor Marcian), stiff, idealized imperial portraits on the splendid gold medallions and coins of late antiquity, a general exaltation of imperial status in painting, in mosaics, in vast, finely worked silver panels and in ivory diptychs. And on the Church's part, we find elaborate, lavish reliquaries, bishop's crosses, ornaments, processional crosses, objects of use in the liturgy and for baptisms, canopies, and sumptuous book covers for Holy Writ.

Private portrait sculptures and free-standing sculpture as a whole became less popular, but the art of relief carving took on new life from the 3rd century, in the form of sarcophagus decoration. Here the most important work at first came from workshops in Asia Minor and Greece but it was not long before Rome and the Western provinces caught up. The subject-matter of these relief sculptures was entirely determined by the person commissioning the sarcophagus; scenes from Greek and Roman mythology were as popular as battle-scenes. Many were on Christian themes.

Late antique Latin literature comprises many very different elements. On the one hand there was a concern for formal continuity and retention of old traditions. It was not only the aristocrats around Symmachus who worried about the preservation of classical texts and the attitude of mind required for understanding them. Rhetoric had long since penetrated into many branches of literature, and in the panegyrics of the great Jubilee speeches (delivered on the anniversaries of emperors' accessions), or at the endless official state functions, it still led a thriving existence. In the field of history, however, the decline – both intellectual and stylistic – is unmistakable. On the other hand, there was a conscious shift towards the needs of new circles of readership, and in more specifically Christian contexts a move to new forms of ecclesiastical literature.

Poetry, by contrast, experienced something of an Indian summer. At the time of Constantine ingenious poems arranged in odd shapes by such poets as Optatianus Porfyrius, with alphabetical acrobatics, were much admired by the emperor and his court. More genuinely poetic work was produced by Claudian and Rutilius Namatianus at the beginning of the 5th century. It is noteworthy that the former (in a poem celebrating the consulate of Stilicho) and the latter (in his *De Reditu Suo*) are still celebrating the destiny of 'eternal Rome' in conformity with ancient tradition. Nevertheless that traditional Rome was not the Rome of the future. In its place rose the Rome of the Christian martyrs, and it was this new city that the following hymn – by an anonymous 10th-century writer, sung throughout the Middle Ages – exalts:

O Roma nobilis, orbis et domina,
cunctarum urbium excellentissima,
roseo martyrum sanguine rubea,
albis et virginum liliis candida:
salutem dicimus tibi per omnia,
te benedicimus: salve per secula . . .

[O noble Rome, mistress of the world, most excellent of all cities, red with the rosy blood of martyrs, bright with the white lilies of virgins, we wish you well in all things, we bless you: hail for eternity.]

The Roman legacy

Although Rome – indeed, Italy as a whole – was virtually a straw blown hither and thither by, successively, Ostrogoths, Vandals, Lombards, Franks, and even Byzantines, and although the now centuries-old political unity of Italy became utterly fragmented, Roman traditions continued to exert a powerful influence. Initially this influence was by no means co-ordinated. In crude terms it was divided into three main strands – republican, imperial, and Christian.

The republican strand can be seen only fitfully and at first made only halting progress. It is evident in the medieval Italian republics and the free German imperial towns, and in Rome itself – at its most fascinating – with Cola di Rienzo. It later revived in the groundswell of feeling at the time of the French Revolution, and had of course been equally powerful in its inspiration of the American Founding Fathers. In this tradition the heroes of the free Roman Republic became magnificent exemplars of history. Their outstanding moral qualities were held up as ideals by such writers as Corneille and Bossuet, while the actual political processes through which their history evolved profoundly influenced Machiavelli, Montesquieu, and (later) Niebuhr, and Mommsen.

The imperial strand of the Roman tradition was taken up much sooner. Ever since the Augustan age the Roman Empire had been seen as the ideal well-ordered state – a historic creation in which world peace was guaranteed and ensured through the just, constructive rule of a great power. Thus it served as a justification of new imperial claims in East and West by both Byzantium and the medieval German empire. Extra-territorial national armies and ambitions have continued, right up to the most recent years, to turn to it as both a model and a justificatory precedent: the Napoleonic empire no less than the British; and the advocates of a worldwide *pax Americana*. (Whether Mussolini's propagandistic proclamation of a new *Impero Romano* comes into the same category is more debatable).

Meanwhile, in Christian Rome, the immediate local continuity of the Roman tradition has persisted, at its most diverse and effective, up to the present day. Through the embodiment of the Christian Church in the papacy, and notwithstanding the new Romans of the Byzantine East, and even the concept of Moscow as a 'Third Rome', Rome in the Middle Ages regained (and in a sense retains) that universal focal position it held, politically, in antiquity. Ancient Italy, condensed into Rome, in its republican, imperial, and Christian guises, conquered more than just its Mediterranean neighbours. Through numerous renascences and humanist movements, it has over the years created a tradition, the strength and greatness of which are still to be felt wherever European civilization has left its mark. It is, therefore, in the cultural and religious – rather than the narrowly political – sense that *Roma aeterna* has indeed become a symbol of historical continuity.

SENATVSPOPVLVSQVEROMANVS
IMPCAESARIDIVINERVAEFNERVAE
TRAIANOAVGGERMDACICOPONTIF

Monumental lettering was one of the legacies of Rome taken up most eagerly at the Renaissance. An impressive example is the inscription on the base of Trajan's Column. Word-spaces are indicated by dots.

The opening lines may be translated: 'The Senate and people of Rome to Imperator Caesar Nerva Trajanus Augustus, son of the divine Nerva, . . .'

·II·

THE MEDIEVAL CENTURIES

500-1350

THE ITALIAN MIDDLE AGES have too often been regarded as simply that – an age 'in the middle' between the Roman Empire and the Renaissance. Such a view not only underrates the vast achievements of these centuries – in the arts, in literature and in philosophy – but it makes it very difficult to understand all subsequent Italian history. For Italy as we know it was born in the Middle Ages. The barbarian invasions of the 5th and 6th centuries began a process that turned a unified centre of empire into a land of small independent city-states fought over by foreign powers, and so it remained for well over a thousand years. The medieval centuries also saw the growth of a division between the wealthy, politically active North and the poor, politically subjugated South. From these political upheavals emerged a characteristically Italian localized and urban culture.

By contrast there was one Italian institution that transcended not only regional but even national boundaries – the Catholic Church. Already by the 6th century the bishop of Rome was the acknowledged leader of Western Christendom, and throughout the whole period covered by this chapter that leadership was never seriously challenged. Theology, when it did not emanate from Italy, was subject to Italian approval; Western monasticism was given its characteristic form by St Benedict of Nursia and Pope Gregory the Great; and Europe's most influential saint, Francis of Assisi, could have belonged to no other country. Christian iconography and Christian music were also very largely Italian in origin.

Two themes will dominate the chapter that follows. One is the continuing influence of ancient Rome. In a sense, medieval Italy was living on its past. The memory of former greatness never died. In law, in political theory, even (as we are increasingly discovering) in the details of urban living, as much as possible of the classical heritage was salvaged and preserved. Even the church, led by a pope whose title was *Pontifex Maximus*, kept Latin as its language and administered its provinces as a spiritual empire. The second theme is the influence of the civilizations to the north (the Germanic) and to the south (Byzantine and Islamic). Italy was the meeting place of ideas, artistic styles, scientific knowledge (as in medicine and physics) and architectural techniques: what other country could contain, within 150 miles, both St Mark's, Venice, and Milan Cathedral?

One more theme – that of continuity – is perhaps the most Italian of all, and will emerge with almost equal emphasis in every chapter of this book. As Virgil could speak to Dante, so Dante can speak to the Italy of today. For here the past never disappears; it merely becomes part of the present.

Christian Rome

stood on the foundations of classical Rome – literally so in the case of the church of S. Clemente (*opposite*). The site had originally been occupied by a Roman house with a temple of Mithras attached to it. In the 4th century this was covered over and a Christian church built, to roughly the same dimensions as the present one. During the next two centuries this church was filled with fine furnishings, notably the marble screen enclosing the choir, an Early Christian arrangement that later became obsolete. In the 11th century this church too was superseded and on top of it the present church was erected. The old choir-fittings, however, were kept and re-used in the new building, with some additions such as the pulpit on the left and the large candlestick. Both the previous levels below the present floor can now be visited, providing a living picture of continuous occupation and worship. (1)

From Roman to Romanesque

The adaptation of Roman models to serve the needs of a Christian community can be followed most clearly in the arts of architecture and sculpture. Each part of Italy evolved its own characteristic version of this style.

Churches developed not from temples, which had relatively small and dark interiors, but from Roman law-courts, basilicas. An extended nave, ending in an apse, flanked by aisles and lit by clerestory windows above an arcade, became the standard arrangement. S. Sabina, Rome (*left*), of the early 5th century, seems to have been the first to use arches on columns instead of a flat entablature; the columns and capitals are re-used classical pieces. The Ostrogothic kings, Arian Christians, saw themselves as the successors of the Caesars, and Theodoric's mausoleum at Ravenna (*below*), of the early 6th century, follows imperial models. (2, 4)

Sculpture retreated from the realism of classical art to a style that was more idealized and more spiritual. This peacock (*left*) from Brescia is a conventional symbol of eternal life; it shows Byzantine influence in the way it resolves itself into two-dimensional pattern. (3)

In 11th-century Pisa concepts of monumental town-planning had not been forgotten. The grouping of cathedral, campanile (the Leaning Tower), baptistery and in the background the cemetery (Campo Santo) is something that is not typical of the Middle Ages but which was to be revived in the Renaissance. The upper parts of the baptistery, with their lacy tracery, are late Gothic. (5)

A conscious revival of classical sculpture came in the 13th century. It seems to have begun in the South, under Frederick II, and to have been carried north by Nicola Pisano and his son Giovanni. Their reliefs on the pulpit of Pisa Cathedral (*right*: detail of the *Betrayal of Christ*) recall Roman sarcophagus carvings. (6)

Medieval townscape

Many Italian towns of today still have the character that they had in the Middle Ages: Genoa with its straight narrow streets between tall buildings, Venice with its bridges and canals, Assisi or Gubbio with their steep steps and alleys.

Fortified hill-towns like those in the background of Simone Martini's Siena fresco of Guidoriccio (*above*) can still be seen all over Tuscany and Umbria. **Pavia** kept much from its Roman past, but by the later Middle Ages (*right*) much has been added. The Roman bridge has acquired fortified gate-towers and a covered passageway. The street-plan is Roman but the houses themselves (including many tower-houses) are medieval. **Verona** deliberately maintained its Roman buildings as items of civic pride. This 10th-century painting (*below*) shows several features that are still recognizable, including the amphitheatre and the bridge across the Adige. (7, 8, 9)

De Summo Montis Castrum Prospectat in urbem   *Dædaleā factum arte Viisque tetris.*

THEATRVM

Nobile praecipuum, memorabile, grande Theatrum, / Quod Deus extructum Sacra Verona tuum.

Magna Verona vale, valeas per secula semper,   *Et celebrent gentes nomen in orbe tuum.*

A prosperous countryside

If medieval Italy was essentially a land of cities, it depended upon a flourishing agriculture for its nourishment. The countryside seems indeed to have been continuously farmed throughout all the great social upheavals, and farming methods remained very much as they had been in the Roman Empire. Virgil's *Georgics* were not to become out of date for many centuries.

The seasons revolved in their endless cycle, and for every season there was the same task to perform, year after year. The great fountain at Perugia carved by Nicola and Giovanni Pisano in the late 13th century (*left*) is only one out of hundreds of representations of these 'labours of the months'. We see here June (reaping and haymaking), July (threshing and winnowing) and September (treading the grapes). (10, 11, 12)

The countryside gave life to the city, a process made memorable by Ambrogio Lorenzetti's great fresco at Siena (mid-14th century). A fashionable hawking party leaves by the gate on the left, meeting as they go a peasant driving a pig and a line of mules carrying grain. In the foreground a vineyard is being tended, while in the middle distance reaping and threshing are in progress. But what did the countryman gain from the town? The answer, according to Lorenzetti, is in the upper register – security, symbolized by a robber hanging from a gibbet. (13)

Field patterns laid down under the Roman system of centuriation remain remarkably intact in many areas of North Italy. This aerial view shows the country near Cesena. (14)

Oxen drawing the plough in
Romanesque Spoleto, 12th century,
might be on a Roman relief of a
thousand years earlier: the similarity to
that illustrated on p. 35 is striking. (15)

Trade,
the life blood

In most parts of Europe wealth and power were concentrated in the hands of an aristocratic landowning class. Such a class existed in Italy too, but it was increasingly challenged by a town-based aristocracy and bourgeoisie which had grown rich above all through trade. Some towns, like Venice and Genoa, built up trading empires overseas. Others, like Florence, developed banking enterprises whose branches also stretched beyond Italy. In any of these cities a successful merchant was the equal of a nobleman elsewhere.

A goldsmith's shop in the 14th century, opening straight on to the street. Here the goldsmith is St Eligius – hence the halo – but the setting is authentic. He is bent over a gilded saddle. To his left and right assistants are busy on a plaque and an incised cross. At the back is the workshop where a man is hammering on an anvil. (16)

In the manipulation of money the North Italian cities led the world. By the 14th century many of the typical modern functions of a bank were being carried out by private firms – lending money at interest, profiting by exchange rates, selling insurance, transferring funds by letters of credit. Among the technical innovations was double-entry book-keeping. Here (*right*) public employees are being paid by the *Comune* of Siena. (17)

72

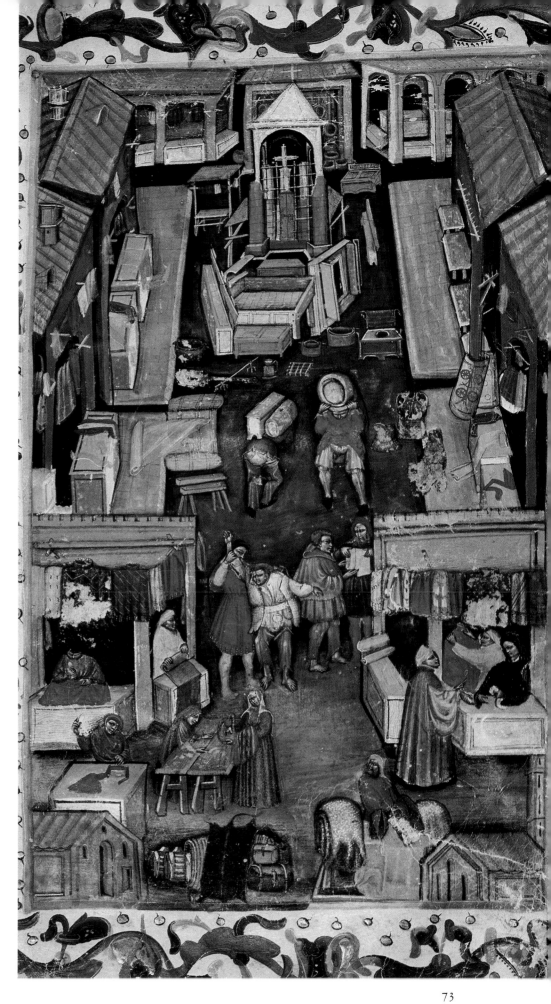

The urban fabric. *Top*: an apothecary's shop. *Bottom*: making spaghetti in a 15th-century kitchen. *Right*: a street specializing in textiles and vestments. (18, 19, 20)

73

The patterns of power

Medieval Italy was shaped by the way power was divided and exercised, a point that can be made by comparing how the patronage of architecture has been represented.

King, pope and merchant present the churches they have endowed to the patron saints to whom they are dedicated. *Left*: Pope Honorius I bearing his church of S. Agnese fuori le mura, Rome, *c.* 625, to St Agnes. *Below left*: William II of Sicily offers the cathedral of Monreale to the Virgin, *c.* 1180. *Below*: the merchant Enrico Scrovegni presents his chapel at Padua to the Virgin – detail from Giotto's fresco in the interior, *c.* 1310. (21–23)

When the towns became masters of their own destiny, they symbolized their status in prominent town halls, the seat of ruling councils. The earliest view of Florence's Palazzo Vecchio is on a fresco fragment of the 14th century (*above*) showing the defeat of the attempted tyranny of Walter of Brienne, Duke of Athens. St Anne hands over flags of freedom to the Florentine militia. The Bargello (*right*) was the official residence of the *podestà*, the chief magistrate of Florence, appointed from outside in the hope that he would rise above warring factions. The coats-of-arms on the stairs are those of the city's wards. (24, 25)

In the South royal power never relaxed its grip, though the ruling dynasty might change. The Hohenstaufen emperor Frederick II's kingdom included Sicily, Calabria and Apulia. It was in some ways their Golden Age and the last time when they would challenge the North in terms of either material prosperity or cultural achievement. Frederick's exquisite castle of Castel del Monte (*left*) – as much a glorified hunting lodge as a fortress – is a monument both to the refined tastes and the military strength of the Hohenstaufen dynasty. (26)

75

The Church and its critics

By the 13th century the papacy had become one of the strongest secular states in Italy. Coupled with the pope's spiritual authority as head of the Church, this gave it immense wealth and power.

The popes were buried with all the honours due to monarchs. The effigy of Honorius IV (1285–7), once part of a magnificent tomb in Old St Peter's and now in the church of S. Maria in Aracoeli, shows the pope reclining in death and dressed in splendid papal robes. Honorius's career illustrates the dilemmas facing a medieval pope. On the one hand he was sympathetic to the mendicant orders who were trying to revive the ideals of early Christianity. On the other hand he was the first to employ banking houses of Northern Italy in the collection of papal dues. (28)

St Francis represented the most radical criticism that could be made of the temporal church. Yet the Church managed to contain his movement and to use his moral energy in its own cause. *Left*: the famous fresco at Assisi attributed to Giotto, in which St Francis, defying his father, strips off all his clothes and dedicates himself to poverty. (27)

Dante's deepest scorn is reserved for the simoniacs, churchmen who sold benefices for profit. He finds them in the Eighth Circle of Hell, buried face downwards in the ground with their legs writhing in the air (*below*). Here he meets the guilty Nicholas III, pope from 1277 to 1280. (29)

The view east

Sicily and parts of South Italy were at various times under Moslem rule. Venice had many trade links with Turkey and the Levant. The Eastern element in Italian civilization is something that can hardly be overstressed.

A turbaned figure thought to represent a Levantine merchant decorates a Venetian house of the 13th century in the Campo dei Mori. (31)

The stalactite ceiling of Palermo's Cappella Palatina (*left*) was made by Arab craftsmen for King Roger II in the early 12th century. Its intricate wooden cells bear Kufic inscriptions. The mosaics, on the other hand, are Byzantine, though the lettering is mostly Latin. (30)

Amalfi and **Palermo** (*right*) were both
so close to Islamic influences that their
own culture became partially
Islamicized. This is most obviously
true in terms of architecture – here the
cloister and campanile of Amalfi
Cathedral and the church of
S. Giovanni degli Eremiti in Palermo –
but it can also be traced in such
features as the scientific and medical
bent of the Southern university of
Salerno. (34, 35)

The taste for Kufic, an ornamental
Arabic script used all over the Islamic
world, is one of the most intriguing
instances of cultural migration.
Christian artists, pleased by its
calligraphic beauty, employed it as a
decorative motif untroubled by, or
perhaps unaware of, the possible
meanings that it might convey. *Above*:
roundel on the bronze doors of the
tomb of the crusader Bohemund at
Canosa, in Apulia. *Below*: detail from
the Virgin's robe in Duccio's *Maestà*,
Siena. (32, 33)

Italy's greatest poet captured the thought and experience of his own day in a work central to Italian culture. Dante's *Divina Commedia*, in which he relates his visionary journey through Hell, Purgatory and Paradise, is at the same time so universal that it can give us an understanding of the whole medieval cosmos and so particularized that it could have been written by no one but a Florentine, living around 1300 and in Dante's own special circumstances. Real places and real people are its subject – Dante's friends, Dante's enemies, figures from history ancient and modern, the saints of the church: all are equally present in God's scheme and in the poet's mind. The circles of Purgatory and the streets of his native city belong to the same universe. This fresco, painted 150 years after his death, represents him holding a book in which the opening lines of the poem are written. On the left is the descent into Hell: behind him, guarded by an angel, the entrance to the hill of Purgatory, where souls expiating their sins by suffering climb to Paradise; on the right are the walls of Florence and Brunelleschi's dome – in Dante's time, of course, unbuilt – of the cathedral. (36)

II

The Medieval Centuries: 500–1350

BRYAN WARD-PERKINS

THE MEDIEVAL Italian world revolved around its cities. They were the centres of political life and the focuses of culture. Many had been founded in the Roman period, like Aosta, Pavia and Lucca, but most looked back through an unbroken history to a remoter past: Villanovan Bologna, Etruscan Perugia and Greek Naples and Syracuse for example.

In the early Middle Ages, the period before AD 1000, some Roman towns disappeared, generally those in the remoter and poorer upland areas, or those on the coast, like Aquileia and Ostia, that faced particular environmental and defensive problems. However, even in the darkest centuries of the Middle Ages, while some towns were disappearing, the seeds were sown for the new growth of others. In the lower Po delta, for instance, as Aquileia, Concordia and Altinum were slowly abandoned, new sites were being settled at Comacchio, Ferrara, Venice and Torcello.

In many towns of Italy that were continuously settled throughout the Middle Ages, and indeed to the present day, there is a period that we know very little about: the 'Dark Ages' of the 7th and 8th centuries. The few surviving sources for this period clearly show, however, that cities continuously dominated Italian religious, military and political life. The bishops and their clergy were present in the towns throughout the Middle Ages, and as visual symbols of this stood the great basilicas of the 4th and 5th centuries, replaced from the 11th century onward by the present cathedrals of Italy. Warfare too was often characteristically urban. The 6th-century war between the Gothic kings of Italy and the Byzantine invaders was one of long drawn-out sieges, such as those of Naples, Rome, Urbino and Osimo. Nor did the Lombards, Italy's least Romanized invaders, interrupt this continuity. From the start they set up their local military and political bases in the towns of the peninsula, and made Pavia, Spoleto and Benevento into major capitals. Like the Goths before them, they too, when threatened, shut themselves up in their cities: Charlemagne in 774 defeated and conquered the Lombards, not in open battle, but by a ten-month siege of Pavia.

A glance at air-photographs of twenty or more Italian towns will show that alongside this continuity of urban administration and urban defence went a continuity of active and populous town life. In Verona, for example, the grid pattern of Roman streets is still almost perfectly preserved in the present town plan, although the paving blocks of classical times are now buried under a metre or more of continuous resurfacings. The forum square – the centre of economic and administrative life in the Roman period – has survived in continuous use as a market place and a meeting place for the citizenry. Such a remarkable survival of a town plan can only be explained by a continuity of relatively dense urban life in the city. The Lombard dukes and the Catholic bishops of Verona were certainly not squatting in the empty ruins of a Roman past, but were in the centre of a flourishing early medieval town life.

Undoubtedly at the beginning of our period there were centuries that were economically and probably demographically far darker than what came before and what came after, but through them all the towns survived. They did so principally because the administration, both secular and ecclesiastical, never left them, and because the Italian aristocracy, whether of Roman or barbarian descent, never lost a taste for urban life and continued for the most part to exploit its rural lands from the towns. Consequently, even if for several centuries their commercial and artisan function may have been of little importance, towns still survived as centres for the consumption of the surplus of the surrounding countryside.

The resilience, even in the Dark Ages, of Italian urban life must also have depended in part on an exceptional degree of agrarian continuity. To match the survival of town plans, there is in the modern landscape of field boundaries a remarkable survival, particularly in the Po plain and Tuscany, of areas of regular centuriation (the division by the Romans of the land into regular rectangular fields). As with urban street patterns, the almost perfect survival of so many of these ancient fields can only be explained by a continuous and uninterrupted history of agricultural use. If the fields had been abandoned, much of the centuriation would rapidly have disappeared. Because towns obviously depended in many ways on a prosperous agricultural hinterland, it is no surprise to find that towns with well preserved street patterns, pointing to continuity of urban prosperity, often sit in the middle of an agricultural territory with well preserved field patterns.

Because of this urban continuity, cities remained the building blocks of power, although on a wider scale there was very considerable change in the politics of the

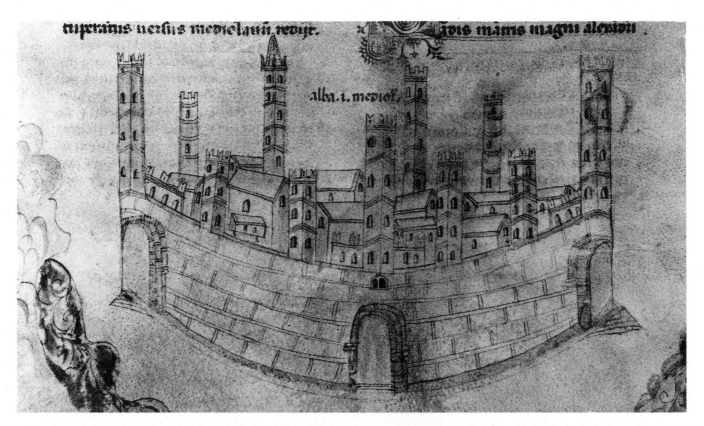

Italian cities dominated the life of the peninsula through all centuries of the Middle Ages because the economy and administration remained firmly urban-based. This early 14th-century drawing of

Milan, from Fianno's 'Cronaca di Milano', shows the city's impressive late medieval walls, with three gates visible, and numerous towers.

peninsula, as Italy in the period AD 400 to 1300 was transformed from being the centre of a great empire into an ever-changing kaleidoscope of tiny bickering states, often fought over by foreign powers. In Northern Italy the cities even achieved complete political autonomy and destroyed any unity imposed by kings or emperors. This was a gradual process, starting in the 10th century and more or less complete by the 12th, when the communes were firmly established and when an observer from feudal and monarchical Northern Europe could comment with astonishment that the Italians were governed 'by the will of consuls rather than rulers'. In Southern Italy the Norman, Hohenstaufen and Angevin kings of the 11th to 14th centuries prevented any similar rise of urban autonomy, but remained firmly city-based themselves, above all in their capitals of Palermo and Naples.

In the intensity and importance of its urban life Italy was exceptional. In the two centuries AD 600–800 it was the only part of Western Europe to have a substantial number of sizable towns, and it was more urbanized even than the Byzantine East. In the later Middle Ages it retained this predominance, and only a very few cities of 12th- and 13th-century Northern Europe matched those of Italy for size and splendour. But the exceptional importance of towns in Italian life was not just a question of size, it was also a question of the relationship between town and countryside.

In Northern Europe the aristocracy remained primarily rural, living in castles and manors, and only rarely in town houses; consequently the focus of landholding and of power was often in the countryside. In Italy, however, except perhaps briefly in the 10th and 11th centuries, landowners were normally urban-based. To illustrate the political and cultural dominance of the towns and of urban life, we need only compare the churches of medieval Italy with those of medieval England. English towns have a magnificent series of great cathedrals and also a wealth of lesser urban churches, but, to get a fuller picture of medieval patronage, we must go out into the countryside and also visit the villages. Here we find, even in poor areas, elaborate and sometimes massive churches built by the local lord, and containing the tombs and memorials of his family. In Italy, by contrast, rural parish churches are almost always a disappointment to the tourist and the art historian, but in the towns we find a plethora of buildings and memorials that more than makes up for this. Wealth was not usually spent in the countryside; rural villas were not the main houses of the Italian aristocracy, but only convenient and occasional retreats from the heat and bustle of urban life.

Commerce and economic life

The continuity of towns from Roman times perhaps depended more on the presence within them of the administration and the aristocracy of Italy than on commercial opportunity; however, their rapid expansion from the 10th century onwards was based largely on a prosperous, and then a booming, urban economy. Much of this was probably a question of developing humble but close economic links between the individual towns and their immediate agrarian hinterlands.

Because this local economic activity is scarcely dramatic, it features far less in the works of both contemporaries and modern historians than another area of Italian medieval pre-eminence: long-distance trade and commerce. But its importance should not be underrated. Except in the case of a few remarkable coastal towns, such as Amalfi or Venice, local trade with the immediate hinterland was probably always of much more importance to a town than dramatic long-distance trade in articles like spices, silks and wool.

In long-distance trade and commerce Italy certainly led Europe and profoundly influenced it. By the end of the 13th century Italians had established a trading empire that stretched from China to Britain. Furthermore they had not only opened the routes of commerce, they had also developed the structures to facilitate it. The merchants of an earlier period had themselves travelled with their goods, at their own risk, and then exchanged them for other goods or coin. In contrast, the great Italian firms by the end of the 13th century had huge funds of invested capital and professional agents stationed in all the major trading towns of Europe, doing business in products as yet unseen and often as yet unproduced, and paying for them in letters of credit.

In the prosperity and the political independence of their cities, Northern and Central Italy were more remarkable than the South. In the early Middle Ages towns in all areas of the peninsula may have had a roughly similar history of limited prosperity, but in the 12th century the towns to the north of Rome began to outstrip their Southern rivals in size, wealth, and political autonomy.

It is relatively easy to see why the political role of towns in the two areas should be so different. All stirrings towards communal self-government in the South were stamped on by a strong Norman kingship in the late 11th and 12th centuries, and then by their Hohenstaufen and Angevin successors. In the North the centralized state almost completely collapsed in the 10th century, and all attempts to reinstate it by the German emperors were to fail, however bloody and determined.

It is much more difficult, however, to say why the Southern towns ended up less prosperous than those of the North, and why in economic terms, from the 12th century onwards, one can reasonably talk of 'two Italys': a rich urbanized manufacturing North, and a

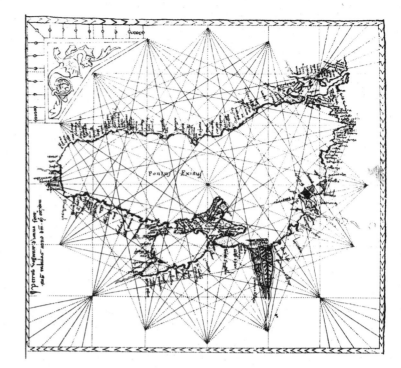

The importance of trade for medieval Italy encouraged cartographical skills; this navigator's map of the Black Sea (north is at the foot) is by Pietro Vesconte of Genoa (1318).

poor peasant South. Perhaps in part this was the price the South paid for strong central government and comparative tranquillity. The existence of such a government could weigh heavily on merchants in taxes, controls and monopolies, while in the Northern towns politics and the interest of trade were often closely combined (as in the Genoese and Pisan contributions to the first crusade, in return for commercial privileges in the conquered land). Undoubtedly too, a strong monarchy helped prevent Southern towns spreading the tentacles of economic and political control over the surrounding countryside. Yet these factors do not fully explain why an apparently flourishing commercial life in the 10th and 11th centuries at Bari, Amalfi, Gaeta and elsewhere should in the end be eclipsed and often dominated by the merchant towns of the North, above all by Pisa and Genoa.

The Italians, particularly from the North, made their mark not only in trade, but also in the closely related field of banking. It was in this area of commercial expertise that they probably had their greatest effect. The large banking firms, principally centred in Tuscany, were happy to juggle with money in a variety of ways: lending it, transferring it across Europe, selling insurance, and even playing complicated games with fluctuating exchange rates. In the late 13th and 14th centuries the Italians were the bankers of Europe. Private citizens, popes and kings depended on them: Edward I of England, for example, borrowed £392,000 from the Riccardi of Lucca in the period 1272–94 (when his ordinary annual income was only about £40,000). The potential profits were huge, but so too were the risks: the commercial world of Italy, and indeed the whole Tuscan economy, were severely shaken in 1342 when Edward III repudiated the massive debts he had accumulated with the Bardi and Peruzzi of Florence, and thereby drove them to bankruptcy.

Italian commercial panache not only opened the way to royal deficit-financing, it also tickled the imagination of Europe with its tales of the mysterious East. Thanks to Italian enterprise and to the peace imposed by the Mongol Empire, the route to India and China began to be regularly followed by Italian traders from the later 13th century onwards. Several of those who traded along this route, including the Venetian Marco Polo, wrote accounts of their journeys that circulated widely in Europe.

The great age of Italian commercial pre-eminence was certainly the 12th to 14th centuries, but its obscure origins can be traced back with reasonable confidence into some of the darkest centuries of the early Middle Ages, the period between about AD 600 and 800. These years saw the first signs of commercial activity in many of the centres that were to dominate the later Italian economy: for instance, Pisa, Amalfi and Venice. In 829 the will of a Venetian doge records that he had 1,200 pounds of gold invested in overseas ventures, and the excavation of an early medieval glass-manufactory at Torcello has shown that the Venetian lagoon's tradition of fine glass-making is much older than the earliest written reference to it in the 10th century. Even Lombard Italy, not normally seen as a centre of prosperity and sophistication, shows signs of a precocious commercial economy. In 715 the Lombard kings negotiated with the merchants of Comacchio the first recorded trading agreement in medieval Europe, and their laws show that merchants of Lombard blood were both rich and prestigious enough to serve in war on horseback alongside the landed nobility.

Urban amenities and urban pride

With this continuous tradition of urban life and prosperity went a survival of urban amenities, and a pride in the buildings of the towns. Medieval Italian towns, and certainly those of the Dark Ages, seldom or never matched the splendour and luxury of the Roman period, when all cities, even the most humble, had been provided by rich patrons with the sophistication of paved streets, buildings for entertainment, temples, piped water, drains, huge baths, public lavatories, and splendid ceremonial and civic buildings. But this tradition of amenities never totally died, and, with the new wealth of the 11th century onwards, it flourished again, though now the buildings constructed were above all churches, *palazzi* of the town government and *piazze* for the citizenry.

In some cases, however, there was a remarkable continuity, not only of the desire to build, but even of the ancient amenities themselves. Roman Pavia, for example, was provided with a complex underground network of drains to carry off ground-water and sewage. This was maintained throughout the Middle Ages, and indeed is still functioning today exactly as it did two thousand years ago. It was evidently a source of some pride to the people of Pavia in the Middle Ages. The 10th-century historian, Liudprand of Cremona, manages to work two references to the drains of his native Pavia into his history of contemporary Italian politics and the 14th-century Pavese, Opicino de Canistris, is careful to include the drains in his encomium of his city's splendours: 'Throughout the city, the roads and lavatory-shutes (which every house is provided with) are cleaned out when it rains into deep underground drains. These drains are like beautiful underground vaulted chambers, and some have vaults so tall that a horse and rider can pass through them.' Liudprand and Opicino had every reason to be proud, since it is very doubtful if any other town in Europe could match such sophistication.

In the provision of piped clean water and baths for its cities medieval Italy was also remarkable. Most Roman aqueducts were allowed to decay, mainly because they were no longer needed for the huge secular public baths, but some were kept up and repaired, largely to provide water for the bath-houses of the clergy, as in Rome throughout the early Middle Ages. The massive and luxurious secular public baths of classical times disappeared; instead there proliferated a large number of smaller baths more suited to the austere patronage of Christianity: baths for the clergy and baths for the poor and sick. A 9th-century commentator from St Gallen (in what is now Switzerland) thought it an unpleasant characteristic of the Italian clergy to be unnaturally clean: this is the best possible testimony to the continuity of Italian water-technology!

In order to drink and wash at home, the towns of the early Middle Ages did not need water to be piped in: they could manage adequately from wells, cisterns and water carried by women or donkeys. However, at least one fountain in Italy played continuously throughout the early medieval centuries. This was the famous Fountain of the Pine-cone (Fontana della Pigna) erected in the atrium of old St Peter's in late antiquity, possibly by Constantine himself. In the 8th and 9th centuries, popes were careful to keep this fountain working – a labour that involved keeping in repair an aqueduct bringing water all the way from Lake Bracciano. This tiny fountain is humble in comparison with the huge aquatic displays of classical, Renaissance or Baroque Rome, but it kept alive a tradition that has always linked Rome with fountains, and certainly it was a wonder that no Northern town could match. Charlemagne, or some later Northern emperor, was so impressed by it that he had a copy made to erect outside the palace-chapel at Aachen.

The Fountain of the Pine Cone, in front of Old St Peter's, Rome, was kept in repair through the darkest centuries of the early Middle Ages. In this 16th-century drawing the unfinished dome of new St Peter's looms over the fountain and the nave of Constantine's church, which stood intact until 1503.

In the later Middle Ages, the cities of Italy built on this early medieval tradition to create some monuments to the importance and beauty of water worthy of the ancient Romans themselves. The achievement was most spectacular in the hill-top towns, partly because the problem of supplying them forced their inhabitants to complete ambitious projects of hydraulic engineering, such as the great aqueduct of Spoleto, but also because the scarcity and preciousness of water on a hill-top encouraged towns to display it proudly once provided. At Perugia in the 1270s the leading sculptor of the age, Nicola Pisano, was commissioned to decorate the fountain at the end of the city's new aqueduct. In 1334 the government of Siena decided to complete its much-loved central piazza, the Campo, with a fountain supplied by a new and ambitious aqueduct. This fountain, the Fonte Gaia, was eventually completed and decorated by Jacopo della Quercia in the early 15th century.

In the hot South and Sicily water was always at something of a premium, and here too it was used and displayed to great effect. The lush pleasure-gardens of the 12th-century Norman kings at Palermo were kept green and fresh by fountains and basins of clear water. In the scorched landscape of Sicily in summer they must have stood out as desirable oases of lush vegetation and coolness.

Even when building types changed, the motivation for building – the conspicuous display of wealth and splendour – often remained very much the same. In 6th-century Italy the Ostrogothic king Theodoric spoke of his palace at Ravenna as 'the fine façade of government and a witness to kingship, which is displayed to the admiration of ambassadors, so that they can see from his dwelling what its master is like'. In 9th-century Carolingian Italy the Frankish emperors expressed very similar sentiments, when ordering repairs to their palaces, 'so that they will be suitable and beautiful for our use and for display to ambassadors who visit us from other nations'. In late 13th-century communal Siena the decision to build a new Palazzo Pubblico for the town government was taken because 'it is a matter of honour for each city that its rulers and officials should occupy beautiful and honourable buildings, both for the sake of the commune itself and because strangers often go to visit them on business. This is a matter of great importance for the prestige of the city.' The political structure had changed remarkably, from sub-Roman Gothic Italy to communal Siena, but a court official of Theodoric would have understood what the Sienese were talking about.

This quotation from Siena shows the pride of the Sienese in their city and in its beauty: a pride that in the late 13th and early 14th centuries was manifested not only in the building and decoration of the Palazzo Pubblico, but also in the commissioning and ceremonial instatement of Duccio's *Maestà*, in the over-ambitious project to enlarge the cathedral, and in the decoration of the Campo. It has rightly been said that the greatest works of art in Italy are the townscapes themselves. These are normally seen to be a product of civic wealth and patriotism, starting with the economic boom of the 12th century. In a sense this is correct, since very few buildings that we see today are any earlier than this date, but it must also be said that the Italian tradition of civic pride, and with it a pride in a city's appearance and a control of its buildings, is far older than this, and indeed probably has a continuous history from Roman times and earlier.

Two anonymous poets praising their native towns, Milan in the early 8th century and Verona in about 800, open with short accounts of the surviving Roman buildings of their cities before moving on to the main theme of their works, the relics and holy shrines. Both open with glowing descriptions of the Roman walls: 'The circuit has tall, roofed towers; it is resplendent and carved with great skill on the outside and within adorned with buildings. The width of the walls is twelve feet. Their foundation is a massive base of squared blocks; above this is an elegant superstructure of brick' (Milan); 'The square shape of the city is strongly walled; forty-eight towers gleam in the circuit, of which eight stand up taller than all the others' (Verona). This evident pride in the carefully maintained buildings of their past, a past that had never been allowed to die, could not be more different from the mournful reflections of an anonymous Anglo-Saxon poet looking at the ruins of one of Roman Britain's cities: 'Roofs are fallen, ruinous are the towers, despoiled are the towers with their gates; frost is in the mortar, broken are the roofs, cut away, fallen, undermined by age.' ('The Ruin'.)

Furthermore Italians did not just feel a vague pride for the appearance of their towns – they also enforced regulations to make sure their cities remained functional and beautiful. Although there are traces of them earlier, these regulations are best documented in the communal statutes of the 13th century onwards, which are full of decrees about street paving and dumping of rubbish, and which occasionally also make reference to more purely aesthetic concerns. In 13th- and 14th-century Siena, for instance, regulations were enforced to make sure that any houses built around the Campo did the piazza credit in materials and in design.

Alongside this pride in a city's buildings stood a pride in the written history of each town. This was true above all in later medieval Northern Italy, where the complete eclipse of the centralized state and the consequent rise of cut-throat local rivalry meant that the record of each individual town's events became of paramount importance. The greatest and most famous of these urban histories, that of Giovanni Villani for

Florence, included a long and glowing description of the wealth and industry of the city in 1338. Many towns, however, even some of the smallest, had in the 12th, 13th and 14th centuries their local historians, annalists and panegyricists. Italians came to see themselves first and foremost as citizens of a particular town and part of a distinctly local history, and only after this as members of any broader racial or geographical group. This created a strength of local tradition that, with all its advantages and disadvantages, is still very present in Italy today.

The strength of local pride and local feeling that had developed by the early 14th century is admirably shown in the meeting in Dante's *Inferno* between Virgil and Sordello, both natives of Mantua. These two men's lives were separated by 1,200 years; one wrote poetry in Latin glorifying the Rome of Augustus, the other wrote love lyrics in medieval Provençal in a period of war between independent Italian communes and a German emperor; and yet it did not seem absurd to Dante that, when the tormented spirit of Sordello by chance heard Virgil say he was of Mantuan birth, the two should embrace: ' "O Mantovano," ' Sordello exclaimed, ' "io son Sordello della tua terra." E l'un l'altro abbraciava.' All differences of time and culture were overriden by a deep and shared love of their home town.

Living with the past

The strength of urban life also meant that medieval Italians lived amidst the monuments of their classical past. Some of these were still performing their original function, some had been altered to a new use, and some had been abandoned; but almost all were prominent in the townscape.

In Verona, for example, the process was one of gradual transformation from within that left much standing, rather than one of destruction followed by new beginnings. The streets and forum, with successive repaving, slowly lost their Roman appearance, though they never wholly lost their Roman shape; the theatre was substantially torn down in order that its materials should be reused, and part of its site was given over to a church in the early 10th century; from the 4th century onwards churches appeared both inside and outside the walls, to replace the abandoned temples and to provide a new focus of worship and building; one of the Roman bridges disappeared before about 900; parts of the amphitheatre were torn down, or fell of their own accord; in the communal period the Roman defensive wall was replaced by a new circuit to protect an enlarged city.

However, through all these changes much survived, even if in an altered shape. Most of the amphitheatre remained, and it still dominates the city. The Roman bridge survived and was the only crossing over the Adige until the 14th century; despite extensive damage in the Second World War, its original form is still preserved and it is still open to traffic. Even the old gates of the Roman city continue to stand, although the wall they were attached to has long disappeared. Furthermore these Roman survivals were not 'dead' tourist attractions, but were an important part of the life of the medieval city, though often in a new capacity: the bridge remained important for obvious reasons; the Roman gates were no longer needed for defence, but were kept up to embellish two of the main streets of the town; and the amphitheatre came to be used for executions, civic pageantry, bull-fights and similar entertainments.

It is one of the main attractions of Italian towns today that they wear their past gracefully, and this is certainly because there was never a break between past and present, but rather a gradual process of adaptation and transformation. We see this process most clearly in the classical buildings adapted to new purposes from the 4th century onwards. The amphitheatre of Lucca, for example, probably no longer functioned for spectacles after the 4th century; in the 10th century its vaults were being used for storage and it had already been divided up amongst private owners; in the succeeding centuries these vaults were slowly built over and adapted; today what appears on the surface is only an amphitheatre-shaped piazza of houses. But just under the surface there are still substantial remains of the Roman structure.

Other buildings were adapted in more or less their original shape, so that their classical antecedents are still obvious. A famous case is the Pantheon in Rome, once a temple of all the gods, built by Hadrian on the site of an earlier building of Agrippa. This was converted into the church of S. Maria ad Martyres in the early 7th century, and so it has remained ever since, though at no point in the building's history was its earlier pagan dedication and name forgotten. The Pantheon is a particularly impressive example, but it was not at all rare. There were in the medieval towns of Italy hundreds, perhaps thousands, of buildings similarly adapted, and scores of them still survive today as, for example, the cathedral of Syracuse and the church of S. Maria at Assisi (both ex-temples).

Even in cases where the classical buildings were ripped apart, their ornamental elements often had a prominent second life, reused in medieval structures in such a way that they were clearly identifiable as ancient pieces. This style of architecture, with *spolia* (as the reused elements are called), went out of fashion in most of Italy in the 11th century, probably in part because the supply of suitable marbles was running low, but in Rome, with its inexhaustible supply, it remained current into the 13th century, as we can see in churches like S. Lorenzo fuori le Mura.

Most of this adaptation and reuse of classical buildings, or bits of buildings, was motivated by purely functional reasons of convenience; it was easier and cheaper than building, quarrying or working anew. However, it played a vital role in preserving many buildings or fragments of them after their original function had disappeared. Ironically, the Renaissance architects of Italy were much more destructive, because they were seldom content to adapt ancient buildings to new functions or to reuse marble without having it recarved. It is also important to realize that even in the Middle Ages a certain amount was done to preserve the monuments of the classical past for historic and aesthetic motives. For reasons of political ideology (in order to seem more Roman even than the Romans whom they ruled) the Ostrogoths were concerned to preserve as much as they could of this monumental heritage. They therefore deliberately granted ruinous public buildings to private individuals, on condition that the new owners maintained and repaired the ancient structures when adapting them to a new purpose.

In the immediately succeeding centuries there is no evidence of unneeded buildings being preserved for such ideological reasons, though there is evidence of antiquarian interest in classical monuments for their own sake, and of a pride in their splendour. A 10th-century drawing of Verona, for example, is above all a record of the Roman buildings of the city – some, such as the bridge and walls, still in use but some, such as the theatre and amphitheatre, by now empty ruins. A verse around the drawing praises the splendours, natural and man-made, of the city.

The primary motive for studying and preserving such buildings was certainly pride in the continuous and ancient history of the city. It was the same motive that made 12th-century Mantua adopt Virgil as a symbol of the city, placing his name, and later his bust, on their coinage. This interest in the past could lead to absurdities. The citizens of Padua, for instance, were not content with a Roman past, but had to have a Trojan one as descendants of Antenor, thereby putting themselves on an equal footing with the Roman descendants of Aeneas. In 1283 a recently discovered sarcophagus was declared to be Antenor's tomb, and it was set up in a prominent place with an inscription to this effect.

Because the past was so present and so impressive in Italy, it is hardly surprising that on many occasions it inspired conscious cultural revivals. The three best known of these are the 9th-century Roman revival of early Christian architecture and art, the 13th-century revival of classical modes of sculpture, and the late 13th- and early 14th-century first stirrings of a desire to revive the study of classical literature for its own sake. The only thing that these three well-known revivals had in common with each other was a conscious desire to seek cultural inspiration in a Roman past. Because the circumstances and needs of those medieval men who looked to the classical world for inspiration varied according to period and place, the aspects of ancient culture that they looked for and what they did with it once found were entirely different.

The early 9th-century popes in Rome, in particular Leo III and Paschal I, seeking to revive a supposed golden age of papal holiness and prestige, looked back to early Christian Rome, to the great basilicas of Constantine's time and to the mosaic decoration of churches like SS. Cosma e Damiano. They imitated these (on a smaller scale, and in a cruder style) in their own buildings, such as S. Prassede and S. Cecilia.

In the first half of the 13th century, Frederick II of Hohenstaufen, king of Sicily and emperor of the West, looked back to a very different Roman past for inspiration. He looked to imperial Rome of the Caesars to glorify and justify his own pretensions. From this past he took inspiration in several ways: imitating the imperial style of law, of coinage and of sculpture. To glorify his rule, he built at Capua a great triumphal gate, decorated with classicizing busts and with a seated and draped figure of himself in the antique manner. The North Italian sculptor Nicola Pisano was probably trained in Frederick's kingdom, and when he returned home to his native Pisa, though of course abandoning the imperial inspiration of the South, retained a profound interest in classical forms of sculpture. Nicola's work revolutionized the sculpture of Tuscany, and, with its classicizing interest in the depiction of mass, was perhaps also the main inspiration for a slightly later revolution in Tuscan painting, led by Cimabue and Giotto.

At the end of the 13th century and the beginning of the 14th, groups of men in Tuscany and especially in the Veneto also looked back to ancient Rome. These men, the so-called 'pre-humanists', were above all lawyers and notaries trained in Roman law and in Latin rhetoric in order to practise their professions. Their interests and training naturally led them to yet another area of the past, classical literature, and they sought out, copied and diffused manuscripts of the classical authors which they found in libraries like that of the cathedral of Verona. The future of what they had begun, humanism, will be studied in the next chapter of this book.

I have selected these three strands of conscious revival because they are particularly well known and because they illustrate well the very varied ways in which a classical past could provide inspiration. They are not, of course, by any means the complete story of the influence of the classical world on medieval Italian culture. There were also other periods of conscious revival, some of which we shall be looking at later – for example, 11th-century Bologna in law, 12th-century Rome in art and architecture, and 12th- and 13th-century Southern Italy in science (via the Byzantine and Arab worlds). It is also true that the Roman past was ever present, and therefore often an inspiration, even outside the many periods and places in which classical influence was sufficiently strong to merit the term 'revival'.

Even when there were centuries of slack or interruption, the survival of works from the past made it much easier to take up again at a later date the threads of an artistic tradition. We shall see in a later section how bronze-casting was little practised in Italy before the late 12th century. However, some of the great bronzes of classical times, in particular the equestrian Marcus Aurelius in Rome and the so-called 'Regisole' in Pavia, were carefully protected, preserved and displayed throughout the preceding and later centuries. This was of great importance in keeping alive a dormant Italian tradition, that was to be awoken and exploited in the 14th century by marble horsemen, such as the Cangrande at Verona, and in the 15th century by the great bronze statues of Gattamelata at Padua and Colleoni at Venice.

Urban culture

Because of their strong urban and mercantile traditions, medieval Italians were likely to have a broader education and be more sophisticated in those skills essential to life in towns and in commerce than their Northern European counterparts. We have seen hints of this sophistication in the drains and fountains of Pavia or Perugia, but we see it most clearly in the powerful traditions of the written word and of written law.

In the early Middle Ages, as usual, evidence is somewhat scanty, and one might at first suppose that in the 6th century an age of illiteracy (outside the privileged ranks of a few clergy) set in with the decline of the cultured senatorial aristocracy and the disappearance of the last recorded secular schools in the classical tradition. Certainly education declined, both in the range of subjects taught and in the standard of basic literacy achieved, but a degree of literacy and of dependence on the written word always remained.

In particular, from at least the late 7th century onwards in Lombard Italy, and continuously in Byzantine Italy, written charters were the normal means of transferring ownership of land and of other chattels. Furthermore these charters were no empty ratification of an essentially oral process: in disputes concerning ownership, charters, when available, were cited as conclusive evidence.

Signatures in the witness-lists of charters show that a surprisingly large number of people amongst the upper classes knew how to write at least their names (instead of signing with a cross). In the charters of Lucca, a Lombard town until 774, 47 per cent of witnesses in the 760s signed their names, and 83 per cent in the 890s. Of the lay witnesses, 11 per cent were capable of signing in the 760s and 77 per cent in the 890s. It is not quite clear where these people acquired their education. In the case of the clerics (and perhaps some of the laymen) it must have been in the cathedral schools that are recorded from the 8th century onwards. For most laymen, one can only assume some professional training or rudimentary private education that have left no trace at all in the records.

A drawing of a disputation at Pisa in about 1400. Disputations were a central feature of medieval higher education; they were formal debates on learned topics and provided exercise in logical argument and the dialectical methods of scholasticism.

By the later Middle Ages the scale of education and the degree of literacy had increased greatly from these tentative early medieval beginnings. In Florence in 1338, according to Giovanni Villani, 8,000 to 10,000 children were receiving elementary education, 1,000 to 1,200 at six different schools were being taught commercial skills, and 500 to 600 were learning Latin and logic at ecclesiastical schools. Even allowing for exaggeration, it is clear that education had become a basic part of any upbringing, professional or aristocratic.

Italian education and intellectual achievement in the later Middle Ages were most successful in the field of professional training. Given Italy's urban and commercial traditions, this is not surprising: the cities of Italy needed, and could afford, a host of notaries to draw up transactions – and a host of lawyers to dispute them!

Probably there was a continuous tradition of training for notaries and lawyers throughout the Middle Ages: certainly when they first appear in charters of the 8th century, they seem to be a recognized and respected class. But we do not know anything about this training before the Italian schools started to pour forth a horde of professionally trained men in the 11th and 12th centuries. In the field of legal and, to a lesser extent, notarial training Italy acquired a European reputation and pre-eminence. An ambitious medieval student who wanted to study theology would go to Paris, or later perhaps Oxford, but to get the best in law he would head for Bologna, or a lesser Italian centre like Pavia.

The Italian communes and their governments were proud and jealous of their schools, and often financed at least part of the necessary salaries. Such pride was partly born of an economic good sense: a successful university might bring troublesome students, but at least these brought with them the cash to pay for their intellectual and bodily needs. It was also born of a sense of the prestige that a great intellectual tradition might bring. The coins of medieval Bologna, for instance, carried on the reverse the proud inscription '*Bononia Docet*' ('Bologna teaches') and the 13th-century legal teachers of its university were given some magnificent tombs behind the apse of S. Francesco.

From the 11th century onwards Italian scholars not only trained the lawyers of much of Europe, but also produced the scholarly works of commentary and the textbooks used also by many who never came as far as Italy for their education. The most famous of all these works was a codification of canon law, Master Gratian's *Decretum*, completed in 1140. This work is more correctly known as the *Concordance of Discordant Canons*, a title that gives a much better idea of the labour and intellectual effort involved in setting order into the chaos of medieval canon law. Almost nothing is known of Gratian as a person, and indeed none of the Italian legal writers and teachers had the fame and flamboyance of the scholastic theologians of Northern Europe, but their work revolutionized both the study and the practice of European law.

The scholars of 11th-century Pavia and Bologna were credited with 'rediscovering' the law of the Roman Empire, above all the Code of Justinian, and as far as detailed intellectual legal study is concerned, this is probably true; but, as in other fields, their achievement had at a humbler level much older roots, stretching back without interruption through Byzantine and Lombard Italy to the legal theorists and legal enactments of the Roman Empire.

The large professional class of medieval Italy, the lawyers and notaries, had on occasion an importance beyond the confines of notarial formulas and legal distinctions. In the 10th and 11th centuries, when we can detect the first stirrings of communal discontent, lawyers and notaries feature prominently amongst the citizens agitating for greater independence from emperors or bishops. Since they constituted a sizable, rich and educated class of citizens, this prominence is not surprising. Much later, in the late 13th and 14th centuries, professional men were once more of great importance, this time in the 'pre-humanist' revival of classical literature in centres like Padua. Again it is not surprising that lawyers and notaries, with their traditions of secular learning and their need for Latin law and Latin style, should be at the forefront of a development towards the study of the classics in their own right.

The presence of highly developed legal study and of a mass of scholarly and well-qualified lawyers unfortunately did not make medieval Northern Italy a well ordered and peaceful place. Until the rise of the autocratic lords, the *Signori*, at the end of the 13th century, the strife-torn communes of the North generally lacked a powerful and effective executive arm to enforce law. As a result, law and litigation were often less a process of carefully regulating society from above (as the Roman lawyers might desire) than tools used by groups and individuals in the constant jockeying for power and influence in an unstable world. Indeed, such was the lack of a firmly imposed order from above that 12th- and 13th-century town dwellers often had to rely on means of self-protection and of settling differences that are characteristic of much more primitive societies: the defensive pact, the clan and the feud.

In Northern Europe, with the rise of the state and of state-imposed order, these mechanisms of self-defence were in decline in the 12th century. In Northern Italy,

on the other hand, despite its cultural and legal sophistication, the chaos of politics and the breakdown of central control forced citizens into a world of tower-houses, armed bands, ties of blood and vendetta. Hence the irony that while the Roman lawyers created on paper their carefully ordered concepts of sovereignty and law, Montagues and Capulets were spilling blood in the streets below.

Southern Italy

While the North, led by Bologna and followed by a multitude of smaller centres, was famous above all for a study of the law, the South of Italy was renowned principally for the medical school of Salerno, and for a tradition of scientific study and scientific writing.

This Southern intellectual reputation grew up in part out of a continuous Italian tradition of medical studies, going back to Roman times. This is suggested by the fact that other areas of Italy also had a considerable, if lesser, reputation for medicine: for example, there was a medical school at Bologna that produced in the later 13th century a noted commentator on the works of Galen and Hippocrates, Taddeo d'Alderotto. It is also certain that medical manuscripts were copied in early medieval Italy, and even that a few minor works were composed, such as a *Liber Medicinalis* written in Milan around AD 700.

It is only from the 10th century that Salerno is recorded as a medical school, and it would be rash to connect its origins too tightly with an old-established Italian tradition and a Roman past. It is likely that Salerno was influenced most, not by native Italian traditions, but by those of two of the former political masters of early medieval Southern Italy, the Byzantine Greeks and the Arabs. These races were responsible in the early Middle Ages for preserving and adding to the scientific writings of the ancient Greek world. In the West, with an almost total disappearance of knowledge of Greek outside Byzantine Italy, this scientific knowledge almost entirely vanished, beyond what was known through a few translators and adapters into Latin, such as Boethius in the 6th century.

The study of medicine in the South may have depended on new influence from the East, but once established it revived traditions that were very Italian. For instance, it gave new life to the medicinal spa at Baia near Naples. This had been a famous health and pleasure resort in classical times, but is not recorded between the later 6th and the 10th centuries. But by the 12th century it was booming again. Benjamin of Tudela, the Jewish travel-writer, in 1165 recorded that it was visited each summer by a large number of Italians for their health. In 1227 the Emperor Frederick II visited it for a cure, and by the 14th century it was famous not only for its medicinal qualities but also, like 18th-century Bath, as a centre of social and amorous activity.

The Norman and later the Hohenstaufen courts of

Southern Italy maintained a tradition of patronizing masters of Greek and Arab scientific and philosophical scholarship, whether of Eastern or Western birth. Roger II, for instance, provided a home for the Arab geographer Edrisi, who in 1154 dedicated to the king his illuminated and entirely Arab geographical work, the *Book of Roger*. Frederick II patronized, amongst others, the Western astrologer and translator of Aristotelian texts, Michael the Scot. The writings of Michael are a reminder that much of the learning was peripheral to what would now be considered scientific research. Frederick himself was almost certainly much more interested in astrology, which he seems to have used to regulate his daily and political life, than in the drier areas of Greek thought. Another of his scholars, Theodore 'the Philosopher', had a responsibility not only for astrology and Greek science, but also for producing new and exotic confectionery to tickle the imperial palate.

Frederick had a considerable curiosity about the natural world, and himself produced a remarkable treatise on falconry, *De Arte Venandi cum Avibus* (*The Art of Hunting with Birds*), which he dedicated to his son Manfred. The treatise consists in part of a synthesis of previous knowledge, such as that collected by Roger II's falconer William and by Arab writers on the subject, and in part of detailed and acute personal observation, accompanied by illustrations.

Frederick's book, with its mixture of the Arabic and the scientific, is typical of the Southern court, with its strong and cultured monarchy and its cosmopolitan traditions. Another venture of his, the establishment of the University of Naples in 1234–9, could also have originated only in Southern Italy. Like the universities of the North, it gave above all a strong practical training, in law and rhetoric; but its aim was very different. It was set up as a state university, with the express aim of producing trained and skilled servants to run the highly organized and centralized Southern kingdom. Furthermore it was Frederick's aim that it should be the only university to provide this training; students and professors were forbidden to leave the South to study elsewhere.

It is questionable whether the Normans and Hohenstaufen were uniformly successful in enforcing their will over the South. But they certainly developed a façade of rule that was uniquely autocratic, and, behind it, an administration that, even if not quite as all-embracing and smooth running as it claimed, was none the less certainly more effective than that of any other Western European state, including even Angevin England and Capetian France. In creating this state, the Normans of the 12th century, especially Roger II, used the whole range of examples of kingship and administration that were available to them, whether Arab, Byzantine, or feudal North European. The Hohenstaufen Frederick II in the early 13th century, after an initial period of civil war, was able to expand

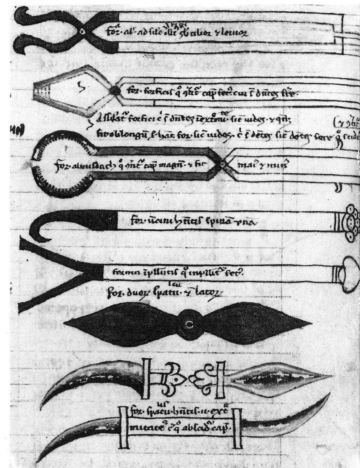

Medieval Southern Italy's high reputation for medical science was partly a result of its Islamic inheritance: these surgical instruments are from a 13th-century Latin translation of an Arabic medical text.

the Norman achievement with an extension of effective royal power backed by a large force of Moslem mercenaries, a string of royal castles and propaganda that harked back to antiquity, as seen in the triumphal arch at Capua, the gold coinage bearing Frederick's bust in the antique manner, and the legal code of 1231, the *Liber Augustalis*.

Courts and the lack of them

Southern Italy in the 12th and 13th centuries was exceptional in that it had a powerful, rich monarch and therefore a court and a court culture. The rest of medieval Italy was much more politically fragmented and mostly under an oligarchic rule: as a result, no individual had the opportunity to patronize scholars on the scale of Norman and Hohenstaufen Southern Italy. This absence of courts and court patronage had a profound effect on the shaping of medieval Italian culture.

As we have seen, in intellectual achievement Italy was mainly remarkable for its level of literacy and its professional training of lawyers, notaries and doctors: people able to flourish in the rich urban environment of the peninsula. Except in the 12th- and 13th-century South, it was much weaker in what might be termed 'high' intellectual achievement, above all in theology and philosophy. There were several great Italian theological thinkers in the 11th to 13th centuries: Peter Damian, Anselm of Aosta, Lanfranc of Pavia, Peter Lombard and Thomas Aquinas. But of these, only Peter Damian wrote most of his work in Italy: the rest all moved north to the French schools and beyond.

In this later period the reason why Europe north of the Alps held the ascendancy over Italy in high culture was probably mainly a matter of tradition. Northern Europe, above all the Ile de France, had the established schools and therefore attracted scholars and teachers. The lack of a similar tradition in Italy probably had its origins as far back as the 8th and 9th centuries, when the Frankish conquest of Northern Italy and the decline of the independent Southern Lombard duchies caused the disappearance of a Lombard court-culture. In the 8th century, at the courts of Liudprand in Pavia and of Arechis II in Benevento and Salerno, we find a patronage of intellectuals, such as Peter of Pisa and Paul the Deacon, of a scale and quality to rival anything in the rest of Europe at that date. But the Frankish conquest destroyed the court of Pavia and drew what talent there was in Italy out of the country towards the courts and monasteries of the North: Peter of Pisa, Paulinus of Aquileia, and, briefly, Paul the Deacon all moved north to the Carolingian court. Italy in the 9th and 10th centuries, under Frankish and Ottonian rule, became a place that ambitious scholars left, or where intellectuals born and trained in the North, like the Lotharingian Rather or the French Gerbert of Aurillac, were given ecclesiastical posts as a reward by Italy's foreign masters. But it had nothing of the intellectual vitality of the courts of Charlemagne, Charles the Bald and Otto I.

By the 11th and 12th centuries great theological scholars of Northern Italy, like Lanfranc and Anselm, however talented, had little chance of gaining plum posts in the Italian church, since by this date the whole network of ecclesiastical patronage had collapsed in the chaos of communal politics. The archbishopric of Milan, for instance, was not in the gift of a ruler, who might spot a talented intellectual, but was being bitterly fought over by the local Milanese. On the other hand, in Normandy and England, where both Lanfranc and Anselm completed their careers, the duke and king were able to give them successively a prize abbacy and the primacy of all England. Not surprisingly, men of their calibre went north.

The high culture of philosophy and theology was particularly dependent on patronage, since it had little practical application, and so was hard to sell in the market place. Because of foreign domination, followed by political disintegration, the conditions favouring such patronage were rare in medieval Italy. However, by the end of our period, courts were returning to Northern Italy with the rise of the *Signori*, autocratic lords of the former republican communes. Not surprisingly, we find that these men were of great importance as patrons of the new humanist learning.

In republican Italy it was possible to pursue a part-time intellectual career while earning a living – Boccaccio, for example, earned his money mainly as an employee of the Bardi bank and as a Florentine ambassador – but it was difficult. Life was much easier as a 'pure' intellectual, fed and supported by a *Signore*. Boccaccio himself tried to escape the grindstone by seeking a position at the Neapolitan court, and the greatest intellectual figure of the 14th century, Petrarch, lived, not in his native republican Florence, but at a series of Northern courts. In 1353 he had to defend himself against criticism of his move to the court of the tyrant Giovanni Visconti of Milan, stating, rightly, that it was necessary to provide himself with the leisure (*otium*) and tranquillity (*solitudo*) that he needed. Republican Florence could only offer him work, in the form of a chair at the University, and this he turned down.

The rarity of courts in medieval Italy also affected literary achievement. Love poetry in the vernacular, the Romance, and the ideals of *courtoisie* all originated in the cultured ease and patronage of the royal and noble courts of 12th-century Europe north of the Alps. Italy was to imitate these ideals with enthusiasm, borrowing the forms and much of the vocabulary of *courtoisie*, but only after a considerable lapse of time. Significantly, some of the very first vernacular literature in Italian also originated in a court, that of Frederick II.

Influence from abroad: the East

The Arab, Greek and Latin culture of the Norman and Hohenstaufen South reminds us that Italy stood culturally and geographically between the Arab and Byzantine South and East and the Germanic and Latin North and West. This uncertain position between two worlds was not just geographical but was also underlined by political and racial conquest and settlement. Ever since the Visigoths marched into Italy in the early 5th century, sacking Rome in 410, the peninsula was at the mercy of a succession of Northern invaders, at first rude barbarians, and then kings and emperors with greater cultural pretensions but with similar territorial ambitions. In the late 5th century the Ostrogoths arrived, in the mid-6th the Lombards, in the late 8th the Franks, in the mid-10th the Germans, and in the South the Normans in the 11th and the Angevin French in the late 13th.

The Eastern connection was just as marked, though in terms of political control it was eradicated earlier. The whole of Italy became a province of the Eastern,

Greek-speaking Byzantine Empire when Justinian reconquered it from the Ostrogoths in the mid-6th century. Much of it, including Ravenna, Rome, Naples and Sicily, resisted the initial Lombard invasion of the 6th century and remained in Byzantine hands. Greek control in the North was gradually chipped away, until Ravenna itself fell to the Lombards in the mid-8th century; though even here Venice with her lagoon continued in a vague allegiance to the emperor in Constantinople. In the South, Greek power lasted much longer. Sicily fell to the Arabs in the 9th century, but areas of mainland Southern Italy, centred on Apulia, remained Greek until the Norman conquests of the 11th century. The Arabs in their turn conquered and settled Sicily, took over parts of the Southern mainland, and even for a time seriously threatened and devastated Central Italy and Rome. Their power in Sicily was only destroyed in the late 11th century by the Normans, with the help of fleets from the North Italian communes.

The Arabs and Greeks brought with them powerful and influential cultural traditions, which long outlasted their political power. We have already seen this in part in the medical and scientific culture of Salerno and of the Norman and Hohenstaufen courts. It is also very clear in the visual arts of the 12th century. Arab influence can be seen in the bulbous domes of Norman Sicilian churches and in details like the elaborately carved ceiling of the Cappella Palatina in Palermo. Byzantine influence is even more marked. Greek mosaicists worked for Roger II in the 1140s at the cathedral of Cefalù, at the church of the Martorana and at the Cappella Palatina in Palermo, and for William II in the 1170s at the cathedral of Monreale.

Greek dominance in Italy in the visual arts can be traced with reasonable confidence to the beginning of our period. The carvings of 6th-century Ravenna, for example, are for the most part the work of Constantinopolitan sculptors. The frescoes of early medieval Rome, such as those in S. Maria Antiqua, were closely inspired by Byzantine developments, and in 8th-century Lombard Italy a Greek painter produced the fine frescoes of S. Maria foris Portas, Castelseprio. In later medieval Italy, Greek influence remained important even in areas that had not been under Eastern political control since the 6th century. Italy did undoubtedly develop its own regional schools of mosaic and fresco decoration, but until the very end of the 13th century these schools can reasonably be termed 'provincial Byzantine'. It was only at this date in painting and mosaic, with the works of Cimabue and Giotto, that Italy developed a style that is very definitely not Byzantine, based as it was on the depiction of mass, rather than on hieratic stylization.

This impression of a gradual loosening of Eastern ties and of the birth of a powerful native school is particularly noticeable in the case of fresco and mosaic but it also holds for other areas of artistic achievement.

Byzantine skills provided models for Italian craftsmen throughout the Middle Ages. The bronze doors (1076) of the sanctuary of St Michael, at Monte S. Angelo, Apulia, inlaid in silver with stories of the archangel, came from Constantinople itself.

For example, in the 11th century, decorated bronze doors were greatly appreciated in Italy, but at this date had to be imported from Byzantium: examples can be seen at S. Marco in Venice, S. Paolo in Rome, Amalfi, and Monte S. Angelo in Apulia. The only native products were the technically crude early panels of S. Zeno at Verona. However, by the late 12th century Italian mastery had taken over, and even in Greek-influenced Monreale it was the work of a Pisan bronze-caster, Bonanno, that was commissioned for the great west door. By the early 14th century, Italian bronze-casters were producing not only doors, but also sculptures in the round, such as the Evangelist symbols on the façade of Orvieto cathedral.

93

In the case of a minor art, decorative pottery, the story is similar, though here the main foreign influence was Arab. In much of Italy from the 11th century onwards it was the fashion to decorate the exterior of churches with colourful and precious pottery plates set into the brick- or stone-work. On 11th-century churches these plates are all foreign: some are Byzantine, but most are Arab, from Syria, Egypt or North Africa. However, in the 13th century Italy developed its own powerful tradition of local fine pottery, maiolica, and from then on it was above all Italian pots that were used to decorate churches and to grace the tables of the rich.

In written culture, because of the language barrier, Eastern influence on Italy was always much less dominant than in the visual arts, until the work of translation in the 12th and 13th centuries. However, here too there is some evidence of continuous contact. In the Lombard Duchy of Benevento, which inevitably had close ties with Byzantine holdings in Southern Italy, Greek manuscripts are known to have been copied in the 8th and 9th centuries, and certainly Greek was known and read not only in Byzantine Ravenna, but also in the South and in Rome, where most of the popes of the late 7th and early 8th centuries were Greeks by birth and culture.

The influence of the North

Whereas the influence from the East was strongest in the visual arts, the North had a powerful influence on scholarship (made inevitable by the links of a common Western European Latin scholarly culture) and on literature (facilitated by the similarity between Romance languages).

Though Italy was supreme in law and medicine, in the queen of medieval disciplines, theology, she took a very secondary position behind France. As we have seen in an earlier section, those Italians who excelled in theology were generally in part French-trained and spent much of their working lives in the North.

Similarly, the development of vernacular literature did not originate in Italy, but only spread there slowly and hesitantly from France, this time above all from Provence. In France the vernacular appeared as a language of written literature in the late 11th century, notably in love poetry, epics and romances. Italians seem to have been attracted to these French works from an early date: the earliest depiction of Arthur in art is on the mosaic floor of the 12th-century cathedral of Otranto in the very far south of Apulia. However, although clearly interested in French developments, Italians were slow to create their own vernacular literature.

Some of the first poetry in Italian was written in the early 13th century at the Sicilian court of Frederick II, who himself wrote love poetry in the vernacular – an example which was followed in several centres, particularly Florence, Pisa, Lucca and Genoa. This nascent poetic tradition was, however, closely dependent for both content and style on the courtly lyrics of troubadour Provence, and indeed much of it, such as the works of Sordello of Mantua, was even written in Provençal.

By the end of the 13th century and in the 14th century, the Italian vernacular was much more firmly established, though even at this date the picture can be greatly exaggerated by concentrating attention on Florentines. Florence undoubtedly produced a flood of great literary figures who wrote much of their work (though by no means all of it) in Italian, and who by now looked not to France but to local precedent. In late 13th-century literature we have the love lyrics of a group of poets that included Guido Cavalcanti and Dante. In his *De Vulgari Eloquentia* Dante provided (in Latin) the first explanation for the use of the vernacular and the first treatise on Italian style. In later life, when in exile, he composed in Italian verse his masterpiece, the *Divina Commedia*, a poetic depiction of the entire divine order. In the mid-14th century, Dante was succeeded as the main Italian literary figure by two more Tuscans, Petrarch and Boccaccio. In the writing of history in Italian, rather than Latin, Florence again excelled, as can be seen in the chronicles of Dino Compagni and of Giovanni Villani.

Because these Tuscan writers have become the official fathers of modern Italian literature, it is easy with hindsight to see the Italian vernacular firmly established as a literary language by 1350. But outside Tuscany and even within Tuscany outside Florence (for instance, in a thriving centre for the visual arts like Siena) the tradition was much weaker. Little poetry was being written in Italian by others than Florentines, and most urban chronicles, such as that of Mussato at Padua, were in Latin.

The reason why Florence should excel in this particular field is very obscure, but it would certainly be an error to see it entirely as a sign of cultural superiority. The weakness of Italian outside Florence is as much an indication of the strength of Latin in other places as of the poverty of the local vernacular. Latin always remained powerful in medieval Italy as a medium of both intellectual thought and literary expression; in fact after about 1350, with the rise of humanism and the influence of Petrarch, it again almost entirely shouldered out writing in Italian.

In the visual arts and in architecture, the main influence from the North came in the 13th and 14th centuries, at the time that Eastern influence was in decline. We see this clearly in painting and sculpture, as for example in the elegant and elongated representations of the human figure in the frescoes and panel paintings of Simone Martini. These have broken away from Byzantine influence, and are clearly inspired by Northern European Gothic art as well as by native precedents.

There are also art forms that can be shown to have

The court of the Norman kings of Sicily displayed strong Islamic and Byzantine influence, partly as a result of Greek and Arab scholars and craftsmen employed by the king. This detail from a 12th-century illuminated manuscript shows the death of William the Good in 1189. The dying king is attended by his doctor Achim and his astrologer, both Arabs.

originated in France. In particular, the tradition of funerary sculpture was very weak in Italy before the 13th century, but well established north of the Alps. Through a series of artists, like Arnolfo di Cambio, who looked north for precedents and examples, this tradition gradually spread all over the Italian peninsula. In the late 13th and early 14th centuries, the cardinals and popes of Rome, the nobles and kings of Naples, and the merchants and artistocrats of Florence were buried in elaborately carved figured tombs in the manner of the North, whereas their predecessors, even as late as 1250, had been buried under slabs decorated only with an inscription, or in a reused ancient sarcophagus. This was an important change, not only for the contemporary works of art it produced (such as the tombs of Boniface VIII in Rome and of Robert of Anjou in Naples), but also because it opened the way for the plethora of splendid Renaissance and Baroque tombs in Italian churches.

The most obvious artistic import from the North was Gothic architecture. In the 13th and 14th centuries this spread from across the Alps all over the peninsula. Even Rome, which was the most architecturally conservative of all Italian cities, has a Gothic church of this period, S. Maria sopra Minerva. In most of Italy the Gothic style was adapted, as we shall see in a later section, to fit local traditions.

In the early Middle Ages, despite greater political dependence, the influence of the North was much less marked than it was after 1100. The Germanic invaders, above all the Goths and the Lombards, brought their own distinctive cultures, but these eventually disappeared almost without trace under the force of sophisticated native Italian tradition. For example, although the Goths and Lombards must have had their own heroic poetry, like the Anglo-Saxons, of their language there survives only a smattering of words and place-names in modern Italy. Only one fascinating building, the Mausoleum of Theodoric at Ravenna (*c.* 526), shows a cross-fertilization between the native Roman and the Germanic traditions; but it stands out as a unique monument to what might have been a fusion of two cultures but never was. The building contains a number of Roman elements: squared ashlar blocks, classical stone decoration, an imperial porphyry sarcophagus and a low dome, in shape similar to contemporary 6th-century structures. But it also contains elements that are totally alien to the classical world and must have originated in a Gothic mind: a frieze of 'pincer' decoration that can be paralleled on Ostrogothic jewellery and a dome constructed of one huge monolith, which is so odd and so un-Roman that it must reflect some obscure Germanic desire for a solid cover to one's tomb. Theodoric lying in his porphyry sarcophagus under a massive monolith represents an eclectic approach to culture which even he did not follow in his other buildings and which certainly had no future in Italy.

A channel between East and West?
Because Italy had close links with both the Greek and Arab East and the Latin and Germanic North, it is not surprising that it was on occasion a point of contact between the two worlds and a channel whereby Eastern intellectual and artistic influence reached Northern Europe.

95

The Norman lords of Sicily, for example, not only had a court based on oriental models, but also maintained close contacts with their kinsmen in both Normandy and England. It was therefore inevitable that a certain amount of Greek and Arab culture should filter into North Europe by way of Italy. At the very end of the 11th century, a verse book on hygiene, diet and healthy living, *Regimen Sanitatis Salernitanum*, was dedicated to a 'king of England', probably Robert Curthose, Duke of Normandy, cured at Salerno in 1099 (at a time when he believed that he was about to claim his rightful English inheritance from his younger brother Henry I). Influence in administration and painting can be shown in the later 12th century, when Master Thomas Brown from the court of Roger II of Sicily held a special seat at the Exchequer of Henry II of England, and when one of the artists of the Winchester Bible was clearly closely influenced by some of the Byzantine mosaics of Sicily.

Cosmopolitan Norman Sicily, not surprisingly, also served as one of the centres of translation of Greek and Arab scientific and philosophical works into Latin, and therefore as a centre of diffusion of ancient Greek thought into the West. A number of scholars, such as Adelard of Bath, Aristeppes of Palermo and Eugenius the Emir, some of Greek or Arab birth and some Westerners, laboured at translation in Southern Italy in the 12th century. But it would be a mistake to exaggerate the role of the Sicilian kingdom as a channel for Eastern culture to the West. The contacts and influences we can document are scarce and spasmodic, and even the importance of the South in the vital work of 12th-century translation can be exaggerated. Spain for instance, divided between Christian and Arab lords, was much more important than Sicily in this achievement.

In the earlier Middle Ages the evidence is, as usual, poor, but it seems that the contacts between East and West through Italy were even less. A large number of Italians certainly understood and could read both Greek and Latin, but there was not yet enough informed interest in Greek thought in Northern Europe to stimulate the work of translation that would eventually make this contact important. Consequently in this period Western scholars relied for their knowledge of ancient Greek thought on references in Latin works and on the few works of translation and synthesis produced by Boethius at the very beginning of our period, when a secular culture in Greek and Latin still survived.

After about AD 500, an effective language barrier kept the Greek East and the Germanic and Latin North apart and mutually suspicious in intellectual thought. Since this barrier did not exist in the visual arts, here there may have been more contact, and much of it through Italy, though sadly the evidence is not really sufficient to allow for more than informed speculation. For instance, it is almost certain that Charlemagne's

court school of manuscript illumination was closely influenced by Byzantine painting. It is also very possible that this influence came not direct from Constantinople, but through Byzantine work in Italy, such as the frescoes at Castelseprio. If so, Italy was a cultural channel between East and West at a very important time in the history of Western art.

Italian and regional traditions

The three preceding sections may have given an impression that Italy was culturally passive – either a channel to transmit influence from East to West, or soft wax on which Byzantines, Arabs and Northern Europeans could stamp their cultural imprint.

This is not of course the whole truth. In earlier sections we have already seen many areas of culture, such as the law, the art of city life and the influence of a classical past, that are strongly and distinctively Italian. We have also seen how native traditions in language, literature, architecture and art were sufficiently strong to survive barbarian invasion and political domination and the Germanic culture that these brought with them. This section will explore more fully the force of native Italian tradition, particularly in art and architecture, in order to show how, even when foreign influence was strong, it did not generally manifest itself as a pure and alien phenomenon, but rather fused with local elements, to create styles that are distinctively Italian.

Even when we find works that were probably produced by foreign artists and craftsmen, we tend to find these used in a distinctive Italian context. For example, in Norman Sicily the mosaics seem to be almost entirely the work of Greek craftsmen, but, because the Normans usually built basilical churches in the Western tradition, and not centrally-planned churches like the 12th-century Greeks, the iconographic cycle of these mosaics has had to be arranged to fit a shape of church that was rare in the contemporary East. The result, for instance in the Cappella Palatina at Palermo and the cathedral of Monreale, is an Italian design of church, with Byzantine mosaics adapted to fit its shape.

The survival, as at 12th-century Monreale, of the long, aisled basilical plan as the main form of Italian church is an excellent example of the strength of local tradition. Its strength is the more remarkable because, as far as we can tell, in Italy between about AD 600 and 800 very few basilicas were built. This was partly because the buildings of these centuries were often tiny if elaborate chapels (like John VII's oratory at St Peter's in Rome, S. Maria foris Portas at Castelseprio, and S. Maria in Valle at Cividale) and partly because there was a vogue for centrally-planned churches such as S. Maria in Pertica at Pavia (since destroyed) and S. Sofia at Benevento (the latter crudely but explicitly based on the shape of its Constantinopolitan namesake).

But even a pause of two centuries and a vogue for central plans in the Eastern manner did not destroy the basilica as the favoured and most common Italian design of church. This was because the great Christian basilicas of an earlier period, the 4th to 6th centuries, stood throughout the Middle Ages and were inevitably a source of architectural inspiration for the ambitious structures built from the 9th century onwards. This is an important point, because it illustrates the extent to which the artistic traditions of a country lie not only in the achievements of a particular period, but also in what is maintained of the achievements of the past.

We have already partly illustrated this theme in the discussion of the classical buildings turned into churches, but it is even more striking in ecclesiastical architecture. We can still form an impression of this by visiting Italy today, since many late Roman churches still stand, such as S. Sabina and S. Maria Maggiore in Rome (both of the 5th century), Ambrose's S. Simpliciano at Milan and the several surviving churches of 5th- and 6th-century Ravenna. Before the great rebuilding of Italy's churches, brought about by the wealth of the 11th to 12th centuries, every Italian town must have had at least one major paleo-Christian basilica standing and continuously used, as a constant reminder of a particular style of late Roman building and of styles of decoration. The late Roman cathedrals of Florence and Milan, for example, stood throughout the early Middle Ages and were only demolished when the present late medieval buildings were begun. (Their marble and mosaic floors, preserved under the present churches, have now been excavated.) In Rome, the huge basilica of St Peter's, built by Constantine in the early 4th century over the grave of the Apostle, remained intact until the architects of the Renaissance demolished it to make way for the new church. The history of old St Peter's gives us some idea of the constant effort required to keep the structure in shape: major repairs to the roof are recorded seven times between 590 and 858, and these often necessitated the felling and transport of huge timbers from Southern Italy or from the Central Italian Apennines, since no tree growing locally could span the broad nave.

Because of this degree of survival and maintenance of the basilicas of early Christian times, it is hardly surprising that the builders from the 9th century onwards (as at S. Prassede in Rome and S. Salvatore in Brescia) built churches on a traditional Italian basilical plan, despite Eastern influence and despite what had been built in the period 600 to 800. The basilica remained a fixed point of Italian architectural tradition, occasionally influencing the North, as during the Carolingian Renaissance, and ensuring that most Western churches even today are recognizable as the same kind of building as those erected over 1,500 years ago by Constantine. It is also not surprising that Italy remained a centre for decorative arts of the type that ornamented the churches of early Christian times: *opus sectile* (marble marquetry-work) and wall- and floor-mosaic.

The mosaics of Sicily are unusually pure instances of foreign influence, since they involved Eastern craftsmen producing the finished article for an Italian patron. Normally outside influence was taken up by native craftsmen, often at second- or third-hand, and the result is generally much more of a fusion of the local and the alien. An excellent example of this is Italian Gothic. The basic forms came from France: the pointed arches, the vaults, the large windows, the thin walls and the tall naves. When these ideas reached Italy they produced a wide variety of local Gothic styles, because they were fused into local traditions of building and decoration. In the valley of the Po, churches had always been in brick, owing to the scarcity of building stone, and consequently the Gothic churches of the area are imposing and austere brick buildings, like S. Petronio at Bologna. In Tuscany and Central Italy, however, building stone and marble were commoner, and here Gothic takes a completely different form in the striped and polychrome cathedrals of Florence, Siena and Orvieto. Only in Naples do we find churches that would not look out of place in France, and here it is only because the Angevin French lords of the city favoured peculiarly pure French styles. Otherwise, the Gothic churches in Italy have perhaps less in common with Northern Europe than they do with local Romanesque buildings – for instance, in Tuscany the polychrome marble of S. Miniato near Florence and of Pisa cathedral, and in the Po valley the brick of Romanesque Pavia and Piacenza.

The example of Gothic shows that at least by the later Middle Ages Italy had not simply a strong national tradition, but a number of others that varied from region to region. This was undoubtedly because both politically and geographically (by reason of the great Apennine barrier) the peninsula was extremely divided and also because it was rich enough to support a large number of local traditions of art and craftsmanship. We see this very clearly in 11th- and 12th-century architecture. In Southern Italy and Sicily we find a peculiar blend of the architectural traditions of the Normans, the Arabs and the Byzantines; in Rome a highly traditional architecture of squat basilicas built on reused columns; in Tuscany churches elaborately decorated in polychrome marble, but recognizably different in style even in such neighbouring centres as Pisa, Lucca and Florence; in Venice a Byzantine-inspired architecture of domes and mosaics; in the Po valley massive brick churches with details, such as capitals and doorways, carved in sandstone or Verona marble.

At the same date we find a wide stylistic variety of floor decoration in marble and mosaic. Decorative marble-work and mosaic were an Italian speciality in the 12th century, partly a continuous tradition arising from the availability of materials, and partly a revival, inspired by the remains of ancient and Early Christian Italy and by the influence of Byzantium. However, this tradition took a very different form in different parts of Italy. In the Po valley and Apulia schools of mosaicists flourished, producing figured tessellated floors, full of heroes, monsters and symbols, like those at Pavia and Otranto. In Venice, Sicily and Rome we find brightly coloured geometric floors of *opus sectile* marble-work, influenced by contemporary Byzantine work, but different in each area: the availability of red and green porphyry, for instance, made great discs of these precious materials a distinctive feature of Roman Cosmatesque marble-work, whereas in Tuscany the style was completely different, with intricate inlays of black and white marble, as at S. Miniato near Florence.

This powerful regionalism in architecture and marble working can be matched in other areas of cultural achievement. In painting by about 1300 there are distinctive stylistic schools recognizable in Rome, Florence, Siena, Bologna, Venice, and elsewhere. There were many contacts between these schools: Giotto, for instance, worked in Rome, Assisi, Florence and Padua. But, despite these contacts, we find, for example, that Sienese painting remains recognizably different from that of nearby Florence. Similarly, in 13th-century intellectual achievement, regional traditions were strong: science and medicine in the South, canon law in Rome, banking and vernacular literature in Florence, the law in Bologna, and the study of classical literature in the Veneto.

This variety at a high level of culture was matched in the humbler details of townscape and domestic architecture, since town sites, local building traditions and the local availability of materials created cities that are profoundly different from each other: Venice with its canals, its marble-faced palaces and its strange chimney-pots; Bologna, with its wooden and brick houses, and its porticoes; hill-top Siena, with its elegant Gothic stone façades; Genoa, cramped into a tiny space between the mountains and the sea, with its five- or six-storey buildings and its narrow dark alleys; Rome, with its houses and palaces carved into ancient ruins or built of reused columns and bricks.

Because so little survives from the period before 1000, whether in church architecture, in sculpture, in fresco or in domestic architecture, it is impossible to say how old each regional tradition is. In this period we can only point to particular differences between certain areas: between, for example, Pavia in the first half of the 8th century, with its classicizing stone sculpture, its Latin court and its Lombard law-codes, and to contemporary Rome, with its Greek popes and its Byzantinizing frescoes.

The degree of regional variation that we can document after about 1000 persisted beyond the Middle Ages because the political divisions remained until 1870; what can be said of Romanesque can equally well be said of the differences between Baroque architecture in Sicily, Apulia, Naples, Rome, Florence or Turin. It is one of the great charms of the peninsula that the natural

differences of the landscape are accentuated in the towns by a multitude of profound and deeply felt differences in local culture.

Italy and the religious life

In the religion of medieval Italy we find some new and important themes, though many of them are linked with cultural and political developments that we have already examined in part.

Of unique importance, not just for Italy, but also for European and world Christianity, was the gradual emergence of the Roman papacy as the spiritual head of the Western church. This was a slow process, helped by a series of great men and by historical accidents so complex that even the sceptic might see in them the workings of a divine plan. The bishops of Rome started from a sound ideological position, both as successors of St Peter, whose grave and church they were careful to honour, and as bishops of the chief city and cradle of the Roman Empire. Given this situation, it is not surprising that even before 500 they emerged as important figures in the Church and had developed grandiose theories of spiritual leadership and superiority, although only further developments over the succeeding medieval centuries allowed these theories to be elaborated and put into practice.

In particular, the bishops of Rome were exceedingly fortunate that the secular political world of Italy and of the West collapsed in such a way as to leave them with a considerable degree of independence. Rome survived as an obscure and largely autonomous frontier area of the Byzantine Empire and its bishops neither disappeared under barbarian lordship, nor fell under tight Eastern imperial control. This saved them from the fate that befell the patriarchs of Constantinople: becoming influential spiritual leaders, but without any degree of independence. The patriarchs in Constantinople were appointed by the Eastern emperors and strictly controlled by them, with violence if necessary. Undoubtedly if Rome had survived as the seat of a powerful Roman Empire or had become the centre of a strong barbarian kingdom, its bishops would have assumed a very similar position. Indeed, in the very few periods when a secular power did firmly control central Italy, as in the mid-6th century under Justinian and in the later 10th century under the Ottonian Germans, popes were appointed, pressurized and even deposed very much in the Eastern manner.

However, for most of the Middle Ages Rome miraculously remained a disputed frontier area between great powers: to the north, the Lombards, followed by the Franks, the Germans and the city communes; to the south, the independent Lombard principalities, followed by the Arabs, the Normans, the Hohenstaufen and the Angevins. This complex balance of power, which survived all kinds of permutations through the centuries, allowed the popes a considerable degree of independence from the sway of any one secular power,

Details from Otranto Cathedral's mosaic floor of 1163–5 show Italy's receptivity to foreign vernacular literature. It includes the earliest representation (above) of King Arthur in art, inspired by Celtic legend and French romances.

Alexander being carried to heaven by griffins attempting to seize the bait he holds above them – a story from 'The Romance of Alexander', a vastly popular story with Greek origins.

and by the 13th century had made them into substantial territorial lords in their own right.

Papal independence was a vital ingredient in Rome's authority, but this also depended on the desire of the peoples of the West to look to the papacy for direction and example. The Western churches did just this, partly because the popes had taken over the force of the name of Rome, once centre of a great secular empire, and had adapted it to aspirations of ecclesiastical supremacy, and partly because of the efforts of a few remarkable popes. In particular, Gregory the Great (590–604) established a personal position of moral authority for the bishopric of Rome which his successors were able to exploit.

Gregory by his writings, in particular the *Pastoral Care*, in which he discussed the office and duties of a bishop, produced some of the basic texts of medieval Christianity and ensured that future popes could bask in reflected glory as the successors of one of the major doctors of the church. Even more important, Gregory extended papal efforts and influence to areas of Europe where orthodox Christianity was again beginning to assert itself, after being badly battered by two centuries of pagan and Arian invasion. (Arianism, the heretical Christianity of the Ostrogoths and Lombards, denied the full equality of the Son with the Father.) Ironically the invasions probably helped to establish papal primacy: while leaving Rome almost untouched, they destroyed much of the force of local ecclesiastical autonomy which had characterized 4th- and 5th-century centres like Arles, Milan and Aquileia. By the time of Gregory, much of this early pride and independence outside Rome had disappeared under the power of foreign domination.

Gregory's greatest long-term success was in pagan Anglo-Saxon England, where St Augustine's mission, although perhaps less successful in converting souls than the efforts of the Irish churchmen, nevertheless firmly established both a tradition of Roman involvement in British affairs and a respect by the English Church for her Roman mother. When the English in the late 7th and 8th centuries began themselves to convert and reform other nations, such as the Friesians and the Franks, they exported a respect for Rome and the papacy that dated back to Gregory's time.

Through its continuous tradition of independence and through the efforts of its bishops, Rome came to be seen in the West as a source of authority on matters of spiritual tradition. Charlemagne, for example, when attempting to standardize Frankish church customs, naturally looked to Rome for the 'correct' forms of liturgy and organization. The emperor sent to Rome for teachers of plain-song and to Monte Cassino for a definitive text of the Rule of St Benedict, the monastic rule espoused by the papacy since the time of Gregory the Great.

Much later, in the 11th and 12th centuries, with the help of some zealous Northerners, the popes were able to assume the leadership of the European-wide ecclesiastical reform movement that set the church's own house in order and tried to define its relationship with the secular powers. This led to some violent confrontations with the princes of Europe, in particular the German emperor, but also led to a slower and more peaceful process, whereby Rome became firmly established as the ultimate appeal court for all matters of church law. While Bologna was supreme in legal theory, Rome became the greatest practising legal centre in Europe. By about 1200 the papal curia and the office of pope itself were dominated by lawyers, experts

Benedict hands his Rule to a group of monks (left). This short but powerful work came to be accepted as the main guide for monastic life in the West. (Right) the story of the raven that carried off poisoned bread given to Benedict by a jealous priest.

in canon law and capable of resolving disputes about ecclesiastical matters as far away as Norway and the Holy Land. As in the days of empire, Rome was again filled with foreigners – but now appealing to the successor of St Peter, rather than the successor of Augustus.

The successful establishment of the papacy as the head of a territorial principality in Central Italy, and of a great jurisdictional empire that stretched across Europe naturally did not endear it to everyone. The political and financial ambitions of the popes, pursued in order to maintain their independence and to provide for their officials and favourites, affected all the West, but obviously hit Italy itself particularly hard. It is not surprising that we find here some of the earliest and most dramatic reactions against it. Dante, a devout and orthodox Catholic but an embittered exile from his native Florence, delighted in consigning to Hell those popes whom he saw as most corrupt in their meddling in Italian affairs and whom he blamed for Italy's tormented politics. In the 1320s Marsiglio of Padua, who had experience of papal interference in the politics of Northern Italy, went even further and produced the first detailed and consistent treatise to state the complete independence of secular power from clerical interference, the *Defensor Pacis*. Even inside the Roman curia there were periods of doubt at the direction that things had taken: in 1294 the cardinals, normally a hardened bunch, elected to St Peter's chair a simple but holy hermit, Celestine V. This experiment with apostolic simplicity was, however, short-lived, and Celestine has the unusual distinction of being the only

pope who has ever voluntarily resigned.

The 12th and 13th centuries in Italy saw reactions not only against the specific abuses of the papacy, but also against the whole character of the church, which, not surprisingly, found it easier to preach Christ's gospel than to practise it. Heresy, fuelled by disdain for the established church, was strong in 12th- and 13th-century Italian cities, particularly in the North. It was helped too by Italy's cosmopolitan contacts: the particular form of heresy that was most prevalent, Cathar dualism, had its roots in the eastern Mediterranean and was well established in Languedoc.

In the early 13th century, Italy produced, in the Franciscans, a movement that might well have become heretical, but which instead, through the guidance of Innocent III, became a vital part of the Western established church. St Francis was born a typical well-off Italian, the son of a wealthy merchant of Assisi, but the ideals he followed form a contrast and complement to much of what we have seen as distinctive of later medieval Italy. While his father and his social equals espoused the cause of profit, Francis wedded himself to extreme apostolic poverty. Amidst the wealth of Italy, Francis made of poverty a virtue, demolishing with his own hands houses given to the Order, and taking no thought for the morrow, even to the extent of forbidding beans to be soaked overnight.

Yet the Franciscans were not just a reaction to the realities of contemporary Italian life; they also fitted in very closely with it. They were above all an urban movement, providing a spiritual focus for the growing number of townsmen, both rich and poor, who had been little served by the religious organization of preceding centuries. Unlike the earlier monastic movements of Europe, which retreated from the world under the patronage of great lords and landowners, the Franciscans maintained a mission as preachers to and servants of the urban population, and through their Third Order, a lay confraternity, encouraged secular participation. Even after the original ideals of devotion and poverty had become somewhat tarnished, the Franciscans remained an active urban movement all over Europe. It is no surprise that this ideal should have originated in Italy.

The spirituality of the pre-Franciscan period was typified by the 6th-century Benedict of Nursia. His answer to the problem of personal salvation was to retreat from the world into a small tightly-knit community of holy men, first at Subiaco and then at Monte Cassino. This was a response found amongst many holy men of the period all over the Christian world, and there is nothing that is distinctively Italian about Benedict's experience. Indeed the document that made him so influential, his monastic Rule, achieved its great success largely because it is so universal and so little tied down to local conditions. It is powerful, and yet short and simple enough to be widely applicable and adaptable. Its success was, however, due not only to these qualities but also to a geographical accident, because a near neighbour of Benedict's foundation, Gregory the Great, picked it out from the many rules available to him as the one that he, and therefore the bishopric of Rome, most favoured. Gregory spread the rule widely by correspondence and exhortation, and also provided all we know about its author, by writing Benedict's life. Had it not been for Gregory and the papacy, Benedict and his rule might well have sunk without trace.

Some elements of medieval religion in Italy did indeed disappear, although of great importance for a time. Arianism played a vital part in Italian life for more than a century. It set up a rival hierarchy of churches, priests and bishops; it removed orthodox clerics from a position of influence and power at court; at its worst it instituted sporadic persecution. Yet, when Arianism was eliminated, its traces were destroyed so effectively by its Catholic rivals that they have left nothing distinctive for us to see: Arian books were burnt, Arian churches were appropriated, and all distinctive decoration removed before reconsecration.

The 'Middle Ages' as a period

The concept of an historical 'middle age' was invented by Renaissance scholars, in order to glorify their own achievement in supposedly getting back to the civilization of classical antiquity. It is a concept so well established and so useful as a short-hand method of referring to about one thousand years of history that we must continue to live with it; but it is a deceptive term for two main reasons. Firstly, because it seems to

belittle the achievements of the medieval centuries, by seeing them only as undesirable and brutal, a gap between two culturally superior epochs. Secondly, because it imposes rigid chronological boundaries, at around 400–500 and around 1350–1450, that are used across all fields of human achievement, and yet are based purely on the survival or revival of Latin high culture and of classical styles of art. In economic, social, religious, political and to some extent even in intellectual and artistic life, the periods of major transition were in fact very different.

It is not, I hope, any longer necessary to stress that the Middle Ages were a period of fruitful and interesting developments in European life and culture. The early centuries gave us our Germanic roots and were essential in the development of our Christian culture and religion. The later medieval centuries (1000–1350) saw the emergence of the political, economic and cultural dominance of Europe. The scholars of the Renaissance may have looked back on these centuries with scorn, but their own achievement depended on and did not shake off the cultural heritage of the Christian Middle Ages; indeed their achievement was made possible only by the economic and political developments of the preceding centuries that had created the rich courts and cities of Renaissance Italy.

In economic life change was always a slow and gradual process, difficult to divide into periods. Even if we try to do so, the main turning-points probably fall much earlier than the traditional dates for the 'descent' into the Middle Ages and the 'ascent' out of them. Roman Italy's economic dominance of the Mediterranean, as the main producer and exporter of manufactured goods like pottery and cash-crops like oil and wine, was lost as early as the 1st century AD. Roman Italy was never again as rich as it was in the Augustan period, and in the 3rd and 4th centuries it suffered the additional strain of paying for the effort of defence against barbarian invasion. Economic prosperity may have reached its lowest point in the 6th and 7th centuries, but this was only the bottom of a gradual descent starting five centuries earlier and never amounted to a total economic collapse: as we have seen, fields continued to be cultivated and towns inhabited. As early as the 8th century there are signs of new growth, which by 1000 was well on the way to making Italy the rich country that we see in the 12th and 13th centuries. The date 1350, if anything, is a date of renewed decline, brought about by the Black Death and by the collapse of several major banking firms.

In political and social life also, the changes were very gradual, but do not always correspond with the traditional 'Middle Ages'. It is true that a vital change came in the 5th century, when Italy fell into barbarian hands and also lost her empire. But this was a slow process, which involved the gradual handing over of the reins of power to new masters and which saw considerable continuity in the basic structure of politics. Politics remained, as under the empire, monarchical and centred on a network of cities and their territories. In a sense the greatest change in Italian political life came only in the 10th and 11th centuries, when in the North the superstructure of the monarchy collapsed, leaving the cities free, while in the South the new and powerful monarchy of the Normans forged political unity out of what had been a very confused jumble of principalities. With relatively minor alterations (the substitution of the Hohenstaufen and the Angevins for the Normans, and of the *Signori* for the communes), this remained the basic structure of Italian politics to 1350 and for a long time after.

In religious life, the great break obviously came well before the Middle Ages, with the conversion of Constantine in the early 4th century and the gradual imposition over the next hundred years of Christianity as the official religion of the empire. The next thousand years saw dramatic developments, such as the rise of the papacy, of monasticism and of the friars; but these changes all grew out of a process started in AD 312 and all of them continued to affect European life well beyond the 14th century.

Even in intellectual life, the concept of a middle age, too rigidly defined, can be deceptive. It is true that Latin secular literature suffered a severe decline after about AD 550, and was treated with renewed respect from the 14th century onwards. However, this humanist view-point totally ignores other areas of achievement and threatens to treat intellectual life as the preserve of a small group of late antique senators and of scholars and antiquaries of the 14th century. It ignores the gradual rise of a Christian culture from the 4th century (and even earlier). In Christian intellectual life in Italy there was undoubtedly a low point when little of genius was produced, but this was in the narrower confines of the 7th to 10th centuries. It also ignores the revival from the 11th century onwards of legal studies in the North, and of Greek medical, scientific and philosophical thought in Southern Italy.

In architecture there was apparently a period around 550–750 when very little of any size was built, but even in these centuries such classical traditions as vaulting, building in brick or decorating in mosaic were maintained. Admittedly in the 15th century ancient buildings and architectural theory came to be more carefully studied and consciously imitated. But arguably a far more important revival came in the 9th to 11th centuries, when buildings of a number and on a scale to rival classical antiquity were again erected all over Italy.

In painting and sculpture, long before the Middle Ages began, the 'classical' style had been abandoned for the more rigid and hieratic approach that we see, for instance, on the arch of Constantine. From about AD 400 there was undoubtedly a decline in the quantity and quality of work produced, above all in figural sculpture. But even the early medieval centuries produced a few splendid examples of mosaic decoration (like S. Prassede in Rome), of fresco (like S. Maria Antiqua), of stucco (like S. Maria in Valle at Cividale), and of bas-relief carving and epigraphy (like the slabs of Lombard Pavia). In quantity and quality a revival probably came, as in architecture, in the 9th to 11th centuries. Even the major stylistic break, with the rise of a distinctive Italian school brought about by Nicola Pisano and Giotto, preceded the emergence of humanist learning.

The realization that the Middle Ages in Italy were neither homogeneous nor self-contained does not only help us to avoid simplistically rigid periodization. More important, by emphasizing the changes that occurred and their links with both past and future, it dispels the notion of the period as an unfortunate and ephemeral hiatus in the inevitable progress of the classical tradition. Within the different branches of human achievement, we can perceive distinctive features in the way the medieval period remodelled its ancient inheritance and contributed wholly new elements to the stream of Italian culture. The resulting synthesis was important not only for the history of the moment, but also for the future and present shape of Italy.

The signs of the zodiac: an intricate marble inlay from the floor of S. Miniato, near Florence. Such exquisite workmanship demonstrates that decorative marble-work in medieval Italy was a native tradition without equal in Europe.

·III·

HUMANISM
AND
RENAISSANCE

1350-1527

THE RENAISSANCE is unusual among historical periods in being defined not by any great political events or chronological divisions but by an intellectual and artistic movement. The term was coined by Vasari to describe the 'rebirth' of the arts, as he saw it, after the Middle Ages. Beginning with a renewed interest in classical Rome and involving careful research into classical texts and classical buildings, it led to a wholesale re-examination of conduct in the light of classical ideas. In a country other than Italy all this might have remained the preserve of a small élite. What caused it to escalate into a major European movement was the status it conferred on the ruling class. To employ a secretary who was a master of Latin prose, to preside over a court where poets and philosophers congregated, to patronize the greatest painters and sculptors, were more than merely intellectual ambitions. They contributed to one's glory and immortality. The result was an unprecedented flowering of talent in almost every field, a combination of forces that was never to be repeated, and which has alone assured it a place in history as one of the great peaks of Western civilization.

In the realm of ideas, too, it was a moment that could never come again. Medieval faith in God, in no way shaken by the revived interest in paganism, was now joined by a new faith in Man – humanism. For a while it seemed as though the values of the ancient world could merge with those of Christianity, a not impossible ideal if both were aspects of the same divine plan. And the most potent images of Renaissance art are those which embody this new vision of heroic, perfectable humanity – Masaccio's Apostles, Donatello's *St George*, Botticelli's nymphs, Michelangelo's athletes.

To the political and social historian the Renaissance is something much less precise. Italy remained what it had been since the early Middle Ages, a country divided between an absolute monarchy in the South, a papal state in the centre, and in the North a collection of independent territories with a variety of constitutions ranging from autocracy (Milan for example) through oligarchy (Venice) to a form of genuine republicanism (Florence). This diversity was clearly one factor in the spread of humanism. Another was the progress made in commercial and banking systems that was making parts of Italy decidedly rich. But as a period with a shape of its own – emerging with the generation of Petrarch (the 1340s–70s), coming to maturity in that of Brunelleschi and Donatello (1420–50) and reaching its apogee in the early 1500s under Michelangelo, Leonardo and Raphael – it is in cultural terms that it has to be defined.

From the point of view of Italy's place in the world, however, the Renaissance can be seen as almost equivalent to a political force. Italy conquered Europe through her thinkers and artists, assuming a dominance (reinforced by her explicit claim to be the heir of ancient Rome) from which she has never afterwards been displaced.

Constantine's Arch
looms over an Old Testament scene in the Sistine Chapel – a striking symbol of the Renaissance philosophical synthesis. The Arch, as we have seen in Chapter I, was itself a monument to that other moment in history when Christianity and classical Rome met and merged. When Botticelli chose it as a background for his fresco *The Punishment of Corah* he was adding yet another dimension, that of the Jewish Covenant. (The story comes from Numbers xvii: Corah and his followers had rebelled against Moses, who raises his rod to call down God's wrath upon them.) Meaningless in realistic terms, the Arch turns the painting into a much wider diagram of ideas. The fact that it is painted on the wall of the pope's private chapel in the Vatican, the scene of papal elections and the hierarchical centre of the Church, makes it all the more compelling. (1)

NEMO·SIBI·ASSVM
AT·HONOREM·NISI
OCATVS·A·DEO
ANQVAM·ARON

The Tuscan breakthrough

Three men, Florentines in the 1420s, following the same principles in different arts, made such an impact upon their contemporaries that no art was the same again: Donatello the sculptor, Brunelleschi the architect and Masaccio the painter.

Donatello was the longest lived of the three and his work shows a marked change from youth to age. St George (*above*) is portrayed as an ideal Roman, poised and confident in his strength but self-aware as a moral agent. At the end of his life Donatello abandoned classical balance and showed the extremes of emotion without restraint. *Right*: Christ rising from the tomb, a detail from one of his two pulpits in S. Lorenzo, Florence. (2, 4)

Brunelleschi created what is still the dominant symbol of Florence, the dome of the cathedral. Crowning a medieval church, it is still Gothic in its form (a ribbed octagon), but the scale, the details and some of the constructional techniques look back to Roman models. (3)

Masaccio died youngest but was perhaps the most influential of the three. His *Trinity* in S. Maria Novella (*right*) takes the medieval memorial painting and transforms it into a Renaissance statement. Framed by classical pilasters, above an altar covering the dead man's skeleton, rises the crucified Christ with God the Father, the Virgin and St John. But now every detail is rigidly subject to the laws of perspective. (5)

'The Courtier'

Castiglione's book is the record of conversations held at Urbino in 1507 on the theme of the perfect courtier. His attainments should be physical (sports and war), intellectual (education, literary accomplishment, music) and also moral and social.

Urbino under the Montefeltro dukes came close to conforming to Castiglione's model. Though in appearance a medieval city clustered on its hill-top, it could boast one of the purest Renaissance palaces, by Luciano di Laurana, containing work by such artists as Francesco di Giorgio and Piero della Francesca. (7)

Federigo da Montefeltro, the man responsible for giving the tiny state of Urbino the status that it enjoyed in the High Renaissance, was one of the most famous generals of his age, making his fortune as a professional *condottiere*, but at the same time a man of learning with a world-famous library and a lavish patron of the arts. This portrait, probably by Pedro Berruguete, represents him in his dual role, dressed in armour and reading a classical manuscript. Beside him is his son and successor Guidobaldo. (8)

The arts of war and peace are similarly balanced in the marquetry panels of the duke's study – armour in the lower half, instruments of astronomy, music and learning above. (6)

Chess players. In the relaxed atmosphere of a humanist court men and women engage in the symbolic war of chess. Painter and provenance are uncertain but the picture no doubt reflects a real background; the time is about 1470. (9)

Women as people in their own right, not simply as the wives, mistresses or mothers of men, are fully alive in Renaissance art – most of all, perhaps, in Leonardo da Vinci's haunting portraits. The sitter here is presumed to be Ginevra Benci, member of a leading Florentine family. Leonardo sets her against a lush watery landscape, the black mass of a conifer setting off the paleness of her face. (10)

Humanism at ease

The society portrayed in *The Courtier* is one where learning is worn lightly, where the sexes meet on equal terms and disputes are conducted with mutual respect: the ideals, in other words, of a liberal education for the next four centuries.

Music had a prominent place among the courtier's accomplishments. *Above*: faience dish with an open book of music surmounted by the arms of the Gonzaga of Mantua. (11)

How far did Castiglione, the author of *The Courtier*, conform to the standard of his own book? Born in 1478, he had a distinguished career at the courts of Mantua and Urbino, visiting England as ambassador between 1506 and 1507, and ended his life in Spain in the service of Charles V. Among his friends was Raphael, who painted this portrait of him. (12)

The Concert by Lorenzo Costa subtly suggests the blending of voices accompanied by a lute. Vocal music still prevailed over instrumental, but Italy was acquiring new ideas from abroad and beginning to evolve its own musical style. (13)

Venice, the model city

The Venetian constitution was often held up as an example to be imitated, for achieving stability while avoiding tyranny. Power was limited to the aristocracy, but within that class was equitably administered.

Civic pride outweighs religious devotion in Gentile
Bellini's *Procession of the Reliquary of the True Cross*. The relic
itself, in a rich gold reliquary, is carried under a canopy in
the centre. Taking part in the procession are members of the

various *scuole*, or charitable brotherhoods, with their
insignia. The setting is the Piazza S. Marco in 1496. The
building line on the right would be set back by the
Procuratie Nuove a hundred years later. (14)

The judgment of time

Familiarity with ancient Rome, and an awareness of their remoteness from it, gave the humanists a new view of history and of man's place in it. It became important to live in men's memory, and to live as an individual.

Fame and Chance are more than mere abstractions – they seem to acquire the urgency of real beings. *Left*: Fame on a globe (her trumpet has been lost) triumphs over Death, while green leaves sprout from the cup of Virtue. *Above*: Youth, anxious to seize Opportunity by the forelock, is restrained by Virtue. (15, 16)

The artist confers immortality and also gains it for himself. **Brunelleschi** (*above*) is commemorated in a portrait bust in Florence Cathedral, **Alberti** (*above right*) on a medal by Matteo de' Pasti. **Pisanello** adds his name prominently to a medal of a knight kneeling at the feet of Christ. (17, 18, 20)

Pinturicchio (*above*) left his name and portrait as part of his decoration of the Baglioni Chapel in S. Maria Maggiore, Spello. (19)

Pietro Mellini (*opposite*), a Florentine of no special distinction, is of interest to posterity – as he no doubt intended – because Benedetto da Maiano carved his portrait; his personality lives on. (21)

The synthesis of Man

Nowhere is the humanist dream of reconciling classical reason with Christian revelation so clearly demonstrated as in Raphael's frescoes in the Stanza della Segnatura, known as *The School of Athens* and *The Disputà*. Here, facing each other as equals, are the two mental and spiritual worlds in their definitive images.

The pagan world is presented as a gathering of the greatest minds of antiquity within a vast classical basilica (based on Bramante's then unfinished St Peter's). In the centre, representing the two main philosophical schools, are Plato, pointing upwards, and Aristotle, pointing to the earth. Euclid, lower right, is expounding a geometrical proof with compasses. Diogenes, the cynic, reclines by himself on the steps. Heraclitus rests his chin on his hand to write on a block of stone. Pythagoras sits surrounded by disciples in the left foreground. For many (perhaps all) of these figures Raphael used models of his own day. Plato, for instance, is Leonardo, Heraclitus Michelangelo, Euclid Bramante. (22)

The Christian world has to be shown more diagramatically. It is divided horizontally into two levels. The link between them is the Eucharist, existing at the human level as the host on the altar and at the divine as the body of Christ, descending vertically through Father, Son and Holy Ghost. The Virgin and St John the Baptist sit to left and right of Christ, who holds up his hands to show the wounds, signifying his redeeming sacrifice. In a half circle round him are the saints, martyrs and patriarchs. On the extreme left: St Peter, Adam, St John the Evangelist, David (with lyre), St Stephen and Jeremiah. On the right Judas Maccabaeus, St Lawrence, Moses (holding the Tablets of the Law), St James, Abraham and St Paul. On earth are the great theologians who have helped to illuminate divine truth, often shown with their books at their feet: St Ambrose (following the pointing hand of the old man next to the altar), St Augustine (with *The City of God*), St Thomas Aquinas, turning towards Pope Innocent III and St Bonaventura; the standing pope is Sixtus IV, and behind him the unmistakable profile of Dante. On the other side of the altar, we find among others: St Jerome (with his lion) and Pope Gregory the Great, wearing the triple crown and sitting on a carved throne – he is given the features of Julius II. (23)

117

Architecture: the rule of law

Geometry, whose perfect shapes reflected the perfection of the cosmos, and therefore of God, ruled supreme; each part of a building was necessary and sufficient; nothing could be added or taken away.

Symmetry was an axiom. The circle, the square and the octagon were the ideal plans, as in Bramante's Tempietto in Rome (*upper right*). In this anonymous design of a whole city (*above*) a modified balance was preferred, since order should never become monotony. (24, 25)

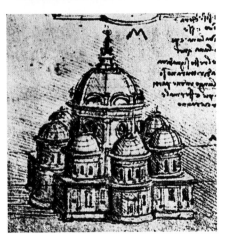

Leonardo's mind played ceaselessly with architectural forms, though he built nothing himself. A design in a sketchbook (*above*) shows a dome rising from a square base with apses on the sides. Whoever built the church of S. Maria della Consolazione at Todi (*below*) – its architect is unknown – must have been close to Leonardo's circle. (27, 28)

Renaissance ornament obeyed less formal laws, and it was as ornament that the new style first conquered Northern Italy. Marrina's façade to the Piccolomini Library in Siena is an exuberant *tour de force* of classical motifs. (26)

In the cool clarity of an interior such as the Library of S. Marco, Florence, by Michelozzo, the Renaissance feeling for space and volume is made manifest. The constituent elements – columns, capitals, arches and mouldings – come from the ancient world, the proportions from geometry and its relation to the human scale. (29)

Michelangelo's genius was of so gigantic and overwhelming a kind that he made it virtually impossible for Renaissance art to continue on the same course. One of the revelations of recent years has been the cleaning of parts of the Sistine ceiling that had lain concealed under layers of dirt and grease. The series of the ancestors of Christ above the windows was painted last, and they show Michelangelo, still the master of heroic forms, turning towards a new intensity and emotional charge. In this family group the mother and baby look back to the certainties of humanism, but the father, wildly open-eyed, seems to belong already to Mannerism. (30)

III

Humanism and Renaissance: 1350–1527

J. R. HALE

As a period in Italian history, the span of time between the early 14th and mid-16th century takes its name from a dominant form of culture. That culture, expressed through the arts, buildings, books – and the ideals and sometimes the practice of personal and political behaviour – will therefore be our chief concern. What was 'the Renaissance'? How and why did it manifest itself?

Moving from the medieval rooms in an art gallery to those devoted to the Renaissance we see the difference at once. Faces become more expressive, bodies more believably weighty and rounded, towns and landscapes more akin to real ones. Art moves nearer to life. Walking through cities like Florence, Venice, Milan or Rome, we can see how in palaces and churches pointed-arched windows or door-frames give way to rounded or square ones; on façades or in interiors a whole repertory of decorative motifs – pilasters, friezes, arcades – show architects referring more and more devotedly to the buildings of classical antiquity. Turning the pages of manuscripts and (from 1465) printed books, we sense an increased interest in personal feelings and experiences, a new, self-conscious awareness of what the process of committing thoughts to paper – via the choice of a literary form, the use of language, the consciousness of an audience – involved. Governmental records and diplomatic correspondence reveal a similar change: towards a more self-conscious explanation of decisions or proposals, a justification of present actions by reference to what those pre-medieval Italians, the ancient Romans, had done.

As for ideals of behaviour, we shall look at this crucial indicator of the change from one period of self-awareness to another by spending much of our time in the company of the author of a book which was actually devoted to behaviour – if only to that of a particular class. Published in 1528, Baldassare Castiglione's *The Courtier* sums up and elegantly popularizes much that was thought and taught during the Renaissance. By reviewing the topics he covers and stopping to assess how they came to be part of the culture he inherited, we shall get, I hope, some sense of how that culture evolved.

An inquiry into the meaning and timing of the Renaissance is fraught with splendid difficulties.

The stubbornly independent city-based political units of the peninsula developed on their own terms and at their own pace. Though there were cross-cultural influences between them, it is not mere habit that divides the painters of the Renaissance into 'schools' – Florentine, Sienese, Lombard, Umbrian, Venetian; in searching for the common denominator of Renaissance culture we must not blur the intense variety of its local modes of expression. And for the same reason there were time-lags between the establishment in one place of an attitude of mind or an artistic or literary style that to us can be immediately dubbed 'Renaissance', and their adoption as a cultural orthodoxy elsewhere.

When Florentines or Milanese or Venetians or men from Lucca or Pisa thought of themselves – as, from time to time, they did – as Italians, it was with the consciousness that they were superior as a race to the inhabitants of France, Spain, England and Germany. But they were also international traders and bankers. So while the culture of the peninsula was progressively drawn into a more unified form by a novel preoccupation with the achievements of its own classical past, it was constantly played upon by influences from outside. Indeed, had the Renaissance in Italy not absorbed so much poetry from Provence, music and pictorial techniques from the Netherlands, fashions and personal deportment from Spain, its contribution to the 16th-century 'renaissances' in other countries would have been far less pervasive.

Nor can we cut off the Renaissance from the medieval past that its spokesmen affected to despise. Many of its scholars, builders, artists and saints remained potent influences within a society that evolved slowly (there is no break between medieval and Renaissance in Italian political or socio-economic history) and was, after all, the paymaster and endorser of the culture it sponsored. It is no coincidence that the country that produced the enormous volume of works of art, scholarship and literature that gives the Renaissance its status as an outstanding phase of Italian civilization was also the richest in Europe. But Italy had been – in terms of the per capita income of its patron classes – even richer in the 13th century.

That Edward I of England hired armies to conquer Wales and to build there some of the grandest of all medieval castles with money (about £13m. or $23 m. in modern values) borrowed from a single Italian bank was because Italians had pioneered such essential

A Renaissance artisan at work: though the great fortunes were made from international commerce and banking, Italian prosperity was based more widely on manufactures: woollen cloth, silk, luxury metalwork, glass and ceramics.

instruments of capitalistic business life as the partnership; the legally liable agent; the insurance of goods in transit; the conveyance of money in paper form through the letter of credit, ancestor of the money-order and the cheque; and accountancy methods, including double-entry bookkeeping, that enabled the entrepreneur to keep track of his balances over the whole range of his personal and business expenditure.

These were the methods – collectively termed 'the Commercial Revolution' – that enabled Italians to dominate international trade and banking throughout Western Europe. This was all accomplished before 1300, and part of their profits went into paying for palaces and churches, altarpieces and sculptures, in the then dominant Gothic style. It was a style as international as was their business empire. Why, beginning with the next century, did their money go into sponsoring a culture that was not only 'Renaissance' as opposed to 'medieval' but was so much more specifically Italian?

And – to raise only one more of the difficulties that confront any attempt to describe and explain the Renaissance – why did so distinctive a culture emerge within, and remain largely the spokesman for, a Catholic faith which remained intact throughout the medieval and Renaissance centuries and continued to be subscribed to automatically and with little discernible change in the degree of average personal involvement?

What we shall be looking for is a new ingredient (or at least an ingredient absorbed in a more massively effective dose than formerly) that while not disturbing the basic economic, religious or political constitution of Italy, brought about a radical change in its cultural complexion.

The political background

Although the Alps remained as little a barrier to commerce and culture as they had during the Middle Ages, Renaissance Italy was, for the most part, politically self-contained. There were dynastic marriage connections with France: from 1494 these led successive French kings to invade on the pretext of securing 'their' Milan and Naples. An Aragonese dynasty ruled Sicily from 1282 and the Kingdom of Naples from 1442. But while the 'mother' countries did on occasion intervene to give armed support, distances were great, and connections were not with the European monarchs themselves (save when Alfonso V of Aragon, after taking Naples from the House of Anjou, ruled in person there 1442–58).

Similarly, while the Holy Roman Empire still claimed to be overlord of Tuscany and Northern Italy as well as (even less realistically) of Naples and Sicily, apart from the invasion by Henry VII (1310–13), the peninsula usually behaved as though successive emperors – even those few who did come to Italy in person – were no more than the sowers of those useful titles, duke and count, or useful temporary allies against a domestic rival. At the beginning of the 16th century Maximilian I, stimulated by the successful invasion of Italy by France and (again) Aragon, did attempt to conquer parts of Venice's territory on the mainland; but 'empire' and 'imperial' are words that earn their fullest significance again only when Charles V, who from 1519 linked the old imperial domains with the kingship of a now united Spain, began the series of massive campaigns that consolidated Spanish control of Naples and inaugurated it in Milan.

The rest of Europe, then, was of greater concern to those cosmopolitan Italians who were, as clerics or merchants, involved abroad in its own intense political affairs, than to those who stayed at home, whether as governors or governed.

By the early 14th century the process was well-nigh complete whereby shared municipal self-government, deadlocked by cut-throat rivalries between citizen interest-groups and between citizens as a whole and the great landowners outside the walls who were determined to control the market places where their produce was priced and sold, had surrendered to the better order enforced by hereditary *signori*. The great dynasties had arrived: Visconti in Milan, Este in Ferrara, Della Scala in Verona, Carrara in Padua, Montefeltro in Urbino. Others were soon to join them: Gonzaga in Mantua, Malatesta in Rimini. If we add the popes of Rome and the kings of Naples, the peninsula begins to look like a jammed mosaic of principalities. But certain cities, and among them some of the most important, hung on to the principle of communal self-government. Of these, Genoa and Lucca did so with the greatest difficulty, often having to call in, or put up with, temporary 'dictators' to give time for civic feuds to simmer down. Florence had to use such an expedient twice, in 1325 and 1342–3, Siena only once, between 1399 and 1404. Venice alone managed to deal with the problems arising from republican, openly debated control – anguish at what was felt to be discriminatory taxation, family and clan rivalries, the clamorous search for scapegoats when a war was lost or a series of harvests failed – without calling in an outside referee with full, if theoretically temporary, powers.

All this is to mention only those cities which, as contributors to Renaissance culture, formed, as it were, the period's ill-matched beauty chorus. There were many other political units which had a *de facto* independent existence from time to time (and a psychological conviction that they had it *all* the time): Pisa, Piombino, Bologna, Perugia, Faenza, Amalfi, Lecce – the list could be extended. And it could be further confused by adding the great baronial families, based on some hill-top fortified complex, whose scattered subsidiary castles and whose dominant call on the loyalty of rural, soldier-like communities, formed a shadow polity filling the spaces (especially in north-western Lombardy, Friuli and central and Southern Italy) left by the effective power of the city-based states.

As the generations passed towards that date, 1494, which was, as we shall see, regarded by contemporaries as a political turning point in the fortunes of Italy, five powers came to dominate the peninsula by conquest or less formal browbeating: Milan, Venice, Florence, Rome and – by simply enduring as a powerful if grossly inefficient focus of authority – Naples.

Space does not permit an adequate treatment of Milan and Naples. Both were odd men out, and in a less politically and culturally relevant fashion than was Rome. The Lombard capital, thanks to its position at the junction of Alpine passes and the local lake and river systems (exploited by means of an elaborate and pioneer construction of canals), was little less prosperous in terms of per capita income than Florence or Venice. That Italian merchants were commonly known in Northern Europe as 'Lombards', however, is due to the same sort of linguistic fluke that has given us 'America' rather than 'Christofera'; the Milanese were the Japanese of the Commercial Revolution, shrewdly adapting the techniques evolved by their Genoese and Florentine rivals. Again, as befits its northerly position, feudalized social texture, court-centred administration and (up to 1454) belligerently expansionist political stance, Milan is better understood by comparing it to Burgundy than to Venice or Florence.

For similar reasons, the Kingdom of Naples, whether Angevin or Aragonese, was *sui generis* within the peninsula. With its unique population imbalance between capital and countryside, its massive dependence on North Italian commercial and cultural expertise, the clogging poverty that held it to the landlord-and-tenant level of that of Poland or Lithuania, Naples was already the ancestor of today's 'Problem of the South'. Because of its man-power, all

too grateful to receive a military wage, it was a force to reckon with in peninsular affairs; but its spasms of political energy were necessarily short-winded. Only in the 17th century did its cultural identity emerge.

We shall concentrate only on three of the five leading powers: Florence as the chief dynamo powering Renaissance culture; Venice, the only truly imperial power; and Rome, the traditional centre of organized Christianity and Western Europe's first artificial capital city. As examplar of many minor independent princely states, we shall add Ferrara. With these four, if we cannot do justice to the hectic variety of Italian political life, at least we shall not seriously misrepresent it.

Florence

'Stingy, jealous and haughty', 'malign' and 'ungrateful', 'wolves', 'discord-ridden', 'beasts'; mongrelized, corrupt, vainglorious and never satisfied.

Thus the most famous of Florentines on the fellow citizens who had exiled him in 1301 and caused the *Divina Commedia* to be the work of a refugee.

Florence was then the richest, if only the fourth largest (after Naples, Venice and Milan) city in Italy. It had shared in the pioneering of those business devices that, as we have seen, have been dubbed 'the Commercial Revolution'. These techniques, employed by personalities who reflected the extraordinary range of practicality, adventurousness and intellectuality that produced Pope Boniface VIII's grudging definition of the Florentines as 'the fifth element', had led to banking and trading activity that stretched from England and France to Syria and Persia. At home, taxable incomes had enabled the municipal government to build a new, extended circuit of walls to protect the population of *c*. 90,000, to re-house itself in the Palazzo Vecchio (as it is now called), to bridge the Arno with the Ponte Vecchio and to begin the construction of a new cathedral and its campanile – 'Giotto's tower'. Pious benefactions had led to the building on a grandiose scale of the other largest churches in the city, the Dominicans' S. Maria Novella and the S. Croce of the Franciscans.

It was money, too, earned from cloth manufacture and artisans' work of all kinds as well as from commerce and banking, that had enabled the Florentines to preserve their communal form of self-government. Elsewhere, it had been the lack of a sufficiently large group of wealthy businessmen that had led communal governments to truckle to, or be seduced by alliances with, the rural magnates that surrounded them. Such liaisons, forced or voluntary, could all too easily lead to political infighting soluble only by recourse to *signori* whom all parties could, if bitterly, agree to support. But the precocity and size of the Florentine capitalist class was such that the magnates had been forced to come to terms, to the point where they found themselves, even when they owned palaces within the walls, debarred from any political role in the city.

The form of government from which they were

excluded is worth a brief description, partly because it resembled that of other republican cities as well as the constitutional machinery that continued to work elsewhere even when its policy-making and taxing aspects had been switched off by the *signori* and their appointee advisers, and partly because it changed only in detail until towards the end of the Renaissance.

The city was divided for purposes of local administration into sixteen districts called *gonfaloni*. From these, in various combinations divisible by four, men were elected to serve on the chief councils of municipal government: the 16-strong council of *gonfalonieri* (standard bearers), the 12-strong council of *buonhuomini* (good men) and the senior council, or (very roughly) cabinet, the *Signoria* of 8, plus a chairman who was known as the *gonfaloniere di giustizia*, or standard-bearer of justice. The *Signoria* gave the original name, Palazzo della Signoria, to the sternly castellated building (now known as the Palazzo Vecchio) where its members had to reside during their period of office. Policy was debated by the *Signoria* and then discussed, before proposals for enshrining it in legal forms were agreed, with the *buonhuomini* and the *gonfalonieri*. In this way decisions were reached which, albeit in token form, represented the topographical spread of the city.

These were then passed down for assent or rejection (but not amendment) to two larger councils whose names represent a much earlier and more 'democratic' era of communal government: the 200-strong council of the *popolo* (people) and that of the *comune*, which had 300 members. A proposal passed into law would thus have been approved by a majority, at least, among bodies totalling 537 citizens – perhaps 10 per cent of politically enfranchized Florentines. What is more, because of the factions that had cost other Italian cities their freedom to govern themselves on a communal basis, and because of the passionate party-feeling that had flung out wave after wave of Florentine families into exile in the past, membership of all these bodies rotated, so that power could never be exercised by individuals, or groups, for a sustained period. Membership of the *Signoria* changed every two months, of the *buonhuomini* every three, of the *gonfalonieri* and the larger councils every four: in each year, therefore, 1,650 different men staffed the conciliar structure of municipal government. And when the membership of executive committees, such as those responsible for security and police, war and diplomacy, currency and the mint, roads, bridges and defences, administering the property of exiles, and so forth, are taken into account, the rotation rule annually involved over 2,000 in some form of responsibility within central government.

Rotation was only one consequence of the principle of distrust that determined the power structure of municipal politics. Others were the period of quarantine before a man could become eligible again to serve on the same body (three years in the case of the *Signoria*); the barring of more than one member of the same family serving on any of the smaller councils or executive committees; and, most remarkably to modern eyes, the selection of men not by personal candidacy or in terms of their experience, but by lot. The names of men qualified by age, guild membership (a device to exclude magnates) and freedom from tax debts were put, literally, into a bag for each organ of government, and drawn out as in any other form of lottery.

The elements of the principle of distrust had been worked out as *ad hoc* solutions to the tendency of Italians to give their loyalty primarily to small interest groups. Even today, city and regional loyalties in Italy keep the local standard of business enterprise and the standard of living high (especially in the Centre and North) at the expense of effective central government. In the Renaissance, when the largest political unit was the individual city (and the adjacent territory it dominated), the instinct was to limit full loyalty to enclaves *within* the city – to a group of interrelated families, to a specific economic interest, to a *gonfalone* where palaces, churches and shops formed a community with the comforting sense of intimacy of a club within a metropolis. It was this preference for the smallest, most personally felt unit that prevented Florentines from advancing from the techniques of the Commercial Revolution to the next stage of capitalist enterprise: the exploitation of large concentrated work forces. The manufacture of wool remained on a putting-out basis spread among a multitude of small masters. Partnerships did not grow into corporations. Labourers on large building projects were split into small, independently contracted gangs. Within a city which was itself on a small, human scale (twenty minutes to walk across in any direction), where everyone knew, or at least recognized, everyone else, there were nevertheless prior and fierce foci of even more local interest.

As time went on, and especially when, from the late 14th century, Florence was threatened by an aggressively expanding Visconti Milan, the principle of distrust was exalted into a republican ideology of personal freedom guaranteed in return for unselfishly serving the state: 'Liberty' became a drumhead on which to send out propaganda messages against the forces of 'Tyranny'. But however neat and rational the Florentine constitution can be made to look, however corruption-proof, the rationale behind its construction – the emasculation of factions – guaranteed that it would not work, for factionalism could not be suppressed at the psychological or local levels. And from those levels there continually arose attempts to subvert the 'distrust' regulations and use government to support sectional interests.

We must not make too much of the contrast between the cities that accepted the control of *signori* and those like Florence which continued to manage their own

Florence, hub of the Renaissance, shown in a 15th-century woodcut. The city retained for long the outward form of communal government, although actual power was increasingly exercised by the great merchants and bankers who had made Florence the richest city in Italy by the 14th century. Left: (above) the emblem of the people of Florence; (below) the device of the Guild of Bankers.

affairs. Most of the governmental structures we have described continued to function under princely rule; the *signori*, wrapped up in their own often turbulent family feuds and frequently absent for long periods earning money as *condottieri*, had no substitute to offer for them. Similarly, communal government was never 'democratic' and became steadily less so in the Renaissance republics. The government that exiled Dante because he disagreed (as a 'white' or soft Guelf) with the desire (that of the 'black' or hard-line Guelfs) to back the papacy to the hilt, was already a mild form of oligarchy in spite of the number of citizens who served within it.

The guild structure of Florence was organized in two distinct tiers. The upper comprised the 'greater' guilds, those of the only two professions recognized as such, lawyers and doctors (for the clergy of all sorts, though accounting for perhaps two per cent of the adult population were excluded from civic affairs), the importers and manufacturers of wool and silk, and bankers and furriers. Far more numerous were the men who belonged to the 'lesser' guides: self-employed master craftsmen of all sorts, innkeepers, the *petite bourgeoisie* who owned shops or workshops – bakers, butchers, smiths, carpenters. But while any guildsman could be eligible for public office, the majority in any department of government – six out of eight members of the *Signoria* for instance – were drawn from the greater guilds. They, as having the major stake in the fortunes of the city, were accorded the predominant voice in its running.

Moreover, the constitution outlined above was the 'normal', peacetime form. When there was a crisis – an impending or actual war, a commercial recession, or a succession of bad harvests which imperilled the ability of the majority of the population to buy bread, other constitutional devices were available and they all increased the influence of the greater guildsmen. The *Signoria* could call on them to give advice in meetings known as *pratiche* or *consulte* – informal discussions. Such meetings, if they led to the formulation of policy proposals, naturally emphasized the interests of the city's top people. Moreover, sanction could be sought for the temporary reduction of the names placed in the lottery bags to increase the likelihood of drawing those of men of proven, relevant experience. Finally, recourse could be had to what was at the same time the most democratic and the most exclusive practice of all, the pronouncement of a state of emergency that temporarily suspended normal constitutional procedures.

The *vacca*, the great bell in the tower of the Palazzo della Signoria, would sound an invitation to the entire adult male population to hasten to the piazza. There assent would be asked (not always audibly) for the establishment of a provisional government with power to circumvent the ordinary constitutional processes. Out of fear, laziness or incomprehension, assent would be given, and a government hand-picked from the city's dominant families would be formed. This would last until the emergency was over – or at least until the increasingly truculent mood of the populace made it advisable to declare it at an end.

The application of these devices, exceptional as they were, helped to emphasize the bias towards oligarchy inherent in any mercantile society which denies political rights to the majority. Power in Florence, as in the other Italian cities, tended to become concentrated in the hands of families who because of their wealth, influential marriage connections, long membership of the key councils (especially the *Signoria*), or tenure of such prestigious posts as ambassadors or governors of important subject cities (for Florence this meant Arezzo, Montepulciano, Cortona, Prato, Pistoia, Pisa and Volterra), came to be called the *ottimati*, 'the best', or the *grandi*, 'the great families'.

This process, which further reduced the difference in social tone between princely and republican states, was accelerated in Florence by a traumatic proletarian revolt in 1378. In that year the *Ciompi*, the workers on whom the cloth industry relied, revolted (with the fleeting support of some of their betters who were out of sympathy with the régime of the moment) and forced the government to grant them guild, and hence political, status. However, after some weeks of panic and barred doors, the establishment, sensing that the impetus of revolt was wearing off, and with the support of members of the lesser guilds who were equally dismayed by the prospect of worker-influenced wage levels, rescinded its concessions. The democratic moment passed, leaving a fear of the masses that ensured that men of middling station would look on more tolerantly than ever while power accumulated in the hands of the men who most impressively represented the principle that financial profit depended on political hierarchy; it was better to toady to the rich than to be victimized by the poor.

This mood was sustained in the generations before and after 1400 by the Visconti wars which both justified frequent recourse to the 'emergency' devices within the constitution and led to an extension of Florence's rule within Tuscany that appeared to justify oligarchical control in the most practical and convincing manner. And because oligarchies squeeze together the most potent of potential rivalries, the chief families agreed to bite their lips and accept the general leadership of one of them; first the Albizzi and then, from 1434, the Medici.

How then was the 'distrust' principle, so carefully, indeed mathematically, enshrined in the constitution, subverted? How, given the conciliar system of policy decisions shared among the three leading organs of state and vetoed or endorsed by the larger councils, is it possible to speak of the 'régime' that banished Dante,

or that of the Albizzi, or more evocatively, of the Medici, when there was meant to be no such thing as a régime, but simply a series of short-service congeries of citizens plucked at random from lottery bags?

Part of the answer lies in the working of the emergency provisions which enabled a comparatively small number of men to be recycled through the conciliar-committee system while retaining a fairly steady political image. But mainly the answer is to be found in the traditional instinct to think of family and neighbourhood first and city second.

This – especially because of the trade recessions which after the 1340s made it more difficult for recent immigrants to found fortunes – led men of modest means to cluster for security within the established shadow of their local merchant- or banker-grandee (most rich men were both). What he could offer was perhaps in itself trivial: a loan to bridge the failure of a minor business venture or to provide one of those dowries without which girls remained unmarriageable, a whiff of influence in a law-suit, an aura of protection which in itself established a certain status. But these favours could make the difference between reasonable security and disaster. They were sought and cherished, and they created a following – if sufficiently extensive, a party.

For many of those so protected were, as guildsmen, part of Florence's political class. Even if the boss himself – for it is legitimate to think in proto-Mafia terms when considering the municipal scale of Renaissance politics – were not in government at the moment, his clients might be, and could be expected to vote as he would have done. And to keep them available for public office he – as did the Albizzi and the Medici – would, among the other favours, pay off the tax debts that would exclude them if their names were to be drawn.

This exchange of uncontractual, informal services gave shrewd political managers the chance to influence the processes of government by remote control. It was punishable at law, but difficult to pin down. Many engaged in it, and from the dominant classes' recovery after the *Ciompi* alarm Florentine domestic affairs can be read in terms of competing clientage groups until politics steadied under the influence of the most successful of all, the one led by the Medici.

So much glamour attaches to the phrase 'Medicean Florence' that it is worth saying at once that Florentine culture would have been much the same had the family never existed. They were highly educated men with a keen sympathy for the intellectual tone of their city. They were in a position from time to time to assist with a reference, occasionally to employ, some of the greatest cultural figures of the age – Brunelleschi, Michelozzo, Donatello, Uccello, the youthful Michelangelo and the writers Pulci, Ficino and Poliziano among them, but only the last two depended on them to a significant extent. As patrons the Medici were but one family among many. And they had no court which could impose a dominant 'courtly' style as happened, as we shall see, at, for instance, Ferrara. They paved the way for the rule of princes, but they were not princes themselves.

Until 1434 Florentine politics had been dominated by groups of families which had come to feel that their common economic interests were best served by granting a measure of leadership to one of them, the Albizzi. Such a family-led coalition was fraught with jealousies which were exacerbated by the sense of its illegality. It was therefore peculiarly dependent on the success of the policies it backed. Failure came to the Albizzi in the form of an unsuccessful and disastrously expensive attempt to conquer Lucca. In a last exercise of power they negotiated the exile of the leaders of the outstanding opposition party, that of the Medici. But within a year the momentum of failure reversed the process and in their turn the Albizzi were banished, the Medici recalled from exile.

They were recalled because they represented not a radical solution to the tensions within the city's fractured ambitions but a more promising alternative to the previous solution. The head of the family, Cosimo, was well aware that he represented a replacement rather than a fresh start and his public demeanour – followed in varying degrees after his death in 1464 by that of his son Piero (d. 1469) and of his grandson Lorenzo (d. 1492) – reflected that awareness. If the Medici came to be more identified with the fortunes of their city than any other family pursuing similar aims in Italian republics, it was because they better observed these imperatives: to stay rich (Cosimo inherited the most prosperous bank in Florence); to cultivate their clients; to prefer manipulation through others to a too obvious personal show of power; to monitor public opinion so perceptively as to be able – through clients alarmed at the threats which crises offered to themselves – to adjust the forms of government so that without too much offence being caused they became less open to the influence of rival interests.

These adjustments were not dramatic, but they confirmed the tendency, observable in other republics – Genoa, Lucca or Siena, for instance – to restrict policy-making to a mercantile oligarchy of the rich: in Florence to some 75 families, most of whom agreed that to support the Medici was, on balance, better than to renew the power struggles amongst one another. But this did not mean that Florence was formally an oligarchy. The constitution, even with the lottery bags restricted (and this device could not be used for long at a time), still allowed lesser men, farriers, leather dealers and the like, to acquire high office. Nor could men of weight who grudged the favour granted the Medici be altogether excluded. Thus it was the clientage system that linked, hazardously, the oligarchical direction of affairs with the constitutional mechanism of broader-based republicanism. And this allowed a face-saving

belief within the city at large that communal traditions were being maintained.

The hereditary succession of unofficial leadership from one Medici to another certainly could not have been established without wealth. Cosimo was probably the richest man in Europe. Piero was a careful manager. Lorenzo – Lorenzo the Magnificent – was not, but by then another unique aspect of Medici influence compensated for the dwindling fortunes of the bank. It arose from the bank's international branch organization which gave its heads a unique information network relating to foreign affairs and a unique opportunity to meet and to influence foreign rulers or their ministers. Acknowledging this, the Florentine government had allowed Cosimo to take initiatives in foreign policy which they subsequently backed. By Lorenzo's time it was accepted that external policy was decided in Palazzo Medici in Via Larga (now Via Cavour) rather than in the Palazzo della Signoria. It was for this reason that other governments looked on the Medici as the princes, rather than – as was the internal view – the political impresarios of Florence.

Wealth and foreign connections were, however, not enough. Ceaseless attention to the clientage, alertness to the persistence in the city of a preference for more widely shared decisions, care to retain an image of the Medici palace as a government entertainment centre rather than the centre of an alternative government – all these precautions were ignored by Lorenzo's son Piero the Younger. And in 1494, after only two years of his brash taking for granted of his special position, the Medici were once more hounded into exile.

This time there was no rival family to replace the banished one. Instead, in revulsion against what was quickly termed the 'tyranny' of the Medici, the constitution was reformed to allow more men than ever to have a chance to formulate and execute policy decisions, to guarantee more firmly even than in the age of Dante that no one family, let alone one individual, could subvert the communal longing for widely shared self-government. At its base was a council with elective and decision-ratifying powers that numbered no less than three thousand.

But the ideological clock had been set back too far. Nothing like that number of men were interested in turning up to the Great Council's meeting. After the French invasion of 1494 and the drastic change in the balance of Italian-European fortunes, experienced hands were needed on the rudder of policy (an image frequently used at the time). The firmness associated with Medicean-oligarchical direction came increasingly to be regretted. By 1512 the Medici were back. And with the election in the following year of Lorenzo the Magnificent's son Giovanni as Pope Leo X the process accelerated whereby the city would allow Medici leadership to develop into – from 1530 – hereditary ducal, indeed from 1569 grand-ducal, rule.

Venice

In spite of Florence's unique mustering of creative talent and its ability to retain so long the forms of communal government, its fortunes are analogous to those of other Italian states: the constant outflow of individuals and companies seeking business in Northern Europe and throughout the Mediterranean, the conquest of surrounding lesser towns, the employment of mercenary armies lest recruitment for war should interrupt normal trade and industry within the city, conflicts within interest groups leading to fewer citizens having greater influence.

Venice, however, was a case, and a place, apart.

It retained, unwaveringly, its republican form of government – retained it, indeed, with changes only of detail until the coming of Napoleon Bonaparte in 1797. The key to this imperturbability was the decision in 1297 to give a legal definition to the governing class which would settle once and for all the problem faced elsewhere by the absorption of competitive *nouveaux riches*. The adult males of some 200 families were given the hereditary right to decide policy and see to its execution. While not suppressing rivalries this restrained them within the common interest of a caste with not only a monopoly of political power but with the governmental means to foster its own dominant economic interest: trade with the Levant and the re-export of the luxury goods – spices, silks, porcelains, dyes and drugs – purchased there to the hungry markets of Europe. And as the state not only guaranteed the status of the patricians, as they came to be called, but tried to support their livelihoods (it could not, after all, teach lame ducks to fly), it induced a loyalty, a suppression of personal interest in the service of the state that, for all its imperfections and exceptions, produced a body of men psychologically different in their attitude to government from any other; vested interest bred a mystique of public duty. If to catch the flavour of Florentine policies it is helpful to think of the Mafia, to catch that of Venetian values it is useful to consider the ethos of the Victorian-Edwardian imperial establishment.

While other Italian maritime states – Pisa and Genoa, for example – had established footholds in the eastern Mediterranean, only Venice established a veritable empire there. From the imperial capital in the lagoon, Venice by 1300 administered a string of land bases and islands down the Adriatic, Dalmatian and Greek coasts that extended to Crete; in 1489 this was extended to Cyprus. Governed by Venetian patricians, these bases and their hinterlands provided ports-of-call for the galleys trading with Constantinople, Aleppo, Beirut and Alexandria. Before the expansion of Portugal and Spain overseas, Venice was the only European state that was also a colonial power.

Venice was also exceptional in being a late-comer to the competition for territorial expansion within the Italian peninsula. Not until 1405 was the realization

fully accepted that the quasi-monopolistic purchase of goods in the Levant would produce maximum profits only if the republic could obtain permanently open and toll-free routes from Venice to the Alpine passes that gave access to the markets of Central and north-western Europe. By 1428, after an unprecedentedly successful series of military campaigns and diplomatic pressure, Venice gained – and then grimly hung on to – a land empire stretching from Bergamo and Brescia to Udine, via Verona, Vicenza and Padua. This abrupt and universally resented appearance as a mainland power still further nourished in the minds of the patriciate the sense that they incorporated the dignity of a special destiny that God – especially through their patron saint, St Mark – had granted them as the continuation of his divinely guided Roman Empire. Had not their ancestors, albeit as refugees from wave after wave of barbarian invaders, kept the idea of that empire alive on the muddy islands of the lagoon and then, centuries later, re-established the notion of empire by sea and land?

All Italian cities cherished the idea that God had singled them out through one of His saints (St John for Florence, the Virgin for Siena) for success. Most could point to some Roman remains (the arena at Verona, the amphitheatre at Lucca, the baptistery – believed to be not Romanesque but Roman – at Florence) that qualified them to be the legitimate inheritors and resuscitators of antique glory. But with a canniness not untouched by real awe, the Venetians' sense of the double validation of their pretensions was unusually fortifying – though the canniness made them seek to establish for themselves through diplomacy the status of a European and not merely an Italian power.

One must not make too much of these ideologies; they were only the fancy dress in which personal and collective self-interest occasionally chose to parade themselves. But here again Venice was a special case. Other states were impressed by what has come to be known as the Myth of Venice. The Myth (so-called because it contained elements of exaggeration) had three main components. The first was that the Venetian constitution contained some ingredient that made it impervious to change. Save that it had an elected permanent head of state, the doge, it was not in fact all that different from that of Florence; the same principle of distrust, for instance, led to rotation and quarantine, guards against members of the same family sitting on the same councils, the use of lottery as a selection procedure in order to avoid party pressure. During the crisis that followed the expulsion of the Medici in 1494, Florence – though Venice's chief adversary – paid it the compliment of copying first the Venetian Great Council (the body which all patricians had the right to attend), then the dogeship, making the previously two-month gonfaloniership of justice an office tenable for life. But this homage to the base and apex of the Venetian system did not work because the key to

Venice, depicted in a woodcut of 1490, when the republic was at the apogee of its maritime and mainland power. In the illustration (left) to 'Hypnerotomachia Polifili', a romance published in Venice by the Aldine press in 1499, the hero faces three doors with inscriptions above in Arabic, Hebrew, Greek and Latin – symbolic of the universal culture of the city.

Venetian stability was in fact the social exclusiveness of its governing class.

But why did this not provoke opposition? In the early 16th century the population of Venice was about 140,000. Only 2,500, as patricians, had power. Yet the second component of the myth was that of a social harmony that made Venice more or less immune from those tensions, which occasionally turned into revolts bordering on civil war, that plagued other Italian and, indeed, other European, states. Necessarily briefly, the answer is this. Non-patrician men of wealth and standing had three outlets for their ambitions: trade (though on less privileged terms than patricians); the civil service, which they entirely staffed and through which they obtained both recognition and the indirect power which comes from permanency; the authority to run those peculiarly Venetian religious and charitable institutions, the *scuole*, to which the government delegated much of what would today be called the welfare services of the state. To the less prosperous, the guildsmen and labourers, the government offered – as alone an easily guarded island community could do – reasonably full employment protected from immigrants, and ready access, through commissions appointed for the purpose, to the consideration of grievances. Finally, the city itself, built up of one reclaimed islet after another, represented a series of social microcosms each with its *campo* or square, church, shops, palace, merchant and artisan housing; communities satisfying in themselves and headed by patrician families whose loyalty, unconcerned with building up a local clientage, were centred in the council rooms of the Doge's Palace.

The third component of the Myth was stability; while other states changed their mode of government as the result of internal crisis or – from 1494 – foreign pressure or conquest, Venice remained unvanquished and unchanged. The seal was put on this aspect of the republic's image when by 1517 it had weathered the military storm released on its domains in 1509 by the alliance of Cambrai, which comprised the pope, the monarchs of France, Spain and Germany, and the dukes of Mantua and Ferrara. By then Venice, the 'newest' power in Italy and therefore the last to absorb its cultural tone (while having the confidence to alter it with the style of its own, delayed Renaissance), was the only Italian state, apart from the papacy, which was granted a diplomatic place above the salt by the greedy dynasts – Habsburg, Valois, Tudor – who jockeyed for power on a continental scale.

Ferrara

Ferrara provides a model for those city-based states of the Renaissance which while not of outstanding economic importance, had a prosperity based on agriculture and crafts and a lucrative control of road or river trade-routes (in this case, the Po) sufficient to enable them to hire troops to support their independence. Like Mantua and Urbino, the city realized

Ferrara in 1490: the centre of the city is dominated by the great square castle of the Este, who ruled Ferrara from 1332 to 1597. The 13th-century façade of the cathedral is opposite.

the implications of its own urban factiousness and from 1332 accepted the rule of the dominant local land-owners, the Este. It was a confession of failure that gave little cause for regret. The Este, governing as marquises from 1393 and as dukes from 1471, determined foreign policy and tax levels and occasionally forced through major changes – as when Ercole I, duke from 1471 to 1505, trebled the area bounded by the city by what has been known since as 'the Herculean Addition' – but otherwise the communal system of conciliar municipal government remained intact. And what is notable is the shift from an initial sense that surrender to the Este was a regrettable act of political necessity to one of identification with a family and its court whose achievements and splendour became a source of general civic pride.

This shift was only possible because of the economically unsophisticated nature of the middling-sized Italian cities. Ferrara was a city of rural aristocrats who kept town houses there, dealers in agricultural produce, shop-keepers and craftsmen catering for the brisk local demand for household goods, clothes and farm implements. There was a bourgeoisie of lawyers and doctors, but no international merchants and bankers to form a group strong enough, as in Florence and Venice, to stave off a signorial take-over of the commune. And when the talent of a lawyer or prosperous corn-chandler became uncomfortably conspicuous, he would be drawn into the service of the Este's growingly complex personal bureaucracy, to oversee the involved organization of their rural estates and the hunting lodges and pleasure villas they were building there, or to steer them through the financial complexities of the profits they aimed for as *condottieri* up for hire by rulers more weighty than themselves.

If princely rule on the Este model was an imposition it was also a partnership between court and municipality. The more splendid the court, the better the livelihood of those who catered for it. The more military engagements the ruler could get for himself the more opportunities there were for the able-bodied poor as soldiers. Moreover the ruler's personal earnings (and this is true for the Gonzaga of Mantua and the Montefeltro of Urbino) meant that he had to lean less heavily on the tax capability of his urban subjects. Though modern democratic sentiment finds perhaps more to admire in Renaissance republics, the time-traveller would not find himself materially worse off in the princely cities, even in the greatest of them, Milan, run internally on similar lines to Ferrara by the Visconti and, from 1450, by their successors, the Sforza dukes.

Rome

The government of Rome was also a form of partnership, between the city's municipal government and the *signori*-like popes. Here, however, there was a third partner, illegal but irrepressible: the great baronial families – the Orsini, Colonna and Caetani conspicuous among them – whose military raids from their country estates and whose feuds among their fortress clan-centres within the city kept political life in perpetual disarray.

With virtually no aristocracy who put the city's interest first and the smallest professional and merchant class of any Italian city of its size (about 25,000 in 1400), Rome had no important resident banks, no industry and no international trade: no body of citizens, therefore, wealthy or powerful enough to keep the barons at bay. It was a local market town, a livestock centre, and a grasping but slovenly host to pilgrims. Needless to say, it had no university. Twice, in 1347 and again in 1354, the eloquent visionary Cola di Rienzo proclaimed himself Tribune of the People and persuaded his fellow citizens to remember that they were the direct descendents of the Rome of the Caesars. But the artificiality of his programme of revived Roman leadership within Italy was shown when the very mob who had supported him hacked him to death and the city reverted to the undergoverned, violent condition that had already caused the papacy to leave for less historically appropriate but calmer headquarters.

This was at Avignon, where successive popes

remained from 1309 to 1377. In itself, this long sojourn was neither surprising nor scandalous. Thanks to its chronic instability, between 1100 and 1309 Rome had been the home of the papacy for a total of only 82 years. Neither the efficiency of Europe's largest bureaucracy, managing the legal, financial and diplomatic services of the Church throughout Western and Central Europe, nor the spiritual leadership that flowed from the popes' succession from St Peter and their power to interpret the will of God, was maimed by residence abroad.

What suffered from the residence at Avignon (its possible permanence symbolized by the vast and lavishly appointed Papal Palace) was, first, the control of the papacy over the Papal States. Throughout that great stretch of territory running from a point midway between Rome and Naples up north and eastwards to the borders of Ferrara, the local families who had been appointed vicars, or proxy rulers on behalf of the papacy, had, as it were, gone native, and treated their roles as implying hereditary ownership rather than delegated authority. This fissiparism, only partially checked by the dispatch of legates to halt it, meant the dwindling of the power base of a papacy that needed the tax income and the soldiers from its own state in order to negotiate with other governments from a position of strength, for popes were secular rulers as well as bureaucratic chieftains and spiritual leaders (a combination of functions incompatible with the instincts of a hermit or the selflessness of a potential saint).

What also suffered was the sensibility of those Italians who, in the moments of wider patriotism induced by humanism's emphasis on the peninsula's common inheritance from Rome, saw papal absenteeism as betrayal. Hence Petrarch's denunciation of French-dominated Avignon (all the popes elected there were Frenchmen) as the 'unholy Babylon' which he likened to the harlot of the Apocalypse 'full of abominations and the filth of her fornication'.

It was primarily the need to restore control over the Papal States, however, that brought the papacy back to Rome. But 1377 was not the beginning of the process that was to establish a political *modus vivendi* in the city and transform its scattered and largely derelict urban fabric into a capital city worthy of its ancient and papal role, a rival of Florence and Venice. That beginning was postponed by the Great Schism. Dissatisfied with the election in Rome in 1378 of an Italian pope, the French cardinals declared it invalid and elected another one. From then there were two popes (from 1401 three) and it was not until 1417 that this confusion was rectified and a unified papacy, in the person of Pope Martin V, was able to begin to restore the prestige of his office and tackle the problems of Rome and the Papal States – problems all the more urgent in that the anti-Roman popes had secured support from the rival powers of Europe by granting them concessions at the Church's expense.

Martin at once began repair work on St Peter's and the Vatican, restored churches and summoned artists: Masolino, Gentile da Fabriano and Masaccio (who died in Rome *c.* 1428). At last, after centuries of neglect, there arose an intention to dignify and embellish the city with new streets and squares. But new threats to Catholic unity in Europe and fresh incursions by the resentful Roman barons put the city's capital status again in doubt. Eugenius IV spent most of his reign (1431–40) in Florence. Only with the pontificate of Nicholas V (1446–55) was Martin's work taken up again. Once more, painters and architects were called from Florence – Gozzoli, Fra Angelico and Leon Battista Alberti among them; once more plans were made for urban renewal and rationalization. By now Rome's future was assured by resident popes who had sufficient wealth and authority to obtain armed help against the Orsini, Colonna and other third parties and to restart the collaboration with a municipality that realized (with Cola di Rienzo's dream forgotten) that its fortunes were entirely dependent on a papacy which by bringing trade, talent and public works could put money into Roman pockets. Even so, news of the creation by Pius II of a tiny ideal city at Pienza to commemorate his birth there caused rumour to suggest that another papal flitting was about to take place. Only with Sixtus IV (1471–84) and the grandiose building plans he spoke of and partly carried out (and an influx of painters to decorate his new chapel in the Vatican – among them Botticelli, Perugino and Signorelli) was it accepted within Rome and without that the popes were back in their city for good. And his determination to accelerate what was to be the long process of regaining central control over the cities of the Papal States – which even led him to war against Florence – proved it.

Rome, then, as an orderly and impressive city and as the permanent headquarters of the Catholic Church, was, like Venice, a late-comer to the full cultural and political life of the peninsula. Because popes were usually old when elected, to get things done without relying on the dubious loyalty of those who were already thinking of what might happen after their deaths, they brought in wave after wave of relations – the *nepoti* who gave their name to nepotism – and dependents from their own homelands on whom they could rely. And these men prospered, built and stayed. Increasingly, too, the cardinals, hitherto resigned to the constant packing of their bags, felt secure enough to build palaces. Rome grew, and went on importing men to see that it grew beautifully. Under popes who appreciated the arts and were not as yet alarmed by 'pagan' humanist scholarship, the most degraded (if most sacred) of urban sites developed by the 1520s into the cultural as well as the political-diplomatic centre-piece of Italy with a speed and majesty and a power to repay cultural debts rivalled by the development of no other city in Europe.

The Renaissance as a cultural period

From Petrarch (1304–74) onwards, contemporaries saw the thin slices of time that constituted their own experience in terms of 'renewal', 'restoration' or 'recovery'. It was not until 1550 that Giorgio Vasari used the term 'rebirth' and then only with reference to the arts, of which he was the pioneer historian. But all these words shared a common assumption: that intellectual or otherwise sophisticated men were being given, and were taking, a second chance – a chance to be 'born again' and to recreate, even to surpass the accomplishments of the ancestral world of classical antiquity that had been ignored or misunderstood over too many spiritually enlightened but (it was thought) culturally barren centuries.

Such a view was blinkered both in space and time. It refused to acknowledge the scholarly and artistic achievements of the Gothic North, and it affected to reject the medieval heritage within Italy itself – the Romanesque style, for instance, which was absorbed so creatively into the classicizing architecture of the 15th century.

For with every allowance for the uniqueness of individual talent and the inevitable changes in appearance that occur when old aims are pursued in a new context, what provided the common denominator within the immense variety of Renaissance style was a literally epoch-making resolve: to discount the achievements of what was seen as a 'dark' or 'middle' age and to match the edges of contemporary culture to those ripped across so long ago by the barbarian, 'gothic' conquerors of ancient Rome.

The urge to do this was provided by the scholarly but readily popularizable programme that has come to be known as humanism – the impulse, that is, to acquire information about the past which would restore a sense of contact with a time when Italians had not only conquered the known world but given to it examples of excellence in every field of human endeavour, from politics and war to poetry and architecture.

This process of imaginative reconstruction was a lengthy one. It involved re-reading the authors known throughout the Middle Ages – Virgil, Ovid and Horace, Seneca, parts of Livy and Cicero, for example – with the aim of understanding them afresh within the context of their own, separate, pre-Christian civilization. It involved the search for works shelved throughout the Middle Ages but unread. And on many manuscripts a ferocious editorial effort had to be expended before they could be written out again in more or less the form which their authors had given them. No more eloquent witness could be called to prove the power of the spell cast over the present by the past than the fact that even before the introduction of printing to Italy in 1465 almost the full range of ancient Roman writers known today was available in reasonably 'clean' texts.

What kept the scholarly drive to locate and edit texts so persistently vigorous was an ever-increasing belief in their relevance. Without social acceptance and financial assistance, uninstitutionally supported scholarship would have faltered (universities were slow to offer perches to humanists). But editorial and copying time and manuscript searches extending from Western Europe to Egypt and the Levant were paid for by men who were not primarily, if at all, scholars themselves, but who felt that part of being alive now was to know something of what it had been like to have been alive then. Most normally perturbed men find the present inadequate and mentally dwell on, and seek standards of excellence within, an alternative society. For the medieval Christian it was that of the City of God; now it may be the City of Marx. Then it was – for a minority, but a crucially important minority for the tone of Renaissance culture – the City of Rome and, perceived more dimly, Athens. 'Invisible cities', all of them, but none the less potent for that.

While the textual history of humanism zig-zagged from find to find within a steadily broadening knowledge of the nature and achievements of the ancient world, the moments at which a positive relevance was seen between contemporary and ancient aims had a chronology of their own. That Nicola Pisano's pulpit of *c.* 1260 in the baptistery of Pisa reflected a response to the Roman sarcophagi displayed in the nearby Campo Santo was the result of a personal taste. That at about the same time a group of lawyers at Padua sought to look back from the medieval commentators on the Roman Law they taught to the actual circumstances within which its decisions had been formulated was a coincidence. Only when they are linked to Petrarch's concern to use Virgil as a literary model (for his epic *Africa*) and his shocked alarm at finding letters of Cicero that showed the 'timeless' philosopher so respected in the Middle Ages to have been deeply involved in the political controversies of his own age, can we twist threads of relevance together so that they start to form the pattern of later development: the checking of contemporary achievements or values by reference to those of antiquity.

Petrarch, in his works of the 1330s and 1340s, was the first to see that ancient society, with its pagan-activist ethos, offered a challenge to Christian contemplative values. Intuitively he sensed both the completeness of a civilization he could glimpse only in fragments and its dangerous majesty: the challenge that Rome offered, as a haven for the lively mind, to Christianity's offer of a heaven for the soul. The comprehensiveness of his vision did not prevent others turning now to the relevance of one aspect of ancient wisdom or accomplishment, now to another as it suited their interests, but it enabled each aspect to be seen as part of a whole.

During the 15th and early 16th centuries the areas of relevance extended: from educational theory, moral and political philosophy and historical writing to the design of medals and coins, town planning, the drama, linguistics and statecraft. By 1513, when Venice's commander-in-chief Bartolomeo d'Alviano proposed that the republic's armies should be organized on the lines of the Roman legions, or by 1515, when Machiavelli reproached his contemporaries for turning to the ancients for models of excellence in sculpture, medicine and law but ignoring the vast fund of experience to be drawn on in their political achievements, humanism, enriched from the mid-15th century by a growing acquaintance with ancient Greek authors, had become not only an enthusiasm but a cult. Collectors' agents were alert to garner the numinous bric-a-brac (pots, gems, statues, coins) turned up by peasants' ploughs. Over baptismal fonts clergymen resignedly intoned such 'Christian' names as Flavia, Livia, Camillus, Aeneas, Achilles, Hector.

We are at this point only concerned with humanism from one point of view: the question of whether its preoccupation with the achievements of classical antiquity was so pervasive as to be the primary reason why we look on the Renaissance as a separate cultural period. Even in the context of the most advanced people in Europe, 'culture' applies only to an intellectual and artistic élite and not to the habitual accommodation to circumstance – whether evidenced by a plough, a cottage or a kinship – of a society coping only with the imperatives of subsistence. Such a society existed within Renaissance Italy; it constituted, indeed, the majority of an overwhelmingly rural population. The changes within its history, however, have no relevance to those of 'the Renaissance'. Indeed, there was little change in the working conditions or the expectations of what life could offer the landless peasant, or the unskilled urban proletariat, between the early Middle Ages and the 20th century.

Around 1450 the population of Italy was approximately nine million. Of these only about 300,000 lived in the cities (Milan, Venice, Verona, Mantua, Ferrara, Florence, Siena, Urbino, Rome) which played a decisive part in shaping the development of Renaissance culture. And of this 300,000, only perhaps 30,000 had the power, leisure, cash, and command over materials and labour to give form to that culture. When to this is added another figure – the estimated 600 painters, sculptors, architects, musicians, writers and scholars who constituted the creative élite between 1420 and 1540 – the extent of the discrepancy between the history of the people and of the culture of the Renaissance becomes glaringly apparent.

Of course the works of the élite were copied and modified by less original men. Because of the patronage and the commissions they could offer, cities sucked in talent from the smaller towns and hamlets of the provinces. But then they pumped it back again in the form of pupils and assistants who could not keep abreast of big-town competition. Moreover, the masters themselves travelled and left works behind

Clio, the muse of history: a 15th-century Florentine engraving. Of all the arts and sciences, history was the one most radically affected by the new perspectives of humanism. Even today, the Renaissance three-tier model of classical antiquity, 'Middle Ages' and modern times is virtually impossible to avoid.

them that challenged other communities to catch up with what was innovatory and fashionable. From Florence, Giotto and Donatello left such challenges to the artists of Padua, Antonio da Sangallo to the mastermasons of Montepulciano; Renaissance Rome owed its emergence as a cultural centre from the mid-15th century entirely to the reverberations registered after the visits of foreigners: Bramante, whose architectural career began in Milan, Raphael from Urbino, Michelangelo from Florence. And a sense of participation in an élite culture sank downwards, at least in the major urban centres. This was only partly in the negative sense that the Renaissance dropped a harness over the work-force that built its monuments. Because of an intensely patriotic inter-city rivalry and the availability for public inspection of not only new buildings but also the majority of new paintings and sculptures, which were commissioned for churches and city halls, the works that make up our notion of Renaissance culture were not created in an atmosphere of élitist stealth.

This suggestion of a general participation in a culture generated by a small minority must not be taken too far. All the same, it was further aided by the fact that many commissions were placed by groups – confraternities, guilds, cathedral chapters, boards of works – knowledge of whose deliberations filtered among those linked to them by the conditions of their membership or employment. A sense of rapport with painters and sculptors and architects of genius was helped by knowing that the great majority had risen from the ranks of craftsmen or tradesmen and were – though many came to kick against the stigma – members of craft organizations. It is true, too, that many of the occasions which assembled a variety of expressions of élitist style were aimed at mass audiences: pageants, processions and entertainments in which painted banners, *tableaux vivants* on ox-drawn floats, rhetorical speeches and musical accompaniments presented opportunities for the periodical recognition of the point attained by culture in the service of civic, princely or religious occasions. But we are still talking of only 13 per cent of Italians, even if we expand our figures to include all the towns, however culturally drowsy, with populations of more than 10,000. And because, whatever the reactions of its audience and the echoes transmitted by its disciples, the tone of a culture is set by its leaders and their financial backers, we are brought back to 300,000 or 0·3 per cent of Italians who, in any one generation of twenty years, were in a position to foster the work of about 100 men who decisively determined the appearance and impact of newly created works of art, music, literature and learned speculation.

These calculations – uncertain as they must be – are reminders of the startling differences between the numbers of men who made the Renaissance as a cultural phenomenon, and those who witnessed or remained oblivious to it. But they suggest that the values of humanism, though radiating from minute foci of scholarship, could, by playing on the imaginations even of small numbers of men sensitive enough to respond to a dominant ideology, unify a culture whose vitality also sucked nourishment from many other sources and expressed itself in creations each bearing a vividly individual imprint.

Periods within the Renaissance

Let us first look back to that marvellous first generation of the 14th century: was it then that the Renaissance 'started'? Giovanni Pisano's pulpit in S. Andrea, Pistoia (1298–1301); Duccio's *Maestà* (1308–11) for the cathedral of Siena; Giotto's frescoes in the Arena Chapel at Padua (*c.* 1304–13); Dante's *Divina Commedia* (1304–21): these are works whose difference from their predecessors' was not merely due to the impact of individual genius. All brought the effects of art nearer to human appearance and emotion.

The question poses a famous problem. Men of genius do not copy but transform their inheritance. But did the transformations of this generation contain the consciousness of a new direction likely to be sustained by others, or did they, rather, reflect an ability to play brilliantly with the hands dealt by the immediate past? Looking from their works forward to those of

the first generation of the 15th century, there is no doubt that the latter answer is the more likely. Earlier medieval Italian painting had little to offer. Vasari was on the whole right in castigating it as flat and repetitive, though wrong in thinking it therefore unbeautiful. But skills remained lively and could react to the call from the new religious orders of the 13th century, the Dominicans and (more especially) the Franciscans, that the tremulous faithful should be assured of the human reality of the Gospel stories. Duccio responded to this call, if in a manner more exquisite and reserved than that of Giotto. Moreover, both had access to many of the works of Giovanni Pisano and his father Nicola, which reflected that astonishing family's interest in ancient sculpture; its suggestions as to how the interest in scattered realistic detail that was an element in medieval sculpture all over Europe might be concentrated in the representation of the human body. Assisi, Siena, Pisa, Pistoia and Florence were all interlinked by the travels of friars, artists and their mercantile and clerical patrons. And Dante too reviewed, in scorn and hope, his immediate inheritance.

In one of Masaccio's frescoes in the Carmine in Florence, St Peter is shown curing the sick with his shadow as he passes. Giotto's earlier figures, though creating through expression, bodily weight and position in space a greater sense of the illusion of being records of real people than had been aimed at hitherto, cast no shadows. Yet Dante portrays himself as recognized in Purgatory as a living man because he casts one – as the shades of the dead could not. But neither here, nor in the multitude of other graphic details in the *Commedia*, is Dante assuming that to create an illusion of reality should be among the aims of art, as Masaccio was to do. His details rise from the pell-mell touches of realistic description in the chronicles and the often bitterly personal poetic squibs of his youth. As a realist Dante drew also on the vivid repertory of personalized mockery and invective that was current in a jostling and competitive society, and on its knack of occasionally focusing in stone or words on a telling natural detail: a branch of the tree of life, the keys of St Peter, a dog as symbol of lechery. But his shadow made a theological point and only incidentally a descriptive one.

In the same way, as a philosopher, Dante set the prose of medieval theological argument to a verbal music that soared ahead of its time because of its quality, not its intention. Of all great poets he is the most awesome. And this is because he presents himself as personally frail but thoroughly aware of the daunting, proven certainties with which he and his readers must come to terms on their march towards salvation as it was conceived in the theology of St Thomas Aquinas.

And what of humanism, meanwhile in the making among a coterie of scholars, learned courtiers and university teachers far across the Apennines in Bologna and Padua? It was too little known to be effective as a bond linking artistic and literary effort to a new sense of purpose. For Dante, who wrote in trans-Apennine exile but whose mind had been formed in Florence, Aristotle was the supreme philosopher, Virgil – his guide to Hell and those terraces of Mount Purgatory accessible to an unbaptized pagan – the greatest of poets. He saw the course of Roman history as divinely guided so that God could choose its most universalist moment under Augustus as that in which to manifest himself as a man to be wrongfully judged by, and therefore able to offer pardon for their error to, the whole human race. But Dante plucked out men and moments from antiquity whenever they could serve the purpose of his art or argument. He, the professed man of letters and thought, was unconcerned with the separateness of ancient culture and the challenges it could issue when revealed in its own image. So we can be sure that craftsmen-geniuses like Nicola and Giovanni Pisano, Duccio and Giotto were similarly unaffected. Their work coaxed out the latent humanity from medieval culture without the benefit of humanism.

Theirs was a generation of late maturity, not of rebirth. Its products, when looked at afresh a century later, would crucially affect the form and pace of the more deliberately motivated course that a humanist culture was to take, but they did not engender it. With hindsight it can also be termed a time of gestation or 'pre-Renaissance'. And its tone was prolonged for a century. Petrarch continued to write, and manuscript copies of his works spread the infection of his by no means single-minded sense of intellectual communion with the world of antiquity. In *c.* 1340 Ambrogio Lorenzetti's 'Good Government' fresco in the Sienese Palazzo Pubblico, an amalgam of energetic figures derived from Giotto and his followers set in a believable landscape hitherto only described by poets, was still within the extended range of late-medieval culture. But then the long aftermath of the Black Death of 1348–9 imposed a curfew on the increasing traffic in humanist studies and recalled artists to their duty to preach austerity and duty rather than delight.

This protraction of the pre-Renaissance was not contradicted by Boccaccio's *Decameron* of *c.* 1350. Because it is on 'this' side of Europe's greatest catastrophe of all time (nearly half of the urban inhabitants of Italy perished), and because its humour and its literary dash, grace and cunning require no effort to appreciate today, the book may seem a portent of a different cultural climate. Boccaccio in earlier works had caught something of the inflection of early humanism, but what he knew of antiquity's mythology through its poets operated on his imagination in the same way as did that other mythology which flowed into Italy from transalpine courtly poetry: he did not respond to the capital 'A' of humanist Antiquity but added the *matière de Rome* to the *matière de France*. But what of the multi-layered sophistication of the most

complicated of his stories – as of that of the work as a whole with its 'voices' of author, author-invented narrators and narrator-invented characters? Sophistication is not a criterion that can distinguish one culture from another. Boccaccio was the super-sensitive collector of every impulse from the medieval past that helped give artistic substance to the portrayal of humanity. His aim was (at least he said it was) to bring a sense of diverting reality to the day-dreaming of bourgeois wives and daughters semi-cloistered by convention from the more fully realized lives of their busily trafficking and philandering menfolk – and of the priests and members of religious orders who ministered, with such earthy duplicity, to the laity as a whole.

Neither the gusto nor the finesse of Boccaccio's extraordinary work could, however, have derived from the nascent humanism of his day. His contemporary and friend Petrarch, whose troubled, exquisitely expressed self-scrutiny as a poet and whose equally passionate but more solid contributions as a scholar were to prove more seminal when the future's mood was ready to catch his, could not, for all the strength of an imagination that identified itself with a civilization separated from his own by a thousand years, match the vigorous literary personality of Boccaccio, whose imagination supped on dishes still warm and whose hero was not Virgil but Dante.

Boccaccio later came increasingly to share Petrarch's interest in humanist studies, as his influential *Genealogy of the Pagan Gods* witnesses. But his contribution to the rapid spread of humanism as a formative influence, which took place shortly after his death in 1375 (a year after Petrarch), was derived from the *Decameron*. And in two ways. First, its genius bore encouraging witness to the ability of contemporaries to parallel the creative power of the ancients. Second, it handed on into the Renaissance the lively acceptance of life that was the side of medieval society largely lost to us through the evaporation of story-telling and gossip and the destruction – by time or replacement with later fashion – of the visual evidence for it. Machiavelli, for instance, serious student of the Roman past as he was, could not have achieved the comic vivacity of his two plays, *Mandragola* and *Clizia*, or of his *novella*, *Belfagor*, had Boccaccio not elevated anecdote to the status of literature. Indeed, the whole range of early 16th-century comedy, rightly called 'erudite' because of the homage it paid to the dramatic work of Plautus and Terence, could have been lifeless imitation were it not that Boccaccio's spirit infused the classical form.

For the values of humanism, as they began to leak into Italian, especially Florentine, life in the late 14th century, were, as we shall see, essentially earnest. The shift from pre-Renaissance to early Renaissance may be tentatively dated around 1375 when, in the year of Boccaccio's death, Coluccio Salutati was appointed chancellor of Florence. This began a long tradition whereby successive heads of the Florentine bureaucracy were classical scholars. Initially this reflected the belief that the persuasiveness and prestige of the diplomatic correspondence for which chancellors were responsible would be enhanced by a correct Latinity based on the study of Cicero and other ancient models: a belief given symbolic endorsement by the remark put at the time in the mouth of Florence's chief political adversary, Giangaleazzo Visconti of Milan, that a letter of Salutati was more powerful than a company of cavalry. And once brought out of the study into the political arena, other advantages of a knowledge of the ancient world became apparent. During republican Florence's wars against monarchist Milan from 1390–1402 both sides added dignity to their cause by citing the benefit to mankind brought by the periods of republican and imperial rule in ancient Rome. Antiquity became politically and, in governing circles not only in Florence and Milan but in Rome and Venice, socially relevant: the moral philosophy that was to be drawn on by Castiglione came to be relished as an endorsement of the better side of the instinctive behaviour of the wealthy and powerful.

By some process of osmosis a classicizing of the values of political and social life was gradually transmitted to the arts. Three men pioneered what can be called 'the Tuscan breakthrough' that ensured that henceforward painters, sculptors and architects would check what they did against not only the example of their contemporaries and immediate predecessors but also the standards set by their opposite numbers in antiquity. All three, the sculptor Donatello (1386–1466), the painter Masaccio (1401–c. 1428) and the architect Brunelleschi (1377–1446), were men of high intelligence, responsive to new ideas. All were Florentines, and in Florence the new ideas were humanist. In 1396 the government even established a Chair of Greek. Humanism, at the turn of the century, was 'in', and the arts could not be left out of the sense of contact with a more fully realized antiquity.

As in the first generation of the pre-Renaissance, sculpture gave the lead. Donatello, with an eye as alert to the most 'classical' elements in earlier work as had been Boccaccio's ear for what was most redolent of day-to-day experience in medieval story-telling, took the still tentative human individuality of Giovanni Pisano's figures and produced in his *St George* of c. 1415 a youthful Roman general, albeit a sensitively chivalrous one, and in his later bronze *David* the first free-standing nude figure since the close of the ancient world. It was the early work of Donatello that helped Masaccio extend Giotto's rendering of reality by imagining his New Testament characters as so proudly at home in their Augustan world that he was moved to define them with a more logically derived flow of light than had ever before given unity and a sense of real presence to painted groups of figures. And it was Brunelleschi's pioneering exploration of how to prepare for the design

of a building by giving accurate interior and external perspective views of it that helped Masaccio to achieve the haunting majesty of his *Trinity* fresco in S. Maria Novella, the supreme image of the Christian drama enacted on a classical stage.

These men were not humanists. Masaccio's career was too short to permit generalization, but it is clear that his chief concern was to bring the real Bible, not a version *al antica* of it, to life. Donatello's preoccupation with his own reactions to bodies, space and narrative led to a series of works that form in themselves a dense period of different modes of expression which record or anticipate almost all those of the longer cultural period he helped to condition. Brunelleschi studied Euclid and the monumental remains of ancient Rome, but his practice was just as much influenced by what survived of the Romanesque – like the Baptistery – among the predominantly Gothic architecture of his native city. And his most prominent work, the very emblem of Renaissance Florence, the cupola of the cathedral, was the work of a mathematician-engineer responding with supreme ease to the Gothic challenge of the octagonal hole that gaped in its roof.

Decade by decade, antiquity came to be accepted more and more habitually as a point of reference for thought and achievement; thus the banker Cosimo de' Medici (d. 1464) read Plato with his scholar-protegé Marsiglio Ficino at the end of his life, and sponsored building programmes in the spirit of Roman *magnificentia*. For a while, indeed, the prestige of Latin – buttressed by that of Greek, which more came to read but none to write – muffled the vigour of the vernacular. And when Italian came alive in a consciously literary form again, whether in the *Della Famiglia* of Alberti or later in the poetry of Lorenzo de' Medici and Poliziano, it was expressed in the voices of men accustomed to time-travelling between the ancient world and their own.

Italy was increasingly calling in the old world to redress the balance of the new – a conscious correction by antiquity, that is, of what had come to be felt as a too routine inclination towards the examples offered by the still vital Middle Ages. The balance was precarious. This is why the Quattrocento has retained an aura of freshness and experiment. Looked at individually, paintings by Filippo Lippi, Uccello, Piero della Francesca, Castagno, Verrocchio and Botticelli, sculptures by Jacopo della Quercia, Luca della Robbia, Pietro Lombardo and Desiderio da Settignano, buildings by Michelozzo and Guiliano da Sangallo, and so many other works, are self-sufficient masterpieces. But the sense of inspired variety only gives way to one of a shared aim at last consolidated when we confront works of the late 15th and early 16th centuries by such painters as Perugino, Fra Bartolommeo, Raphael, Giorgione, Andrea del Sarto, sculptors like Michelangelo (whose youthful sculpture of a sleeping cupid was successfully passed off as a classical statue), Riccio and Andrea Sansovino, and such architects as Bramante and the elder Antonio de Sangallo. Some of these men only hit this target – the relaxedly harmonious but ennobled view of man and his setting that has been called the style of the High Renaissance – in a single phase of their careers, faltering after reaching it (as did Perugino) or moving through it in pursuit of more entirely personal modes of self-expression as Michelangelo did as architect (the vestibule of the Laurentian Library, started in 1524), painter (the *Last Judgment*, begun in 1536) and sculptor (the late *Pietà* in the Florentine cathedral). By then he had passed through the time zone we associate with the *fin-de-sièclisme* of Castiglione and his contemporaries, the temperamental shift from a High to a 'late' Renaissance. And it was with this late phase that the difficulty of an inquiry into the meaning of 'renaissance' becomes most acute.

Castiglione's *Courtier* as a portrait of Renaissance culture

Before looking in more detail at the strands that composed Renaissance culture, the political circumstances within which that culture grew and the economic base – money garnered from trade, banking, industry and taxes – which supported its growth, let us enter the period at a point when its culture was mature, mature almost to the point of finding itself played out.

Castiglione's *The Courtier*, written by a Mantuan who died as a papal nuncio in Spain, was published in 1528 in Venice and claimed to describe conversations that took place over four successive evenings in the spring of 1507 at the court of Urbino. The cast of characters came from Florence, Genoa, Verona and Rome, as well as Mantua and Venice, and from smaller towns in Liguria, Lombardy, Tuscany, Emilia and the Kingdom of Naples. The book is up to date; its dialogue form pays homage to Plato and Cicero. It also respects tradition: its setting is the *au dessus de la mêlée* framework within which the tales of Boccaccio's *Decameron* were told. The subject of discussion, presented as a 'game' whereby to divert the leisurely evenings of the court and its guests, is the formation of a courtier so widely cultivated and so charming in manner that he will captivate and thus be in a position to influence his prince to be a better ruler. The discussion of the qualities desired in him and the talents he must master provides an opportunity to bring together topics that represent a wide range of Renaissance preoccupations. Cosmopolitan in its cast of characters, eclectic in its choice of literary models and encyclopaedic in its range of interests, *The Courtier* permits us, as does no other single source, to eavesdrop on a culture (albeit a very exclusive segment of it) reviewing its opinion of itself. And because Castiglione intended his book to be a commemorative group 'portrait' (his word) of his friends, its intention was to ring true; every subject discussed is known from other sources to have been a perfectly likely topic of conversation on those evenings. At the very threshold

The Renaissance gentleman: in all his activities, from hawking to literature, he should, argued Castiglione in 'The Courtier', exemplify 'sprezzatura' – that air of nonchalant superiority that has distinguished the gentleman in Europe ever since.

of the book, in its preface, we are introduced to the humanist ideas-bank from which so much of Renaissance culture drew its intellectual working capital. The theme is to be 'the perfect courtier'. But no one can be perfect. Indeed, the very notion of perfection is hidden from the blunted feelers of our senses. But we know that it exists. Aristotle posited that everything has as its purpose the achievement of its own sort of perfection. Plato had suggested that 'out there' exist pre-ordained modules of perfection, and that men should so refine themselves as to understand and aim towards them. The reader was meant to catch these currently prevalent resonances. We remember that Raphael, Castiglione's friend and portraitist, had written that 'I make use of a certain idea that is in my mind'; that Michelangelo (whom Castiglione cited as one of the great artists of his day) was to write of a perfect form hidden in a block of marble that waited to be freed by his chisel; that in 1513 Machiavelli in *The Prince* had poured scorn on this too-prevalent idealization, enjoining us to deal with not what ought to be but what is, with 'the actual condition of things'.

The preface ends with the author's modest assertion that he is happy to submit his book to the truest of all judges, time. Apparently jejeune, the remark had a specifically Renaissance significance. The revaluation of classical works misunderstood or neglected during the Middle Ages gave authors an acuter sense of the reputation of their own works in the future. Indeed, while the Renaissance did not invent the psychological need both to seek comfort in ancestry and to leave behind a reminder of one's own career to others – whether in the form of written advice to heirs, a tomb or a pious benefaction – the rediscovery of the ancient past gave it a sharper emphasis. That past would not exist had it not left behind the materials which could recall it to memory: inscriptions, buildings, works of art and, above all, books. As from such evidence others consolidated the vision of Petrarch and presented ancient civilization in the now recoverable completeness of its beginnings, glory and downfall, the desire to leave comparable evidence grew stronger. Alongside the wish to be called after death to God was the desire to be recalled by Man. Diaries, memoirs, biographies, histories and chronicles, portraits in paint or stone multiplied. Those unable to commemorate themselves paid others to do so. More and more artists signed their works, and not just to distinguish the cash value of their own labour from that of their assistants. Coats of arms and inscriptions on buildings and tombs called out to an audience wider than that of family or locality. Nourished by men who found employment in giving them currency, the concepts of earthly 'fame' and 'glory' became commonplaces. A different apprehension of the future emerged, fostered by an enhanced awareness of the past.

Castiglione's confident appeal to the future as judge of his book corresponded to his anxiety to preserve the memory of what to him had been the most talented of all possible societies meeting in the most delightful of places and at the best of all possible times: an optimistic young manhood (he was twenty-nine in 1507) before his life had been clouded by the death of wife and friends and the spectacle of most of Italy firmly subjected to foreign rule.

He was looking back over a period of only twenty years: he sent his manuscript to the printer in 1527. But they were decades of sobering import to sensitive Italians. From the mid-14th century, humanist studies had encouraged them to emphasize their superiority to other peoples in the light of the progressive revelation of their illustrious ancestry. They got on jealously with one another but on another level of consciousness were aware that they were the clever, cultivated Europeans; the rest were barbarians. But the barbarians had overwhelmed ancient Rome. An invasion by the

French in 1494, which led to the conquest of the Kingdom of Naples, caused a temporary shock, but the French withdrew in the following year. Worse came with the French conquest of Milan and Genoa in 1499 and the Spanish occupation of Naples in 1504. Even these events could be borne with some equanimity (especially by those not directly concerned), but with an invasion by yet a third barbarian power, Germany, in 1508, and a fourth, the Swiss, in 1512, Italy increasingly became the place which, because of its central position, its wealth and its weakening rivalries, was chosen as the arena in which foreigners, with scarcely a by-your-leave, could fight out their own grander rivalries. While Castiglione was revising his manuscript in 1527, Rome itself became a casualty of these conflicts. Its sack by a Habsburg army was not only appalling in terms of human suffering and the set-back it gave to the then most vigorous cultural environment in Italy, but also deeply humiliating as being not even the result of a political plan but of an unpaid army's desire to recoup its arrears from an obviously vulnerable prey. The rape of Rome, doubly a capital city, with the imperial past in its cellars and Christianity's promise in its skies, might have tickled the *Schadenfreude* of rabid anti-clericals and political opponents of the papacy, but it confirmed Italy's subordination. The barbarian had returned and triumphed. Culture, it was clear, was not enough.

We must not portray the process that led up to and past the Sack of Rome too darkly. Life went on. Venice preserved its independence. Florence was to pull itself clear from the shadow of Habsburg domination. Rome recovered. Exchanging native for Spanish masters made little material difference to the inhabitants of Milanese Lombardy or the Kingdom of Naples. Men of genius, such as Michelangelo, Titian, Palladio, Tasso or Galileo, still had their chance to amaze and influence the rest of Europe. Through books, engravings, personal contacts and emigré artists, the Italianization of other peoples' cultures became more pervasive than ever after the manuscript of *The Courtier* was sent off to the press. But the wound to the peninsula's political self-esteem was registered in the book through references, made as lightly as possible so as not to disturb the agreeableness of the discussions' mood, to Italy's miserable condition: 'There is not a nation that has not made us its prey.' And why? Investing too heavily in learning, luxury and pleasure our moral fibre has slackened, leaving us helpless when faced by true courage and determination.

In spite of the author's protest that he is not one of those who think the present inevitably inferior to the past, there is a strong whiff of *fin de siècle* about his book. Other writers, too, expressed the sense of a great age closing. In his *Art of War* of 1522 Machiavelli accused Italy's rulers of putting self-cultivation above public duty, as though the barbarian could be charmed into keeping their distance simply by receiving an elegant letter. His friend Francesco Guicciardini had as early as 1509, in his *Florentine History*, looked back nostalgically to 'those happy times before 1494'. The events that followed 1509 deepened his conviction that with 1494 a period had closed. Starting in 1536 his great *History of Italy*, he wrote: 'It is indisputable that since the Roman Empire, weakened largely by the decay of her ancient customs [he is pointing up the relevance of that age to his], began to decline more than a thousand years ago from that greatness to which it had risen with such marvellous virtue and good fortune, Italy had never known such prosperity or such a desirable condition as that which it enjoyed in all tranquillity in the year of Our Lord 1490 and the years immediately before and after.' But then began 'the calamities of Italy' which were to be his theme.

In the 14th century the recognition that a new phase of cultural achievement was opening had been sustained by an alliance between the scholarship that revealed ancient achievements, the genius of writers and artists who showed that those achievements could be matched, and a buoyant patriotism which, though manifested in terms of individual cities, had led to the conviction that the Italians as a whole were the civilized leaders of Europe. This triple source of cultural confidence had weathered not only major blows of circumstance like the Black Death of 1348, the loss of the papacy to Avignon from 1309 to 1377, and the conquest of Naples by Aragon in 1422, but minor inter-state wars and changes of government that make the history of Italy during the Renaissance most handily dealt with in a dozen parallel columns. It was only the events that followed 1494 that split the triple alliance, leaving the arts and literature as adventurous as ever, prompting a more cautious, counting-the-gains rather than innovatory mood in scholarship, and destroying political confidence.

The Courtier is the perfect reflection of this shift, commemorating a band of spirited, confidently talented men and women by making them sum up, as they harangue and argue with one another, the long, increasingly 'Renaissance' saga of their intellectual inheritance. Intended as an elegy on a past generation it reads as a commemoration of a cultural era approaching its close. Topic by topic *The Courtier* demonstrates that humanist concern for rethinking the present with reference to the ancient past without which the peninsula's culture would still, no doubt, have had vitality (because there was the money to pay for art and ideas) but would have been too diffuse or too unspecifically Italian to be readily definable.

Let us only for a moment imagine what the great fund of creative talent in Italy would have achieved without humanism. Would there have been a develop-ment of purely local styles? Looking across the vast lawn on which the 13th-century Pisan baptistery, cathedral and leaning tower are spaced as in the closing stages of some wonderfully eccentric ecclesiastical board game, we can wonder: was there scope here, and in other cities, for the long-term development of local styles? And what of France? It was the natural trading partner of Italy. Its universities passed on ideas across the Alps. Its poets had deeply influenced Dante and his predecessors. A French dynasty, the Angevin, ruled in Naples. Popes, a potent source of patronage, were to live in Provence for most of that 14th century which saw the girding-up period of Renaissance culture. Without humanism, would Italy have become a dependency of Gothic France? Or take another commercial partner: the Netherlands. Here was the country with the most nearly comparable degree of urbanization, literacy and the marshalling of talent in the service of intelligent patronage. Without human-ism, would Italy have developed on the lines of that equally marvellous – if briefer, less various and far less influential – culture? Was it not humanism, generation by generation, releasing into the cultural bloodstream of Italy knowledge and challenge derived from the vast reservoir of the classical past, that kept the Renaissance vital for so long, so multifarious in its manifestations, so appealing that when others chose to look to it they could adapt freely what was, after all, an interpretation of a shared European inheritance?

Be that as it may, *The Courtier* reflects values which could not have taken on the literary form Castiglione gives them without their having become pliable through long usage. He feels justified in writing about the 'perfect' courtier because Plato had written of the perfect republic, Xenophon (in his *Cyropaedia*) of the perfect ruler, Cicero in the *De Oratore* of the man qualified by knowledge, character and style to be the perfect orator. In the Middle Ages the only perfect type was the saint, or the devout ruler who was as good as one. Humanism produced a whole range of 'perfect' models: Virgil as a poet, Cicero as a prose writer, the *pater familias* described in the 1430s in Leon Battista Alberti's *Della Famiglia*, or the ideal (and by no means saintly) cardinal of Paolo Cortese's *De Cardinalatu* of *c.* 1510.

Humanism reinstated the notion that 'the best' was a concept applicable to the here-and-now. It was the courtier's role to 'bend all his thoughts and strength of purpose to loving, almost adoring his prince'. This involved acquiring intellectual and social skills for an active life of primarily political purpose: helping the prince to be a better ruler. A notable feature of early humanism was the support it gave to the idea that the conscientious pursuit of an active social and civic life was as respectable as a life devoted to Christian contemplation. For Petrarch the two had seemed irreconcilable. He was preoccupied with the tension between his desire for physical love and secular fame and his belief that the Christian's duty was to forsake earthly things and bend all his thoughts to God. He had begun by revering Cicero as a philosopher sage who happened to write like an angel. When in 1345 he discovered Cicero's letters to Atticus, which showed that the sage had also been deeply involved in the political life of the 1st century BC, Petrarch's sense of personal rapport with the world of antiquity – the essential breakthrough in the new attitude to the past – led him to write a letter of bitter reproach to the shade of Cicero. It was, however, the continuing study of Cicero as a moral philosopher who took his duties as a social animal seriously, coupled with the employment of more and more humanist scholars in government bureaucracies, that by the mid-15th century had taken away most of the unease from a life of immersion in practical affairs.

The courtier's aim in life, then, needed no special pleading by Castiglione. Instead discussion concentrated on a purely secular variant of the active *versus* contemplative controversy. The courtier should prepare himself by physical training, riding and jousting for the most active part of his career: serving his prince in war. He should also prepare his mind by being able to read Latin and Greek authors and to write fluently and correctly in the vernacular. But which in itself was the nobler calling: arms or letters? This, too, was a well-established conundrum; and so was its answer. Would Caesar the warrior be remembered were it not for Caesar the writer? Sword and pen were mutually dependent. The issue was, in any case, summed up by a painting which hung in the very palace where the discussion took place. It showed the *condottiere* Duke Federigo of Urbino in 1476 studying a manuscript from his great library while wearing armour and with a sword at his belt. However, the question retained its charm partly because it was given to few to be a Caesar or a Federigo and partly because it touched on one of the true revolutions humanism introduced during the Renaissance: a liberal education devoted to the balanced ideal of *mens sana in corpore sano*.

In the great commercial cities, schools had long been teaching the skills necessary for employment and self-improvement. In the 1340s, for instance, when Petrarch was digesting his discovery of Cicero's 'active life' letters, 20 per cent of the male population of Florence (at a time when a low average life-expectation produced a notable imbalance between young and old) were at school. Of these some 2 per cent proceeded from reading and writing to arithmetic, book-keeping and the calculating machine of the period, the abacus; about 1 per cent switched to the Latin, logic, and rhetoric which would qualify them for the vocational courses, chiefly law and medicine, offered by universities.

It was in the smaller, less economically thrusting cities of the North where such education as was offered was in clerical hands and ungeared to practical life, that the idea of a liberal education, first developed *c.* 1402 by Pietro Paolo Vergerio, tutor to the lord of Padua's children, was institutionalized in the curricula of schools. The earliest and most notable was the one established for Vittorino da Feltre by the ruler of Mantua in 1423. Vittorino's concern was with preparing the sons of noble families for the duties that would

fall to them as soldiers, diplomats and court functionaries. The mind was to be formed by the poets, historians and moral philosophers of antiquity, the body developed through such sports as running, jumping and swimming. This was, in fact, the educational programme that was gradually to condition, with unimportant variants, the education of gentlemen all over Western Europe until well into the 19th century. As far as Italy was concerned, Castiglione, who had experienced it as a youth at Duke Lodovico Sforza's court in Milan, caught it at its flood and his book helped make of it an international intellectual currency. Already recognized in the peninsula, the need was soon to be felt elsewhere for men who could do more than fly a falcon, ride a horse and follow a hound. Castiglione's particular flair was to popularize, and thus make available for export, the gains established by humanist learning and to free them from any smell of the scholar's lamp. Nowhere else in his book was this so persuasively argued than in his well-born characters' discussion of the educational formation of the ideal courtier.

Devotion to antiquity as a source of practical wisdom and of a mastery of flexible and persuasive forms of expression – the active man as rhetorician-of-the-world – was not to be pursued at the expense of neglecting the vernacular. The aim was, after all, not to make gentlemen into scholars but to put scholarship at the service of contemporary experience. So in what language should the courtier express himself and establish his influence? It is a question that seems dusty enough today. Then it glinted with challenge. Humanism had complicated matters by revealing the purity and range of classical Latin. Should an author, before setting down his ideas, especially his more serious ideas, resolve, then, to use Latin? If so, the Latin of Cicero or something more eclectic? If he decided against Latin, what form of Italian should he use? The Tuscan of Petrarch and Boccaccio, who had become almost instant classics of the vernacular? The language of the writer's own province (and there were some dozen forms of vernacular spoken and written in Italy)? Or, as Dante had recommended – but in a treatise written in Latin so that it could be widely read! – should he use a vernacular that was a version chosen from current spoken usage among sophisticated people in especially cultivated cities? For Castiglione, reporting conversations among laymen, the choice had to be a form of vernacular. But his decision to chose the third alternative was less a tribute to Dante than to Cicero, who had already mocked those who imported words from a 'dead' language, Greek, to give a spurious dignity to their Latin, and who had urged the case for a written language kept flexibly, if discreetly, abreast of contemporary speech. Humanism thus in part hindered the development of regional vernaculars into a standard Italian by stressing Latin as an alternative and by encouraging a veneration for fossilized literary expression – whether couched in the language of Virgil and Cicero or of Petrarch and Boccaccio. But it also provided terms of reference within which the relationships between one or another form of written vernacular, and between the spoken and written language, could be argued. And because debate on this very 'questione della lingua' was going on in other countries at the moment when translations of *The Courtier* appeared in France, Spain and England, the welcome afforded the book was strengthened by Castiglione's moderate and unpartisan contribution.

As an argument against following an exclusive literary model, he turns the discussion towards painting: Mantegna, Leonardo, Raphael, Giorgione and Michelangelo all work in different styles, yet all are perfect masters of their art. It was perhaps Castiglione's friendship with Raphael that made him put among the necessary accomplishments of a courtier an understanding of the painter's craft and the ability to draw. He has to justify the first because painting 'may seem today to be a mechanical skill and scarcely suited to men of birth', and the second by pointing out that drawing can have a practical value as for instance through a sketch of a fortress or of the terrain a captain will have to fight over. Indeed, throughout this section there is a sense of special pleading not found elsewhere in the conversations. It is true that the discussion assumes some familiarity with the work of Pliny the Elder, whose 1st century AD *Naturalis Historia* contained an account of the development of the arts in antiquity which showed the respect in which they had been held by the Greeks and Romans. This was a work, endlessly cited, that helped artists to feel less socially trapped by their craft status as guildsmen, just as it encouraged patrons to sympathize with their aims, whether realistic or idealizing (both warmly praised by Pliny). The importance of this source was all the greater because with Pompeii and Herculaneum unexcavated, almost no ancient painting could be seen, and Pliny's descriptions not only challenged but justified a serious concern with producing and fostering painting and sculpture. All the same, Castiglione's hesitant tone is a useful warning against transporting backwards our own inclination to assume that the culture of the Renaissance is above all to be assessed in terms of its art.

This becomes clearer when the discussion moves to music. The courtier must be able to read it, sing, and play an instrument. And this is taken for granted. Even more revealing is the greater range of warmth and critical empathy shown in the description of musical rather than of artistic styles. As far as emotional reaction is concerned, Renaissance culture, with its civic bands, court orchestras, cathedral choirs and *Hausmusik* (aided from 1501 by the introduction of printed scores) was essentially a musical one. And nowhere else is Renaissance humanism's grip on the imagination shown more strikingly than in Castiglione's references to the place of music in the

The conclusion of Cicero's 'De Oratore', written out in 1428 by Poggio Bracciolini, an early Florentine humanist and a papal secretary. He was the first to write a humanist script based on the Carolingian hand of classical manuscripts, for which he spent much time searching.

culture of ancient Greece. From Pliny's descriptions ancient painting could at least be fairly clearly imagined. But of music not only the sounds but even the notation had vanished. Yet Castiglione was able to draw on a lively debate about the nature of Greek music. From Plato onwards, classical authors had paid tribute to music's power, for better or worse, to stir the emotions. But how had these effects been achieved, by what instruments and in what compositional modes? This inquiry was sufficiently widely shared to affect the nature of contemporary music. It was suspected that the lyric poetry of the ancients had been composed with musical accompaniment in mind; this encouraged the development from the 1480s of the solo song, or *frottola*, and it also encouraged, more generally, the notion that musical expressiveness should closely support the emotions expressed in the words of all forms of vocal music. It was not until the next generation that experimental instruments were built to reproduce what *may* have been the sounds that fell upon the ears of the ancients, but in Castiglione's lifetime 'humanist music' joined those other arts which reflected the practice and values of antiquity.

The Courtier goes on to discuss other talents which should be cultivated: dancing, conversation agreeably adjusted to the company taking part, skill in games (especially chess) and the telling of a carefully categorized range of jokes, anecdotes and puns. Even at this apparent nadir of triviality, we do not part company with the influence of humanism. For Cicero, in what was perhaps the most constantly cited work throughout the Renaissance, the *De Officiis (On Public Duties)*, had stressed the importance in social life of leisure, and the legitimacy of just such diversions if conducted with discretion.

Humanism gains ground

Humanism would never have engaged the interest of a circle wider than that of scholars, antiquarians and writers and (perhaps) artists of scholarly bent had it not resurrected texts bearing on the actual conduct of life. It was the recapture through moral philosophy of the ancient spirit in its guise of councillor to men who seriously wanted to live honourably, productively and profitably that turned classical studies into a shared cast of thought, a 'movement': humanism. Four texts predominated in this linkage of scholarship to life: the *Ethics* of Aristotle (never neglected, but re-read with a new sense of its relevance); the *De Officiis* and the *De Oratore* of Cicero and the *Institutio Oratoria (The Formation of an Orator)* by the 1st-century author Quintilian – a text first rediscovered in its entirety in 1416. Add the *Lives* of Plutarch (d. AD 120) and the moral-philosophical tracts of Seneca (d. AD 65) and we get a cluster of texts which, through precept and example, presented a reasoned code of behaviour suited to the times which, in its emphasis on self-control, moderation and service to others was not seen as conflicting with the standards expected of laymen by the Church.

This humanist core of exemplary texts only featured as a whole in the libraries of collectors of manuscripts. Two of them, Cicero's and Quintilian's works on oratory (conceived as a programme of wide-ranging self-education and deportment as well as of influential modes of discourse), were formidably long. But their message was widely disseminated among the social élite of urban Italy by tutors and schoolmasters and through such Florentine republican works of *haute vulgarisation* as Matteo Palmieri's *Della Vita Civile* and Alberti's *Della Famiglia*, both produced in the 1430s. The spreading dye that gave a classicizing tint to Renaissance culture flowed from patrons (including ecclesiastics) secure in a stance of neo-Graeco-Roman personal rectitude.

The Courtier, then, represents a genial up-dating of Ideal Ciceronian Man, now imagined in a courtly setting. But there is a more original aspect of its role in popularizing the culture that its author inherited. Palmieri and Alberti had written too soon to reflect the interest, growing from their own day, in ancient

metaphysical, as opposed to moral, philosophy. This speculative strain, more interested in defining the meaning of existence than in dealing with its consequences, became an activating part of Renaissance culture only with the publication in 1484 by Marsiglio Ficino of Latin translations of the whole range of Plato's works. And because Ficino, in his editorial matter, drew on an intermediary stratum of comment, that of the 3rd-century AD scholars (notably Plotinus) who added their own mystical vision to the intellectual rigours of Socratic discourse, the 'neo-Platonism' of the later Renaissance was the forerunner of Romanticism. What is the 'essence' of an individual? What is the relationship between man and nature? What is the meaning of love in all its stages from lust to the selfless service of what, ultimately, the beloved stands for? Such speculations were no more than luxurious emanations from the securely established pragmatic Aristotelian-Ciceronian core. But they released a vein of fantasy reflected in the work of medallists like Sperandio, the paintings of Botticelli, poetry from Lorenzo de' Medici to Michelangelo, prose from the *Asolani* (1505) of Pietro Bembo to the closing section of *The Courtier*.

It was into the mouth of Bembo (who became a highly reputed cardinal) that Castiglione put his own homage to such neo-Platonism as he had absorbed. Men, as Aristotelian social animals, are born to love as well as to live. But what place has love in the life of a courtier when he has grown beyond the age when it is suitable to indite sonnets to a mistress's eyebrow? Plato takes over in Bembo's soaring tribute to a love that ascends the *scala d'amore*, rung by rung, from physical attraction to a comprehension of love's creator: God manifesting Himself through beauty as the source of all truth. Guided by love, Bembo concludes, the soul, in a purifying ecstasy of contemplation, can pass wholly into the hands of God.

'Bembo having spoken up to this point', wrote Castiglione, 'with such vehemence that he seemed raptly forgetful of himself, remained motionless and silent, gazing upwards as though in a trance – when the Lady Emilia (companion to the duchess of Urbino) who, together with the others, had listened to his speech with the closest attention, took the hem of his gown and gently tugging it, said: 'Take care Pietro lest these thoughts separate your own soul from your body.'

This lovingly mocking deflation of a mood that has become too intense is entirely characteristic of the way in which Castiglione conducts the discussions in *The Courtier*. No one is allowed to go on too long or too seriously before some humorous intervention changes the subject or lightens the tone. For the courtier must never be boring. All he does, all the talents of body and mind he has acquired, must reflect what Castiglione calls *sprezzatura*, a graceful ease of demeanour, a nonchalance in the display of a skill which conceals the labour or pain with which it has been acquired. This is the behavioural ingredient that distinguishes the accomplished amateur from the dogged professional: the air of effortless superiority that came to denote the gentleman within European society for centuries.

The Courtier documents a class acutely aware of its separateness and its superiority. As such it influenced the hundreds of etiquette books that catered for the hobbledehoy rustic nobles and aspiring bourgeois who hoped to commend themselves through their behaviour to princes. Even here, though, contact is not lost with ancient moral philosophy. Slave-based societies had taken social distinctions for granted. The cultivation of certain virtues, like magnanimity and justice, required the possession of power for their display; others, like generosity, required the possession of wealth. Aristotle and Cicero might have blenched at the courtier's narcissistic concern with creating an impression favourable to the advancement of his career within his own circle, but would have approved the assumption that such a circle represented what was potentially best in society.

When Castiglione wrote, the age of lively social mobility in Italy was long past. It had been above all in the 13th and early 14th centuries when booming trade and, before the Black Death of 1348, a growing population made rags-to-riches-in-two-generations careers not uncommon among urban immigrants: those 'new men' whom the aristocratic Dante Alighieri so fastidiously despised. Since then the merchant oligarchies whose members played the dominant part in the running of republican governments, and the noble functionaries who formed the ruling groups within the princely states, had steadied into fairly stable groups, not readily penetrated by outsiders.

Though by no means fossilized, these groups had acquired a stability which did not welcome displays of the blatant 'individualism' that later historians wished to see as a hall-mark of Renaissance society. Rational, tradition-conscious, Italy's ruling circles preferred the norm to the exception, the well-groomed and self-disciplined man to the eccentric, however gifted. Through works on moral philosophy and conduct, humanism had offered, as medieval culture had not, a workable model for the conduct of everyday life, a model calculated to make men increasingly confident in this world without panicking over their status in the next. It caught the religious overtones of antiquity, which were explanatory and supportive rather than hortatory, squared them – again on classical lines – with an ethic derived from antiquity's practical observation of the self-discipline required for orderly, satisfying life in families, cities and states, and represented them as in accord with the promises and demands of Christianity. Attentive to the latent contradictions within the model, its spokesmen pitched its moral and behavioural demands high, as, indeed, had the pre-Christian sources whence its adaptations were derived.

Such a model, however, derived its confidence from men who, whether Greeks or Romans, wrote from the viewpoint of unchallenged political and cultural leadership within their worlds. Master race spoke to master race: the race of Aristotle to that of Cicero, that of Cicero to that of Petrarch. But when Italy was politically mastered in its turn by the 'barbarians' after 1494, a continuing sense of cultural superiority could not on its own keep the model in focus. And the focus was jarred again by the pangs of Christian conscience which first saw Catholicism as having lost its moral leadership, and then re-envisioned its standards in the light of the imperatives of a crusade to counter the inroads of the next wave of *barbari*, the Protestant sects of Northern Europe.

There was nothing dramatic about either the beginning or the close of this process: the borrowing of pagan to supplement Christian standards of behaviour from the mid-14th century or the restoration of precedence to those of Christianity in the mid-16th. Castiglione wrote at a time of political humiliation, not yet a time of counter-reform. It is the way in which he decorates his themes of balanced, responsible, learned public service with grace notes of finicking super-refinement that gives his work its tone of *fin-de-sièclisme*. The toga'd ancients hold the structure aloft while his characters discuss the rival merits of French and Spanish fashions and suggest that Leonardo da Vinci, by changing from graceful painter to dogged searcher-after-truth, has ceased to be acceptable in the deft new world of *politesse*.

With its inner contradictions *The Courtier* reflects wider changes. The humanist total vision of idealized social man was faltering. While steady in his reverence for, indeed his preference for, the way the ancients of republican Rome had handled their problem, Machiavelli in *The Prince* (1513) was scornful of the bland pieties that humanism had offered as Rome's contribution to the art of dignified living. The belief expressed by Raphael's frescoes in the Stanza della Segnatura in the Vatican (1509–11) in a perfect congruity between the aims and temperaments of the pagan philosophers shown in his *School of Athens* and those of the Christian theologians shown on the opposite wall commenting on the significance of the sacraments was never again to be recorded with such easy confidence. Indeed, Raphael himself in his unfinished last work, the nervy *Transfiguration*, moved away from the spacious style precociously announced in Masaccio's *Tribute Money* of c. 1425 and rephrased, after much challenge and experiment in the meantime, in the Stanze. And here he was in line with younger contemporaries like Beccafumi, Pontormo, Rosso Fiorentino and Parmigianino who were reacting against a tradition which threatened to put the achievement of classically derived norms above the expression of an individual manner. In literature, Ariosto's *Orlando Furioso* (1532: the first version, published in 1516, was being revised while Castiglione was reworking *The Courtier*) used his knowledge of ancient poetry – Virgil, Horace, Ovid – to an ironic, charmingly ebullient effect quite different from the more reverent use to which his most like-minded predecessor, Poliziano, had put them in his *Stanze per la Giostra* of 1475–8. In architecture, Giulio Romano's Palazzo del Tè, begun in 1527 for the ruler of Castiglione's native city, the Marquis Federigo II Gonzaga, played proportional and dimensional games with the rules of classical architecture which would have seemed irresponsible to the Francesco di Giorgio of S. Maria di Calcinaio (begun 1484) or the Antonio da Sangallo of S. Biagio, begun in 1518. By the time Castiglione had sent his book to the press, Renaissance culture had shifted beyond the values taken for granted in his cherished spring of 1507 and for a while thereafter.

Perhaps no work of art represents so close a harmony between the ideals of painter and subject as Raphael's portrait (1514) of Castiglione himself. Equally agile in mind and hand, Raphael caught the calm but unsolemn mastery of self that Castiglione was in the process of describing, while Castiglione prompted in Raphael that concordance between liveliness of outline and confident marshalling of form that was the hallmark – shared by both of them – of ancient ideals relaxing in the assurance that they had been at last naturalized within the changed circumstances of their original home. Their aesthetic – Castiglione's of behaviour, Raphael's of art – was identical: that of the 'perfect' courtier in total accord with that of the 'perfect' painter.

Such a match between what was considered best in life and art was rare. The two men were, however, friends and, in the survey of the surviving monuments of ancient Rome that Pope Leo X called for in 1519, collaborators. Moreover, the portrait, together with the fact that Castiglione's subsequent turn (registered in the last draft of *The Courtier*) to a pessimism alleviated by mystical neo-Platonism matched Raphael's move towards Mannerism, does suggest that life and art, although in the normal course seldom seen to observe one another's rhythms, did for a moment fall into step.

The periods reviewed

I have suggested that as a long phase within Italian culture the Renaissance proceeded through three stages. The first was the pre-Renaissance stage, *c.* 1300–*c.* 1375, when sporadic interest in classical antiquity and a concentration on the most 'human' elements in medieval culture produced modes of thought and art which were recognizably different from what had gone before. The second was that of the early Renaissance, *c.* 1375–*c.* 1480, a time of avid but unequally shared resolve imaginatively to resurrect the ideals and to imitate or surpass the achievement of antiquity. The third, *c.* 1480–*c.* 1520, was that of actual and widely shared mastery of this resolve, a stage for

which the word 're-birth' has at last a real validity; it is not ridiculous to suppose that had the hero thinkers, writers and artists of antiquity been reincarnated, their nature – qualified by their nurture in the kaleidoscopic and tradition-conscious political and social world of the early 16th century – might have produced something like the culture of the High Renaissance, or at least a significant part of it. And after 1520?

With re-birth, surely, there comes a new life; so while the term 'late Renaissance' has a certain retrospective usefulness and does convey the sense of a classicism still aesthetically vital but morally less concerned, of the lingering relinquishment of hard-won ideals, in fact of an often beautiful aftermath, it is quite inappropriate as a label for the extraordinary outburst of re-directed talent in the second generation of the 16th century.

Of course scholars continued to edit classical texts, patrons to commission mythological subjects from artists, statesmen to dignify their pronouncements by drawing on the enormous fund of respect for antiquity that had accumulated during the Renaissance centuries. But political disillusion and an increasingly conscience-searching Catholicism came at a time when men of creative genius were (like their post-medieval ancestors) picking and choosing among the aspects of their inheritance that they found most stimulating rather than endorsing it as a whole. This conjunction produced a mood and a manner – indeed, a Mannerism – that looked for new solutions to the expression of changed feelings.

When we look at the successors of Raphael and Castiglione – at paintings by Lotto, Bronzino, Giulio Romano or Correggio, at buildings by Michele Sanmicheli or Jacopo Sansovino, or when we read the letters of Pietro Aretino or the *History of Italy* by Guicciardini – we can no longer feel that we are in the Renaissance. The gains of the past are recognized, but as things to play with, contradict or, especially in music and architecture, take advantage of with an easy mastery that forgets a long apprenticeship.

Conclusion: a five stage 'model'

Any significant aspect of historical change can be explained in terms of a rough-and ready five stage 'model'. What were the preconditioning factors without which change would have had no base to rise from? What were the new, general factors which precipitated the likelihood of change? The 'trigger' that actually produced it? The sustenants that kept it in motion? The brakes that eventually slowed it to a point where it was subsumed into the preconditions for another change?

Given the wide differences that we have sketched between the urban milieux in which Renaissance culture developed, the vagaries of individual genius (increasingly recognized as such and given its head) and the diverse needs and expectations of patrons, no explanation in terms of this model can be, or should try to be, complete or foolproof. But let us see what pattern it suggests.

The preconditions are straightforward: the urbanized prosperity of 12th- and 13th-century Italy, the predisposition to spend profits on cultural artefacts – buildings, sculptures (almost always associated with churches as tombs or façade decorations) and paintings (also largely associated with public places of worship); the love of learning (largely 'scholastic' in tone), of recording (chronicles), and of poeticizing feelings about martial valour, sex and (at the bottom of the heap) nature.

Three precipitant factors can be isolated, but all worked upon one another: first, a more calculated estimate of the ties between self and others; second, humanism; and third, a preference for illusion over allusion, for the specific over the general.

During the pre-Renaissance of the 14th century, a number of earlier conditioners of personal feeling were strengthened. Business partnerships and dependence on agents broadened the need – hitherto mainly required in military and family relationships – to gauge the abilities and trustworthiness of others, a process necessarily involving a degree of selfconsciousness. In political life, too, automatic loyalties or resentments gave way to a more pondered, calculating stance. Consciousness of self and of others was enhanced by, for instance, the choices involved in the slide from communal to signorial rule; it was essential to the gradual development of the clientage system, wherein men had to become aware of their own personalities in order to play them effectively against potential allies. Wider literacy, encouraged by the increased number of men entering careers in business, bureaucracy or law, increased the opportunities to review feelings and relationships more clearly by having to express them on paper. And these changes took place at a time when the vivid religiosity of the mendicant orders, Dominican as well as Franciscan, was urging a more personal reaction to clearly realized biblical characters than had been within the emotional compass of the exhortations to repent and pay up of the average parish priest.

It was upon this first precipitant factor that the second, humanism, played; its call to link society with society, present with ancient past, re-echoing across its vaster arena the thinner, local cries of man to man. To relate oneself to the past, through gossip, chronicle, genealogy and the recounting of tales, had long been a characteristic human impulse. Now, as later in the Reformation, when calls to a New Testament or early papal past jarringly produced a novel religious fervour, this impulse was quickened. And – to emphasize humanism's importance by another analogy – it not only related present to past but promised to explain, through this confrontation, both the present to itself and its possibility of self-improvement – just as for later generations Freud and Marx were to promise an explanation of current behaviour and a programme for

Formulario di lettere & di orationi uolgari con la
proposta & risposta cōposto p Christofano landini

A humanist lecturer: Cristoforo Landino taught poetry and rhetoric in Florence between 1458 and 1492. He wrote imaginary dialogues in which Lorenzo de' Medici discusses with Ficino and Alberti such quintessentially humanist topics as the good life, activity versus contemplation and the allegorical meanings of Virgil.

that of the future by reference to the individual's and society's previous experience.

Blending with both was the third factor, the inclination towards an art and a literature that proffered an illusionistic, or quasi-realistic, view of man and nature rather than one that alluded to them through symbols or other forms of coded hints. We are well-placed to understand this shift. We too live in an age which is coming to prefer an art that mediates only gently, representationally, between ourselves and reality, to the allusive or more-or-less abstract art that has dominated informed taste and artists of genius over the last seventy years. The desire to bring art nearer to life reflects, perhaps, a lack of confidence, a desire to make every aspect of human endeavour cosily cohere. A more demanding perception of human relationships and a clearer apprehension in a Christian society of the glories of a pre-Christian civilization were sources of perturbation as well as challenge and delight. As with humanism, in this respect, too, irradiation from the prophetic, uniquely gifted source – Petrarch for humanism, Giotto for art – was slow, fettered by epigoni and by patrons who had not quite seen the point as well as by natural disasters, war and plague, which then as now sent novelty scuttling to the shelter of tradition.

And the trigger that released the explosive potential within these three long-term precipitants of change? We have reviewed it under a different label: the Tuscan break-through. It was thanks to the overlapping careers of two men who identified humanism with the successful conduct of high political office (both headed the Florentine civil service), Coluccio Salutati and Leonardo Bruni, and to the stylistic and expressive advances in painting, sculpture and architecture made by Masaccio, Donatello and Brunelleschi that the hesitancies of the pre-Renaissance were consolidated into the assured and sympathetically supported experimentalism of the major talents of the 15th-century early Renaissance.

The sustenants that maintained the change and carried its influence throughout the peninsula were, chiefly, the precipitants in a more established form. The consciousness of self in relation to others was extended by warmer feelings within families and between friends, a clearer apprehension of the connection between individuals, power groups and governments – all, under the influence of ancient authors, expressed through letters and in books. The consciousness that, with all its uncertainties and necessary routines, life afforded more opportunities for savoured pleasures was fostered by the building of more domestically comfortable palaces, the designing of gardens and the building of villa-like farms in the countryside. If what the Venetian ambassador reported Leo X in 1513 as saying – 'Since God has given us the papacy let us enjoy it!' – is not literally true, at least it expresses the accumulation of here-and-now interests that give many (but by no means all) aspects of the Renaissance a secular, worldly cast.

Of humanism's influence on men's interests and the way they expressed them, and of artists' determination to master the means of reproducing faithfully what they saw, even if they then chose not to subordinate art primarily to that aim, enough has been said earlier in this essay. But the point can be made that though during the early and the High Renaissance there were wars and outbreaks of plague and other epidemic diseases, there was no psychological blow, such as the Black Death administered to the culture of the 14th century. Thanks to the use of mercenaries and the difficulty of storming or starving large cities, urban cultural life was hardly disturbed. Wars were expensive, but culture was – except for buildings and bronze equestrian statues, more of which were planned than completed – cheap, taxation did not halt the flow of patronage and production, nor the increasing sense of intellectual rapport between those who made and those who paid for works of art that culminated in the 'learned' mythologies of Botticelli and Raphael's and Michelangelo's frescoes in the Vatican.

What, finally, were the 'brakes' that checked the momentum that carried the Renaissance from its early to its 'full' phase and enabled its culture to turn thenceforward on to a fresh route?

We have noted some: wars that came to be seen in terms of national humiliation and of foreign occupations that were apparently permanent; a realization that humanism did not, after all, provide the solution its protagonists had apparently proffered for the conduct of everyday life and that it had failed to resolve the contradictions between classical and Christian cultures into an arm-in-arm dialogue between ancients and Christians during the walk towards eternity; the sense of 'enough' that made artists, writers and thinkers turn to an eclecticism vulnerable to the attraction of newer and more energetic goals.

Those goals were to be set by the emergence of princely courts at once more remote from and more invasive of the imagination, a less genially permissive religiosity, a response to individuality that saw it less in terms of actions than of a private state of mind – and a need for forms of escapism more erotic, violent or arcane than had been desired hitherto. Culture veered from the highroad of Renaissance, and another phase of its ever-fascinating relationship with life began.

The anchor and dolphin impresa of Aldo Manuzio (1450–1515), whose press at Venice printed some of the finest editions of the classics published during the Renaissance.

·IV·

DISASTER AND RECOVERY

1527-1750

THE SACK OF ROME was the climax of three decades of violent struggles for the control of Italy in which, increasingly, the chief protagonists were non-Italian powers. In 1494 Charles VIII of France had crossed the Alps in order to revive a moribund claim to the throne of Naples. A second French invasion in 1499 provoked the intervention of Spain, which in turn provoked invasions by the Swiss, the Spanish and even the Turks. In 1527, at the conclusion of one of these campaigns, the undisciplined armies of the Emperor Charles V laid siege to Rome. The commander-in-chief, Charles, Duke of Bourbon, was killed just as the walls were stormed; and, completely out of control, the unpaid mercenaries – Italian, German and Spanish soldiers of fortune with no ideological commitment to any political or religious cause – proceeded to perpetrate a tragedy far worse than the one the city had suffered at the hands of the Goths eleven centuries earlier. Estimates of the dead ran to well over 10,000. Churches were desecrated, convents violated, houses and palaces ransacked, citizens tortured in expectation of ransom or a lead to hidden treasures. The shock wave spread throughout Italy: even the seat of the Universal Church, it became evident, was not immune from the kind of brutal violence that had already ruined most of the rest of the country.

It has long been assumed that the Sack of Rome spelled the end of the Renaissance, that Italian artists and writers after this event suffered a 'loss of nerve', that the serenity and confidence of humanism gave way to the tortured doubts of a wholly new artistic style, 'Mannerism'. But such assumptions can no longer be sustained. However elusive the term Mannerism may be, when applied to the letters and arts of the decades after the Sack it must refer to a movement dedicated principally to elaboration upon and to experimentation with the cultural achievement of the High Renaissance. It was this elaboration and experimentation that eventually prepared for the scientific revolution of the following century and for a new style in the arts that has never been surpassed for eloquence, forcefulness and energy: the Baroque. The continuity between Renaissance and Baroque means of expression was assured in part by the restoration of ecclesiastical institutions under the inspiration of the Tridentine Reformation (from the Council of Trent, 1545–63), and in part by the remarkable economic recovery that followed the final end of the Italian wars in 1559. It was assured also by the consolidation of Italian political institutions in the form they were to maintain for another two centuries. How the Baroque then gave way to the more decorative styles of Rococo and eventually to the Enlightenment is the theme of the last part of this section.

Two years after the Sack, Charles V, the most powerful prince in Europe and the nearest to a universal monarch since the time of Charlemagne, arrived in Italy. He was reconciled with Pope Clement VII, whom he assisted in putting down an anti-imperial, anti-Medici régime in Florence. The other states rallied to his support at the Congress of Bologna in 1530–31, and thus took the first essential steps in passing from disaster to recovery.

Charles V conquering discord.
Hailed in Genoa, where he landed, as 'the ruler of the world', Charles was able by a combination of force, persuasion and compromise to evolve a solution to Italy's problems that – against all expectations – was to prove long-lasting. This bronze by Leone Leoni shows him as an allegorical warrior of peace, binding in chains the savage figure of war. As a tribute to the man partially responsible for the Sack of Rome it is not without irony. (1)

The Medici restored

The surrender of 1530 placed Florence again in Medici hands and although the Emperor had initially promised to preserve the 'liberty' of its citizens, they soon realized that such terms were relative. First came the indecisive rule of Duke Alessandro de' Medici, then (1537–74) the long and successful reign of Cosimo, created first grand duke of Tuscany in 1569 and the founder of a dynasty which lasted until 1737.

Cosimo I, a shrewd and calculating statesman, has benefited in the eyes of posterity from his judicious patronage of the arts. *Left*: Cosimo with architects and engineers, by Vasari, in the Palazzo Vecchio. *Right*: his triumphant entry into Siena, handed over to Florence in 1555 and incorporated into the Duchy of Tuscany (a fresco by Il Volterrano in one of Cosimo's villas near Florence). The marble roundels *below* and *opposite* are part of a series representing the blessings of Medicean government. (2, 9)

Most of the subjects, described here from top left to bottom right, are based on classical models. **Water-supply:** Ammannati's Neptune Fountain with its aqueduct. **Naval strength:** a fortified port on Elba, seen here with classical boats, the entrance closed by a chain. **The army:** Cosimo had reorganized the Florentine *milizia*; here he appears as a Roman soldier leading his troops. **Learning:** the Laurentian Library, which Cosimo opened to the public in 1571. **The family seat:** Palazzo Pitti, bought by Duchess Eleonora in 1549. **'Offices':** the Uffizi, seat of the bureaucracy, with the Palazzo Vecchio in the background and Justice in front. (3–8)

Chivalry: the Order of S. Stefano was founded to defend Italy from the incursions of the Turks. **Government** by the prince. Ducal hands unravel the skein of politics. Cosimo assumed absolute power in 1537. **Union** of Florence and Siena – the lion (Marzocco) and the wolf (of Romulus and Remus). Tuscany, with cornucopia, guards both. (10–12)

Art and anxiety

In spite of increasing political stability, the years between the Sack of Rome and the last quarter of the century were for many artists and writers years of tension. The escapist Utopianism as well as the ethical ideals of Castiglione's *Courtier* were more fully explored, while the makers of culture reached out to new audiences with the help of such technological innovations as the printing press and the etched copper plate.

The setting, which in High Renaissance painting had served to define and dramatize the subject, now moves forward to overwhelm it. In Paris Bordone's *Annunciation* (*right*) the angel is almost lost in a forest of elaborate columns. Vasari, in his mural of Pope Paul III bestowing cardinals' and bishops' hats (*below*), creates a claustrophobic space with real people in the background (including Michelangelo) and a huge allegorical nude stretched in the foreground. (13, 14)

The human body – exalted by the
High Renaissance as the supreme
symbol of dignity and beauty – has
now to bend before the new aesthetic
criteria of 'grace'. Parmigianino
abandons realistic anatomy in his
Virgin and Child: the Virgin's neck and
hand, the Child's torso and limbs, are
elongated for the sake of a graceful
composition. In Rosso's *Moses
Defending the Daughters of Jethro* the
pattern is even more contrived, while
the muscular effort is so intense that
the pose could only be held for a split
second.

Neither painter, however, would
have seen himself as rejecting the
standards of the High Renaissance.
Parmigianino was continuing the
elegance of Raphael, Rosso the
physical force of Michelangelo.
(15, 16)

153

The city as work of art

The early Renaissance had played with the idea of the 'ideal' city based on geometry. In the 16th and 17th centuries many such schemes were put into practice, but with an ulterior political motive. Grandiose design was to reflect the power and prestige of the ruler. Architecture became the art of spectacle, a stage-set for the drama of power.

Fountains grew in elaboration and prominence. In Florence the old Piazza della Signoria was given the Fountain of Neptune (*above*) with central figure by Ammannati. At the same time the city of Palermo erected the Fontana Pretoria (*below*) by pupils of Ammannati – Tuscan Mannerism superseding local tradition. (17, 19)

In Florence too Vasari connected the Palazzo Vecchio to the Arno by two parallel blocks of municipal offices (*uffizi*) with a loggia to the river. Contemporary **Genoa** (*below*) was building the Strada Nuova (now Via Garibaldi) lined with magnificent palaces. Both schemes show the Mannerists' love of converging lines. (18, 20)

It was in Rome that the idea of the consciously constructed city was taken furthest. Michelangelo laid out the Campidoglio (*above*) with its three palaces, monumental staircase and groups of classical sculpture. A century later Bernini's piazza in front of St Peter's (*below*) uses similar principles to draw the spectator into an organized space dominated by the great basilica. The Vatican palace stretches away to the right. (21, 22)

Venice: the public image

The picture of a society which posterity sees in its works of art is generally the one that it wishes posterity to see. This is transparently true in the case of Venice. Through all the changes of style, Venetian painting for several centuries projects a consistent image of prosperity, grandeur and the glory of the Republic.

Veronese in the 16th century gave even religious pictures an overtly Venetian setting. *Left*: detail from his huge canvas *The Marriage at Cana*. (23)

Canaletto in the 18th century fixed the stereotype of Venice for the rest of Europe. *Below*: a festival in the Piazzetta – note the tall Baroque pavilion specially erected, the pyramid of athletes to the left, and the ropes leading to the Campanile down which it was possible to slide, to land at the Doge's feet. (24)

Tiepolo represents the end of the great Venetian tradition. His *Banquet of Antony and Cleopatra* looks back to Veronese; but the tone is lighter, the touch yet more brilliant. (25)

Classicism and realism

The return to the forms of the High Renaissance, spearheaded by the Carracci, did not mean loss of contact with the real world in which the artists worked, even with those aspects of the real world that were aesthetically the least pleasant. As the prophets and apostles of the Tridentine Reform gloried in serving the most basic needs of the less fortunate, so Caravaggio went beyond the 'realism' prescribed by Albertian and Carraccian formulas with spotlight techniques that approach surrealism.

Naples, 1647: resentment over ever-increasing taxes imposed upon the necessities of life for the support of the ever-more exhausted Spanish war treasury flared into open rebellion under the leadership of the charismatic fishmonger Masaniello. Thanks to the support of discontented peasants elsewhere in the kingdom, the rebels managed to set up a short-lived independent republic. This detail from a contemporary painting shows Spanish officials being lynched. (26)

Plague returned to most of Northern Italy in 1630 after more than half a century – in some areas after an entire century – of dormancy. A series of Florentine waxworks carries the realism of Caravaggio to bizarre and frightening heights – as in this detail of a dead mother with a living child at her breast. (27)

Realism of an equally direct kind
motivated the artists of the Sacri Monti
of Northern Italy. *Above*: detail from a
tableau at Varallo showing Christ and
St Veronica; behind her one of Christ's
persecutors has a monstrous goitre, a
condition actually prevalent in the
area. (28)

Common humanity was for Caravaggio part of the nature
of holiness, although to those who thought differently he
was degrading holy subjects to the condition of humanity.
For *The Death of the Virgin* (*above*) he used not only barefoot
peasants as models for the apostles but (it was said) the body
of a prostitute dragged from the Tiber as the dead Mary.
The picture was rejected by the church that had
commissioned it and sold to a secular buyer. (29)

159

A world of marvels

The scientific method, as it evolved in the 17th century, sprang from a restless curiosity about the universe. One symptom of that curiosity was a new interest in cosmology and metaphysical systems; another was the accumulation of data on all subjects from anatomy to anthropology and from coins to crystals. A typical collection of such curios is illustrated on p. 179. Here we show the impact upon art of this sense of discovery, not only of remote times and places but also among familiar things.

The element of fire: Arcimboldi's fantastic personifications of the elements stand halfway between science and magic. Fire is made up of guns, candles and blazing brands. (31)

The connoisseur represents the exploration of the past. Titian's *Jacopo da Strada* (*opposite*) is portrayed with choice items from his collection – an antique statuette, a torso, coins and medallions. (30)

The riches of the sea: Jacopo Zucchi makes painting a sort of visual encyclopaedia to display the treasures of the submarine world – shells, pearls and coral in a setting that characteristically mixes the classical and the barbaric. (32)

The drama of faith

The Tridentine Reform produced a new vision of the relation between man and the Divinity, and artists readily came forward to serve it with the latest aesthetic techniques – all for the purpose of heightening the emotional response of the viewer.

A new kind of saint arose to consolidate and enrich the reforms of Trent. *Below*: Carlo Borromeo, whose restructuring of the diocese and province of Milan became a model imitated all over Catholic Christendom. *Bottom*: Filippo Neri, founder of the Roman Oratory that bound clerics and laymen together in a common vocation – and in which was born both the musical 'oratory' of Palestrina and the great historical and theological *summa* of the Tridentine Reform. (34, 35)

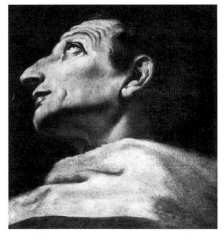

Illusion in the service of Truth. Baroque painters achieved on the ceilings of churches what Galileo achieved with his telescope: they burst through the boundary between the finite and the infinite. Here in the Gesù in Rome the beholder is lifted into the realm of the saints gathered in joy around the glowing monogram IHS, while at the edge of the frame painting turns into sculpture and sculpture into architecture. (33)

Volume and space were moulded by Baroque architects to express spiritual energy. *Above*: the cupola of Borromini's S. Ivo della Sapienza, Rome. *Right*: Guarini's dome over the Chapel of the Holy Shroud, Turin. (36, 37)

The moment of ecstasy: in works such as this, *The Death of Ludovica Albertoni*, Bernini expresses in marble the highest forms of religious feeling – as well as the fascination that mystical experiences held for the piety of the Baroque age. (38)

Pope Benedict XIV greets Charles III of Naples after the Battle of Velletri. Our period ends as it began, with a political settlement. During the first half of the 18th century Bourbons and Habsburgs used Italy as the arena in which to carry on their apparently endless quarrel. In 1744 an Austrian army moving south with the intention of occupying Naples was defeated by Charles III. The victory consolidated his dynasty; four years later the Treaty of Aix-la-Chapelle stabilized Italian boundaries for the rest of the century. (39)

IV

Disaster and Recovery: 1527–1750

ERIC COCHRANE

BY MIDNIGHT of 10 August 1530, when the anti-Medici party inside the walls of Florence finally accepted the terms dictated by the pro-Medici commissioners of the papal-imperial army outside, most of Italy lay in ruins. Ever since the first French invasion of 1494, it had been struck by a relentless series of calamities. The eastern half of the Venetian mainland state – though not Venice itself – had been devastated by the Turks in 1499, the western half by the French and Germans in 1509. Ravenna and Prato had been sacked by Spanish troops in 1512 – many of the citizens killed, many more tortured, much of the real property destroyed and almost all the moveable property carried away. Brescia had been sacked in 1513, Fabriano, Como and Genoa between 1519 and 1521, Rome – most disastrously of all – in 1527, the majority of the towns of Apulia and the Abruzzi in 1528. The population of most cities had fallen to half or a third of what it had been before 1494. Many small towns and villages had been completely abandoned. The survivors had been further decimated by several serious outbreaks of the plague and by the rapid spread of the most recent disease to be imported into Western Europe, syphilis. Much of Italy's accumulated wealth had been drained off in the form of ransoms and extraordinary tax levies. Most of the wool and silk looms upon which the smaller towns of Lombardy depended for a livelihood had been destroyed. Fields everywhere had long been left untilled and systematically ravaged by frequent use of that favourite Renaissance military tactic, scorched earth.

The year-long siege of Florence, the destruction of its suburbs, the ruin of its export business and the confiscation of its citizens' wealth were therefore only the most recent of over thirty years of man-made and natural calamities. The siege also marked the last attempt on the part of Italians to halt the calamities by political and military action. One by one the states of Italy had crumbled, many of them less than a century after they had been founded or consolidated. Florence had lost much of its territorial domain between 1494 and 1502, Venice all but a fragment of its empire on *terraferma* in 1509. The Duchy of Milan had been seized by the king of France in 1499; shorn of several of its major cities, it had later been passed back and forth between the kings of France supported by the anti-Sforza Milanese on the one side and the descendants of the Sforza dukes with the backing of a Swiss or an imperial army on the other. The lordship of Genoa had passed from a Milanese governor to a French one, then to a coalition of artisans and textile workers, then to an aristocratic oligarchy, then back to a French or imperial governor, depending upon the vagaries of the ever-shifting balance of military power. The dukes of Ferrara had regained the lower Polesina from the Venetians; they had lost and then reconquered Modena and Reggio. The Kingdom of Naples had been seized by one king of France, recaptured – except for the cities of Apulia, which he had ceded to the Venetians – by the current successor of the Italianized Aragonese dynasty, partitioned between the king of Spain and the king of France, conquered by the king of Spain and then almost won back again by another king of France. The Papal State, tripled in size as the result of the nepotistic policies of two popes, had been financially ruined by the similar but abortive policies of a third. Within a few days of the sack of 1527 – and the beginning of a year-long imprisonment of still another pope – it had virtually dissolved into its component parts. By now all governments, native or foreign, had come to be looked upon as oppressors. Political authority – what there was of it – relied solely on military strength. Frontiers – even those of the regional states that had emerged a half-century earlier from the ruins of the last attempt to create a nation-state – were now regarded as merely provisional.

Reconstruction

What nobody realized was that a somewhat less unhappy issue out of their afflictions was just then being arranged – not indeed by any of the Italian princes or potentates, but by the prince who had emerged as the victor in the thirty-year contest for the hegemony of Italy. He was Charles V, the hereditary ruler of the Burgundian Netherlands, of the Habsburg lands in Germany, of Aragon with its dependencies in the Mediterranean, of Castile with its rapidly expanding empire in the New World and, in Italy, of the kingdoms of Naples and Sicily. After 1519 Charles was also Holy Roman Emperor, a rank that gave him theoretical suzerainty over much of Northern Italy together with considerable prestige as the current inheritor of the great medieval dream – a united empire of all Latin Christendom. That Charles was not an Italian bothered no one, at least before the 19th century; the inclusion of Italian generals in foreign armies, the presence of non-Italian mercenaries in most Italian armies and the impossibility of distinguishing the behaviour or the misbehaviour of Italian from foreign soldiers had broken down any discrimination between Italians and foreigners. Even the humanists discarded the prejudices, adopted from the ancient Romans, against transalpine 'barbarians', particularly when they found themselves honoured and subsidized by transalpine princes. Thus when Charles induced his chief rival, Francis I, to recognize the futility, at least for the moment, of further adventures in Italy (Treaty of Barcelona, 1529), and invited all the powers of Italy, great and small, to join him for a two-month celebration of his reconciliation with, and his coronation by, the pope at Bologna in the winter of 1529–30, they all gladly accepted.

The Congress of Bologna marked the first major step toward the establishment of the political order in Italy that was to last, with only minor changes, for the next two centuries. In return for abundant subsidies, loans and gifts, of which his overdrawn treasury and his underpaid armies were constantly in need, Charles settled the affairs of the Italian states in such a way that, if not all were fully content, none was so dissatisfied as to risk open opposition. He gave the cities of the Romagna back to the papacy in return for the pope's recognition of the Venetians' protégés, the Della Rovere, as dukes of Urbino. He returned Milan to the penitent rebel Francesco II Sforza and the city of Asti to the duke of Savoy. He rewarded the Medici pope, Clement VII, for accepting the return of the Este to Modena by assuring him of the restoration of Florence to the Medici. Two years later, again at Bologna, he confirmed the settlement with a formal alliance, pledged to the maintenance of peaceful relations among the Italian states – after four centuries of almost constant warfare – and to the prevention of any further interference by the two most threatening powers outside Italy, France and the Ottoman Empire.

That the imperial, or pan-Italian, alliance worked as well as it did was due only in part to the emperor himself and to the army he kept stationed near the French frontier in Lombardy, for Charles's pressing obligations elsewhere in Europe did not permit him to yield to his advisers' proposal that he should settle permanently in what had become the geographical centre of his far-flung empire. The alliance depended primarily on his personal representatives in Italy – his ambassadors in Rome and Venice, his viceroys in his kingdoms of Naples and Sicily and, after the death without heirs of the last Sforza duke in 1534, his governor in Milan. But it also depended on those independent Italian powers who were most committed to the imperial cause – Duke Alessandro de' Medici of Florence, to whom Charles married his illegitimate daughter Margherita; Alessandro's successor, Duke

Cosimo, who married the daughter of his viceroy in Naples; his wife's brother-in-law, Duke Charles II of Savoy; and the admiral of his Mediterranean fleet, Andrea Doria, who after the *coup d'état* of 1528 became the Periclean 'first citizen' of the Republic of Genoa. It depended finally upon the benevolent, or self-interested, acquiescence of the two Italian powers with major commitments outside Italy. The first was Venice, mistress of Cyprus, Crete and the Ionian Islands, who, having reconquered most of her former mainland domain, tacitly agreed to recognize her current frontiers as definitive. The second was the pope, Paul III, whose grandson Ottavio became Margherita's second husband and whose position as the spiritual head of Latin Christendom frequently led him into quarrels with Charles over European ecclesiastical politics.

This alliance was subjected to several major crises during the first thirty years of its existence. But after Ottavio Farnese's success in saving his new duchy of Parma-Piacenza from the double attack of the governor of Milan and Pope Julius III, and after Pope Paul IV's failure to bring in the French in order to drive the Spanish out of Naples, the alliance at last managed to fix the borders of the Italian states in the shape they were to maintain, with very few exceptions, for another century and a half. At the same time, the alliance succeeded in putting an end to invasions from abroad. After failing to conquer Malta in 1565, the Turks were forced by an almost impregnable system of fortifications to limit their aggressive operations to occasional raids along the Tyrrhenian coast; and after the destruction of their fleet at the celebrated (if ultimately insignificant) Battle of Lepanto in 1571, they moved the focus of their military operations from the Mediterranean to Hungary. Even the kings of France finally came to realize that their three-century-old dream of a Mediterranean empire was no longer practicable. By the Treaty of Cateau-Cambrésis in 1559, Henry II agreed to withdraw not only from his remaining outposts at Mirandola and in the Sienese Maremma, but even from Savoy and from Bresse, on the French side of the Alps.

The new political order

Italy in 1530 thus entered upon a period of relative and then of total peace that proved to be far longer than any it had enjoyed since the fall of the Ostrogothic kingdom. This peace was won and maintained at a price much lower than that exacted by all previous attempts to create a pan-Italian polity – the hegemony of the Hohenstaufen in the mid-13th century or of Angevins in the early 14th, the empire of the Visconti in the late 14th or the alliance of Lodi in the mid-15th century. The legally independent states of the peninsula were expected to recognize the supremacy of the Emperor Charles V and, later, of his son and heir, Philip II of Spain; otherwise they were left to regulate their internal and most of their external affairs with the degree of

The entry of Charles V and Clement VII into Bologna, where the pope crowned Charles as emperor in 1530. The coronation was the occasion of magnificent ceremonial embodying the new-found friendship between the two heads of Christendom (the Sack of Rome conveniently forgotten). The Congress of Bologna, held during Charles's stay in the city, determined the political boundaries of Italy, which, with only minor changes, were to remain for almost two centuries.

CLEMENS VII · PONT · MAX · IMP · CAES · CAROLVS · V · P · F · AVG ·

independence that could be expected of small and medium sized members of what had become, after the invasion of 1494, a European system of states. At times they could even get away with annoying the hegemonic power. That is what the Venetians did in 1540 and again in 1573 when they concluded separate peaces with the Turks. That is what the grand duke of Tuscany did after the destruction of the Spanish Armada, when he married a French princess, arranged for the reconciliation of Henry IV and the pope and drew up plans for a Tuscan colony in Venezuela. Even in the legally dependent states local government was divided, *de jure* as well as *de facto*, between an externally appointed and usually short-term governor and several self-perpetuating, self-sufficient constitutional bodies, like the Parlamento of Sicily, the Seggi of Naples and the Senate of Milan. These bodies did not hesitate to undermine the authority of the governor by appealing directly to the king – who was thus assured of their loyalty – whenever the governor threatened their rights and privileges.

Limited, and then permanent, security enabled the rulers of the Italian states to embark upon extensive programmes of internal reconstruction. They established a number of important political and constitutional innovations. First, they transformed the secretaries and notary-chancellors inherited from the late-medieval communal governments into professional and relatively permanent *auditori*, whose sole qualification for appointment was a law degree and whose sole qualification for retention was efficiency. These they then allowed to take over much of the real work traditionally entrusted to patricians elected for short terms to the constitutional magistracies – most of which they allowed to remain. They thus took the first major step towards the creation of a modern bureaucratic state, administered by salaried professionals rather than by amateurs owing their positions to birth or wealth. The rulers also transformed the traditional communal charters and statutes into something approaching 18th-century written constitutions – the Genoese in 1528, the Florentine in 1532, the Milanese in 1541. And they did so with such care that most of these constitutions lasted, with few major modifications, until the reforms of the late 18th century.

Similarly, the rulers of the Italian states sought to diminish the differences between privileged and unprivileged orders – between patricians, nobles and

Mannerist architects were encouraged to create ordered cityscapes, to display their rulers' power; Palmanova, designed by Giulio Savorgnano, is a planned city that, unlike most such projects, was actually built (1599).

members of the equally privileged 'citizen' class on one hand and the disenfranchised artisans, manual labourers and peasants on the other. They did so by insisting upon equality before the law – a notion reinforced by the increasing interest among jurists in the sources of Roman jurisprudence – by removing as far as possible the role of influence in judicial procedure and even, at times, by providing legal counsel for those unable to afford it. It thus became ever more difficult for well-born thugs like Piero Strozzi and Galeazzo di Tarsia to beat up their inferiors or dependents without ending up in the Bargello or on the island of Lipari. The first step was thus taken toward the creation of a 'state of right' in place of the traditional state of privilege and toward the broadening of the social basis of political authority to include all those dependent upon it. The rulers also sought to diminish the legal distinctions between city and country and between dominant and subject cities. They did not abolish these distinctions, to be sure; provincial governorships, foreign embassies and domestic bishoprics remained the preserve of the patricians or nobles of the dominant cities. But they did create a system of appeal courts in which 'subjects' could obtain justice on the same terms as 'citizens', and they opened the administrative corps of the *auditori* to all subjects regardless of provenance. The first step was thus taken toward the transformation of a communal or city state into a unified territorial state.

In order to ensure the permanence of the reforms they introduced, the rulers of Italy followed the example of all their predecessors since the advent of

humanism: they turned for assistance to the artists, the poets and the men of letters. Since antiquity still implied timelessness, they had themselves identified, in Horatian odes and Demosthenian orations, with Spartan ephors and Etruscan *lucumoni*, with Caesar, Scipio and Augustus. Since political authority was still identified with persons rather than with institutions, they had their portraits painted by Titian, Bronzino or Giovanni Battista Moroni, or carved in marble by Benvenuto Cellini or Giovanni da Nola. Since the symbol of a person was considered to be almost the equivalent of his actual presence, they left their domains everywhere blazoned with their emblems – like the Medici balls that appear on public fountains in the remotest villages of Tuscany and the lions of St Mark that guard the ruins of former Venetian fortresses all over Greece. Since success in ruling was held to be proportionate to the beauty of the ruler's city, they resuscitated and perfected the urban-planning projects left from the generation of Sixtus IV, Alfonso II, Alberto Pio and Filarete. They pulled down the stalls and awnings that made smaller streets dangerous and impassable. They turned open areas and unhealthy slums into geometrically harmonious squares: Vasari's Piazzale degli Uffizi in Florence, Michelangelo's Campidoglio in Rome, and Jacopo Sansovino's enlarged Piazza S. Marco in Venice. They carved broad straight streets through mazes of winding alleys: Via Toledo in Naples, Via dei Cestari and Via dei Baulari in Rome. They encouraged their richer subjects – by giving them rights of eminent domain – to build or rebuild palaces along the new thoroughfares, like Via Maggio in Florence, Strada Nuova in Genoa and the Grand Canal in Venice, in accordance with the latest Roman and Florentine models. Medieval cities thus came to incorporate many elements of the ideal Renaissance city. And some smaller towns, particularly those that were built or, like Aquila after the earthquake, rebuilt at the time, were made to incorporate all those elements: a grid plan inside circular or square walls with two principal streets crossing at a central square, as at Portoferraio and Livorno, or with the grid plan shifted several degrees off the axis formed by the city gates, for greater protection against invaders, as at Guastalla and Sabbioneta.

The age of Mannerism

Fortunately, Italian culture was well able to lend effective support to the task of political reconstruction. The years of the calamities had coincided with the completion of the major masterpieces of what is today known as the High Renaissance. The impression made by these masterpieces even at the time was such that those who judged current history according to cultural rather than political events spoke not of a deplorable age of calamities but of a golden age of the arts, which they named after Pope Leo X, who succeeded his uncle Lorenzo de' Medici as the greatest patron of all Italy.

The early 16th century witnessed the creation of literary works that were instantly accepted as classics, matching or even excelling the works of ancient Rome and 15th-century Tuscany. Below, the title-page of the 1538 edition of Pietro Bembo's 'Prose della Volgar Lingua' which argued for the elevation of Tuscan as the literary vernacular. Right, the opening of Canto 35 of Ariosto's 'Orlando Furioso', showing the warrior-maiden Bradamante defeating Rodomonte. Ariosto's revisions to his epic poem moved it towards the purified Tuscan encouraged by Bembo.

Era quel uecchio si espedito , e snello ,
  Che per correr parea , che fosse nato :
E da quel monte il lembo del mantello
  Portaua pien del nome altrui segnato .

Oue n'andaua ; e perche facea quello ,
  Ne l'altro canto ui sara narrato ;
Se d'hauerne piacer segno farete
  Con quella grata udienza , che solete ,

IN QVESTO TRENTESIMO QVINTO LO AVTORE LEG-
giadramente esforta i Prencipi ad hauere in pregio i Poeti & gli huomini uirtuosi , dannando i pes-
simi costumi de le corti. NEL fine racconta alcune laudeuoli proue, che con i caual-
lieri d'Agramante spinta da la gelosia fece la innamorata Bradamante.

CANTO TRENTESIMO QVINTO.

HI SALI=
ra per me ,
Madonna in
cielo

A RIPOR=
tarne il mio
perduto in=
gegno ?

Che poi , ch'usci da bei uostri occhi il telo ;
Che'l cor mi fisse ; ognihor perdendo uegno .
Ne di tanta iattura mi querelo ;
Pur , che non cresca , ma stia a questo segno:
Ch'io dubito , se piu si ua sciemando ;
Di uenir tal , qual ho descritto Orlando .

Per rihauer l'ingegno mio m'è auiso ;
Che non bisogna , che per l'aria io poggi
Nel cerchio de la Luna , o in Paradiso ;
Che'l mio non credo , che tanto alto alloggi .

Ne bei uostri occhi , e nel sereno uiso ,
Nel sen d'auorio , e allabastrini poggi
Se ne ua errando ; & io con queste labbia
Lo corrò ; se ui par , ch'io lo rihabbia .

Per gli ampli tetti andaua il Paladino
Tutte mirando le future uite ;
Poi c'hebbe uisto su'l fatal molino
Volgersi quelle , ch'erano gia ordite .
E scorse un uello ; che piu , che d'or fino ,
Splender parea ; ne sarian gemme trite
S'in filo si tirassero con arte
Da comparargli a la millesma parte .

Mirabilmente il bel uello gli piacque ,
Che tra infiniti paragon non hebbe ;
E di saper alto desio gli nacque ,
Quando sara tal uita , e a chi si debbe .
L'Euangelista nulla glie ne tacque ;
Che uenti anni principio prima haurebbe
Che col M, e col D, fosse notato
L'anno corrente dal Verbo incarnato .

PROSE
DI
MONSI
GNOR
BEMBO

CON PRIVILEGI.

These masterpieces were accomplished in accordance with the aesthetic ideals induced by a careful observation of the surviving masterpieces of ancient Greek and Roman culture – a process known as *imitatio*, 'imitation'. For those forms of expression which were not derived from classical models, like love poetry and prose *novelle*, imitation could be directed instead to the masterpieces of the equally 'classic' age of Italian, or Tuscan, literature, the 14th century, in particular to Petrarch's *Canzoniere* and Boccaccio's *Decameron*. Many of the High Renaissance masterpieces were held to have surpassed the models they imitated: Michelangelo's *Moses* and his Medici Chapel, Raphael's Vatican fresco cycle, Lodovico Ariosto's epic romance *Orlando Furioso*, Ariosto's, Machiavelli's and Pietro Aretino's comedies, Baldassare Castiglione's dialogue *The Courtier (Il Cortegiano)*. Those artists and writers who had not yet surpassed their models were expected soon to do so. For as Michelangelo had discovered all the rules for great art, so Pietro Bembo, the leading linguist of his day, had restored both the perfect language of the ancient Latin literary masterpieces and, in his *Prose della Volgar Lingua*, the language that had generated the Italian masterpieces of the 14th century. Go, admonished Bembo and Michelangelo's spokesman Giorgio Vasari, and do thou likewise.

That is just what many of the leaders of Italian culture did during the next two generations. The greatest of the 16th-century *novella* writers, Matteo Bandello, scrupulously adhered to the formal structure

169

Palladio's design for Palazzo Iseppo Da Porto, Vicenza, (begun c.1550) from his 'Four Books of Architecture', first published in 1570. This, the earliest of Palladio's palaces in Vicenza, combines the influence of Vitruvius with the High Renaissance architecture of Raphael and Bramante.

of the *Decameron*. Gaudenzio Ferrari in his *Crucifixion* (now in the Sabauda Gallery, Turin) carefully followed the formal arrangement of figures he had learned in Milan from Raphael and Leonardo da Vinci; his Milanese associates Gian Pietro and Aurelio Luini multiplied the statuesque figures that their father Bernardino, the leading representative of High Renaissance painting in Milan, had previously put on the walls of the Monastero Maggiore of S. Maurizio. At Palazzo Farnese in Rome, both Michelangelo, the chief architect, and his successor Giacomo della Porta respected the basic design prescribed by Antonio di San Gallo in the years after 1514 for what became the most spectacular monument of High Renaissance architecture. Even those who departed from their masters'

lessons did so in conformity with their masters' principle of 'imitation': Anton Francesco Doni made his unlettered tavern keeper speak in passages lifted verbatim from Machiavelli's comedies, while Giovanni Battista Gelli made his philosophical animals speak in dialogues patterned on those of Lucian, the most recent addition to the pantheon of ancient 'models'. Andrea Palladio justified his imposition of austerely classical structures on the very unclassical cityscape of Vicenza by appealing to the authority of Vitruvius, or rather to Vitruvius's descriptions of late republican buildings in ancient Rome.

Yet what the masters had supposed to be eternally valid principles, the disciples often demoted to the rank of proposals for further experimentation. Some lyric poets introduced startling un-Petrarchan metaphors into impeccably Petrarchan verse forms, as when Galeazzo di Tarsia (the bully baron) compared love to a wiggling fish. Some applied the Petrarchan love themes canonized by the Neo-Platonist philosophers to very non-Petrarchan subjects, like a none-too-Platonic relationship between two men and the frankly salacious passion of an old pedagogue for his pre-adolescent pupil. In the place of Petrarch's abstract mistress they put personified abstractions, like Bernardo Tasso's (and Michelangelo's) 'Sleep', or very concrete absurdities, like Francesco Beccuti's pet cat. Some *novella* writers expanded the morbid aspects of certain stories of Boccaccio to the point where the abnormal and the monstrous prevailed, as in Giovanni Brevio's account of double incest and in the description of the love gestures of mutilated corpses in Antonfrancesco Grazzini's *Cene*. Other *novella* writers expanded the 'frame' of a series of stories until the stories themselves became merely particular instances of theses proposed during a conversation among the story tellers. The playwrights sought to overcome the frequent reduction of personages to stock figures in the early imitations of Plautus by making them speak in the language they normally used in real life – in mixtures of Spanish and Italian, in Brescian or Paduan dialect or even, in one case, in *Romaïco* – an Italianized modern Greek.

The most striking departures from High Renaissance standards took place, however, in the realm of the visual arts. Paris Bordone in his *Annunciation* (now at Caen) brought Raphael's architectural setting so far forward that it swallowed up the subject. Some artists carried the doctrine of natural realism to its utmost limits: Tintoretto made the legs of the paralytics at the Probatic Pool wither away from disuse and put the spectators at chin-level in the pool itself; Jacopo Bassano restored Jesus's disciples to their social status as low-born fishermen; Giovanni da Nola tilted the head of Pedro de Toledo's wife so that her eye could look exactly perpendicularly at the page held slightly at an angle by her finger in the middle of the book. Other artists carried to its limits the equally Albertian technique of attracting the viewer's attention to the action – Vasari, for example, by stretching along the bottom of a mural a huge male nude, propped upon one elbow with the back of his head towards the viewer. Some artists, like Pontormo, maintained a credible spatial relation among their figures but reduced their colours to incredibly flat washes; others maintained Leonardo's triangular arrangement of the figures but endowed them with such apparent motion – for example, the violent fury of Rosso Fiorentino's *Moses* – that they would have shattered the triangle the moment the scene was put into time; still others made anatomically correct muscles unnaturally large and tense, like those of Baccio Bandinelli's *Hercules and Cacchus*. Many artists sacrificed anatomy altogether for 'grace' (*grazia*): Parmigianino's Christ Child is as gracefully unanatomical as is the famous 'long neck' of his mother.

When separated still further from the example or the memory of their masters, or when set to work on a relatively new form of artistic expression like grotesques, the artists could experiment with even greater freedom. They could indulge fully in what E. Battisti was to call 'hedonism' and 'sensuality', as Giulio Romano did as soon as he moved from Rome to Mantua and as Primaticcio did as soon as he arrived at Fontainebleau. Or they could make fun of these things, as Luzio Luzzi did on the ceiling of the Sala di Apollone in the Castel S. Angelo, where an elderly merman up to his thighs in a swamp points a gigantic erection in the direction of two placid swans.

The diversity, or the audacity, of such experiments baffled the critics of the time. But diversity, or individuality, was only one aspect of Mannerist culture. Whenever several Mannerists gathered together in order to collaborate on a single project, they had no trouble blending – without sacrificing – their individual proclivities into an admirably harmonious whole. S. Sigismundo in Cremona, S. Giovanni Decollato in Rome, the Palazzo Vecchio in Florence and the magnificent, if, alas, short-lived display put on for the funeral of Michelangelo in the same city provide ample justification for the inclusion of all the collaborators – stucco workers, wood carvers, papier mâché technicians, musicians and scholars as well as painters, architects and poets – as representatives of the same distinct age in the history of Italian culture.

The foundations of Mannerism

The reasons for the success of this unity in diversity are not hard to find. Arts and letters in the age of Mannerism benefited from the same system of public and private patronage that had supported the culture of the early and High Renaissance. That is, works were commissioned and paid for not only by princes and courts, as is supposed by certain modern anti-Mannerists, but also by merchants, patricians, land-owners, guilds, confraternities, religious orders and

Orpheus, from the pavement of the Cappella di S. Caterina in the church of S. Domenico, Siena, designed by Domenico Beccafumi (1484/6–1551), who spent most of his life in Siena. He was one of the few great Mannerist artists not to have his origins in Florence or Rome.

urban magistracies. The arts flourished equally well in turbulent popular republics, like Siena at the time of Beccafumi, in well-regulated monarchies of unlettered princes, like the Florence of Duke Cosimo, and in such semi-public imitations of Castiglione's paradise at Urbino as the 'courts' of Cardinal Roberto Ridolfi and of the ambitious wife of the governor of Milan. They were also encouraged by the creation of a new kind of institution: voluntary but formal associations of producers and consumers of culture, governed under written statutes by regularly elected officers and called, in deference to the earlier if much less formal imitations of Plato, 'academies'. These, whether wholly private like the Infiammati at Padua or recognized and partially subsidized by political authority like the Accademia

The title-page of 'De Re Anatomica' (1559) by Realdus Columbus (c.1510–69), an anatomist who taught at Padua, Pisa and Rome. This book contains the substance of his lectures. Columbus was the first to describe the pulmonary circulation.

Fiorentina, were soon founded in all cities of Italy, and remained, in forms varying according to the exigencies of time and place, the principal form of collective cultural activity for the next two centuries.

The arts and letters also drew strength from the reform or revival of a much older institution: the universities, which the governments now charged within the training not only of doctors and lawyers, but above all of administrators and technicians. Young men of good family and humanist education began to seek university degrees, which were increasingly required for entrance into public office. It was the humanists, even in traditionally non-humanist disciplines, who acceded – at the ever higher emoluments offered on the increasingly competitive Italian job market – to professorial chairs. They and their students then undertook to report on what they taught or learned to the non-university audiences that had traditionally supported the humanist disciplines. In doing so they were forced for the first time to translate the technical language comprehensible only to the initiate into the language of their audiences. The long maintained

distinction between a university culture based on science and philosophy and a humanist one founded on literature and rhetoric at last broke down. Aristotelian cosmology and Galenic biology were incorporated into the realm previously reserved for poetry, oratory and political philosophy. They therefore became subject to the rules for the verification of hypotheses established by the humanists: reference not to an authoritative text, but to observation of the relevant data. In the work of the anatomist Andrea Vesalius and of that irrepressible investigator of all disciplines, Girolamo Cardano, the Mannerist practice of experimenting with norms thus laid the methodological bases for the scientific revolution of the following century; Varchi's scientific lectures before the Accademia Fiorentina created the nucleus of the informed lay public that was to provide the revolution with its chief social support.

Finally and most important of all, the arts and letters benefited immeasurably from the great technological innovation of the age, the printing press. The establishment of presses in most of the major cities brought much nearer to realization the hope expressed in one contract (Torrentino) of keeping the cities 'abundantly supplied with every kind of book on every subject'. The perfection of the art of copper engraving, particularly in the hands of such masters as Marcantonio Bolognese, made possible the rapid transmission of the latest aesthetic experiments from one artist to another. Printed books, particularly the inexpensive and often defective paperbacks that profit-conscious publishers preferred to the artistically and philologically impeccable tomes of Aldo Manuzio, made possible the diffusion of humanist culture to a much broader public. They also made possible the multiplication of schools: by the 1530s, sons of modest families in the remote towns of the Marche could obtain a preparatory education of sufficient quality to enable them to compete with their peers when they moved to the cities. Above all, printing made possible the development of a new kind of literature: stories, poems and dialogues that were meant to be read rapidly and silently rather than declaimed, and that sought to amuse or entertain rather than to inspire or elevate.

Thanks to this support, some men of letters managed to go beyond experimentation and created substantially new forms of expression. Francesco Guicciardini and Paolo Giovio expanded the kind of municipal history sanctioned by Livy and the 15th-century Livians into, respectively, a history of all Italy and a history of the whole world that included Turks and Aztecs as well as Latin Christians. Carlo Sigonio extended the methods he had perfected for the study of classical antiquity to post-classical times and wrote the first history of medieval Italy. Giorgio Vasari fused Plutarchan and Suetonian biography with his own extensive observations to produce the first great monument of the discipline later known as art history. Giovanni della Casa, downgrading the elevated conversations of

Castiglione's courtiers to the level of a homey but impeccably Tuscan-speaking old gentleman, produced a classic of Tuscan prose that was also a witty and useful guidebook to good manners, the *Galateo*.

These and other writers and artists also succeeded in bringing to fruition a process that had begun with the first wave of emigration of talent from Florence: they transformed, or elevated, previous regional and local idioms into a single national culture. Mannerist painting had been born in Rome, Florence and Cremona; it was soon diffused by the Campi to Milan, by Parmigianino to Emilia and by Pino da Siena, a former pupil of Beccafumi and a collaborator of Perin da Vaga in Rome, to Naples. Mannerist architecture had its beginnings in Rome at the time of Baldassare Peruzzi; Galeazzo Alessi soon took it to Genoa and Milan as well as to his native Perugia. The very uncanonical and experimental character of Mannerist art facilitated its amalgamation with still vital local artistic traditions, engendering such spectacular variations on the standard themes as the rectangular façade of S. Bernardino in Aquila and the irrepressibly fantastic combinations of mensolated balconies, convex–concave ellipses and vine-covered spiral columns that Tarantino and Gabriele Ricciardi spread through the Terra d'Otranto. Wherever local traditions proved to be adamantly hostile, as they seem to have been in Casale Monferrato, Mannerist art wiped them out. Eventually even the Sicilians succumbed. When the commission for the huge Fontana Pretoria in Palermo was given not to a native sculptor trained in the traditional Catalan gothic but to Florentine pupils of Bartolommeo Ammannati, Sicily too became a full member of the Italian cultural community.

To be sure, regional specialization did not disappear. Poets tended to gather in Ferrara, the city of Ariosto, and later in Naples, the city of Sannazaro. Comic playwrights congregated in Siena, Padua and Venice, where performances of their works were assured by permanent theatre companies. Vernacular philologists found their way to Florence, where the best Trecento manuscripts were available. But all now wrote – some at the cost of considerable study – in the same Trecento Tuscan prescribed by Bembo, adopted by the Accademia Fiorentina in its campaign to translate the ancient classics and eventually formalized by the Florentine Academy of the Crusca (1582). Medieval Latin was relegated to the lawyers and the pre-Tridentine theologians; classical Latin, which had once threatened to obliterate Tuscan, was reserved for Tridentine theology, classical scholarship, schoolboy exercises and books aimed at a specialized transalpine audience. All currently spoken languages, not only the charming Paduan with which the classically educated comedian Ruzante had entertained Venetian patricians in the 1520s, but even the bitterly defended vernacular of Florence, were demoted to the rank of dialects. Bembo's *Volgare* became the official written language of all Italians, the spoken language of all Italian diplomats, statesmen, administrators and preachers, and the principal vehicle by which Italian culture spread across Europe.

Italy was thus constituted as something more than just the area circumscribed by the borders of an ancient Roman province or by Dante's Alps and Apennines. It was now a single linguistic and cultural entity, one which included all those communities that recognized as their own the current embodiment and the official language of humanist culture. This 'Italy' still included isolated pockets elsewhere in Europe, for the various Florentine, Lucchese and Genoese colonies in Seville and Antwerp, Lyon and Cracow, scrupulously guarded their special national identities. It excluded on the other hand several enclaves within the geographical limits of Italy, like the Jewish ghettoes in Venice, Ferrara, Livorno and even Pitigliano; the Greek and Albanian settlements in Sicily, Calabria and along the Adriatic coast; and the much larger and more consciously Hellenic colony clustered around its national church of S. Giorgio dei Greci in Venice. It embraced Corsica along with the rest of the Genoese dominions, but not yet Sardinia; Piedmont, but not the Valle d'Aosta (where French, not Tuscan, was the official language); Trent and Trieste, where the urban patriciates used Italian culture to defend their privileges against German-speaking bishops and governors; and the greater part of Dalmatia, including the independent Republic of Ragusa (Dubrovnik), where all educated Slavs learned to write Italian. Finally, it overlapped with Greek culture in Crete and the Ionian Islands, notwithstanding the efforts of Venetian bishops and administrators to prevent marriages between Catholics and Orthodox.

A scene from Vecchi's 'L'Amfiparnasso', a commedia dell'arte story tricked out with witty madrigals, first performed in Venice in 1597.

The Tridentine reformation

Now that the myth of a 'pagan' Renaissance has at last been banished from the realm of serious historiography, it is not surprising to observe that many of the creators of High Renaissance and Mannerist culture were also men of deep religious piety. This piety, nurtured in part by their exposure to the recently recovered works of the Greek Church Fathers, was also inspired by the efforts of the 15th-century humanists like Lorenzo Valla and Marsiglio Ficino to infuse Christianity with the wisdom of the ancients. It was further reinforced by the example of those many persons of all social ranks – women as well as men, humble as well as high born – who attained the highest levels of spirituality: Paola Antonia Negri, the 'divine mother' of the Angeliche, Battista da Crema, the spiritual advisor of the founder of the Barnabites, Caterina Fieschi of Genoa, Caterina de' Ricci of the Prato Dominicans, Girolamo Savonarola, the 15th-century Ferrarese prophet of Florence, and Filippo Neri, the 'Socratic' apostle of mid-16th-century Rome.

This piety was manifested in many different ways. Some of its adherents retired from the world and became hermits, like the aristocratic graduates of Padua who settled at Camaldoli in the first decades of the century. Others, like the Venetian statesman Gaetano Contarini, sought to project their personal religious experiences into the world by assuming an active role in civic affairs. Some gathered in informal circles around such charismatic figures as the emigrant Spanish theologian Juan de Valdés in Naples and the Petrarchan poetess Vittoria Colonna in Viterbo. Others sought to restore the observance of an original rule in one or another house of an old religious order – the Dominicans of S. Marco in Florence and Lucca, the Olivetans in Pavia and all those Augustinian congregations that heeded the call of their energetic general, the patron of the Neapolitan artists and writers, Girolamo Seripando.

None of these religious leaders paid much attention to the formal theology still taught in the seminaries of the principal religious orders, for it had come to consist of little more than refinements upon formulas set down two or three centuries earlier and proved capable of generating nothing more relevant to the problems of 16th-century Italy than interminable quarrels about the still hypothetical doctrine of the Immaculate Conception. Few religious leaders took much interest in the formal structure of the Church. The reputation of the conventual and mendicant orders that had been responsible for the religious revivals of the 10th and 12th centuries had by now sunk to a level that fully deserved the bitter satire of Machiavelli and Aretino. Bishops and abbots seldom resided in or even visited their sees and abbeys, which they regarded chiefly as a source of income while they engaged in more important activities elsewhere. Often the same cleric was bishop, abbot, cannon and rector of a long list of benefices. When occasionally a man of conscience attempted to fulfil his pastoral duties, he found himself powerless to act in the face of the exemptions enjoyed by almost all the ecclesiastical institutions within his jurisdiction.

Realizing, however, that religion was still of great concern, both to 'the most rough and simple men' and to 'the most profound men of letters', the religious leaders of the early 16th century set out to create new forms of corporate religious life more consonant with the needs of their times. Some of these organizations were patterned on the guilds and the lay confraternities of the 14th- and 15th-century communes. Others represented the institutionalization of what had begun as informal groups of friends, like those who gathered around the Basque immigrant Ignatius of Loyola in Rome to found the Society of Jesus (1540). All were primarily concerned with promoting – or, more exactly, augmenting – the spirituality of their members. To this end they engaged in common liturgical ceremonies, like the Oratorians' pilgrimages to the paleo-Christian shrines of Rome. They transformed the still inchoate rites of the sacrament of Penance into a means of spiritual direction. They worked out patterns of methodical prayer, like the Jesuits' 'spiritual exercises', with which to assure the constant progress of the individual to ever higher levels of religious sensitivity. At the same time, all were committed to propagating the spirituality they engendered among themselves to others through works of service and charity. The Genoese, and later Roman, Oratory of Divine Love built and administered hospitals. The Theatines taught secular priests to become pastors. The Capuchins preached in public squares. The Barnabites provided elementary education for poor children. The Archconfraternity of the Visitation of Rome took care of abandoned orphans. The Archconfraternity of S. Giovanni Decollato ministered to condemned criminals. All buildings erected for these activities conformed to the highest contemporary standards of architecture and painting.

Yet those who promoted piety on their own initiative found it increasingly difficult to ignore the formal structures of the church. Ever since Pope Nicholas V had adopted humanism as the chief ideological support for religion and Pope Leo X had made literary as well as political accomplishment a chief criterion for promotion in the Curia, the Church of Rome had become identified with what became in the age of Mannerism the national culture of Italy. After a catastrophic experience with two Catalan popes and after one disappointing experience with a Flemish pope, the century-long process of Italianization was brought to fulfilment. The Church of Rome became the most eminent, or at least the most visible, pan-Italian national institution, to which all the states and all the great families turned in search of employment for their favourite sons. When Pope Paul III, turning from the

St Ignatius Loyola (1491–1556), founder in 1540 of the Society of Jesus, the largest missionary order of the Tridentine Reform. The armour refers to Ignatius's early life as a soldier and to the Jesuits' military spirit of loyalty to their captain, Christ.

either directly through Venetian book dealers or indirectly through such apparently innocent manuals of piety as the crypto-Calvinist *Beneficio de Cristo*. The theologians of Italy were baffled by the questions raised by the Protestants; the answers they suggested ranged from strict Augustinianism to semi-Pelagianism. A few accepted the answers given by Luther, Calvin, Melanchthon, Bullinger or even the Anabaptists. Several – most notably Lelio and Fausto Sozzini of Siena, from whom derived the later Socinians of Poland and the Netherlands – raised questions concerning the nature of the Trinity that not even the Protestants had considered. When the philo-Protestants then deduced from these answers propositions that were antithetical to the very existence of the established Church, and when they began speaking no longer as individuals but as members of organized communities – in the Veneto, at Modena, at Naples, at Siena – several of the civil governments became alarmed and issued anti-heresy decrees. Finally, when yet another official attempt – at Regensburg in 1541 – failed to reach an agreement on doctrine with the German Lutherans, the Roman Church became alarmed as well. In 1542 Pope Paul resurrected the long-defunct office of the Inquisition for the explicit purpose of keeping at least Italy free of heresy.

The margin of theological toleration was thus abruptly narrowed. Some of those whose opinions proved to be unacceptable to the civil, diocesan or Roman inquisitors either recanted or were fined and imprisoned. Others fled abroad – to the Grissons, Geneva, Basle, Wittenberg, England, Poland, Transylvania, or to any other part of Europe in which their opinions might be judged orthodox. Still others kept their opinions to themselves and conformed outwardly to those of the inquisitors – at the risk of being denounced by the Protestants as 'Nicodemites'.

Determining which answers to current doctrinal questions were compatible with Catholic Christianity thus became a matter of great urgency. So did the long-postponed projects to correct what both Catholics and Protestants denounced as intolerable abuses in the administration of the Church. Realizing that neither the bishops, the pope, the civil governments nor even the new religious organizations could alone undertake both institutional reform and doctrinal clarification, almost all the Italian religious leaders eventually accepted, with varying degrees of enthusiam, the means finally chosen by Paul III for accomplishing both: the ecumenical Council of Trent. Their acceptance was well rewarded. After many years (1545–62) of argument with each other and with their transalpine colleagues, after frequent interruptions and after the expense and discomfort involved in long periods of residence in a small, distant, ill-supplied town, they finally arrived at a definition of Catholic doctrine – one that included the Fathers and the councils as authoritative interpreters of the Scriptures, that recognized all the books of the

traditional policy of passive toleration to one of active collaboration with the leaders of Italian religious life, promoted several of them to the rank of cardinal, they willingly accepted the call – and thereafter joined with the established church authorities in reforming the old institutions they had ignored in accordance with the standards of the new institutions they had created. Indeed, one of the old institutions turned out to be surprisingly amenable to such a transformation: the diocese. When the Sack of Rome put an end to his political career in the Curia, Giammatteo Giberti set forth, with a grant of special powers from the pope and assurances of co-operation from the Venetian government, to change his diocese of Verona from a 'benefice' into a 'church', a church much like the ones he had read about in the works of St Ambrose and St John Chrysostom. His programme was so promising that it was soon imitated by several of his episcopal colleagues – by Jacopo Sadoleto at Carpentras near Avignon, by Girolamo Vida at Alba in Piedmont, and by 'the most learned and even more pleasant and gracious' Galeazzo Florimonte at Aquino.

These efforts on the part of Italian religious reformers became particularly urgent after the writings of the Protestants began to permeate the peninsula,

Bible as canonical, that allowed for a degree of human initiative in the process of salvation, that accepted the sacraments as channels of divine grace. They also succeeded in incorporating many of the results of their own religious and ecclesiastical experience into church law, a law now binding upon all those other Christians throughout the world who chose, or were forced, to remain in communion with the Church of Rome.

Economic recovery

Political reconstruction, ecclesiastical reform, cultural elaboration – all cost money; the fact that money was available can be attributed largely to another product of the imperial peace: economic recovery. The original stimulus to this recovery seems to have come from those private men of means who, once the wars were over and the fortresses paid for, set about rebuilding their once profitable enterprises. By the middle of the century the principal Florentine commercial houses had established branches in even the smaller towns of Apulia and the Capitanata. Many businessmen took advantage of recent incorporation laws to form *società in accomandita*, which could attract capital from many small as well as from the traditional few big investors, and which permitted the resultant societies to last without changes in management for longer than the usual three-year profit-dividing period. One Florentine firm doubled its capital in eight years. The total investment in Florentine silk manufacturing rose from 15,000 florins in 1540 to 155,000 in 1590. Wool production multiplied ten-fold in Venice between 1500 and 1602 and in Pavia between 1540 and 1589. Admissions to the silk guild of Naples rose from 195 in 1561–5 to 255 in 1591–5.

What private investors initiated, governments at all levels hastened to support. Given the narrow-mindedness of many corporate owners, observed one innovative entrepreneur, the state 'can accomplish in three years what private persons, even at great expense, can barely accomplish in twenty'. Most states agreed with him. The Farnese of Parma-Piacenza certainly did. By shifting the tax burden to their less productive, and less disciplinable, feudal vassals, they enabled their more productive immediate subjects to produce so much new wealth that the state budget rose from 8,000 *scudi* to 32,000 in half a century without the imposition of new taxes.

Fortunately, this increase in industrial production was accompanied by a parallel increase in population – indeed, by the most spectacular demographic upsurge in the history of Italy between the 13th and the 19th centuries. The return of peace happened to coincide with the exhaustion of one major plague cycle, and the next hundred years were marred by only two or three local, albeit locally disastrous, outbreaks, of which by far the most severe was that which struck Venice in 1575–7. The continuing fertility of the rural population, which probably approached that of Prato where

there was an average of 6·1 inhabitants per household, made up for the inadequate fertility of the cities, where, to take Florence as an example, as much as 10 per cent of the population was composed of celibate religious and 6·5 per cent of usually unmarried domestic servants. The population of Lecce in the far south rose from 20,400 early in the century to 36,000 in 1595; that of Verona in the far north from 26,000 in 1518 to more than 53,000 in 1577; that of the province of Calabria Ultra from 29,281 in 1505 to 59,778 in 1595; and that of the city of Venice from 115,000 to some 180,000 on the eve of the plague – which, incidentally, is twice the figure for 1981.

This rise in population provoked a sharp increase in the demand for agricultural products, which in turn combined with what may have been an Italian reflection of the European inflation brought about by Spanish importation of silver from the New World, stimulating a long-term rise in agricultural prices – almost 300 per cent for grain in Milan and 75 per cent for all foodstuffs in Pavia between 1550 and 1580. Rising prices benefited not only the middlemen, for whom transportation costs remained constant, but also the producers – or so it appears from the almost equal increase of 275 per cent in wheat prices in the wheat exporting province of Apulia.

Proprietors were thus encouraged to incur enormous expenses for new farm buildings in Lombardy and Umbria. The grand duke of Tuscany hired the best architect of his day to design the farm houses (*case coloniche*) that are still one of the most characteristic features of the Tuscan countryside. The Venetian patrician Alvise Corner founded a company to drain the marshlands along the Brenta. The citizens of Ravenna, with encouragement from Pope Gregory XIII, brought under cultivation some 40,000 hectares of wasteland around the city. Where wheat yields were too low, proprietors experimented with labour-saving machines, like the seeders and harvesters introduced, not very successfully, into the Romagna or those waterless mills in Sicily of which improved designs were registered almost yearly at the Palermo patent office. They also tried out new crops – linen, *canapa*, mulberry trees and, above all, maize, which, thanks to its much higher yields, became the staple diet of all Italy north of the Apennines. The resulting rise in productivity is illustrated by the 304 per cent increase of land under cultivation over a twenty-year period in Lombardy, a similar 220 per cent increase over a fifty-year period in the Basilicata and – making due allowance for the importance of land ownership as a means of social advancement – by the comparative prices of one particular feudal domain near Naples: it was bought for 3,556 ducats in 1533, and was sold for 20,000 in 1609.

Economic recovery did not occur without setbacks, especially since, like political reconstruction, it took place in the almost total absence of a theoretical

The street cries of Rome: a detail from a lengthy series by the Bolognese artist Lorenzo Vaccaro (1580). The flourishing trades of Rome were a symptom of the revived economy of Italy in the second half of the 16th century.

framework. Far more money was poured into public and private architectural monuments than would ever be tolerated by the much richer communities of the late 20th-century USA or EEC. Much of it was drained from dependent territories, especially in the Papal States, to pay for the exaltation of the metropolis. Even more money was extracted in the form of tax grants (in Naples) or loans (in Tuscany) to fill the ever empty treasury of the Spanish monarchy. Almost as much went out of Rome to finance those projects abroad – the support of the Catholic League in France and of the imperial armies in Hungary – to which the papacy was committed in its role as head of the universal Church Militant. Money available to small rural borrowers was often so inadequate that the government had to intervene to limit interest rates, as the Venetians did in Friuli.

Usually, however, the typically Mannerist spirit of experimentation and the long tradition among Italian businessmen of accommodating themselves to new circumstances succeeded in overcoming these setbacks. When the demand for woollen cloth tapered off in Monza, the cloth-makers turned to the manufacture of felt hats. When Turkish pirates interfered with trade by sea, the Venetians and the Anconitani opened overland routes to the east through Spalato (Split) and Ragusa. When Philip II of Spain defaulted on his enormous debt in 1575, the great Genoese bankers, who had transformed Genoa into the credit capital of Europe, moved their annual money market from Besançon, in Philip's Franche-Comté, to Piacenza. They then ostentatiously opened negotiations with Philip's chief enemy, William of Orange. Thus they soon obtained a promissory note on all that was owed them – at a lower interest rate but with still more guarantees on tax revenues in Castile and on silver shipments from America. Similarly, when in the late 1580s many of the smaller private banks failed, the formerly charitable Monti di Pietà became interest-paying and interest-receiving credit institutions, and several states established public banks, one of which, the Banco di Santo Spirito, is still in operation. When in the early 1590s the whole Mediterranean basin was struck by a series of severe crop failures, the grand duke of Tuscany sent ships to buy grain in Poland and the Ukraine – at no small profit to himself and to the Florentine bankers who helped finance the operation.

The age of consolidation

While experimentation in the economic field continued to reward its practitioners, in several other fields it reached a point where it was becoming an end in itself, rather than a means to further creativity. Mannerist sculptors could still get away with stringing bas-relief sea shells and apples across the façades of Palermo; Mannerist architects could continue for another half century to carry out the plans of 1549 for the jutting portico and the outsize cornices of S. Paolo Converso in Milan. But the spatial and anatomical deformities in the frescoes with which Pontormo covered the interior of S. Lorenzo were too much for Vasari to understand; they were subsequently destroyed and are known today only from the surviving sketches. Similarly, the withered limbs and squirming seascapes that Vasari's pupils painted on the panels of the Studiolo in the Palazzo Vecchio in Florence surpassed the tolerance even of the 'Mannerist' prince who commissioned them, Francesco de' Medici. And the pretentious depiction of the heavenly hosts that Vasari himself began painting on the underside of Brunelleschi's dome annoyed the magistrates in charge of the cathedral so much that they hired as successor not the faithful disciple Vasari had designated, but the first prophet of Roman anti-Mannerism, Federico Zuccari. Similarly, Mannerist comedians tried again and again to put life into one version after another of the well-worn plots of Plautus and Aretino, only to discover that the audiences would pay attention to nothing but the musical interludes (*intermezzi*) – which consequently became a dramatic form of their own.

Painters had much less trouble finding a way out of the dilemma. They simply turned again for inspiration to what the Mannerist theorists themselves had constantly recommended as guides to lasting artistic values: the images on early imperial Roman coins (which the archaeologists were turning up in ever increasing numbers), the frescoes of Correggio in Parma, and the *istorie* of Masaccio and Andrea del Sarto, which Vasari made his students at the Accademia del Disegno copy for practice. They soon learned once again to create unified, three-dimensional spaces, anatomically correct human figures and geometrically arranged forms. The architects adopted much the same solution: they returned to Bramante, Brunelleschi and

177

Vitruvius. Jacopo Barozzi da Vignola perfected at the church of the Gesù in Rome the severely sober forms he had tried out earlier at the villa of Pope Julius III. When his criteria of sobriety turned out to coincide with the Jesuits' criteria of visibility, audibility, size and economy, the Jesuits' own architects spread them all over Italy in the form of the barely disguised dormitories of their elephantine colleges.

The philosophers and scientists found the problems rather more difficult. What corresponded in philosophy to experimentation in the arts consisted of an ever expanding mass of new data: the writings of the ancient mathematicians recovered by such non-university scholars as Niccolò Tartaglia and Federico Commandino; the strange plants and animals brought back by the overseas explorers; the abdominal muscles of which the anatomist Gabriele Faloppio found 'not a trace in Galen'. Such was the quantity of this new data that collecting it became a major enterprise; and many of the collections were subsequently displayed, along with pieces of ancient and modern sculpture, paintings and miscellaneous bric-a-brac, in especially constructed 'museums' and 'galleries' for the admiration, rather than for the instruction, of impressionable guests. Some of the contents of these collections were turned over to the encyclopaedists, who published them under such arbitrary titles as Tommaso Garzoni's *Professions* and Luigi Contarini's *Delightful Gardens*. But whenever they fell within the borders of an established academic discipline they had somehow to be accounted for, lest the discipline itself be swept away by one of the alternate metaphysical systems then being worked out by such speculative geniuses as Bernardo Telesio, Francesco Patrizi and Giordano Bruno.

The *summa* of the philosophers turned out to be somewhat brittle. Not so that of the politicians. Any doubts still nurtured in the late 16th century concerning the merits of what had been accomplished a generation or so before were drowned in the massive response to Machiavelli's dilemma about the morality of politics. Politics and religion were perfectly compatible, proclaimed the new political philosophers, and no religion was more conducive to good and successful government than the Catholic. Venice had always acted on commission from St Mark and Pope Alexander III, and would continue to do so even if it should revert, as Paruta recommended, to its former policy of territorial aggrandizement. Whatever could not be fitted into a Christian re-reading of Tacitus was locked up in a cabinet called 'reason of state', to which princes alone were given access. Since most princes sincerely strove to keep their consciences clear in such matters, no one objected – not even their occasionally riotous subjects, who always blamed not them but their subordinates for what seemed to have gone wrong.

The *summa* of the ecclesiastical reformers were yet more solid. Whatever the Council of Trent had not managed to resolve was turned over to committees of experts who soon produced equally definitive solutions to all the theological and ecclesiastical problems that were of concern to Italians: the corrected calendar that still bears the name of Pope Gregory XIII, the definitive church history of Cesare Baronio, the precise calculation of the relation between grace and free will and between temporal and ecclesiastical authority by Roberto Bellarmino, a catechism, an expansible *Index* of heretical books, and standard editions of such fundamental texts as the Roman Missal, the Breviary, the Vulgate Bible and the works of the Church Fathers. At the same time, the bishops who had been converted to Tridentine Catholicism during the last enthusiastic days of the Council set out to put its decrees into effect. Some of them, with the help of local scholars and artists, adapted these decrees to the particular historical traditions they found in their dioceses – Gabriele Paleotti in Bologna, Paolo Bisanti in Friuli and Braccio Martelli, the Florentine patron of the Academy of the Transformati, in Lecce. Others, most notably Pope Pius IV's young nephew Carlo Borromeo in Milan, stamped out, with the help of professional reformers brought in from outside, whatever local traditions they deemed to be incompatible with the decrees. All of them summoned diocesan synods, personally visited the parishes and monasteries within their jurisdictions, erected seminaries for the training of a new generation of collaborators and prescribed penalties for recalcitrant members of the older generation.

The friars, nuns and cathedral canons who had been the beneficiaries of the pre-Tridentine régime howled – and sometimes threw stones – in protest, but the mass of the faithful responded with enthusiasm. Charmed by the appearance of models of sanctity in the very episcopal palaces where they least expected to find them, and captivated by the public relations techniques that the bishops had learned from their humanist rhetorical texts, they founded countless new confraternities, organized processions, turned Carnival into a preparation for Lent and built ever more churches, chapels and hospitals. They endowed and staffed the most innovative of Tridentine institutions, Sunday schools, which at last brought the art of reading, Trent's prerequisite for a full Christian life, within the reach of even the rural poor. They turned up by the thousands to hear such popular and polished preachers as Francesco Panigarola. They absorbed edition after edition of such manuals of practical piety as Mattia Bellintani's *Mental Prayer* and Lorenzo Crupoli's *Spiritual Battles*. And they applauded as the censors and the inquisitors rooted out not just heresy, which by then had all but vanished, but what Trent denounced as 'superstitions' and what modern anthropologists hail as 'popular religion': the three-day pentecostal orgies in Cuneo, the nocturnal witch-hunts in Friuli, the bull-resurrecting ceremonies in the Veneto backwoods.

In one field, historiography, those who meant to write theoretical *summa* made the mistake of ignoring

The zoological museum of Ferronte Imperato: an illustration from his 'Dell Historia Naturale Libri XVIII' (Naples, 1599). Such collections became common in late 16th-century Italy and were a manifestation of a growing scientific interest in the natural world.

current practice, thinking that they had only to repeat what had been said about history by the ancient rhetoricians and forgetting that the rhetoricians themselves had paid no attention to the practice of their own day. The historians were thus forced to resort to the traditional Renaissance method of surpassing the models; and this they did with such success that no one dared write other histories of the Italian cities for another century. In another field, poetry, the theoreticians could fall back on an ancient *summa* by an author who did indeed take account of all the poetry that his contemporaries regarded as 'classic': Aristotle's *Poetics*. Once it had been translated into Latin and Italian and bolstered with adequate philological and philosophical commentaries, the *Poetics* enabled the theorists to dictate to the poets. True, these theorists often quarrelled among themselves about what Aristotle actually meant and about what he would have said if faced with yet uninvented forms of poetry such as the currently popular madrigal. They also spent much time and paper trying to fit such obviously great modern masters as Dante and Ariosto into Aristotle's categories. Still, their dominion was so absolute that only one major poet managed to escape it, and he emerged rather bruised. That was Torquato Tasso, who happened to be a learned critic as well as a gifted poet and was therefore able to yield to some of the criticisms provoked by the manuscripts he circulated all over Italy and to defend his rejection of others. After several bouts of insanity, caused in part by the critical furor that surrounded him, he finally produced the second greatest Italian epic: *Gerusalemme Liberata*, a fantastic reconstruction of the first crusade. But most of the would-be poets were terrorized into reducing the Petrarchan heritage to what Edoardo Tateo describes as 'cold, austere, introverted [lines] totally divorced from reality' – or into abandoning poetry altogether for poetics. Their retreat was encouraged by the imposition of similar theoretical categories upon every other aspect of contemporary life: letter writing, ball playing, dog raising, hunting, cooking, gymnastics and 'civil conversation'.

179

Stefano della Bella's title-page for Galileo's 'Dialogo' (1632), the first popular exposition of the Copernican theory. Its publication caused Galileo to be brought before the Inquisition and forced to recant his arguments insofar as they conflicted with Scripture.

Cracks in the systems

Fortunately, the heavy hand of theory occasionally fell short of the ambitions of the theorists, and the rules prescribed for one discipline were almost never transferred to another. Whoever had the imagination to combine two or more disciplines could create a new one at will. Bernardo Buontalenti and Giambologna put together architecture, sculpture and botany and turned gardens into a work of art – first at the Boboli in Florence, then at Pratolino, then all over Europe. Battista Guarini put together comedy, tragedy and pastoral poetry and produced one of the most original and most acclaimed of Renaissance dramatic works, the *Pastor Fido*. The friends of the wealthy music patron Giovanni de' Bardi put together dramatic poetry, architecture and what his music master Vincenzo Galilei claimed to be a revival of Greek monody and they came up with what has remained one of the most popular of all Italian arts, the *dramma in musica* or opera.

The philosophic system began to crack when its various defenders failed to supply a satisfactory explanation for motion – and, more practically, for a correct projection of the course of cannon balls. The crack widened as the astronomers and the mathematicians became increasingly dissatisfied with the role assigned to them by the physicists as mere calculators. This dissatisfaction led one student of both mathematics and Aristotelian physics, Galileo Galilei, son of the musician Vincenzo, finally to abandon Ptolemaic astronomy, which agreed with Aristotelian physics only in locating the earth at the centre of the universe. He adopted instead both the Copernican heliocentric astronomy and Copernicus's faith in the physical reality of the universe he had described. Galileo thus combined two formerly separate disciplines, physics and astronomy. To them he added what had previously been relegated to mere artisans – technology. In 1609 he pointed toward the heavens the combination of lenses which he and a group of mechanics had constructed according to the theory of optics. When he found that the resulting observations could be explained only in mathematical terms, and not in syllogisms, the entire Aristotelian-Ptolemaic system collapsed – as well as all the Platonic, Neo-Platonic and hermetic systems that had been proposed as alternatives. The old cosmos staggered on in the seminaries of some religious orders and in a few university faculties for another century; but among all the educated heirs of humanist culture, ecclesiastical as well as lay, the new cosmos rapidly replaced it.

Meanwhile, the political, religious and economic bases upon which both the systems and the counter-systems rested began to show signs of severe strain. The wars against the Austrian archdukes and the Adriatic pirates sapped the economic as well as the military strength of the Venetian Republic, while the War of Monferrato (1613–17) put an abrupt end to half-a-century of peaceful co-existence among the Northern states. The controversy over the Valtellina – at once Spain's land route to Germany and Venice's land route to France – caused the incipient Thirty Years War to spill across the Alps. The sudden recurrence of long-forgotten pre-1530 horrors – the sack of Mantua in 1630 for instance – turned the Spanish monarchy from the guarantor of internal peace into the protagonist in a pan-European war on Italian soil. Similarly, the abortive attempt of Pope Paul V to browbeat Venice over a question of rights to ecclesiastical property led to a rapid dissipation of the prestige that the papacy had won as the leader of reform in the decades after the Council of Trent. It also revealed the anachronistic nature of its claims to supreme temporal jurisdiction, claims that were vigorously attacked by the ascetic Tridentine theologian of the Venetian Republic, Paolo Sarpi. The papacy's efforts to recover some of its prestige during the succeeding pontificate of Urban VIII were based on the mistaken premise that the pontificate of Leo X was still a viable model. Papal and

The coronation of the Virgin Mary: a chariot for a pageant in Reggio Cathedral (1674). Baroque artists were spectacularly inventive in their designs for the theatrical machinery of religious festivities.

curial megalomania, combined with a withering of the reforming spirit among the descendants of the Tridentine reformers, encouraged a substitution of private for corporate forms of religiosity. Diocesan synods became rarer, more and more ecclesiastical institutions escaped episcopal jurisdiction, ever greater numbers of clergy were charged with non-pastoral occupations – some 110 of them in Lecce alone by 1625. The focus of religious devotion shifted away from the parish mass towards miracles, hagiolatry, indulgence-counting, rosary recitals and the studiously promoted pageants of the religious orders.

Finally, guild regulations and soaring insurance rates for large vessels frustrated the efforts of Italian, and especially of Venetian, manufacturers to meet the challenge of the cheaper if qualitatively inferior products with which Dutch and English merchants began flooding the eastern Mediterranean in the first years of the 17th century. Syphoning off capital into private as well as public debt funds (*luoghi di monte*) and into the sky-rocketing deficits of those states expected to pay for the Spanish war effort – from 835,000 ducats to 1,802,000 in Naples between 1616 and 1626 – left

Italy's industrial economy particularly ill prepared to face the European recession that struck suddenly in 1619–21. In response to a 26 per cent drop in prices, wool production in Milan alone fell by 90 per cent in a decade. The number of printing firms in Venice dwindled from 125 to 40. A return of the plague from 1630–3 wiped out much of the demographic growth of the 16th century in most Northern cities. Another plague in 1656–7 radically reduced populations in the others – 55,000 died out of a population of 73,000 in Genoa, 250,000 out of 450,000 in Naples, 40,480 in five months in Rome alone, according to contemporary estimates. Domestic demand collapsed just at the moment when war and protective tariffs were cutting into the foreign demand for Italian manufactured goods. Much of what capital still remained was sidetracked into feeding the entire populations that were kept shut up in their houses, unproductive, for months on end by quarantine regulations. The shock was such that Italy did not begin to emerge from a long-term economic and demographic depression for another hundred years.

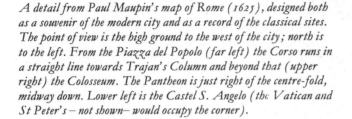

A detail from Paul Maupin's map of Rome (1625), designed both as a souvenir of the modern city and as a record of the classical sites. The point of view is the high ground to the west of the city; north is to the left. From the Piazza del Popolo (far left) the Corso runs in a straight line towards Trajan's Column and beyond that (upper right) the Colosseum. The Pantheon is just right of the centre-fold, midway down. Lower left is the Castel S. Angelo (the Vatican and St Peter's – not shown – would occupy the corner).

The Baroque

Most Italian governments made considerable efforts to meet the crisis. They ordered committees of experts to find ways of preventing the peasants of Pisa from leaving their fields, and preventing the free communes of Naples from spending over half their annual income in interest payments. They covered their own soaring debts by selling demesne lands as feudal domains and then permitting the inhabitants to redeem them; by fixing exchange rates for debased coins imported from other states and then debasing their own coins; by rewarding pre-paying tax farmers with civil jurisdiction and by reconverting their funded debts at lower interest rates. Since no one could think of any better remedies at the time, no one objected – no one, that is, except the people of Palermo, Naples and Apulia, who rose in revolt in 1647, and the citizens of Messina, who did the same in 1674. But these uprisings were products of extraordinary circumstances: the severe internal crisis of the Spanish monarchy provoked by the secession of several of its constituent members after 1640, the attempt of the French monarchy, once freed of its involvement in the Thirty Years War, to tear up the Mediterranean settlement of 1559, and the appearance of a charismatic popular leader in Naples in the person of the fishmonger Masaniello. By combining a policy of repression with one of prudent reconciliation and seeking the sympathy of the various sections of the population rather than playing on their mutual antipathies, the viceregal governments emerged stron-

ger, less impeded by local constitutional bodies and, eventually, more popular than before.

More important, all the governments, together with all those individuals and institutions that aspired to the exalted rank of patrons, responded to the crisis in a typically Renaissance manner: instead of cutting back, they increased their investments in the arts. Unemployed artisans were put to work building the Villa Poggio Imperiale above Florence (which served no more productive a purpose than housing the dowager grand duchess) and digging yet another rectilinear boulevard, appropriately named after the enterprising

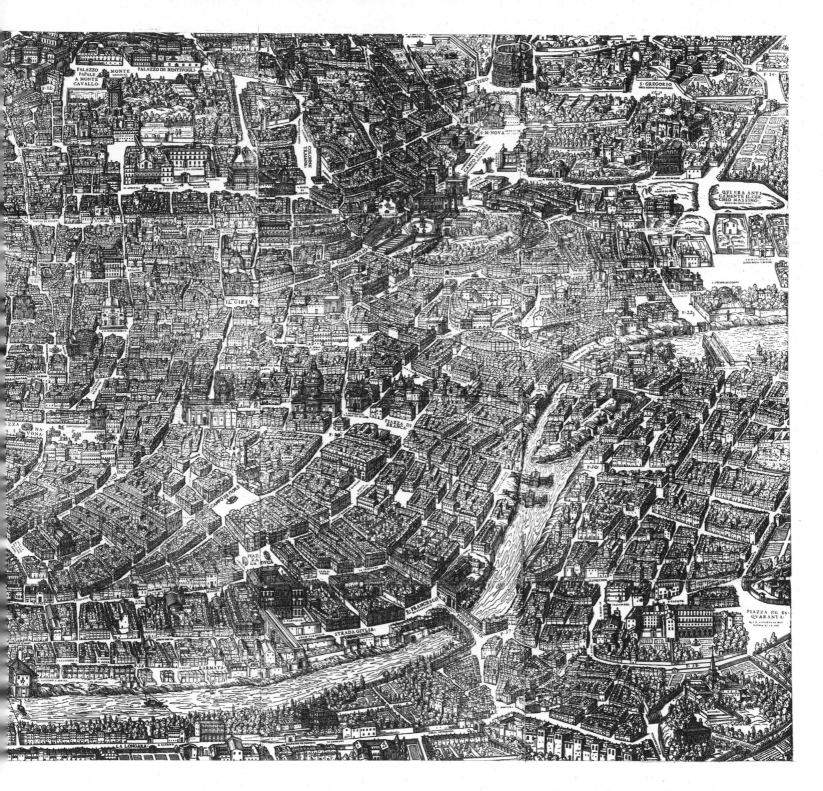

viceroy Manqueda, through the walls of Palermo. The three hundred-odd silversmiths of Naples were kept busy with such technically exigent displays of costly ingenuity as Gian Domenico Vinaccia's solid silver panorama of a procession in honour of St Gennaro. The owners and employees of some five thousand workshops in Rome were charged with completing the still unfinished urban planning projects of previous pontificates. They then went on to transform the rest of the city into the succession of stage sets that made it, when fully illustrated in a score of printed guide-books, the greatest tourist attraction of the day.

Art had long been used to manifest glory. It was now used also to cover up weakness. Those Venetians and Florentines who could afford the price of admission could forget about economic depression by attending the new commercial theatres, like the San Cassiano (1637) and the Pergola (1656), which thereafter replaced private and princely palaces as the homes of creative drama. The Barberini could forget about the increasing reluctance of great powers to include the papacy in their deliberations by having their artists make their emblem, the Barberini bees, crawl first up the twisted columns of Bernini's great *baldacchino* in St

Peter's and then across dozens of façades all over Rome. The Chigi could find solace for the failure of the diplomat who was the head of their family to gain admittance to the European conference at Westphalia in 1648 by paying scores of musicians, sculptors, grandstand-builders and float-designers to celebrate the great contribution to Catholicism he made after becoming Pope Alexander VII: the conversion of the wealthy and petulant Queen Christina of Sweden. The grand duke of Tuscany, with the help of his scientist brother Leopoldo, comforted himself for the loss of his claim to his wife's inheritance in Urbino by gathering Galileo's disciples into the informal Academy of the Cimento, thus re-establishing his city of Florence as a centre of the most advanced scientific activity of the age. The Theatines compensated for the metamorphosis of their name into a synonym for 'bigotry' by sending their gifted philosopher-architect Guarino Guarini to add even more sumptuous façades to their churches in Messina and Modena and to transform Turin into a northern version of Rome in brick. The Jesuits made up for their questionable role in the condemnation of Galileo and for their part in the persecution of the Galilean brothers of the new teaching order of the Scuole Pie by sending their most polished preacher, Paolo Segneri, into the still barely Christianized villages of the Apennines. They also commissioned their most elegant writer, Daniele Bartoli, to divert attention from the defects of their Italian schools to the spectacular success of their missions in China, Japan and America.

The artists themselves, however, were motivated chiefly by the desire to amaze, startle, inspire, and to overcome all the previously recognized limitations of artistic expression. Pietro da Cortona prised open the ceilings of Palazzo Barberini in Rome and Palazzo Pitti in Florence so that his spectators could gaze upward through swirling clouds to infinity. Gian Lorenzo Bernini, in his sculptures *David* and *Apollo and Daphne*, both in the Borghese Gallery, Rome, showed the figures at a split-second in the midst of action. In Rome too, Francesco Borromini made the façade of the Oratory of S. Filippo Neri in the Chiesa Nuova undulate and the lantern of S. Ivo della Sapienza spiral upward from the top of the cupola. Mattia Preti turned the young John the Baptist into a playful four-year-old with nothing but a tiny elongated cross to remind him of his future career in the desert. Guido Reni all but abolished landscape in order to fix Atalanta in a pose exactly contrary to that of Hyppomenes just at the moment when she stooped to pick up the apple. Salvator Rosa let his stormy landscapes swallow up the minuscule shepherds and fishermen hidden among crashing breakers and dark forests. Jacopo Ligozzi painted botanically correct flowers – and medically correct skulls and aged flesh.

All this was done in the name of the 'ideas' supposedly abstracted from the masters of the High Renaissance by such art theorists as Giovanni Pietro Bellori and such literary theorists as Scipione Errico. But they did so with such a profusion of technical virtuosity and thematic originality that they won over – as they learned from – the many non-Italian artists, from Nicolas Poussin to Hans de Jode and Jusepe Ribera ('Lo Spagnoletto'), who helped make Rome the art capital of Europe. So studiously did they violate the rules they proclaimed and so iconoclastically did they make fun of the models they pretended to follow that they were denounced by critics in the late 18th century as 'baroque' – the name thereafter applied to them.

Baroque writers and artists sought to increase the rhetorical force of their work by surprising and shocking the audiences they were trying to inspire and teach. To this end, they carried the geometric forms prescribed by their masters of the age of the Carracci to their limits – by twisting straight lines into convex and concave curves; by combining circles with progressively receding hexagons, like those over Guarini's Chapel of the Holy Shroud at Turin; by stretching circles into ellipses, like those of Bernini's S. Andrea al Quirinale; and by fitting ovals into round-angled rectangles, like those of Borromini's S. Carlo alle Quattro Fontane. They exaggerated the natural realism prescribed by Caravaggio to the point where Carlo Dolci managed to turn even Jesus into a wholly convincing incarnation of passive pathos: slightly parted reddish lips, slightly watery eyeballs and delicately tapered fingers. They juxtaposed logical antitheses, played on double meanings, strung out extravagant metaphors and infused accepted forms with inappropriate subjects – as Giuseppe Artale did when he addressed a Petrarchan sonnet to a flea crawling on his lady's nude breast. They incorporated the real into the purely imaginary, painting stucco to look like marble, inlaying marble to look like painting and putting lions next to two-headed beasts – like those that still look down on meetings of the Florence Provincial Council from Luca Giordano's ceiling in Palazzo Medici-Riccardi.

All the representatives of Baroque culture thus joined in abolishing one of the most essential Renaissance critical principles, the distinction between the true, the false and the *verosimile*, and in putting in its place Torquato Accetto's principle of 'honest deception'. In the theatre they did away with the distance between actors and audience – with such success in the case of Carlo de' Dottori that his tragedy *Aristodemo* is worthy to be ranked with Shakespeare's *King Lear*. Even historians were encouraged, by the most prestigious *ars historica* writer of the age, Agostino Mascardi, to 'invent' truths if they found documented truths boring. The archaeologists and antiquarians who flourished on the ruin of Renaissance municipal historiography were too fascinated by the parchments and stones they uncovered to bother fitting them into historical theses. The Galileian scientists of the

Cimento and even of the more speculative Accademia degli Investiganti of Naples were too fascinated with the specific data revealed by their tireless observations to bother with the less empirical aspects of their master's methodology – with the happy result that they avoided complications with the defensive officials of the Holy Office. They repeated with ever more refined instruments Evangelista Torricelli's experiments with a mercury tube. They repeated with ever more powerful telescopes the observations of Saturn's rings that the Dutch mathematician Christiaan Huygens had dedicated to their patron, Leopoldo de' Medici. They examined the decaying flesh of the hundreds of different domestic and exotic animals that Francesco Redi collected at Pisa, before and after exposure to the fly-filled air. They hiked through the hills of Tuscany and Calabria in search of fossils and rowed round the harbours in search of corresponding living marine fauna. If all this seemed to suggest that atmospheric pressure accounted for the effects formerly attributed to a 'fear of a vacuum', that the planets moved in a matterless void about the sun, that living organisms were generated not spontaneously but from 'seeds', that matter was composed of atoms rather than of four elements – in a word, that Aristotle and Descartes were wrong and that Galileo and Democritus were right – that was something for others to worry about.

Arcadia

However, even deception eventually lost its charm, and in 1690 a group of poets and critics in Rome founded a new academy for the explicit purpose of getting rid of it. They called the academy 'Arcadia' in honour of Virgil and Sannazaro, whom they held up as exemplars of good poetry in opposition to the 'Marinist' poetry characteristic of their century. So timely was their initiative, and so quickly was it buttressed by theoretical treatises and critical literary histories, that 'colonies' of Arcadia soon sprung up in all the cities of Italy, which thus became, in the words of one promising 'shepherd' (*pastor d'Arcadia*), Ludovico Antonio Muratori, a single 'literary republic'. Arcadia engendered very little real poetry, with the possible exception of the frequently performed tragedy *Merope* of the Veronese historian and critic Scipione Maffei. But it did produce reams of correct Virgilian and Petrarchan verse and many editions of the long-neglected pre-Baroque Italian literary classics. It thus paved the way for the successful adaptation of Renaissance forms to the particular social and aesthetic problems of the generation of Giuseppe Parini, the first great poet of the Italian Enlightenment. Similarly, when the architects of Sicily were summoned in 1693 to reconstruct the cities of the south-east that had been destroyed by an earthquake, they decided – apparently independently and with very little guidance from the art centres of the mainland – that the elegance required by the municipal reconstruction committees could best be

effected by toning down the forms they had been taught to regard as rhetorically indispensable. At the same time, in the centre of Italy, Ferdinando Fuga and Alessandro Galilei began returning for inspiration to the window-casings and simple columns of the Florentine High Renaissance. When commissioned to erect façades in Rome worthy of the Florentine ancestors of Pope Clement XII, they imposed what they claimed to have been a continuous and uncontaminated Florentine tradition in the very heartland of the Baroque – for example, at Palazzo Corsini and S. Giovanni in Laterano.

Baroque art still exerted a considerable fascination, particularly in the Venetian version that Giambattista Tiepolo was spreading all over the Veneto and southern Germany. But by the 1740s Italian artists had reached a point in practice that was not far removed from the theory proposed to them a decade later by the immigrant German archaeologist and philosopher Johann Joachim Winckelmann. The rebuilt streets of Catania, Noto, Ragusa and other Sicilian towns turned out to be faithful anticipations of the Neoclassical constructions that were soon to spread from Rome, still the art capital of Europe, as far as the royal palaces of St Petersburg and the courthouses of Ohio.

Deception was thus found to be less effective than the truth. The greatest theatrical designer of the age, Ferdinando Bibbiena, accordingly abolished the 'metaphor' that had once drawn spectators onto the stage and built new stages that projected the action out among them. Deception was also found to be psychologically frustrating, and increasing numbers of courageous men of letters began to opt for the undisguised truth. It was one thing to mask atomism in the form of an updated translation of Lucretius and to republish the works of Galileo as 'language texts' for the Crusca lexicographers. But as early as 1670 one Agostino Scilla of Messina felt impelled freely to denounce all the 'caliginous abstractions of the metaphysicians' that persistently misrepresented the thousands of specimens in his fossil collection as something other than what his senses assured him they were: genuine remains of once living animals. By the 1690s the philosophers of the Medinaceli Academy in Naples were seriously discussing the theses of Grotius, Descartes, Leibniz and many other hitherto unknown authors of Northern Europe, whose works poured into Naples – and, through the efforts of that tireless international letter-writer, Antonio Magliabecchi, the founder of what later became the Biblioteca Nazionale, into Florence as well. It was enough, proclaimed the eminent physician Antonio Vallisnieri, just to laugh at the remnants of Aristotelianism. For the 'obstinate defence of Aristotle had put the minds [of Italians] to sleep', and 'maintaining sterile sophisms and erroneous ideas' had prevented them from adding substantially to the available body of 'certain knowledge' (*Dialoghi ... insetti*, 1696). It was positively pernicious, observed the

Neapolitan author of a treatise on pastoral visitations, to suppose that the Tridentine Reformation had accomplished its purpose, for most priests in the rural areas of the kingdom were no better informed about Christianity than the peasants whose life they shared. The religious level of most laymen, observed Ludovico Antonio Muratori in his treatise *Well-ordered Devotion*, was such that they could not defend themselves against the sponsors of practices that he considered un-Christian, such as the blood-oath on behalf of the doctrine of the Immaculate Conception. Several bishops and theologians reacted to these revelations by refurbishing the long-neglected ideals and instruments of Trent, particularly diocesan synods; they thus prepared the ground for the introduction of what has since been called the 'Catholic Enlightenment' into Rome itself after the election of its most eminent representative, Pope Benedict XIV, in 1740.

If deception was counterproductive, then the truth might be actually useful. Such was the thesis proposed to the antiquarians of Italy as early as the 1670s by the itinerant Benedictines of the Parisian congregation of Saint-Maur and then promulgated, in volume after folio volume of historical texts, by their greatest Italian disciple, Muratori. For the truth about the past could at last free Italians from the domination of an eternal present, and the truth about the present, which Muratori expounded in detail in a subsequent essay, *The Defects of Jurisprudence*, could enable them at last to construct a better, or at least less defective, future. Such was the thesis also of the founders of the Venetian *Giornale de' Letterati*, the first of the many literary, scientific and eventually political journals that were soon to narrow considerably the gap between writers and readers. Italians, the editors proclaimed, stood to benefit from being kept informed of all the new truths about all subjects currently being discovered in all the countries of Europe, and they pledged themselves to perform this service by providing their subscribers with critical reviews of all the latest books. Much the same thesis was sustained by Pietro Giannone, the illustrious representative of the lawyer-intellectual class that had come to dominate the civil administration of the Kingdom of Naples. Only by resuscitating the work of patient historical inquiry exemplified by his 16th-century model, Summonte, said Giannone, could modern Neapolitans rid themselves of such abuses as ecclesiastical immunities that still marred their otherwise advanced civil society. He went into exile rather than yield to the violent protests his revelations aroused by covering over his theses. Giannone's compatriot, the philosopher Giambattista Vico, agreed, despite his aversion to the current interest in the natural sciences and notwithstanding his demand for a return to the literary and ethical values of Renaissance humanism. For, he warned, unless the 'philosophers' of the present age of enlightened monarchy were fully aware of how much effort had been required to lift them out of the barbarism that marked the age of Homer and the age of the Goths, barbarism might easily return.

Meanwhile, the death of the last Habsburg king of Spain in 1700, the accession of the first Bourbon king, Philip V, and the counter-claim by the German descendant of the Emperor Charles V's brother, once again turned Italy into a battleground for the great powers – particularly after the Austrian conquest of Milan and Naples provoked a series of counter-offences inspired by Philip V's wife, Elisabetta Farnese, heiress of the Duchy of Parma-Piacenza, on behalf of her son, who eventually reconquered the Kingdom of Naples. The few resources that had been accumulated during a century and a half of relative peace and not dissipated during the succeeding century of economic depression were rapidly consumed by the marches and counter-marches of Spanish, Austrian and French armies, which Italians could do nothing to prevent.

When, forty-eight years later, the powers finally decided to take their quarrels elsewhere, the political face of Italy had been substantially altered. The Venetians had earlier lost Crete, after an expensive thirty-year war; they had now been robbed of their short-lived but still more expensive conquests on the Greek mainland. Naples and Sicily had been deprived of their viceroys and united, for the first time since 1502, under a single resident monarch. The Spanish hegemony in Northern Italy had been replaced by an Austrian hegemony. Tuscany had become, after the extinction of the Medici in 1737, an appanage of the consort of the empress in Vienna. The Duchy of Milan, now under an Austrian governor, had been expanded in the east by the addition of Mantua and shorn in the west of the cities of Alessandria and Novara. The Duchy of Savoy-Piedmont had grown by a third in western Lombardy and had been elevated to the rank of a kingdom by the annexation of Sardinia, which thus passed from the Catalan to the Italian sphere of culture. As Italy then entered into another half-century of peace and stability – to the relief of Italians, but not because of any concerted action on their part – the disciples of Muratori and Giannone and of their even more vociferous successors suddenly found themselves in a position to introduce some of the profound changes in the social, political, economic and religious order of their various states that they had come to regard as both possible and necessary. The age of Arcadia gave way to the age of the reforms.

·V·

THE AGE OF
ROMANTICISM

1750-1860

THE MIDDLE OF THE 18TH CENTURY, like the years around 1530, marks a period of calm after turmoil and the establishment of an order that was to last for many decades. Under the Treaty of Aix-la-Chapelle, Austrian domination was strengthened. Lombardy was ruled directly from Vienna. Other dukedoms nominally independent were connected by family ties with the Austrian house of Habsburg. Piedmont, Venice and Rome remained autonomous. Sicily and the South (known as the Kingdom of the Two Sicilies) were under a Bourbon monarchy heavily dependent upon Spain. This was an age of reforms, in which enlightened rulers, notably in Lombardy and Tuscany, attempted to solve the problems of widespread and acute poverty, an excessively wealthy clergy, and barbaric judicial systems.

For the most part the boundaries of mid-18th-century Italy endured until 1860. The French Revolution sparked off isolated uprisings; the invasion of Napoleon was enthusiastically greeted by many liberals. They were rapidly disappointed. By 1810 the French ruled the entire mainland but it was clear that Italian interests would always be subordinated to those of France. The unpopularity of the new governments strengthened the independence of native thinkers, forcing them to turn their hopes to Italian self-determination. None the less, many of the changes made by Napoleon – the beginnings of a system of public education, common obligations of military service in all territories and the imposition of a single legal code – were not only beneficial in themselves but were absorbed into the ideals of Italian patriots at the outset of the Risorgimento.

The fall of Napoleon was followed by the return of rulers who did their best to nullify changes introduced by the French. But there could be no real return to pre-Napoleonic Italy. The peninsula was divided into eight separate states. French domination was replaced by Austrian. The repressive new régimes soon caused many Italians to regret the end of Napoleonic rule. The movement for unity and independence – ideals upon which all Italians could agree, even if they disagreed about the terms by which they should be realized – made slow progress. Only the unlikely collaboration of Garibaldi, a revolutionary leader of genius, and Cavour, a shrewdly realistic politician with the weight of Piedmont behind him, finally brought it to fruition.

Some have been tempted to see a reflection of this historical progress in the cultural move from Neo-classicism, as embodied in Canova, Batoni, Alfieri and Cimarosa (cosmopolitan, enlightened, rational) to Romanticism, represented by Manzoni, Leopardi and Bellini (which was nationalist, nostalgic and charged with emotion). Such links are more apparent than real, but Romanticism, indeed, became in many ways deeply identified with the struggle for national identity, and in the operas of Verdi it achieved one of those universal utterances in which a whole tradition, popular as well as intellectual, finds passionate voice.

The South never shared
in either the political responsibility or the intellectual ferment that marked the North. From 1738 to 1860 (with a brief Napoleonic interlude) the Spanish-descended Bourbon monarchy ruled with a strong if erratic hand. In 1751 Charles III ordered Luigi Vanvitelli to design a palace at Caserta, between Rome and Naples. The exterior of this vast and magnificent building is influenced by Neoclassicism, then just coming into fashion; the interior, most notably the grand staircase (*right*), is the last great achievement of the Baroque in Italy. Its splendour was intended to impress the visitor with the power and prestige of the Bourbon dynasty. (1)

Cities: unity and diversity

Although the movement toward Italian unification was gathering strength at the beginning of the 19th century, Italy's cities remained as they had been for centuries – highly individual centres of culture with sharply contrasting ways of life.

Naples from the sea, with the Castel S. Elmo on the hill to the left: after the fall of Napoleon the restored monarchs of the Kingdom of the Two Sicilies returned to the autocratic methods of the *ancien régime*. The final years of the Bourbon dynasty – called by Gladstone 'the negation of God erected into a system of government' – were notorious throughout Europe for corruption and repression. (2)

Venice: the last decades of the republic (it ended in 1799) were marked by political laxity, a world-wide reputation for licentiousness and the end of a remarkable artistic flowering. This painting by Francesco Guardi shows the pope blessing crowds in the Campo S. Zanipolo. Verrocchio's famous equestrian statue of Colleoni is visible on the right. (3)

Milan in this period was characterized by intellectual vitality: Volta, Manzoni and Foscolo lived and worked there. Architecture flourished and benefited from an interest in town-planning. Piermarini's Teatro alla Scala (*above*), built 1776–8, is one of Italy's most distinguished Neoclassical buildings. (4)

Rome continued to attract artists and tourists. Now they were drawn by the modern city as well as by the classical antiquities. This Carnival scene (*left*) by Pinelli illustrates the new taste for a romantic, colourful life that had vanished from the cities of Northern Europe. (5)

191

The age of revolution in politics was an era of chaste refinement in the arts. Neoclassicism, a style with a European vogue, was perhaps most at home in the land that had produced classicism itself.

Parnassus (*left, above*), painted by the German Mengs (1761) on a ceiling in the Villa Albani, Rome, embodies Winckelmann's new ideals: 'noble simplicity and calm grandeur'. Although vapid when set beside the vigour of Baroque – prolonged by Rossi in the Villa Borghese, Rome (1782; detail *left, below*) – it was Mengs who attracted the attention of Europe. (6, 7)

Neoclassicism found its finest Italian exponent and Italy her most famous sculptor in Antonio Canova. His tomb for Alfieri (*right, above*) includes a personification of Italy in mourning for the tragedian. *The Three Graces* (*right, below*) inspired a poem by Ugo Foscolo. Although in 1797, to escape the French invasion, Canova had fled to Vienna, where he made the tomb of Maria Christina (*opposite*), he later became one of Napoleon's admirers. (8, 9, 10)

VXORI · OPTIMAE
ALBERTVS

A mourning procession, consisting of the three ages of man, moves solemnly towards the door of death: Canova's tomb for the Archduchess Maria Christina of Austria, in Vienna. Napoleon invited Canova to Paris in 1802 and the sculptor made several portraits of him and of his family, including (*right*) his sister Pauline Bonaparte Borghese as Venus. (10, 11)

Passionate melody

Of all the arts it is opera that most dominates our impressions of 19th-century Italy. A succession of composers of genius created a repertoire of highly expressive works, totally Italian in character, that appealed to every level of society.

The flowering of Romantic opera was initiated by Rossini, here shown (*right*) in about 1815, the year of *The Barber of Seville*. His brilliant career was brief – although he lived until 1868, he wrote no operas after *William Tell* (1829). Donizetti (*above*) wrote 64 operas before his premature death in 1848. He speed of composition was phenomenal – the final act of *La Favorite* (1840), one of his finest works, was written in a single night. The presiding genius was Verdi. His early works roused passionate admiration partly because they were held to embody aspirations to national independence. *Far right:* Pauline Viardot as Azucena in *Il Trovatore* (1853). (12, 13, 14)

The Teatro alla Scala, Milan, was from the time of its building (1776–8) an opera house with a European reputation. This view of about 1830 (*above*) shows the auditorium as it appeared when Donizetti and Bellini were staging their early operas here and Verdi was attending performances as a student. Opera houses were prominent in the lives of all 19th-century Italian cities not only as musical but also as social centres. The auditorium was brightly lit and the audiences talked throughout performances, much to the annoyance of foreign visitors – and composers. (15)

The Risorgimento's aims of unity and liberation from foreign rule were achieved by the brilliant talents of a diverse range of personalities. The two very different men most directly responsible for the movement's triumph were the prime minister of Piedmont, **Cavour** (*top, right*), a devious diplomat of genius, and **Garibaldi** (*bottom, centre*), a charismatic military leader introduced to the cause of Italian liberty by **Mazzini** (*top, left*). The republican Mazzini was elected to the first Italian parliament, but felt unable to swear loyalty to the king, **Victor Emmanuel II** (*top, centre*). But long before political unification the heroes of Italian culture had united the peninsula in popular devotion. **Manzoni's** efforts to create an Italian literary language made him an apostle of unity (*bottom, right*). The early operas of **Verdi** (*bottom, left*) were imbued with the spirit of the Risorgimento. (16–21)

V

The Age of Romanticism: 1750–1860

FRANCIS HASKELL

In 1773 Charles Burney, the historian of music, wrote that 'music still *lives* in Italy, whilst most of the other arts only speak a *dead language*'. In fact, during the hundred years or so covered by this chapter Italy gave birth to the most admired sculptor in Europe; to a novelist of equal standing to any in England or France; to her finest poet since the Renaissance; to scientists whose names (Galvani and Volta) have passed into everyday language; and to soldiers and politicians who brought her back to the very centre of universal attention for the first time since the 16th century. Yet it remains true that music was the supreme art of the period: Burney's contemporaries could enjoy Paisiello's *Barber of Seville* in St Petersburg (1782), Cimarosa's *Secret Marriage* in Vienna (1792) and Cherubini's *Medea* in Paris (1797); or they could listen to Boccherini's string quartets in Madrid and Clementi's piano sonatas in London; while later generations were to be hypnotized by the violin playing of Paganini and to weep (or laugh) at the operas of Rossini, Bellini, Donizetti and the young Verdi. It is thus hardly surprising that Italy should have made her greatest impact on the world of the late 18th and early 19th centuries through an extraordinary outburst of musical genius, which even today colours most people's vision of the period more than anything else.

In 1748 the Treaty of Aix-la-Chapelle between the great powers (France, England, Holland, the Holy Roman Empire and Spain) brought peace to Italy – peace which was to last for fifty years – and confirmed a degree of nominal independence which had not been seen since the 16th century. Spain had been expelled from Naples and the South, though she retained a controlling influence on the recently installed Bourbon Kingdom of the Two Sicilies; the direct rule of Austria was confined to Milan and Lombardy, though the Habsburgs made themselves strongly felt in Tuscany; Piedmont was wholly autonomous and powerful; Venice retained a precarious independence; while in Rome the popes were increasingly having to back down under pressures from the great powers and their Italian allies – the symbolic climax of this process was reached in 1773 when Clement XIV was compelled to suppress the Jesuits. In fact, however, well before this, under Benedict XIV (1740–58), an autonomous, if limited, series of reforms had been brought into effect even in Rome, and we will shortly see that, whatever may have

been happening in the political arena, in some cultural matters Rome began to regain an ascendancy which, for a time, she had appeared to have lost to Paris and London.

Indeed by the end of the previous century observant men in all the states of Italy had recognized that her intellectual (and even artistic) supremacy had long since been overtaken by developments in France, England and elsewhere in Europe. Foreign military intervention in the peninsula helped to disrupt stagnation; thereafter peace and stability provided an opportunity to narrow the gap. Despite the Inquisition and censorship small groups of intellectuals studied and helped to make known the work of Newton and Locke and, later, of Voltaire, Rousseau and the *philosophes*. By the 1750s, especially in Milan, Tuscany and Naples, they were themselves beginning to make serious contributions to the thought of the Enlightenment. It was, however, not until 1764 that there was published (in Livorno) the first serious book by an Italian since the death of Galileo to attract – and deserve to attract – the attention of all educated Europe (as distinct from the more restricted circles of scholars): *On Crimes and Punishments* (*Dei Delitti e delle Pene*). Its author, Cesare Beccaria, was a Milanese aristocrat aged twenty-six, and in less than a hundred pages of heartfelt, persuasive and logical prose he exposed the absurdity – as well as the cruelty – of judicial torture and the death penalty. And during the course of the demonstration he also helped to undermine the basis of the 18th-century social order. Beccaria himself was a timid man by temperament who failed to live up to the expectations of the *philosophes* when, with extreme reluctance, he took up the inevitable invitation to visit Paris; but it was largely under the impact of his book that, in 1786, Tuscany (whose government, until the accession twenty-one years earlier of Grand Duke Peter Leopold, had been renowned for bigotry and incompetence) became the first state in Europe to abolish the death penalty.

This was at a time when England's reliance on the gallows was notorious throughout the world, only to be surpassed in extent a few years later by the use of the guillotine in Paris – despite the proposals of many deputies in a debate of 1791 (during the course of which the name of Beccaria was frequently invoked) that the death penalty should be abolished along with other barbarities and anomalies of the overturned régime.

Capital punishment is rejected: the frontispiece to Beccaria's 'On Crimes and Punishments' (1764). This polemic against the death penalty was soon translated into twenty-two languages.

As early as 1768 Voltaire had noted that 'it may well be that the Italians are ahead of us', and, in the years that followed, the Italian contribution to theories of legislation, politics and economics attracted increasing surprise, attention and admiration in Paris, London, Stockholm and elsewhere. None the less, the original impulse had not come from Italy. There was, however, one branch of civilization in which Italy did not need to look to others for inspiration.

Cultural pilgrimage

Widespread and imaginative collecting of art and antiquities had been endemic ever since the Renaissance, and it had long been essential for foreigners wishing to acquire cultural sophistication to visit the churches and palaces of Rome and Venice, the Gallery of the Grand Duke in Florence and similar establishments in other cities. But in the middle years of

the 18th century new factors combined to inspire quite new developments in the acquisition and display of art. Those same travellers from the great powers of Europe – England especially but also Russia, Poland and the German states – who had formerly come largely to admire, were now showing increasing signs of wishing to buy the magnificent works of art that Italian owners showed less and less interest in retaining (or at least more and more reason for selling). Faced with the threat of a catastrophic dispersal the popes decided to intervene. Thus Cardinal Albani's collection of antique marbles was acquired by Clement XII in 1733, despite lucrative offers from abroad. But whereas at any time over the two previous centuries the reigning pope would have bought treasures of this kind for himself and his family, now – in a spirit that can only be called enlightened though it predates the spread of the Enlightenment in Italy, let alone in Rome – the antiquities were purchased for the city itself and placed in one of the palaces on the Capitol which Michelangelo had designed, though it was built long after his death, where they attracted the unqualified enthusiasm of antiquarians and visitors.

A third of a century later the pace had quickened. Excavations were yielding spectacular results; the resources of noble families were declining ever more rapidly; foreign wealth was becoming ever more menacing. In 1769 Clement XIV inaugurated a great new museum in the Vatican, and this was energetically developed by his successor Pius VI. The creation of the Museo Pio-Clementino marks the final climax of papal patronage of the arts in Rome, and constitutes one of the noblest contributions of the genius of Italy to European culture. Precedents for the opening to the public of princely collections can be (and have been) traced in quite large numbers, but the Museo Pio-Clementino was exceptional in the brilliant virtuosity displayed by a series of architects (notably Michelangelo Simonetti) who adapted and added to a group of existing buildings in order to show off the antiquities to most telling effect. Long galleries lined with standing figures led the pilgrim to some of the more outstanding pieces, just as in the city's churches carefully illuminated altarpieces glowed at the end of darkened naves; a circular room, filled with niches, was specially built to house a (largely reconstructed) Roman chariot; in the alcoves surrounding another domed hall, intended to evoke the Pantheon, stood huge statues presiding over a colossal porphyry basin in the centre; there were recesses and corridors, some lavishly decorated and others quite austere, an octagonal courtyard (containing the most celebrated sculptures in the world), a hall in the form of a Greek cross, large rooms and small, an uncovered loggia and a round vestibule – as the museum developed over the reigns of several popes, it created a setting which has never been rivalled for the clarity and excitement with which works of art have been presented to public view.

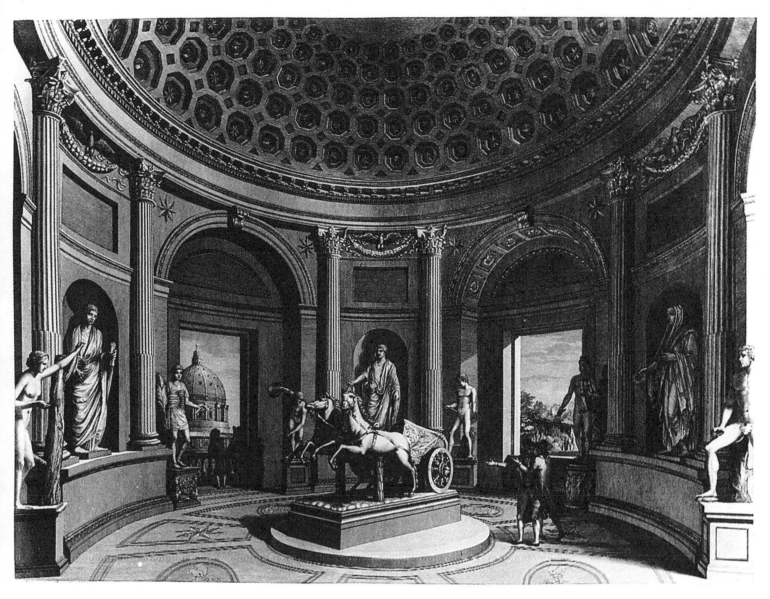

The Museo Pio-Clementino, founded in the Vatican in 1769, was one of the first purpose-built museums in Europe. Its designers contrived an impressive setting for remains of the city's classical past

– many recently excavated. In this room, the architecture, evoking ancient Rome, sets off treasures of sculpture and a reconstruction of a Roman chariot. Visitors lean out to admire the view of St Peter's.

But the Museo Pio-Clementino was not significant only for its methods of display or even for its contents. Between 1782 and 1792 Ennio Quirino Visconti, the most sensitive as well as the most erudite antiquarian in Europe, successor to his father (himself successor to Winckelmann) as Prefect of the Papal Antiquities, produced in several volumes a superbly edited and illustrated catalogue of the collections which set entirely new standards for international scholarship, though catalogues of equally splendid appearance had already been published in Florence, Venice, Naples and elsewhere.

During the period that Visconti's preservation, organization and publication of the heritage of Rome were helping to maintain the city in the very forefront of the cultural development of Europe, in Florence Luigi Lanzi and Giuseppe Bencivenni Pelli (a particular admirer of Beccaria) were revitalizing the museums

there in a spirit that – to later generations at least – may seem even more remarkable, for (among many other reforms) they were actively buying, or at least putting on display, those 'primitive' pictures (by Botticelli, Piero della Francesca, Uccello and others) which were at that time neglected or despised but which are today probably more highly regarded than any of the other contents of the Uffizi. It is hardly surprising that Lanzi (who was also a fine Etruscan scholar) wrote what is the best general history of Italian painting that had yet appeared and that the period around the turn of the century witnessed a remarkable flowering of art-historical scholarship.

For the overwhelming majority of visitors from all over Europe the Museo Pio-Clementino and the Uffizi constituted only subdivisions of the museum that was Italy as a whole. They had come to see the past, and on the rare occasions when they commented on the present

199

it was with slighting condescension. Indeed, the most admired and influential Italian artist in Rome between about 1760 and his death in 1778 was Giambattista Piranesi who combined his genius for etching the (principally ancient) glories of the city with a profitable practice of dealing in (and manufacturing) 'antiquities' – to the advantage of both foreign travellers and the Museo Pio-Clementino, for they were often more beautiful than the real thing. In fact Piranesi's awe-inspiring vision of the ruined baths and palaces in which the treasures of the museum had been unearthed, his vertiginous viewpoints and sense of scale, and especially his imaginative reconstructions of what he believed the capital of the empire to have looked like in its heyday, all probably played some part in influencing the design of the museum. Yet, as an artist, he himself was exceptional in revealing little appreciation of the formal beauty of ancient sculpture: except where topographical accuracy requires them to be shown with some precision, the world-famous statues to be seen in his prints tend to be half hidden by ruins or dizzily perched on inaccessible sites. For, unlike most of his contemporaries, Piranesi had an almost sadistic as well as a nostalgic attitude to antiquity: he loved the rough rather than the smooth; he preferred portraying bas-reliefs – on triumphal columns and arches and vases – to showing fully-rounded figures complete in themselves. He revelled in those very mutilations which he and his fellow restorers were busy repairing for their customers.

Piranesi thought of himself as primarily an architect, and the fanciful ornamentation he designed for the apse, the ceiling and the lunettes round the windows in the church of S. Maria del Priorato on the Aventine which he rebuilt in 1765–7 for the Knights of Malta make its interior one of the most elegant and attractive in Rome of the second half of the 18th century. Yet it was little visited, and it must be acknowledged that from about this period onwards there was a notable decline – both in quality and quantity – of new architecture and painting everywhere in Italy.

The arts of grandeur

The previous half-century had witnessed the erection of many of the most beautiful and familiar buildings in Rome, of which only a few need even be mentioned here: the Spanish Steps, the Fountain of Trevi and the Piazza S. Ignazio, the façades of the Lateran church and of S. Maria Maggiore. In and around Turin Filippo Juvarra had built the façade of Palazzo Madama as well as the pilgrimage church of the Superga and the country palace of Stupinigi, and both he and Bernardo Vittone had made of Piedmont one of the most imaginative architectural centres in Italy – though it was rivalled by Naples, where Fernando Sanfelice had built palaces whose staircases can still dazzle us with their beauty and daring long after the buildings in which they stand have decayed into tenements or slums.

Outside Italy, meanwhile, Italian architects had helped to transform the appearance of Munich and St Petersburg, Lisbon and Vienna. Now all this was changing. In Rome only the creation of the Museo Pio-Clementino added a building of international significance to the city; for, however distinguished, this can hardly be claimed for the sacristy of St Peter's designed by Carlo Marchionni, who had earlier built the villa designed to house the sculpture collections of Cardinal Albani, or for the superbly bombastic staircase which, towards the end of the century, Cosimo Morelli produced for Palazzo Braschi, the last palace commissioned for a papal nephew – a class of building which had given employment to the most talented architects for nearly three centuries.

The most spectacular commission of the period was also the last of its kind – not only in Italy, but in the world. In 1751 Luigi Vanvitelli was summoned from Rome to Naples to build for the king a country palace at Caserta. The example of Versailles haunted both the architect and his royal patron, and, as was to be expected of so recently installed a court, a spirit of competition played a notable part in determining the nature of the building: 'Our palace is much better, there is no comparison', exclaimed Charles Bourbon characteristically when shown plans of the new royal palace proposed for Stockholm. It was certainly bigger: indeed the vast scale required (247 by 184 metres, and twelve hundred rooms) presented Vanvitelli with the great (and not wholly resolved) problem of how to avoid making the façades too monotonous.

It is the gardens and the interior that make Caserta one of the most splendidly awe-inspiring and thrillingly designed of all royal palaces. From the moment that he entered it through the great central arch, the visitor to the king would have found himself being led between octagonal vestibules and galleries, and at every step he would have had differing and partial views of the four large courts which open up on each side, and of the vast grounds beyond which lead eventually to the Fountain of Diana and her Nymphs, some two kilometres away, behind which the great cascade crashes down the hillside. From the central octagon he would have seen not only all four courts and the cascades and formal gardens, but also the grand staircase rising dramatically to his right and then dividing into two and doubling back at the half landing. Though the ornamentation and the decoration are restrained, in every other way the palace belongs to the fantasy worlds evoked by theatre design and by the prints of Piranesi. If architecture can convey a message, Caserta proclaims loudly to the second half of the 18th century that

The frontispiece to Piranesi's 'Della Magnificenza ed Architettura de' Romani' (1761) presents his vision of the splendour of Roman civilization as a prelude to a cultural and architectural defence of Rome against connoisseurs' growing interest in Greek architecture.

DELLA
MAGNIFICENZA
ED ARCHITETTVRA
DE' ROMANI

OPERA
DI·GIO·BATTISTA·PIRANESI
SOCIO·DELLA·REALE
ACCADEMIA
DEGLI·ANTIQVARI
DI·LONDRA

absolute monarchy survives intact in all its pomp and ritualized mystery and that no concession is to be made to reform or enlightenment or even relaxation (it was, we realize with a shock, contemporary with the Petit Trianon and not with Versailles).

Elegant, but much smaller, buildings were erected in these years in Venice and many other cities, but it was only in Milan that there developed a consistently handsome style of modern architecture and a concern for town planning: it is now that Milan first assumes the role (which it has never lost) of being the proud centre of Italian intellect and fashion. It is certainly not fanciful to see its architecture as reflecting this new status, for the internationally-minded poets and philosophers who flourished under the Habsburgs took a direct interest in the buildings which were put up in such large numbers at a time when Rome and Venice appeared to be stagnating. For example, the satirist Giuseppe Parini was an adviser and friend of Giuseppe Piermarini, by far the most influential, admired and prolific (though not the most original) architect among the remarkable constellation of talent that was attracted to the city. Piermarini's compromise between new and old, his lack of interest in any distinctive Milanese style (he had been an assistant of Vanvitelli), his rather thinly-modelled, quiet and somewhat impersonal palaces which avoid both the extreme grandeur and the extreme austerity which were already popular in some circles soon led to his being despised as boring. But for the quarter-century that preceded the French invasion of 1796 he dominated private and public architecture in Milan, and his refined buildings maintain a very high standard of elegance: in the opera house of La Scala he created a monument which has convinced generations of visitors that it is the centre of the operatic world.

Painters and patrons

Italian painting was everywhere – not least in Italy – thought to be on the decline. Artists who worked in the grand manner and who had already made names for themselves before the Treaty of Aix-la-Chapelle – such as Giambattista Tiepolo (1696–1770) and Corrado Giaquinto (1703–66) – continued to produce masterpieces in the second half of the century (though these were often painted abroad), but – as with the architects – no names of comparable stature were to emerge. The last fresco in Rome to attract international attention was painted by a German, Anton Raffael Mengs. His anaemic *Parnassus* (1761) on the ceiling of the main hall of Cardinal Albani's villa is probably his least satisfactory work, and from the vantage point of today it is evident that the cardinal could have chosen any one of a number of Italians capable of producing something much more beautiful. But Mengs's ceiling, which was enthusiastically welcomed by Winckelmann – by far the most influential connoisseur as well as antiquarian and historian in Rome – appealed to a widespread longing for simplicity and for the rejection of illusionism. Its

echoes of Raphael, its antique subject matter and its turning away from the language of allegory that was so prevalent in Italian secular frescoes made it seem both new and adventurous and particularly appropriate for the decoration of a private museum of ancient art. For many other influential connoisseurs the work of Mengs came to be seen as a standard by which to gauge the art of the past, the present and the future.

Pompeo Batoni was considered to be Mengs's only rival, and had he painted in fresco or engaged in large-scale decoration he might well have won for himself the position held by the German. For his compositions lack Mengs's gaucheness, while his feeling for colour, drawing and texture was much greater, and he too exploited that vein of tempered, chastened prettiness combined with echoes of the High Renaissance which, for a time, seemed to be the epitome of a new classicism. But (even more than Mengs) Batoni was forced by economic pressures to devote most of his time to painting portraits of the international Grand Tourists, especially the English. And although these are often supremely elegant and highly evocative, they did not usually call for (or receive) profound commitments of any kind from the artist.

Other Italian painters also worked largely for the foreign market. In Venice, the views that Canaletto had been painting ever since the middle '20s declined in quality, though not in fame, towards the end of his life; but as from 1747 his nephew Bernardo Bellotto (1720–80) – who had at first worked with him – produced a series of remarkably impressive views of Dresden, Vienna and Warsaw. In many of these the artists was fascinated not just by the fine buildings, squares and parks in these cities (which had only recently been created by Italian or Italianate architects) but also by their crowded and sometimes drab side streets and by those aspects of urban life – including the life of the poor – which are so neglected in 18th-century painting of the top quality (though they are much to be seen in the many engraved collections of street cries and similar compilations). Bellotto is unusual – 'enlightened' it is tempting to claim – in showing us stall-holders and beggars, monks and nursing mothers with great freshness and intensity (emphasized by strong contrasts of light and shade), yet without sentimentality, facetiousness or (like Piranesi) an undue concentration on the picturesque. He is the Italian artist of the day who gives us our most telling impression of ordinary life in the last years of the *ancien régime*, for the drawings by Giandomenico Tiepolo, the highly talented son of Giambattista, which concentrate on such life (rather than on the brilliant fantasies for which he is better known) are caricatures and thus – like all caricatures – are both timeless and one-sided. And Francesco Guardi (1712–93), the last real master among the Venetian view-painters, seems to convey the pattern and texture of a crowd rather than to single out the individuals who compose it.

A caricature of a man wearing a domino, by Giambattista Tiepolo. Tiepolo's caricatures, like those of his son Domenico, often poke fun at social life in the Venice of the ancien régime.

Guardi was, in his lifetime, little known except to a relatively small group of local civil servants, lawyers and doctors who made up most of his clientele, and there is not the slightest reason to believe that 'the melancholy sense of the decay of Venice' which later connoisseurs have found in his pictures was noted by those who bought them from him. On the contrary. It seems likely that his appeal lay in the fact that he was not sensitive to the changing times and that his art looked back, neither self-consciously nor with nostalgia, to earlier conventions of colour and fantasy – conventions which were unaffected by the rationalism, or even by the sententiousness, which had been altering the climate of European opinion ever since he had first begun to attract attention in the 1760s. His strength lay in the fact that he was a provincial working for provincials.

Guardi was painting in what was considered to be a minor genre, but provincialism (or, rather, the bypassing of international fashions) is also to be found in many major decorative schemes of the last decades of the *ancien régime*, and it can give them a strength, beauty and conviction which seem to indicate the beginning rather than the end (as turned out to be the case) of a tradition. Thus although the huge fresco painted in 1782 by the Sicilian Mariano Rossi (1731–1807) on the

ceiling of the entrance hall of Prince Borghese's sumptuously redecorated villa in Rome does assimilate a few recent stylistic developments, it nevertheless belongs in spirit far more to the High Baroque of a hundred and fifty years earlier than to the 'classicism' of Mengs's *Parnassus* in the Villa Albani of only one generation before – or to the strident austerity of the almost exactly contemporary Jacques Louis David who, like Rossi, turned back to the legendary history of early Rome for inspiration.

A stifling tradition

Tradition, in fact, weighed heavily on all fields of Italian life – on political thought as on painting, on drama as on agriculture; society was relatively stable and, to a large extent, sheltered from the wars, ambitions and industrial changes that abounded elsewhere. There was therefore little pressure exerted on the artist for any form of radical renewal and such radical renewal as there was could meet with violent opposition. Thus the Venetian playwright Carlo Goldoni (1707–93) made a deliberate and successful attempt to reform the theatre and to substitute for the old, improvised and ruthlessly stylized commedia dell'arte fresh comedies at least partly based on observation of the life he saw around him and on the construction of credible characters. For a time his highly entertaining plays enjoyed great success in Venice and elsewhere in Italy, and the modern historian often turns to him for a lively, if not very penetrating, impression of 18th-century manners. But the traditionalists, led by Carlo Gozzi (1720–1806) – whose *Fables* later came to be so highly appreciated in France and especially Germany – attacked him with remorseless savagery: his break with the past was not only indecorous, almost sacrilegious, but even – it was implied – amoral, perhaps subversive. In 1762 Goldoni accepted an invitation to go to France for two years; he stayed there for the rest of his life. Despite innumerable frustrations in Paris and Versailles (where he gave Italian lessons to the royal children), this most unpolitical of writers, whose most potent source of inspiration was his native city, clearly found himself suffocated by the atmosphere of obstruction and anti-intellectualism that prevailed in Venice.

The autobiography and career of the tragedian Vittorio Alfieri (1747–1803) also give us a vivid impression of the self-consciousness (and the difficulties) involved in trying to shake off what was felt as the stifling and sterile lethargy of Italian life. We see him travelling restlessly throughout Europe in order to expose himself to fresh experiences of every kind: rejecting the *philosophes* as soulless; weeping over Plutarch; scornful in Vienna that the Italian court poet Pietro Metastasio should find it necessary to bow quite so humbly when addressed by the Empress Maria Theresa; dismayed in 1782 that nearly seventy years after its first production Scipione Maffei's *Merope* should still 'be regarded as a model of perfection to all

A pro-Goldoni faction disrupts a performance of a play by a rival, in protest against Goldoni's departure from Venice in 1762.

A B C D
E F G H
I K L M

Lettering from Giambattista Bodoni's 'Manuale Tipografico' (1818), published in Parma five years after Bodoni's death. It contains specimens of the large collection of types which he had put to use in his superbly designed books.

future tragic writers'; above all, trying to master an Italian literary language which barely existed (he himself was brought up in French-speaking Piedmont) by turning back several centuries to Dante and Petrarch, Ariosto and Tasso (none of whom had written tragedies which could guide him). From his autobiography we sometimes derive the impression that Alfieri was more interested in seeing his plays finely printed than actually performed on the stage. Perhaps he was right. The style that he fashioned with such difficulty only rarely has much vitality and his powers of characterization are not great, while it is not surprising that he should have been deeply impressed by the superb new standards of printing that Giambattista Bodoni (1740–1813) was introducing into book production. The memory of Alfieri stimulated a whole generation of Italians as a personal example more than as a great creator – an example of energy, of independence, of the cult of liberty and hence of patriotism.

Canova: stillness and simplicity

When Alfieri died in 1803 his tomb, which was carved by Antonio Canova, included an allegorical figure of Italy mourning over his sarcophagus – the first appearance, so it is believed, of such a figure in the visual arts. Canova (1759–1822) was the last Italian artist to win overwhelming international fame – indeed he was, during his lifetime, probably more acclaimed both in Italy and abroad than any other artist had ever been. And it is appropriate that he should have been commissioned to design the monument, for he, like Alfieri, had, by a determined effort of will, forced himself to adopt a new style which broke with current conventions – conventions within which he had in fact already excelled in his youth. Canova's break with the elaborate naturalism of his Venetian years was accomplished soon after his arrival in Rome in 1780. He renounced movement in favour of stillness, emotionalism in favour of restraint, illusionism in favour of simplicity. In theory these changes were designed to conform to the virtues of antique art which had been so influentially proclaimed by Winckelmann, and to some extent they did. But, as a number of his contemporaries recognized, Canova's finest works are rarely inspired directly by the antique. At its most moving the nature of his talent was no less 'feminine' and graceful than the 18th-century tradition which he sought to displace (his small plaster sketch models remained well within that tradition) and utterly alien to the stern, grandiose and moralizing austerity which marked the masterpieces of David at just the same time – despite the warm respect each felt for the other. Canova's exquisitely finished, delicately mannered (and, occasionally, coy) nudes, so exposed and so sexually teasing; his gracefully tender bas-reliefs; his sensitive, but non-committal portraits – all these bring his 'classicism' (if that is the right word) closer to that of David's pupils, such as Ingres and

French troops under General Championnet entering Naples on 10 January 1799. The Parthenopean Republic was declared on 23 January. Counter-revolutionaries rapidly brought about its downfall and the Bourbons returned in July. As the troops were evacuated, their leaders were captured and executed, sometimes with the connivance of Nelson who was willing to support the Bourbons' corrupt and repressive régime while they remained allies in the war against Napoleon.

Girodet, than to the great, almost violent, archaism that David (and Alfieri) had promoted. Moreover, unlike David, Canova appealed to connoisseurs throughout Europe: he pleased the uncompromising theorists of an antique revival, the fashion-conscious aristocratic collectors of England, Austria and Russia and the new, tough, down-to-earth romantics, such as Napoleon and Stendhal, who were coming to the fore in France. Canova was at his least compelling when he tried to be most forceful, and – as is often the case with very refined talents – his occasional lurches of taste can be disconcerting (this is especially true of some of his paintings and drawings), but a number of his inventions – notably the straggling file of mourning figures who make their way into the pyramid raised to honour Maria Christina of Austria in the Augustinerkirche in Vienna – are among the most moving and imaginative in the whole of Italian sculpture.

Revolution and after

Canova was prepared to use his talents to glorify both Nelson and Napoleon. Since the climax of the Reformation artists had not been expected to make political choices, but the tumults that followed the French invasion of Italy in 1796 brought about a drastically new situation. The two most famous Italian composers, Cimarosa and Paisiello, were both implicated in the disturbances directed against the Bourbons of Naples and, after these had been suppressed, Cimarosa was imprisoned for a time; a sculptor, Giuseppe Ceracchi, was guillotined for taking part in a conspiracy of radicals against Napoleon; Alfieri, writing his autobiography in Florence, refused to meet a French admirer who came to pay his respects; after Napoleon had fallen, the poet Ugo Foscolo settled in England to avoid living under Austrian rule. Artists took different sides in the scattered civil strife that broke out almost everywhere, and some – like Canova – refused to take sides at all, but French domination did ultimately (and indirectly) change the concept of Italian nationalism from a rhetorical flourish to a real political force.

All Italy was affected in varying degrees by the French incursions, but attitudes changed with events. For some the Treaty of Campo Formio (1797) under which Napoleon handed over a recently 'liberated' Venice to the dominions of Austria proved too much; for others the breaking point came with the realization that the French were far more interested in organized looting and exploitation than in putting into effect their high-sounding proclamations about liberty and fraternity; yet others were dismayed to see that Napoleon, far from encouraging the ideals of the French Revolution, was actively supporting rather conservative régimes in those states which he controlled. But many people swallowed their pride and remained faithful to him, as General and Consul and King, until near the end; and many made substantial fortunes out of the upheavals that followed his arrival.

Revolts and revolutions broke out, but lasted only briefly, in Rome, Naples and elsewhere; one of them was described in a controversial literary classic which sounds a note of clear thinking, rigorous expression, moral seriousness and tragic grandeur, not heard in Italian political or historical literature for some two centuries. Vincenzo Cuoco's *Historical Essay on the Neapolitan Revolution of 1799* was first published in 1801, when the author was aged thirty-one. He had been trained as a lawyer and had participated in the 'Parthenopean Republic' whose collapse he recorded in his book, though he was not an eye-witness of events in Naples itself. Cuoco acknowledged his debt to ancient

Napoleon, after the portrait by the Italian artist Appiani. The French invasions were enthusiastically greeted by many Italians, who believed that Napoleon brought freedom from tyranny.

historians, to Machiavelli and to Vico, and the speed of his narrative, the trenchancy of his judgments and the originality of his analysis demonstrate that he had put these mentors to valid use, even if he himself lacks the sustained control over his material which is necessary to a great historian. Although he can jump rather disconcertingly from topic to topic, his conclusions are of the highest relevance to anyone interested in the Italy of his day – or of our own. The Neapolitan Revolution failed, in his view, because it was based on abstract (and imported) ideas which bore little relation to the situation in Naples itself. The intellectuals and the people shared no common ground: 'they had different ideas, different customs, even two different languages'. Moreover the French had been wrong about their own revolution: 'they attributed to the effects of philosophy what was in fact due to the political circumstances in which their country found itself'. As an analyst of the Europe of his day Cuoco rivals Burke. His devotion to moderate, realistic reform made him influential in Napoleonic Italy and at other periods in Italian history when liberal hopes were high: today he seems to be much despised.

But Cuoco is not merely an incisive political analyst. He shares with some of the greatest historians the ability to tell an anecdote or describe a character with great precision, and yet in such a way that both

anecdote or character appear familiar to us living in wholly different circumstances. For instance, under the *ancien régime* there is an ambitious politician who wins support from his Bourbon masters through hounding the incompetent, but wholly innocent, prince of Tarsia, director of the royal silk manufactory: 'What an incorruptible judge! See the zeal, the firmness with which he confronts the prince of Tarsia, a grandee of Spain, a great official at court' – as if, comments Cuoco mordantly, 'injustice committed against the great cannot derive from the same motives and be just as base at that which is committed against the weak'. The end of the book is equally memorable. The Revolution has failed; the Bourbon authorities return. Some bargaining has to be done with the executioner: so many are to be hanged that, in the difficult economic circumstances of the time, it will be cheaper to pay him a monthly stipend rather than the usual fixed sum for every killing. The roll-call of the victims and of their last words and deeds is unforgettable – and achieves the exceptionally rare distinction in this kind of literature of being genuinely eloquent without a hint of false rhetoric.

Although Napoleon's interest in Italy derived essentially from what he could get out of it for himself, his family and for France, many Italians realized that the smashing of the jealous and tenacious dynasties and aristocratic families who had for so long divided the peninsula between themselves had helped to clear the way for eventual unity – in one of his rare notes of optimism Cuoco commented that 'the destruction of that old, imbecile Venetian oligarchy will always be a great advantage to Italy'. It had been accepted ever since Machiavelli that an Italian nation could not be brought into being as long as the international organization of the papacy laid claim to large territories in the very centre of Italy, but now two successive popes had been driven out of Rome into exile in France. It is true that unity was not brought nearer in either case (and that the second only proved to be temporary) but the precedent was significant. And in the republic (later kingdom) of Italy, which brought together the old Venetian empire and Austrian (previously Spanish) Lombardy, a group of remarkably talented writers were bringing about a striking cultural revival in the face of appalling economic difficulties. When, after the downfall of Napoleon, vindictive and embittered rulers returned from exile to reclaim their former possessions, bringing with them the censor (not that there had ever been a lack of censors) and the hangman to suppress the hopes that had flourished during the previous decade, disillusionment soon prompted action. In the light of later developments we can no longer view with quite the same enthusiasm as was once almost universal in liberal circles the enrolments into secret organizations that soon followed in the wake of the Restoration, accompanied by bizarre rituals and oath takings, all designed to bring about the transformation of existing society; nor does the achievement of having largely destroyed a rich variety of deeply-rooted cultures in the name of an almost arbitrary concept of nationalism have the same appeal for us as it did for many people in the 19th century. It would, however, be quite unhistorical to project such scepticism back to the years between 1815 and 1870 (or even 1918) and fail to recognize that the cause of Italian unity and independence attracted many of the most generous and honourable talents in all fields that flourished in Rome and Milan, Naples and Venice. Nor is it possible to discuss any aspect of Italian high culture during these years without realizing that nationalism formed an integral part of it.

Yet the ramifications of high culture had their limits. We have come to realize more and more clearly how restricted were the circles of students and intellectuals who struggled, and sometimes sacrificed themselves, for the unity and independence of Italy. The vast majority of peasants and artisans, even of merchants and members of the professional classes, were little affected by the dreams and aspirations that stimulated the creation of secret societies – though capitalists and entrepreneurs were among those who realized that unification would lead to bigger markets. Misgovernment and oppression were tolerated because they were traditional and inevitable; subordination to the pope or to Austria remained a far more natural state of affairs than the prospect of allegiance to an 'Italy' which – in Metternich's well-known phrase – had never been more than 'a geographical expression'; language and coinage

The artist encounters the spirit of ancient Rome amid the ruins of the Forum: the frontispiece to Pinelli's 'Historia Romana' (1818), etchings illustrating scenes from Roman history. The inspiration of Italy's classical past fired the imaginations of the men who in the early 19th century sought to make real the centuries-old dream of a united Italy.

differed from province to province; customs barriers separated town and town; and literacy itself was a rare accomplishment. It is not entirely perverse in a short essay on these hundred years of Italian history to attribute at least as great significance to an aria by Verdi as to all the theories underpinning the Risorgimento, for we will see later how extensive was the impact of music and how relatively limited the appeal of political change.

'How beautiful are the fine arts', wrote Alessandro Verri (with his brother Pietro and Beccaria one of the great figures of the Milanese Enlightenment) after a visit to the Uffizi: 'here we are giants, and the English and French are only dwarfs'. This comment was no longer true by the beginning of the 19th century – and was exaggerated even when it was made in 1767. For some four hundred years Italian architecture, sculpture

and painting had played a dominant role in the cultural life of Europe. With the death of Canova in 1822 this supremacy came to an end. Talented artists certainly survived, and until 1838 the most famous sculptor in the world was still to be found in Rome, but he was a Dane (Berthel Thorwaldsen) and in that year he returned to his native Copenhagen. By then, however, the Italian genius had found expression in other forms: in music, and also in literature. Writing about these presents the foreign historian with exceptional difficulties, but they must be faced, for three great writers of the first half of the 19th century – Foscolo, Manzoni and Leopardi – not only played a decisive role in recreating Italian pride and creating Italian self-awareness at a time when such a stimulus was much needed, but also help to give us an insight into Italian sensibilities which is not available to us from any other source.

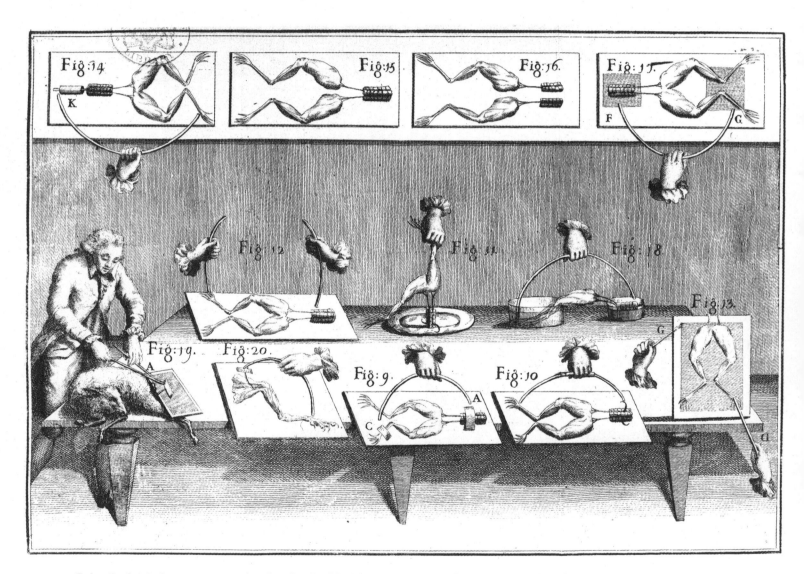

Galvani's electrical experiments: a plate from his 'De Viribus Electricitatis in Motu Musculari' (1791). The conclusion drawn by Galvani – that he had been stimulating an innate electricity in animals – was successfully challenged by Volta, who developed Galvani's observations in the construction of the first electric battery (1800).

Milanese vitality: Volta, Foscolo and Manzoni

It has already been pointed out that even during the last years of the *ancien régime* Milan was the centre for many of the liveliest minds in Italy and this supremacy became even more marked under the quick succession of régimes that followed, for it was encouraged by a tolerant attitude to fresh ideas on the part of the authorities. The vitality of Milan during these years (and even under the Restoration) has been memorably recorded by Stendhal, who had himself called Milanese on his tomb.

For a time between 1801 and 1802 the newly-created Cisalpine Republic toyed with the idea of creating in the city a Foro Bonaparte which would have been the most imaginative (but also megalomaniac) example of town planning since Bernini's St Peter's Square of nearly a hundred and fifty years earlier. Among those approached for the decoration were the finest Italian painters to have emerged in the previous few years, Andrea Appiani (1754–1817) and Felice Giani (1758–1823). Shortage of funds put an end to the project, though many fine buildings were put up in the following decade and both Appiani and Giani (especially Appiani) were extensively and very fruitfully employed by Napoleon and members of his court.

The welcome given by Milan to talents of all kinds can be seen in the honours paid to Alessandro Volta (1745–1827), most of whose life was spent at the nearby University of Pavia. It cannot be said that this great inventor and pioneer of electrical studies had in any way been neglected by the Habsburg authorities of the *ancien régime*. On the contrary. As his fame grew and quickly became international, he was treated with immense respect, but his greatest achievements occurred when Austrian rule was on the verge of collapse. Volta had studied the experiments of the distinguished Bolognese anatomist Luigi Galvani (1737–98), among them one carried out in 1786 (published 1791) which showed that when a dead frog was attached to the two wings of an arc, each made of a different metal, one of them in contact with muscular tissue, the other with a nerve, the muscles began to twitch. Galvani concluded that this was due to external stimulation of some innate electricity in the animal. Volta challenged this theory and successfully demonstrated that in fact the nerve and muscles of the frog had merely acted as a conductor for the electricity generated between the two dissimilar metals of the arc. He then proceeded to construct a primitive electrical battery on the basis of the conclusions he had drawn. This battery was shown to Napoleon, and Volta was among those who in 1801 attended the Congress of Lyon held to endorse the republic of Italy. Galvani's end was very different. He had refused to take the required oath of allegiance to the Cisalpine Republic, and he died in poverty.

It was in Milan that Cuoco published his *Historical Essay* in 1801, and it was there that six years later Ugo

Ugo Foscolo: his poetry was fuelled by a patriotic fervour that led to him becoming politically suspect. When the Austrians entered Milan in 1813 he fled to Switzerland, never to return; he died in London in 1827.

Foscolo (1778–1827) published his *Dei Sepolcri (Tombs)*, the greatest Italian poem for more than two hundred years. Foscolo, whose mother was Greek, was born in Zante in the Ionian islands. He moved to Venice in 1793 and at first welcomed the arrival of the French, though his admiration for Napoleon soon became very qualified. He had drawn attention to himself with an epistolary love novel *The Last Letters of Jacopo Ortis*, much influenced by Rousseau and Goethe. *Dei Sepolcri* was inspired by a French law, which was soon applied to Italy, enforcing burial in public cemeteries outside city walls, and Foscolo said that his verses were written 'to demonstrate the influence exerted on the customs and independence of nations by memory of the dead'. His poem is the finest contribution to the culture of urns and cypresses which assumed such importance all over Europe in the second half of the century; it also celebrates the great men – Dante, Michelangelo and Galileo – as well as recent heroes who could serve as an example to the new Italy, men such as Alfieri and Parini (the Milanese poet who had devoted much of his talent to satirizing aristocratic idleness and selfishness but who, at the end of his life, when asked to join in the cry 'Death to the aristocrats' is reported to have answered 'Long live the republic, but death to no-one'). The strength of the poem derives from its combination of moral seriousness, characteristic of all that was finest in the late flowering of the Italian Enlightenment, with a sentiment of melancholy which is at times slightly self-indulgent but which none the less just avoids self-pity. The framework is classical, but the world of Homer is approached with a new, personal sensibility which owes little to conventional antiquarianism, as can be seen in the beautifully grave lines with which the poem closes:

> *Un dì vedrete*
> *mendico un cieco errar sotto le vostre*
> *antichissime ombre, e brancolando*
> *penetrar negli avelli, e abbracciar l'urne,*
> *e interrogarle. Gemeranno gli antri*
> *secreti, e tutta narrerà la tomba*
> *Ilio raso due volte e due risorto*
> *splendidamente su le mute vie*
> *per far più bello l'ultimo trofeo*
> *ai fatati Pelidi. Il sacro vate,*
> *placando quelle afflitte alme col canto,*
> *i prenci argivi eternerà per quante*
> *abbraccia terre il gran padre Oceano.*
> *E tu onore di pianti, Ettore, avrai*
> *ove fia santo e lagrimato il sangue*
> *per la patria versato, e finchè il Sole*
> *risplenderà su le sciagure umane.*

[One day you will see a blind beggar wandering under your age-old shades and stumbling through them to the tombs where he will embrace the urns and ask questions of them. The secret caves will moan, and the tomb will tell of Troy twice razed and twice splendidly risen above the silent ways so as to render yet finer the final trophy of the fated sons of Peleus. The sacred bard, soothing those tormented souls with his song, will immortalize the Argive princes through all the lands which are embraced by the great father Ocean. And you, Hector, will receive tear-stained honours wherever blood shed for one's country is deemed holy and is mourned and as long as the Sun returns to shine over human miseries.]

Foscolo refused to collaborate with the Austrians when they returned to Milan after the collapse of Napoleon and he settled instead in London where he captivated Whig society and laid the foundations for that English devotion to the cause of Italian freedom and unity whose political consequences were to be so significant in later years.

Among the young writers who had come to know and admire Cuoco and Foscolo in Milan was Alessandro Manzoni (1785–1873) who – largely on the strength of one novel – has become celebrated in Italy as the greatest Italian writer since the Renaissance. Like so many of his contemporaries Manzoni had mixed feelings about the French invasion, and the superb poem he wrote on Napoleon's death in 1821 will inevitably recall to the English reader Marvell's 'An Horatian Ode upon Cromwell's Return from Ireland' in its celebration of a very great man, without wholly commending his policy – or personality:

> *Fu vera gloria? Ai posteri*
> *l'ardua sentenza ...*

[Was it true glory? That hard judgment will have to be made by the future ...]

Manzoni spent some years in Paris during the Napoleonic period, and when he writes of the dead emperor:

> *Ei si nomò: due secoli,*
> *l'un contro l'altro armato,*
> *sommessi a lui si volsero,*
> *come aspettando il fato;*
> *ei fè silenzio, ed arbitro*
> *s'assise in mezzo a lor ...*

[He named himself: two centuries, armed against each other, turned to him in their subjection, as if awaiting destiny; he imposed silence, and as a judge sat between them ...]

it is difficult not to think of the author also as being involved in the 'two centuries, each armed against the other'. He started life as an unbeliever, and – as the grandson of Beccaria – he was the direct descendant of the greatest figure of the Italian 18th-century Enlightenment, many of whose ideals he always maintained. But he became converted to Catholicism, wrote historical dramas under the impact of Shakespeare and ended by being revered as the apostle of Italian unity.

To some extent this is understandable. In its final form his novel *The Betrothed* (*I Promessi Sposi*), which was first published in 1827, constituted among other things a deliberate, self-conscious attempt to write a masterpiece in a living Italian language that did not as yet exist. Like Alfieri before him Manzoni had to go to Tuscany in order to master an idiom and a style which would be as expressive and intelligible in Milan as in Naples, in Venice as in Rome. His triumphant success in doing so earned him a natural place among the founders of united Italy. But in other respects his subtle historical evocation of 17th-century Milan under Spanish rule recreates an Italy of superstition, cowardice, famine, plague and tyranny which could hardly have been thought inspiring by the younger generation fighting for a brighter future; moreover, the 'message' that comes through to most readers is that these terrible evils can only be overcome by submission to the will of God, and that direct participation in events is less likely to lead to happiness and virtue rewarded than is flight – unless one happens to be a well-connected saint. But to consider *The Betrothed* only in relation to its role in the creation of Italian unity is to see it from too limiting a viewpoint. Just as Gibbon claimed that Fielding's *Tom Jones* would outlive the Habsburg Empire, so it seems safe to predict that *The Betrothed* may survive the disintegration of Italy as an independent nation. No great novel relies more on the most basic of all fictional plots: two poor, virtuous, young people – Renzo and Lucia – are in love and want to get married. After meeting every conceivable obstacle they eventually manage to do so. Against their love are set the intrigues and struggles for power of a ruthless and incompetent society which quite fails to live up to the noble and high-sounding forms and rituals that it uses to disguise its greed and ambitions. The contrast between ideals and reality provides Manzoni with an opportunity to display his sometimes sardonic humour to telling effect.

Though the comparisons that are sometimes made with Tolstoy are wildly exaggerated, it is true that *The Betrothed* is surpassed only by *War and Peace* in the wholly unpedantic and wholly unforced image of the past that it brings to life – and this past was, of course, very much more distant and could not have been known to the author through immediate contacts. This remote setting of Milan under Spanish domination gives credibility to episodes and characters which would otherwise be thought of as mere fictional tools for advancing the story: the sudden conversion of an arch villain into a paragon of virtue, for instance, or the elaborate treachery of a proud woman of noble birth who has been forced into a convent against her will. Such episodes are described with an immediacy, vividness and persuasive power that show the genius with which Manzoni was able to transform the enormous documentation which he had absorbed with all the zeal of contemporary Romantic historians; yet his scenes totally lack those painstaking reconstructions of the past which are so familiar in the literature and painting of the 19th century and which now seem so artificial. Other characters in the novel belong to Manzoni's own time (or to ours) just as much as to the 17th century. Of these none is more famous than the well-meaning but vacillating and cowardly priest Don Abbondio whose (easily understandable) reluctance in the face of threats to keep his word and perform the marriage ceremony between Renzo and Lucia leads directly to all the troubles that are to follow, so that a trivial act of timidity affecting two people who, in any earlier work of Italian literature, would themselves have been considered only trivial leads us into wider and wider circles and brings before us a whole world of violence and sanctity.

Leopardi: nostalgia and regret

A third great writer – perhaps the greatest of the three, indeed perhaps the greatest lyrical poet in the Europe of his day – emerged in these years. Like Foscolo and Manzoni, Giacomo Leopardi (1798–1837), the son of a provincial nobleman who had closed the shutters of his palace at Recanati to avoid seeing the French troops who had come to 'liberate' the Papal States, was to be acclaimed for his contribution to the cause of Italian unification, and, like Foscolo and Manzoni, he was a man of vast culture and scholarship. But he touches our hearts now by his uniquely personal response to private grief. Ill health and failure in love poisoned his life, and what seem to us to be his most moving poems record unfulfilled dreams and fleeting visions of a time that once seemed full of hope but that was, as the very

The title-page of the illustrated edition of Alessandro Manzoni's 'I Promessi Sposi' (1840). By choosing to write his novel in the Tuscan dialect, Manzoni contributed to the growth of a unified Italian literary culture.

rhythms make clear, doomed to disappointment from the first. To compare the nature of his genius, let alone the scale of his accomplishment, with that of Proust would, of course, be absurd, but it is perhaps worth mentioning the name because it may just convey a hint of the most accessible aspect of his verse. 'The remembrance of things past' – a theme commonly termed 'Proustian' – plays a dominating role in his creative achievement, as is shown even in the opening lines of some of his most wonderful poems:

Sempre caro mi fu quest'ermo colle . . .

[This solitary hill was always dear to me . . .]

or

Silvia, rimembri ancora
quel tempo della tua vita mortale . . .

[Sylvia, do you still remember that time in your mortal life . . .]

or

O graziosa luna, io mi rammento
che, or volge l'anno, sovra questo colle
io venia pien d'angoscia a rimirarti . . .

[Beautiful moon, I remember that a year ago I came full of anguish to this hill to look upon you once more . . .]

– a poem which closes with the lines:

> *E pur mi giova*
> *la ricordanza, e il noverar l'etate*
> *del mio dolore. Oh come grato occorre*
> *nel tempo giovanil, quando ancor lungo*
> *la speme e breve ha la memoria il corso,*
> *il rimembrar delle passate cose,*
> *ancor che triste, e che l'affano duri!*

[And yet it helps me to recall and to relate this time of my grief. Oh how welcome in youth, when hope still has a long course and memory a short one, is the recollection of things past, even when they are sad and the pain still lasts!]

Even more 'Proustian' are the lines in which Leopardi recalls lying in bed as a child listening to the noise of a public holiday outside:

> *Nella mia prima età, quando s'aspetta*
> *bramosamente il dì festivo, or poscia*
> *ch'egli era spento, io doloroso, in veglia,*
> *premea le piume; ed alla tarde notte*
> *un canto che s'udia per li sentieri*
> *lontanando morire a poco a poco,*
> *già similmente mi stringeva il core.*

[In my earliest childhood when the holiday is eagerly awaited, when once it was passed, I lay awake, sadly, pressing my pillow; and late at night a song that was heard far off in the streets gradually, gradually died away, just in the same way my heart oppressed me.]

Leopardi could, like the greatest artists, transform his private unhappiness into a vision of cosmic grief. Some of his most memorable, and musical, effects are achieved by generalizing abstraction:

> *Così tra questa*
> *immensità s'annega il pensier mio:*
> *e il naufragar m'è dolce in questo mare.*

[So my thoughts drown in this immensity; and it is sweet to me to be shipwrecked in this sea.]

The concision and the sombre, 'witty' closing line remind us that Leopardi was a fine classical scholar, but echoes of antiquity do not with him (as they sometimes do with Foscolo) interfere in any way with the direct expression of the most spontaneous, individual feeling. To the English-speaking reader of today, who has probably been brought up on romantic 19th-century poetry, Leopardi is likely to be the first Italian poet since Dante whose genius can be felt, even if not always fully understood, with absolutely no sense of strain. He can be as concrete and 'real' as he can be abstract, and his melancholy response to life can evoke an immediate response even in those whose own attitude is the opposite of his. No previous Italian writer, artist or composer prepares us for the kind of impact he makes on first reading.

Leopardi was admired in his lifetime by small, discriminating groups in many part of Italy, for he travelled frequently between the principal cities, and he had even begun to win a reputation abroad before he died at the age of thirty-nine. But his was not, of course, the name that would have come to mind in any discussion (whether held in or out of Italy) about the greatest Italian talent of the day. That tribute would probably have been paid to Gioacchino Rossini (1792–1869).

Opera – the universal art

Italian music was, as has been already mentioned, famous and admired all over Europe (even in Paris) throughout the 18th century, and was acknowledged to be flourishing even when the other arts were little appreciated. Yet after the upheavals that followed the French invasions it seemed to many that here too the genius of Italy had finally exhausted itself. After the death of Cimarosa in 1801 the only composer of the first rank left in Italy was Paisiello, and he was in his sixties. The growing posthumous reputation – in Italy as elsewhere – of Mozart seemed yet one more proof that 'the talent of instrumental music has altogether sought refuge in peaceful and patient Germany', as Stendhal was to write a generation later, and even new composers of opera had ceased to appear.

All this changed, quite unexpectedly and with quite unexpected consequences, in 1812–13, when Rossini, then aged twenty, achieved his first outstanding successes in Milan and Venice with three comic operas and one serious one, *Tancredi*. Of the aria '*Tu che accendi*' in the latter, Stendhal could write within ten years of the opera's first production that it was 'perhaps the aria that has been sung more than any other ever in the world, and in more different places'.

If the extraordinary quality of the operatic talent that was to be brought into being by Rossini and thereafter followed up for a century or so by a succession of composers who still dominate the repertoires of the world's opera houses was unexpected to contemporaries, to the historian it appears all but incredible.

Architecture, sculpture and painting had, during their long heyday, been encouraged by wealthy and aristocratic patrons of remarkable culture, highly conscious of the role that tradition had assigned to them ever since the early Renaissance. The genius of Michelangelo, Caravaggio, Bernini or Tiepolo cannot of course be explained in this way, but the opportunities which these men were given and the discriminating enthusiasm with which they were welcomed throughout their careers allowed them and many other supreme artists to develop their talents to the utmost. Court musicians had received similar treatment. The flowering of literature which has been alluded to above also seems in the light of hindsight (and did so even to contemporaries) to be partly explicable by the huge political changes that had overwhelmed Italy, for here,

The Teatro S. Carlo, Naples, founded in 1737 and rebuilt in Neo-classical style 1816–17. Operas by Rossini, Bellini and Donizetti *had their premières here; Verdi visited Naples in 1845 for the production of his 'Alzira' in this theatre.*

of course, questions of patronage were not overriding. With the collapse of the *ancien régime* and the hopes that this raised, men of letters could feel that they were at last in a position to make a serious contribution to the cultural heritage of Italy which would be capable of extending beyond the walls of a palace drawing-room or the pages of an album of society verses. But we have many vivid accounts of the cut-throat commercial conditions which governed the production of Italian opera in the first half of the 19th century, and reading such accounts hardly prepares us for the creation of such imperishable masterpieces as *The Barber of Seville, Norma, Lucia di Lammermoor* or *La Traviata*.

We read of the incredible speed with which operas had to be composed for each new season; of the capriciousness of singers and managers, so that costumes had to accord with the whims of the soloists and sometimes whole acts might be sung in the wrong order; of the absurdities of political censorship which led to plots and characters having to be readjusted or changed at the last moment. And what perhaps shocks us most of all is the failure of the public to respond adequately to what was offered. A visit to the opera was a social, rather than a musical or theatrical, occasion. Talking in the boxes was incessant, and few members of the audience would arrive at the beginning and remain till the end. No doubt such behaviour was prevalent throughout Europe, and it is easy enough to trace reflections of it even today. But the fact that visitors to Italy all commented on it so scathingly suggests that it

was more marked in the home of opera than elsewhere.

But although not contradicting what has just been said, other contemporary accounts – notably those of Stendhal, that most uninhibited enjoyer of Italian customs do also show how deeply rooted opera had become in Italian life. Again and again operas were composed with particular singers in mind, and their absence might lead to the cancellation of some project. Reputations could be made and spread at dazzling speed so that Rossini could be welcomed like a prince in half the cities of Italy, and a new work by him could be the most important event in the life of some small town, as Stendhal wrote in his *Vie de Rossini*: 'eight to ten thousand people discuss for three weeks the beauties and weaknesses of the opera ... with all the power of their lungs'. Such conditions stimulated the production of opera, but also greatly distressed the leading composers. Once they had achieved success, Rossini, Bellini and Donizetti all went to live in Paris (from which the dying Donizetti was carried back to his native Bergamo). Verdi too was constantly threatening to retire (as Rossini did for the last forty years of his life), and as soon as he was in a position to do so, he accepted commissions only from foreign opera houses – Paris, St Petersburg and Cairo. Only when he could work as he wished did he produce for La Scala his last great operas.

Rossini was the least political of men, but none the less played his part in promoting that unity of Italy for which he cared so little – and not only on the social level, where his popularity transcended all distinctions of class. His early triumphs were achieved in Venice and Milan, but between 1815 and 1822 he worked mainly, and with outstanding success, in Naples. Venice and Naples had hitherto been the great musical rivals of the Italian schools. With far greater ease than writers such as Alfieri and Manzoni, and with absolutely none of their self-consciousness or sense of duty, Rossini was able to do for music what they did for literature and to produce operas which were as much admired in Bourbon Naples as in Austrian Milan and Venice; in papal Rome as in the Florence of the Habsburg-Lorraine grand dukes of Tuscany. And Rossini also brought Italian music back to the centre of the European stage.

As Stendhal makes quite clear, Rossini was able to catch the ears of the world through his gift for creating instantly memorable melodies. Byron, for instance, not the most musical of men, would, after breakfast, lounge about 'singing an air, generally out of Rossini'. But though he is today remembered chiefly for his comic operas, in his own time his serious works were just as popular, and they are now considered to have been of greater historical importance. Byron's mistress recalled that it was at a performance of Rossini's *Otello* – 'in the midst of that atmosphere of passionate melody and harmony' – that she told her lover that she would have to leave Venice. But his genius extended far beyond the invention of good tunes or opportunities for emotional self-indulgence.

Rossini transcended the conventions of comic opera which he had inherited. The arias he gives to his leading soloists do not merely provide an excuse for virtuosity or melody (though they certainly do so also); at their best, they illustrate character, advance the plot and create variety of mood. He is able to move with ease from the farcical to the sentimental without ever giving the impression that he does not have in mind some overall design. Not for nothing did he study and profoundly admire the operas of Mozart. He thus broke down some of the more artificial barriers which divided the differing categories of opera, and partly through his use (some complained that it was an abuse) of rhythmical repetition he introduced a feeling of unity into each of his masterpieces – and all despite the fact that commercial pressures often compelled him to 'cannibalize' earlier works. His principal comic operas have never been equalled not just for sheer high spirits, but also for speed and wit, and these ingredients were of fundamental importance in establishing his contribution to the genre. The tradition that he disciplined his singers by writing out their parts in full in order to prevent too much improvisation has been disputed – but even if false it conveys the nature of the real reforms he did bring to opera. The composer of *The Barber of Seville, The Italian Girl in Algiers, William Tell* and very many more started life as a craftsman and improviser, and he was treated as such by his contemporaries. But

he was also a true, if totally unself-conscious, artist who left a direct and profound mark on music in Italy long after he had given up composing there, and he remains today as fresh for us as he was for his earliest and most articulate admirer, Stendhal.

After Rossini had abandoned the Italian theatre at the age of thirty-one his place as the leading composer was taken first by Vincenzo Bellini (1801–35) and then by Gaetano Donizetti (1797–1848). It is through their music that Romanticism (about which there had already been impassioned debate in literary circles) makes its most valuable contribution to the culture of Italy. With them opera becomes 'operatic'. History, very often English history, is ransacked for suitably melodramatic plots and Walter Scott provides a new source of inspiration. Madness and early death take their toll. Happy endings become rare.

Bellini was born in Sicily, but his greatest triumphs were achieved in Milan. He wrote no comic operas but he learned much from Rossini, whose lyrical style he adapted into long curving lines of melting beauty. Indeed, few composers have revelled in sheer beauty of sound more than Bellini and he sometimes achieves his effects at the expense of convincing characterization. None the less the passionate scenes of love and jealousy in *Norma* (1831–2) strike a new note of emotional authenticity in Italian opera, and it is not surprising to learn that Bellini took far more trouble over the choice of suitable librettos than had Rossini and that he was to win the particular admiration of Wagner. Bellini, whose operas had first captivated the public when he was twenty-six, died at the age of thirty-four. The early death of so magical a talent is always a tragedy, and in any society less full of musical genius than early 19th-century Italy it might have proved an irreparable loss. As it was there were others of equal, and later even greater, talent waiting to take his place.

Donizetti took longer to establish himself than Bellini, but he secured a triumph with *Anna Bolena* in 1830, and in 1835 – the year of Bellini's death – his greatest opera, *Lucia di Lammermoor,* was first performed in Naples and ensured him the rights of succession. To discuss great music in such competitive terms and to grade so superficially one unique talent against another, as is being done in these pages, arouses some repugnance in the reader (and the writer) today. It is worth doing, however, for it is in just such terms that Italian operas were discussed in the early and middle years of the 19th century. *Lucia di Lammermoor* made it absolutely clear that Donizetti's abundance of melody was as great as had been Bellini's and that his power of narrative and dramatic intensity was even greater. Moreover, his range of expression was much wider. What Italian composer before him could, with equal conviction, give us the unbearable poignancy of Lucia's mad song and the brilliantly slick sales talk of the quack doctor in *L'Elisir d'amore*? For as well as his great melodramas Donizetti wrote the last comic master-

Posters advertising the premières of 'Rigoletto' (1851) and 'La Traviata' (1853), both now among Verdi's most popular operas – but 'Traviata', poorly performed, was coolly received by the public at its first performance.

pieces of Italian opera before Verdi's *Falstaff* of 1893.

By the 1840s, when Donizetti was dying of syphilis, Giuseppe Verdi (1813–1901) had established himself as the most admired and popular composer in Italy and he retained this status until his death. Posterity has fully endorsed the verdict of his contemporaries. Verdi's greatest masterpieces were composed after the period covered in this chapter, but even before 1861 such familiar works as *Rigoletto* (1851), *Il Trovatore* and *La Traviata* (both 1853), *Simone Boccanegra* (1857) and *Un Ballo in Maschera* (1859) had already been performed, and these and other early works played a crucial role in the cultural development of Italy. As very few great artists have ever managed to do, Verdi incarnated and gave not temporary but undying expression to the public issues which were of greatest concern to his immediate audiences. The cause of liberal Italian nationalism was a fortunate one. Whereas the revolutionary movements of 1789 and 1917 have left behind barely a single cultural monument of lasting consequence, the emotions that stirred Verdi's contemporaries before 1860 live for us still in the Hebrew chorus 'Va pensiero' of *Nabucco* or in the hatred of cynical

tyranny expressed in *Rigoletto*. When Italy was united in 1861 Cavour understandably persuaded Verdi to take part in the newly-formed parliament.

But Verdi's achievement was of course very much greater than the sustenance he gave to nationalism – or even to the cause of freedom. It has been suggested that his peasant birth (strictly speaking he was the son of small landowners) gave him some special insight into those fundamental, unchanging human emotions – love, hatred, the desire for revenge, the pain of separation – which he was able to express with such absolute authority. This may be. What is more certain is that for all their apparent spontaneity of effect, Verdi's operas were, even in his early years, created with extreme care. He knew exactly what he could and could not do. He cared deeply about the plots of his operas and their librettos, and he always collaborated on their production. If the subject or the treatment of the subject failed to satisfy him he refused to write the music. He supervised the staging of nearly all his works and he took a keen interest in the scenery. And though the advocates of more 'modern' music came to denounce him because he did not (until very late in life) change the basic concepts of opera that he had inherited from his predecessors – and he always retained a deep reverence for Rossini and 'the old Italian masters' – some of the views he expressed, quite undogmatically, seem surprisingly close to those of Wagner in their striving for an art form which should embrace all the others into a unified whole.

Verdi most admired those writers – Shakespeare, Schiller, Victor Hugo – who aroused his strongest feelings, while at the same time revealing the complexity of human emotions. He was a master at creating characters at odds with themselves, and as he moved from grandiose to more personal themes, he explored more and more the ways in which our feelings contradict each other or overlap or are reinforced in surprising ways. *La Traviata* – surely the finest operatic plot in existence – is more real and moving to us than any of the masterpieces by Rossini or Bellini or Donizetti mentioned above, partly because Verdi's music is even more melodious than theirs and far more evocative in the creation of character and situation, but chiefly because those characters and situations are given a past as well as a present. Moods are subtle and varying. Memories of past happiness, or unhappiness, are never far away: in this respect, but only in this respect, Verdi is close to Leopardi. A truer comparison is with Shakespeare.

Re-emergence of Rome

Among the censors who gave Verdi particular trouble was the poet Giuseppe Gioacchino Belli (1791–1863) who in 1853 insisted on changes being made to Piave's libretto of *Rigoletto*, which had been adapted from 'Victor Hugo's putrid play *Le Roi s'amuse*': he insisted on the removal of 'the ugly word *vendetta* which is most

The Age of Romanticism: 1750–1860

'*Li Piferari*' – *pipe-players from the mountains, an etching by Pinelli (1810). This is one of a number of etchings he produced illustrating folk-costumes of Rome, in response to growing interest in the 'picturesque' aspects of the modern city.*

dangerous, especially today when spoken by the people'. Such an attitude hardly prepares us for the fact that Belli had himself been a great poet of the people and in fact the last great creative spirit to emerge in papal Rome – and one of the very few ever to have been born there. But his instinct about the nature of Verdi's opera was a sure one.

The Rome in which Belli was brought up and wrote his masterpieces must have been more beautiful than at any time in its long history. During the French occupation excavations had brought to light many splendid monuments which had hitherto lain half buried. These excavations were continued after the Restoration, and a new wing (by Raffaello Stern) of quite exceptional elegance was added to the Vatican museums to house some of the statues which had been uncovered. Giuseppe Valadier (1762–1839), the last architect in a line of great names – running almost without interruption from the middle of the 15th century – to be sensitive at once to the grandeur and to the informality of the city, had designed for it the Piazza del Popolo and the gardens of the Pincio. But the artists who flocked to Rome from all over Europe were now for the first time just as fascinated by the inhabitants as by the architecture: bandits and gipsies, peasants and pilgrims are recorded in innumerable pictures of the

first half of the century; while Bartolomeo Pinelli (1781–1835) engraved scenes from the Carnival and also the folk costumes which seemed so colourful to travellers from England and France where industrial and political changes appeared to be sweeping away such relics of the past – at least from the big towns.

But Rome also had a reputation (and not only with bigoted Protestants) for being one of the worst governed cities in Europe. When Pius VII returned from exile in 1814 some of the reforms introduced by the French were cautiously retained; but as subversion spread and revolutions broke out sporadically in various parts of Italy, repression was intensified. Under Leo XII (1823–9), for instance, the Jesuits were given almost total control over education and the Jews were driven back into the ghetto. Gregory XVI (1831–46) was equally harsh, intolerant – and inefficient. Theirs was the Rome that has been immortalized in the sonnets written in dialect by Belli, who has brought the city as close to us as is the London of Dickens or the Paris of Balzac and Daumier. We see, chiefly through the eyes of the popular classes, processions and jubilees, inns and churches, epidemics and earthquakes, as well as tourists and beggars, popes and criminals. The spontaneity with which their activities are recorded is hard to parallel anywhere in European literature – and especially in the literature of Italy. Belli was a wonderfully witty and perceptive poet whose attitude sometimes of extreme bitterness, sometimes of compassion, sometimes of mockery, but always fundamentally of fascinated resignation in the face of clerical misrule was very widely shared, which is no doubt partly the reason why clerical misrule lasted so long. Belli often found it impossible to publish his sonnets (which however were widely circulated in manuscript), but this does not alter the fact that his poetry has often found particular admirers among the more reactionary members of the Vatican hierarchy.

When reading Belli's sardonic picture of Rome it is difficult for us to conceive that among the many suggestions for solving 'the Italian problem' in his day, one of the most popular (propagated by Vincenzo Gioberti) visualized the pope as leader of a federated, but independent and united, Italy which would be defended by the Piedmontese army: in the 1840s, as in the 18th century, Piedmont shared with the papacy the distinction of being the most repressive and 'unreformed' of any of the Italian states. Yet the idea had a certain perverse logic because (as has already been pointed out) the problem of what to do about Rome lay at the heart of all discussions of Italian unity, and also because only Piedmont – which had self-consciously modelled itself on Prussia – had an army powerful enough to defend the new nation. The ideas put forward in Gioberti's *On the Moral and Civil Primacy of the Italians*, first published in 1843, also made a strong appeal to that mystical and dangerous sentiment, so beloved and so widespread in the 19th century, that there existed a chosen people, superior to all others, whose destiny still had to be fulfilled.

Giuseppe Mazzini (1805–72) certainly shared this view of the Italians, and he also saw Rome as the inevitable centre of the new nation. But his Italy was to be a republic, and he constantly stressed that federation represented the greatest threat to his plans. The 'third Rome' which he envisaged would symbolize the unity and independence of Italy, and would also act as a centre for the whole of a free, unified Europe.

The Force of Destiny

These two examples, out of dozens that could be chosen, show that there were fundamental disagreements among those who were concerned with the future of the Italian states. Recruiting into the secret societies continued; revolts broke out, some serious as in 1820–1, 1830–1, and above all 1848; but there was no unanimity as to exactly what purpose was served by them or by individual acts of doomed heroism. Was Italy to be a kingdom or a republic? A single nation or a group of federated states? Were the necessary changes to be social as well as political? Were they to be imposed from above or were they to be an expression of the popular will? And what happened if – as usually seemed to be the case – the people did not particularly want change?

Certain factors dominated the scene, and the dogmatic and charismatic Mazzini who for many years was the most influential of the revolutionaries (abroad, if not always in Italy) ultimately failed because he refused to take adequate account of them. In the first place only France was powerful enough to pose a successful challenge to Austrian rule in Italy – and this meant that (as the French fully realized) France, rather than Mazzini or any Italian, was likely to have the final word in any new Italian settlement. When the French government was primarily interested in peace as it was under Louis Philippe (1830–48) the sacrifice of Italian lives was, in the last analysis, only a rhetorical gesture – though this is not to deny the heroism or sincerity of such gestures. When the French government was interested in military adventures as it was under Louis Napoleon (1848–70) it would keep its own interests essentially in mind, and those interests, as the occupation of Rome in 1848 showed only too well, were just as likely to include the appeasement of Catholic voters as the urge to strike a blow against Austria. Moreover, if France wanted a slice of Italian territory, such as Savoy, this was a necessary price to pay for her support. Some astute Italian politicians saw this – however reluctantly. Mazzini did not.

In the second place, within the Italian peninsula only Piedmont was potentially strong enough to try and impose its will on the other states. The trouble was that Piedmont's motives were very ambiguous. It was not clear whether the cause of unity meant more to her than her more traditional cause of self-aggrandizement. Nor

The triumphal arch erected in the Piazza Venezia in Rome to celebrate the return of Pius VII to the city on 24 May 1814. He had been in France, a prisoner of Napoleon, since 1809.

was her extremely oppressive régime likely to make an appeal to liberals. To add to these problems there was the vacillating character of her king, Charles Albert, who was forced to abdicate in 1849, after he had finally decided to invade Austrian Lombardy and had then been soundly defeated at the Battle of Custozza.

For all these reasons it proved as difficult for many patriots to accept the leadership of Piedmont (the most French of Italian states) as it was to accept that of France. It is true that when Daniele Manin, a lawyer of Jewish origin whose understanding of reality matched the nobility of his ideals, led a successful republican revolution in Venice in 1848, he realized that an alliance with (even submission to) the house of Savoy was essential; but it is said that when the Piedmontese army was briefly in control of Lombardy, the local peasants – hard pressed by increased taxation and other abuses – would shout '*Viva Radetsky*' (the Austrian general who was leading the victorious counter-attack).

In fact, the situation changed radically in these years. As time passed, demands for unity reached wider and wider circles so that in some of the uprisings which took place in 1848 workmen and even peasants were involved as much as students and professional revolutionaries. It cannot be said that the cause of the Risorgimento became a 'popular' movement as later propaganda tried to make out, but it is true that it did not in the end have to be forced on to an actively hostile population as would have been the case earlier. In this way some degree of social reform went hand in hand with political change, and the new nation was able to retain its (somewhat tarnished) liberalism far longer than could Germany which achieved unity at much the same time.

All this coloured the nature of independence. That independence was itself largely the achievement of two remarkable (and wholly antagonistic) men, who recognized the fundamental importance of the two pressures on Italy – the French and the Piedmontese – which have been outlined above. Count Camillo Cavour (1810–61), the prime minister of Piedmont, shrewdly acknowledged that France had to be gratified and appeased at all costs, even when this led to personal or national humiliation: hence his sending of an expeditionary force to fight in the Crimean War – a cause of no intrinsic interest to Italy, though the soldiers who died there of gangrene and bullet wounds did more for the cause of Italian unity than did most of the heroic adventurers who have given their names to streets and piazzas; hence too his impotent acquiescence when Napoleon III decided to make peace with Austria before Venice had been freed. Similarly Giuseppe Garibaldi (1807–82), 'the hero of two worlds' – South America and Italy – a republican by temperament and a simple sailor by birth who had been introduced to the cause of Italian independence by Mazzini himself and who served uneasily under him during the Roman Republic of 1848, always acted as a loyal subject of King Victor Emmanuel II (successor to Charles Albert as king of Sardinia, i.e. king of Piedmont).

Cavour, who was a genuine liberal – though not a democrat – also saw that liberal reforms in Piedmont itself were necessary if the king was to allay the fully justified suspicions about his motives which were felt in other Italian states. By carrying out these reforms and by his alliance with France and his war against Austria in 1859–60, Cavour was at last able to unite all Northern Italy (except Venice) into a single kingdom. With this achievement he would probably have been satisfied.

Garibaldi had other ideas. He could not accept the notion of an Italy without Venice (still in Austrian hands because of France's withdrawal from the war), Rome (under French protection and therefore safe from Cavour) and the South. Garibaldi captured the imagination of his compatriots and of all Europeans – from duchesses to dustmen – more than any other Italian in history. His absolute personal integrity, his tactical genius, his good looks, and above all his spell-binding personality made of him a hero in an age which lacked them. His soldiers adored him, and his very popularity with the peasants persuaded them to give their support to a cause which was not necessarily in their interest. Garibaldi was aware of this. He too had his share of cunning. Ostensibly he supported official Piedmontese policy, but when he thought it necessary he was quite ready to defy it, while still proclaiming his allegiance. The epic invasion of Sicily by him and his 'Thousand', followed by the equally astonishing capture of Naples, marks the climax of the constructive antagonism between him and Cavour. By these actions he made it impossible for Northern and part of Central Italy to remain a separate united kingdom under Piedmontese tutelage. Cavour and Victor Emmanuel (who, as a simple soldier, felt more at home with Garibaldi than with his own devious prime minister) felt compelled to invade the Papal States – though not, of course, Rome itself – in order to bring the South under control. When Parliament met in Turin in 1861 only Venice and Rome were excluded from the kingdom of Italy and these exceptions were to disappear within ten years.

The new Italy represented a decisive break with the past, most obviously in political terms. It should, nevertheless, have been clear to the perceptive observer that it still incorporated many of the values that had been the glory of the old. Some of the military operations which led up to this great moment were painted by Giovanni Fattori, a member of the most brilliant group of artists to emerge for many generations. The first session of the new parliament, as we have seen, included Giuseppe Verdi among its members. Soon afterwards he began work on *La Forza del Destino*.

·VI·

MODERN ITALY

1860
TO THE PRESENT

ITALY, at last, was free and united. But the euphoria of 1860 was rapidly replaced by uncertainty about the future. The problems facing the new nation were immense. The creation of a unified system of government and administration required heavy expenditure; Italy's industrial capacity lagged far behind that of Germany or Britain; her urban density was slight and her agricultural efficiency small; the problem of the South, backward and poverty-stricken, remained. Advance was rapid: huge sums were expended on industrialization and armaments; cities, at least in the North, grew quickly; new firms – Fiat, Pirelli and Ansaldo among them – won world-wide reputations.

Yet this was not enough to satisfy the aspirations of many Italians. The country's history as the centuries-old supreme source of Western European culture seemed alone sufficient to justify her expecting an important position in world politics. This position was, however, as yet unattained. Italy's political history between the 1880s and 1922 produced a succession of strong leaders who, promising a restoration of Italian prestige, urged Italy to seize its rightful place amid the great powers by embarking on colonial expansion. One result was Italy's humiliating defeat in Abyssinia in 1896: a bitter memory exploited by Mussolini when he too, twenty years later, began to urge his countrymen to win back their former greatness.

The shadow of Fascism falls across the 20th century and obscures the variety and vitality of modern Italian culture. Mussolini's régime, followed by the Second World War, produced a fragmentation of loyalties. Some effects of this fragmentation have been prolonged into the present; the variety of allegiances in modern politics is, at least to the non-Italian, of bewildering intricacy. South and North retain their distinct personalities. The North is as famous today as it ever was for the flair of its designers and the brilliance of its craftsmen. Italian cars, clothes and films project an image of international *chic* that has often eclipsed that of France. Italian culture has never been limited in its manifestations to Italy alone – Roman armies, humanist scholars and Romantic poets have carried it far beyond Italy's borders. The emigrations of the 19th and early 20th centuries took the Italian way of life to every city of Europe and America and beyond – 'Little Italys' everywhere fiercely preserve a sense of Italian identity – in language, cuisine and (in the case of the Mafia) even crime. Equally, Italian culture is carried out of the country by visitors: more than ever it seems true that everybody wishing to understand the sources of Western civilization feels the need to visit Italy. They take away with them an experience of the country that affects all aspects of life: pizzas are eaten in New York, Sydney and Bombay; the images of the Italian Renaissance have become a part of the world's visual currency. Italy's grip on the imagination shows no sign of slackening.

Garibaldi entered Naples

to a tumultuous welcome on 7 September 1860 (*opposite*). It was the climax of a swift campaign whose success took everyone by surprise, except possibly Garibaldi. In May he had sailed from Piedmont with his legendary 'thousand' volunteers, landing on the west coast of Sicily. In four months the ancient Kingdom of Naples, or the Two Sicilies, was overthrown and Garibaldi took possession of it in the name of the new king of Italy, Victor Emmanuel. Most of the other states had already made common cause. Soon the whole country except Venice (still held by Austria) and Rome (still ruled by the pope with French support) accepted Piedmontese leadership, and both these exceptions were removed within ten years. (1)

North and South: the continuing gulf

Unification made Italians free; it did not make them equal. In particular, nothing in the short term could alleviate the contrast between the prosperous, industrialized North and the backward, rural South.

Turin's position as the industrial capital of Italy was already secure in 1860. In 1898 a large exhibition was held there to coincide with the 50th anniversary of the granting of the Piedmontese constitution (see the tablet held by the allegorical female, *Statuto 1848*). The extension of this constitution to the rest of Italy, however, was not an unmixed blessing. (2)

Milan was the scene of one of the first aircraft shows, the Concorsi Aerei, in 1910. Monoplanes were about to overtake the older biplanes, though these were still in service in 1914. (Symbolizing Milan is the central pinnacle of the cathedral.) (3)

Pirelli and Fiat (Fabrica Italiana Automobili Torino), based in Milan and Turin respectively, put Italy in the forefront of the motor industry. *Left*: a Pirelli advertisement of 1910, showing its already vast factory. *Right*: a poster celebrating Fiat's winning both the first and second prizes in the Gran Premio d'Europa, 1923. (4, 5)

Naples could almost be called the capital of non-industrial Italy. Crippled by its long history of bad government, the South did not have the resources to industrialize and so constantly suffered in competition with the North. The teeming streets of Naples (*below* and *right*) became proverbial for overcrowding and poverty. One main consequence, emigration to the North and overseas, perpetuated the problem by reducing its resources still further. (6, 7)

Even the agriculture of the South was handicapped by the division of the land into large estates, *latifundi*, owned by indifferent landlords. Cammarano's genre painting *Leisure and Work* of the late 19th century (*below*) reflects the still basically peasant way of life, with dozens of farm labourers bringing in the landlord's harvest – while a carefree tramp trudges by. (8)

Italy Transatlantic

During the 19th and 20th centuries many thousands of Italians, the great majority from the South, left their homes to seek their fortune elsewhere. Some went only to Northern cities like Turin and Milan; others to France and England; most of all to the land of opportunity, the United States. Here the Italian immigrants, unlike those from Eastern Europe, nursed happy memories of their homeland and kept a strong sense of national identity.

'Il Libro del 'Emigrante' was a textbook published in 1860 for Italian immigrants to the USA to learn English. The jacket gives an optimistic picture of the benefits to be expected from this instruction. The immigrant arrives poor and shabbily dressed; he goes home rich and prosperous. (9, 10)

Italian cuisine has conquered the modern world as thoroughly as Italian art did in the past. The Anglo-Saxon countries, having succumbed to pasta in all its forms (spaghetti, lasagne, cannelloni) are now being conquered by the pizza. Italian wines, olives, cooked meats and cheeses are also part of the normal American diet. Here an Italian grocery in New York ('established over 90 years') opens its doors to customers of all nations. (11)

Italy transplanted. It is interesting to compare the contents of this New York shop window (*opposite*) with the Roman postcard stall shown earlier (p. 24). The expatriate selection is more self-consciously patriotic – 'Little Italy' T-shirts, Italian and Sicilian badges and records of Italian music (Pavarotti singing 'Favourite Neapolitan songs'). The foreground reminds us of one more Italian gift to the world, the espresso coffee-machine. (12)

The belle époque

The years between 1880 and 1914 were a time of increasing prosperity for many Italians: industrialization advanced; liberal reforms were introduced. Italy seemed to relax in a new atmosphere of pleasure seeking and intellectual freedom.

The liberal government of Agostino Depretis (1876–87) initiated the economic growth which brought a higher standard of living to many. This relief (*above*) from Depretis's tomb shows the king asking him to form a new government on 18 March 1876. (13)

The Socialist movement was born and flourished during the Depretis years. This poster (*left*) is for the Socialist daily paper *Avanti*. (14)

The prosperity of Milan in the *belle époque* is embodied in the Galleria Vittorio Emanuele (*right*), an elegantly splendid shopping arcade with many fashionable cafés and restaurants (Biffi's is still an important Milanese social centre). The architect, Giuseppe Mengoni, fell to his death from the roof in 1877, shortly before the Galleria was opened. (16)

Posters capture the style of the age: (*right*) fashionably dressed members of society drink Campari; (*far right*) Giovanni Pastrone's film *Cabiria* (1913), scripted by D'Annunzio, was a famous and provocative spectacular; (*left*) all the European *beau monde* flocked to the Italian Riviera; this poster advertises the delights of its principal resort, Sanremo. (15, 17, 18)

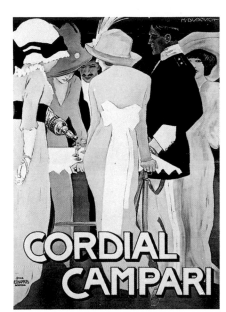

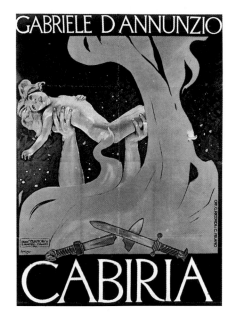

Dynamism and dreams

The two main schools of modern Italian art at the outbreak of the First World War could not have been more different: Futurism, led by Marinetti and Boccioni, sought new ways to express the dynamism of the machine age; Metaphysical Painting, by contrast, looked inwards, and produced mysterious images from the subconscious world.

Energy was at the centre of the Futurist architect Sant' Elia's vision of the 20th-century metropolis. Every aspect of city life was to be organized around one great powerhouse. His 1914 drawing (*left*) of a hydro-electric power station is architecturally innovative – his ideas had great influence after the war – and an exhilarating justification of Marinetti's belief that 'Nothing is more beautiful than a great humming power station . . .' (19)

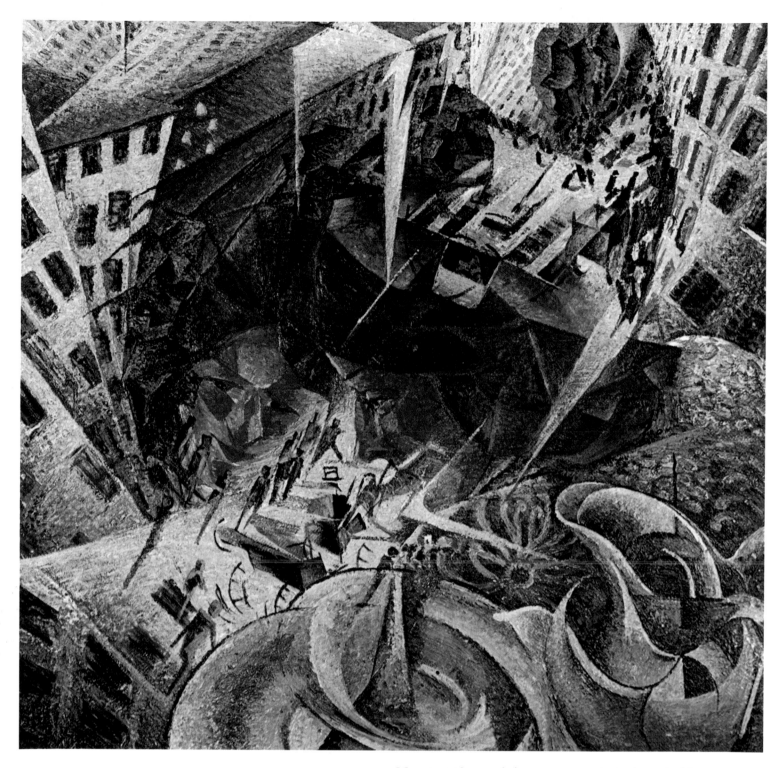

Stillness and a sense of foreboding are the haunting qualities of Giorgio de Chirico's metaphysical paintings. This example (*left*) is entitled *Place d'Italie, 1912*. Disconnected images from the world of dreams fill his carefully rendered settings, which usually embody memories of classical Italian architecture. De Chirico lost interest in Metaphysical Painting after the war, but he did go on to produce a memorable dream-novel *Hebdomeros* (1929). (20)

Movement has rarely been more convincingly evoked in two dimensions than in the paintings of Futurism's leading artist, Umberto Boccioni. *Simultaneous Visions* (*above*), like many of his works, depicts the noise and action of a modern city. Movement is shown not for its own sake, but to express what Futurists saw as the spirit of the modern age – 'universal dynamism' in Boccioni's words – an aim he achieved as successfully in sculpture as in painting. He shared the Futurists' belief in war as the supreme expression of dynamism; like Sant'Elia he died in action in 1916. (21)

The Fascist experience

Mussolini's ruthless seizure of power seemed to inaugurate a new era. Cutting through the tangle of parliamentary government, he did at first succeed in uniting a whole range of public opinion behind an active programme. But his régime soon lost all pretence of legality. His downfall was precipitated by the temptation which Italian governments had earlier (to their cost) failed to resist – aggressive military campaigns to win national prestige.

Prestige and prosperity were Fascism's twin aims; a poster (*above*) shows troops marching into Abyssinia in 1935, guided by the spirit of Italy; much-needed agricultural reforms, including land reclamation, were introduced, encouraged (*below*) by rallies urging greater productivity. (24, 25)

All aspects of life had to conform with Fascist ideals. Architecture, represented (*above*) by the Palazzo della Provincia, Naples, developed a plain version of classicism that was still capable of conveying imperial grandeur; boys were formed into the Avanguardisti – members (*below*) are reading their own paper *Giovenezza* (*Youth*). (22, 23)

Fascism's success was in great part dependent on Mussolini's energy and charisma. He was an orator of great power and his exploitation of Italy's imperial Roman heritage in the symbols and settings of his régime shows a sure instinct for powerfully emotive propaganda. At this rally in Rome (*right*) he appealed for 90,000 more young Fascists capable of carrying a gun, to bring his militia up to strength. (26)

The gift of style

'Style' is a word that recurs like a *leit-motif* in discussions of Italian design of all periods. Whether one is speaking of an Etruscan vase, a Romanesque relief, a Renaissance fresco or a Romantic portrait, there is something supremely assured in the Italian handling that makes it unique. It is just this quality that attracts admiration in present-day Italy.

A counterpoint of past and present has been an ingredient of Italian style almost from the beginning. Carlo Scarpa, at the Castelvecchio Museum, Verona (*left*), uses an old building to display medieval art with the crisp functionalism of contemporary technology. (27)

Edys stacking chairs by Olivetti: the component parts are reduced to the barest minimum before being reassembled in a way that satisfies the eye. (29)

Fiat's assembly line for the Mirafiori 131 (*opposite*), with its various robot units picked out in primary colours, has an undeniable aesthetic power that is like a Futurist dream come true. (30)

Olivetti openly challenge comparison with the past (*left*) by placing their latest piece of electronic equipment in the Baroque park of Bomarzo. (28)

232

Since 1945

The political configuration of post-1945 Italy was determined by the last years of the war, when liberal and left-wing groups competed for power over the dying body of Fascism.

The partisan movement brought together sections of society that had previously had no political definition. Women, having fought beside men against Nazism and Fascism (*above*), could not be denied a voice in the post-war settlement. (32)

Middle-class parties chose a variety of 'middle ways', often precarious compromises between more extreme views. Democrazia Cristiana (the Christian Democratic Party) represents liberal Catholicism (its poster features Liberty on a crusader's shield); Fronte Democratica seeks to unite Communism and Socialism (Garibaldi against a red star); while the Blocco Nazionale (National Block) campaigns for 'neither reaction nor revolution'. (31)

The Communists form a more closely integrated party, though significantly their ties with Russia have grown progressively weaker. Ideologically self-sufficient and deeply committed to local loyalties, Communism here has a distinctively Italian identity. *Right*: a rally (Festa de l'Unità) in Venice, 1973, proclaimed on a banner hoarding of the newspaper *Unità*. (33)

234

The post-war film grew directly out of the Italian wartime experience. De Sica's *Bicycle Thieves*, 1949 (*top*), takes an unsensational working-class story and presents it realistically. Antonioni, in *L'Avventura* (*centre*), ten years later, introduced a new sophistication which has been taken further by a new generation in such films as Pasolini's *Porcile* (*bottom*) of 1969. (35, 36, 37)

Freed from the restraints of classicism, post-war Italian architecture took full advantage of new techniques and materials. The reinforced concrete structures of Pier Luigi Nervi have an effortless beauty that owes nothing to any previous tradition. *Above:* supports for the Palazzo dello Sport, Rome, built in 1960 to seat 16,000 spectators. (34)

The Second Vatican Council of 1962–5 initiated a ruthless modernization of the Church that shocked many of its own members. Giacomo Manzù made a set of bronze panels for a door of St Peter's showing John XXIII welcoming participants – here the black Cardinal Rugambwa. (38)

235

VI

Modern Italy: 1860 to the Present

FRANCO ANDREUCCI

ITALY's emergence as a united country failed to bestow upon her that status for which her history and achievements might have been expected to qualify her. The last of the European 'Great Powers' to come of age, she was looked upon with condescension, with indulgence, and sometimes even with suspicion by the chanceries of Berlin, Paris, London and Vienna. Having for so many centuries occupied the centre of the stage, she found herself relegated to supporting roles. Economically and socially, her development could not match that of her rivals. Venice, Florence, Rome, Milan, Naples – cities that even in the years of 'decadence' had kept at least something of their past splendour – now seemed sleepy and provincial, not to be compared with the other European capitals. Italy became little more than a pleasant stop on the modern equivalent of the Grand Tour, and few people were prepared to consider it one of the principal centres of 20th-century civilization. The country of Machiavelli and Pulcinella (to name only two of innumerable stereotypes) now presents to foreign observers a kaleidoscope of cliché images – all distorted but each reflecting a true aspect of the country, from highly-flavoured, multicoloured pizzas to the posters of Sophia Loren or of Mussolini on a horse that one sees decorating the shop windows of New York's Little Italy.

And yet, looking deeper, all the great problems and dreams of the 20th century have left their mark – often their stigmata – on Italy and sometimes are even revealed to have originated there. Fascism, for example, was born and developed as a model in Italy, succeeding to the point where the term is used today to denote any reactionary, totalitarian policy. Communism, in its turn, finds in Italy its most fertile terrain in the West, even though it seems to have developed somewhat differently there than in other countries. Outside the political sphere, Italy tends to give the impression of a country of brilliant artists and designers, masters of refined and aristocratic elegance, whether expressed in superbly-engineered sports cars or the ultimate in *haute couture*.

Does there then exist an Italy which is unique, which is different from all other countries, economically backward and with a contorted and contradictory political history, but still capable of 'miracles'? About a century ago, Pasquale Villari, an acutely intelligent Italian Liberal, took strong exception to such opinions:

If we Italians consider all the branches of human civilization one by one, we shall agree that in each we are inferior to all other civilized nations. No one doubts that our science, literature, industry, commerce, education, discipline and energy for work are inferior to those of France, Germany, England, Switzerland, Belgium, Holland or America. But when we add everything together we find a certain something which persuades us that we are superior to the others. Now if this certain something exists at all, and if we want the world to believe us with consequent advantage to ourselves, we must demonstrate its existence with facts. If, on the other hand, we only want to use it as a pretext for not making the enormous effort that other nations have had to make to become civilized, then it would be better not to have this mysterious, fatal gift.

Villari's purpose here was to criticize that sector of Italian opinion which was too optimistic or enthusiastic about the difficult birth of a united Italy; and we must begin with the time of that birth to reconstruct some aspects of the complex and contradictory history that has followed it over the past century.

The new nation: 1860–76

All scholars agree that the first fifty years in the life of united Italy, from its foundation in 1861 to the First World War, are of decisive importance in the country's history. This is true for a number of reasons. In the first place, the country began to industrialize, a process whose characteristics continue today to influence Italian economic life particularly with regard to the location of the focuses of development – the so-called industrial triangle Milan, Turin and Genoa – and Italy's role in the international division of labour. In the second place, on the social and political level, the methods of construction and consolidation of the unified state produced a series of long-term effects in the relationship between governors and governed, giving rise to strong opposition and widespread

Autostrada between Siena and Grosseto. The motorway system with its breathtaking series of tunnels and bridges, has been one of the great feats of post-war Italy, inevitably provoking comparison with the achievements of ancient Rome. (39)

interest in politics whose consequences, for good or ill, are evident even today in Italian life. Finally, in the history of culture, the alliances which were born – or died – in those years and which divided Italian intellectuals have remained for a long time a point of reference for Italian culture. The example of Benedetto Croce and his intellectual heritage should be enough to testify to this: the extent and nature of his influence were much discussed during the years before the First World War and are still matters of debate.

Let us now try to reconstruct some of the aspects of the political and economic life of the kingdom that was born with the Risorgimento. At that moment, compared to those countries with which it had been in closest contact during the 19th century, united Italy was poor and backward. Whereas Prussia emerged substantially richer from its victories in the war preceding German unification, Piedmont had spent a large part of its resources on the wars of 1856 and 1859, and its annexation to the rest of Italy hardly improved its financial position. In the first place the completion of unification, with the conquest of the Veneto and the much more complex conquest of Rome, imposed a huge military expenditure; in the second place the real unification of the country – on a level of administration, transport and of infrastructures in general – required resources which were beyond the means of the new kingdom. Finally, and perhaps most important of all, the regions with which Piedmont combined to form the kingdom of Italy were poor and backward. While Piedmont and Lombardy had undergone, at least in the first half of the century, some degree of the economic and social revolution that had transformed the more advanced European countries, the Kingdom of the Two Sicilies and the Papal States, which with Tuscany made up the central and southern parts of the new nation, presented a desolate picture indeed.

If even in 1944, almost a century after unification, the English historian Christopher Seton-Watson, at that time an officer in the British army, was struck by the 'African squalor' of the South, it is not difficult to imagine what things were like in the years after 1860, when illiteracy was about 90 per cent, infant mortality a public disgrace, the communication network almost non-existent (of the 2,200 kilometres of railway that had been built by 1862, 1,600 were in either Piedmont or Lombardy) and when the unproductive *latifondi* (large estates) constituted the basic economic structure.

In general Italy appeared as a country that still had a long way to go even to begin the process of industrialization. The national income was less than a quarter of England's at the same time (though, as Gladstone pointed out, Italy's national debt was greater than England's entire budget); industrial production represented only 20 per cent of the national income; and despite the fact that about 60 per cent of the national product was agricultural, Italy's 22 million inhabitants largely depended upon imported food.

With the exception of some restricted areas of the North, productivity was among the lowest in Europe – lower than that of Russia – while in the non-agricultural sector the transition from artisan to industrial production was no more advanced than in the outlying Balkan areas of the Austro-Hungarian Empire, and commerce and services were almost totally confined to the northern and urban areas. Throughout the country, however, urban population was far less dense than that of the large European centres: in 1861 less than a fifth of the population lived in cities with more than 20,000 inhabitants.

The Italian ruling class, the landowners of the Northern and Central areas, were moderate Liberals who under Cavour's leadership had given excellent examples of balanced and wise pragmatism in the salient phases of the Risorgimento; but they were not equipped to deal with the enormous problems posed by the new situation. It was only very slowly, in the course of their first experiences of government, and thanks largely to numerous parliamentary investigations, that they began even to understand these problems to the full. Thus, in the new and youthful Italy, the honesty and rectitude, the restrained and measured style of government and sense of political responsibility that are usually attributed to the early prime ministers (men such as Quintino Sella, Giovanni Lanza, Marco Minghetti, Urbano Rattazzi) and the representatives of the 'historic Right' which governed the country for fifteen years after 1861, were simply not sufficient to guarantee a balanced and consistent economic and social development. The cumbersome methods and the length of time needed for the first post-unification government to carry out its economic and political programme make this point all too clearly.

A balanced budget, if not the principle objective, was certainly the one pursued with the greatest determination – particularly by Quintino Sella, who was minister of finance several times between 1862 and 1873. It was to be attained by two convergent roads which in the end proved to be effective: a very high indirect tax burden and the imposition of rigorous limits on public spending. If we consider that in 1866 the deficit was still over 60 per cent of the entire State budget and that in order to pay the interest on the large debts contracted Italy was forced to take the lira off the gold standard, we can understand what a formidable task this was. Fifteen years after unification the goal was reached, but the price paid was high – perhaps too high. In a country as poor as Italy, a balanced budget and expensive infrastructures could be achieved only through an indiscriminate and severe indirect taxation. Such a violently unpopular policy had profound consequences not only on the economic level, by preventing the formation of a lively market and the development of a satisfactory level of consumption, but also on the political level of the relationship between the government and the population; to most citizens,

Victor Emmanuel II opens the first parliament of united Italy in Turin on 18 February 1861. Cavour, the first prime minister, died four months later, bequeathing to his successors the difficult problems of creating unified systems of law and administration and transforming fierce local loyalties into a new spirit of national co-operation.

the State became a vast collector of taxes and very little more.

The administrative unification of the country, too, was achieved by tortuous and often ill-advised methods. The wide economic and social variations within the country, and in particular the profound economic differences between North and South, suggested a large measure of decentralization – an idea which Cavour had long supported in opposition to the centralistic plan put forth by his Bonapartist adversaries. It was the centralists, however, who prevailed in the governments that succeeded each other under Ricasoli and Rattazzi, ever concerned with guaranteeing state pre-eminence and state control of the periphery, particularly for reasons of public order. There were good reasons for such concern. One was the fear of a possible return of reactionary pro-Bourbon or clerical sentiment, a possibility that could never be discounted. Another was the need to eliminate highway robbery in Southern Italy, a phenomenon that was complex and endemic largely because it expressed the justifiable demands of the peasants, strangled by taxes and reduced in manpower by the military draft. All this gave rise to a centralist policy that for over a century

was to make the prefect the personification of Italian official life. These men were delegates of governmental authority, endowed with wide formal powers ranging from control and approval of the budgets of individual cities to responsibility for public order, and in addition able to influence local political life by acting as the focus of local relationships.

To this must be added the phenomenon – just as undesirable – of the 'Piedmontization' of Italy. The old Piedmont constitution of 1849 was now extended to the whole country, together with a code of laws which was not conceived according to the needs of Italy as a whole but was based simply on the usages and customs of the piedmont region. Nothing could have been more short-sighted; for example, the forestry laws which in Piedmont permitted the cutting of timber up to the level where the chestnut trees began were now extended throughout all Italy as well; but what was valid for Piedmont, where the chestnut timberline was reasonably low because of the climate, was absurd for the warm Mediterranean areas of the country, where the timberline was much higher, with chestnuts often covering only the mountain tops. Thus there was introduced a much more permissive policy than that enforced by the Bourbons, allowing speculators and absentee landowners to destroy a great part of the country's forestland. Faced with one of those ecological disasters that frequently strike Italy, we should do well to remember that its origin probably lies far back in the foolish deforestation policy that began with unification.

Where the policies of the Right achieved their greatest success, however, was in the completion of the process of unification with the conquest of the Veneto and the realization of the old plan for making Rome the capital city. The pressure of public opinion, and in particular of the Left, from Garibaldian and Mazzinian quarters, was very strong. In the first half of the 1860s there wre numerous incidents, provoked in particular by Garibaldi who even tried to invade the Papal States. But the European powers that had favoured unification were putting equally heavy pressure on Italy to find a diplomatic solution to the problems of the Veneto and Rome. The Italian Government followed two separate but congruent policies: on the one hand it assured France and England that Italy would not be the first to disrupt the *status quo*; on the other it sought opportunities to modify it to her advantage. And those opportunities did in fact present themselves. The first was the war of 1866 between Austria and Prussia which, despite Italy's military defeats at Custoza and Lissa as an ally of Prussia, permitted the annexation of the Veneto; the second was the defeat of Napoleon III at Sedan, which entailed the departure from Rome of the French garrison that had hitherto guaranteed the pope's rule. On 20 September 1870, General Cadorna's troops shelled the walls of Rome and, passing through the

space opened at the Porta Pia, took possession of the city. Shortly thereafter Rome was proclaimed capital of the kingdom of Italy, and the country's unification could be said to be complete. Yet this very act once more created a body of public opinion that was hostile to the Italian State: many decades would have to pass before Catholics could forget the sacrilege perpetrated on the papal city and abandon their attitude of opposition or indifference to Italian political affairs.

The Depretis years: 1876–87

At the same time an alternative was being prepared to the government of the Right, which ended in 1876. Executive power passed into the hands of a constitutional and monarchist Left, composed of former Garibaldini, ex-Democrats, and moderate Republicans. Contemporary witnesses called this a 'Parliamentary Revolution'. In fact there was nothing revolutionary about it, either in how it came about (a shift in vote of a group of deputies) or in the political consequences it occasioned.

In the first place, it must be remembered, the Left and the Right were neither proper parties nor political associations with contrasting mentalities and programmes; rather they were manifestations of social and geographical differences within the upper classes of society. The Right, because of its exceptional social homogeneity, expressed the interests of a class of aristocratic landowners who were inflexible Liberals; the Left – and this is one of the reasons for its historical importance – represented for the most part the union of vast sectors of the Northern middle class with the

Garibaldi's efforts to draw Rome into the newly united Italy were at first unsuccessful: the citizens were content under French rule and gave his besieging army no support when it was defeated by Napoleon III in 1867. In 1870, however, the Franco-Prussian War brought an end to Napoleon's empire and the French garrison was withdrawn from Rome. General Cadorna captured the city after token resistance from Pius IX. A plebiscite in October gave overwhelming support to unification with Italy. Here Garibaldi congratulates the king and points to the triumphant figure of Italy. Only the Church (left) was aggrieved by the Vatican's loss of temporal power.

The catafalque of Victor Emmanuel II in the Pantheon, Rome, specially decorated for the occasion, 16 February 1878. Far more than a figurehead, the king's shrewd grasp of foreign affairs had been of great importance for the successful outcome of the Risorgimento. The succession of his son Umberto confirmed Italian acceptance of the monarchy.

'galantuomini' ('gentlemen') of the South. In the second place, the Left's opposition platform – a fight against taxes, extension of the vote – was never fully realized. And finally, under the influence of Agostino Depretis, the man who would dominate Italian politics for over a decade, there began a process of parliamentary alliances and formation of majorities, the so-called 'transform-ism', which involved men and groups from both sides, united not by mutual support for a programme, but only by a temporary convergence of interests.

The grave economic crisis which struck Europe in the mid 1870s, due above all to a decline in farm prices following the entrance of American cereals into the European market, did not spare Italy; indeed its effects were more serious there than in other countries because of the already difficult Italian economic situation. Some of the social imbalances were even increased by government policy: the adoption in 1878 of a protective tariff on Northern textile and mechanical products, while giving an important boost to industrial production – people actually spoke of a boom – ultimately drained the resources of farmlands and accentuated the transfer of capital from the South to the North and from the country to the city. Adoption of a new customs tax in 1887, which extended protection to other industrial products and also affected important agricultural sectors such as grain production, was only an apparent solution since in reality the tax resulted in an advantage for the great absentee landowners in the South, and thus confirmed the South in its subordinate, backward condition. State intervention, both in the form of protectionism, and also through contracts to such sectors as shipbuilding, turned out to be the principal factor in Italian economic development, but rather than promoting free enterprise on the part of the more capable, it gave an unfair advantage to the groups that happened to enjoy political favour – one consequence being the major role assigned to banks and investment capital. This series of economic and political choices would have a lasting influence on the

241

French occupation of Tunisia in 1881 made Italy determined to end its diplomatic isolation and thus avoid further humiliations (she claimed Tunisia on the grounds that it was essential to the security of Sicily). In 1882 Austria, Germany and Italy – shown in this German cartoon with their backs to the stove – joined in the Triple Alliance, which lasted until 1915. France and Russia, their common enemies, feed the flames of the pact, while the Ottoman Empire looks on, warm but detached.

life of a country; it meant the formation of a strong industrial-agricultural social bloc which would dominate Italy for many decades.

The Depretis era (1876–87) was also the time when a first barely perceptible but significant widening of the political base of the Italian State began. The electoral reform of 1882 multiplied the number of voters from 200,000 to about 2 million – still less than ten per cent of the population – and allowed the urban lower middle class and the upper working class to participate in elections for the first time.

In general, however, the Italian ruling class was oriented in the last quarter of the 19th century toward a pattern of political and social development along 'Prussian' lines, like that realized by Bismarck. Its characteristic features were repression of popular initiatives, an authoritarian domestic programme and an imperialistic foreign policy. This was the orientation not only of the crown and military and court circles, but also of industrialists interested in government contracts and of Southern farmers – all strongly committed to the maintenance of social order and of protective tariffs.

In the great debate on Italian foreign policy that followed the conquest of Rome, furthermore, the example and the authority of Germany had made their weight felt; the Left in particular favoured a closer alliance with Germany rather than a continuation of the attitude of non-interference in international conflicts – the 'clean hands' policy – which had kept Italy on the margin of European politics. This had two important results: the Triple Alliance of 1882, in which Italy was united in a pact of mutual defence with Germany and Austria-Hungary, and (in combination with a protectionist commercial policy whose major goal was to discourage French imports) a progressive worsening of relationships with France, to the point of acute tension between the two countries.

The beginning of Italy's policy of colonial expansion in the 1880s coincided with the renewed interest in colonies on the part of all the great powers, especially in the Mediterranean area and in Africa, and contributed to making overall foreign policy more conflict-ridden. In 1870 an Italian trading company had acquired some territorial rights in Eritrea. These were taken over and extended by the government in 1882, and by 1883 the 'protectorate' comprised a substantial length of coastline. But the beginnings of Italian colonialism were unfortunate, just as her later 'imperial' experiences during Fascism would be. Through inefficiency and irresponsibility, numerous officers in search of fame did not hesitate to put their troops into difficult situations. After occupying the port of Massawa, Italian troops became involved in a series of operations against Abyssinia, and in January 1887 an Italian contingent of 500 men was attacked and completely destroyed at Dogali. In Italy the news was received with horror, and an aversion to colonialism became another of the components of popular opposition, first to Depretis and later to Francesco Crispi. Meanwhile discontent was also growing among those who favoured colonial expansion; and after a series of disappointments, especially following the French occupation of Tunisia, there was pressure on the government to be more aggressive.

Dissatisfaction with Italy's subordinate role in international politics; impatience with the provincial and small-minded aspects of Italian society; demand for a bigger and stronger fatherland – all these were assuming increasingly grand proportions, and the signs of this developmment were expressed first of all in the birth of a true middle-class environment. It is in the Depretis years – boom years, years in which gas lighting was replaced by electricity in Milan – that cities begin to live an intensive and even convulsive life: construction industries developed enormously (in Rome the Vatican was among the biggest speculators in building areas), the possibilities for jobs in State administration increased, commerce and public services developed: in short, the urban dimension of contemporary life was affirmed. The population of the

The Machinery Gallery at the National Exhibition of 1881. After unification Italy made great efforts to advance industrialization, but her lack of iron and coal put her at a disadvantage in comparison with the other industrial nations of Europe. Nevertheless, to establish her strength in the eyes of the world, she spent heavily on manufactures – and on armaments in particular. For a time her shipbuilding industry was the largest in the world. Most of her industry was under the control of two firms – Ansaldo of Genoa (shipbuilding and armaments) and Fiat of Turin (for motor vehicles, agricultural machinery and aircraft).

ten principal Italian cities increased in aggregate from a little over one and a half million inhabitants in 1861 to almost two and a half million in 1881, and the city of Milan alone, now becoming the so-called 'moral capital', increased from 192,000 inhabitants to 320,000.

A national culture that was quite distant from the heroic years of the Risorgimento was asserting itself; its principal exponent was Carducci, and even he, like the majority of his generation who had experienced the Risorgimento in their twenties, abandoned the seductive and sanguine rhetoric of Republican anti-clericalism for a more tranquil life, signalled by moderation in politics and a professorship in a university. The students who booed him in class at the beginning of the 1880s because of his betrayal of Republicanism (in fact the whole of Italian Freemasonry, of which Carducci was a member, passed from Republican to Monarchist) were the young representatives of a vivacious wing of Italian culture that was just then reaching its peak, and of which the main ingredients were faith in the sciences and the systematic study of criminology, but which also combined a certain sentimentalism with bohemian tastes and Socialist beliefs.

Even though the glamour of Wagner was beginning to invade Italy from Bayreuth, on the wave of Germanophilia that was influencing public life more and more, the figure of Giuseppe Verdi continued to represent what was strongest and most typical in Italian musical culture. The choruses of his operas seemed to reflect the collective effort of a people trying to assert themselves, the librettos expressed the more diffuse trends of contemporary literature (Victor Hugo; populist themes, bourgeois drama), while his Requiem Mass in memory of Alessandro Manzoni symbolically linked two vital movements of traditional Italian culture.

But while Italy was slowly starting to compete with the bigger powers on economic and political levels, a large and solid opposition movement was growing. One of its consequences was to favour the development of democratization of the country; but in the longer term it was to express with great force the discontent and the desire for a more just society that no amount of democratization could achieve, and in this respect it was to represent a constant thorn in the side of the Liberal State.

Some of the opposition came from the Catholics; this was fairly widespread and uncompromising, but – though it involved the refusal to participate in elections – it never went to the lengths of actual insubordination against the State. Much more serious was a new and profound phenomenon in Italian society coinciding precisely with the Depretis years: the birth of a Socialist-inspired worker's movement.

The phenomenon was European, but its manifestation in Italy was peculiar from several points of view. It was, first of all, a working-class movement in which factory workers were less in evidence than peasants. Its origins went back before industrialization to the discontent of the stonemasons and artisans, the farm

Agostino Depretis (left) became prime minister in 1876; his liberal policies included extension of the franchise, decentralization of government and anti-clericalism. His successor, the autocratic Francesco Crispi (right), led by his conviction that Italy was a great military power, involved the country in the disastrous Abyssinian campaign of 1894–6.

workers, rice-pickers and miners, and to the inhuman living conditions of the lower classes as a whole. Having expressed itself in earlier times in other forms, such as banditry and farmers' revolts, this dissatisfaction was now following new roads. It was becoming actively political.

Now even those who had been leaders in the anarchist movement, like Andrea Costa – who had become the first Socialist deputy – were convinced that they must participate in the political conflict. The large-scale farmers' strikes of the early 1880s that accompanied the formation of a strong union organization seemed to be following the scenario of those – like Friederich Engels, a careful observer of Italian things – who suggested organizing the class revolt on three fronts: politics, unions, and culture. On the political level the disappearance of anarchist tendencies coincided with the birth of the Socialist Party, founded in Genoa in 1892 (just at the time when the fourth centenary of Christopher Columbus's discovery of America was being celebrated there). On the union level the first *camere del lavoro* were being formed, around which the associations of the various categories of workers were united. On the cultural level the young Socialist movement was proving itself both strong and weak at the same time. Strong because its influence was making itself felt in environments that were traditionally not inclined towards the labour movement, like university classrooms in which many professors did not hide their sympathy for Socialism (among the most notable were the sociologist Enrico Ferri, the historian Guglielmo Ferrero and the psychologist and criminologist Cesare Lombroso). Strong too because in the South it was bringing together thousands of students. But weak because it was a Socialist culture made up of rather worn-out elements: a sentimental Socialism, veined with a Positivism against which Antonio Labriola, the only Italian interpreter of Marxism in the Second International period, was to fight unsuccessfully. With the turn of the century a few strong personalities and one or two solid initiatives like Benedetto Croce's journal *La Critica* were enough to sweep away the Socialist culture.

Right and Left, the widening gulf: 1887–1903

In the meantime, in 1887, the same year as the massacre in Dogali, Depretis died and Francesco Crispi became his successor. A contemporary commented that in place of the régime of an old fox there followed the dictatorship of an old wolf. That it was a dictatorship, or at least an Italian imitation of the German Iron Chancellorship, was immediately evident when Crispi produced a series of institutional reforms aimed at increasing the power of the prime minister and of the prefects, thus strengthening the executive at the expense of the elective bodies, whether Parliament or the town or provincial councils. If we add that fact that Crispi combined the office of prime minister with that of foreign minister and minister of the interior, and that more than once, in order to assuage mass demonstrations or movements, he declared a state of siege and the suspension of constitutional rights, the term dictatorship does not seem out of place. Thirty years later the Fascists were to talk of him as their forerunner.

In the field of foreign affairs, relations with France became strained to the point of war, owing to the heated nationalist sentiments that prevailed in both countries – aggravated in Italy by the bellicose rhetoric of Crispi himself. Commerce declined between the two countries, blocking about 40 per cent of Italian exports and creating a serious crisis for grape farmers and silk producers.

But the most relevant economic fact in the Crispi era was the succession of bank scandals that brought to light a whole network of intrigue and collusion between politics and finance. This was a sign of the growing influence exerted by the banks in economic development, but pointed also to the fact that the State, in its methods of granting financial aid and favours, was becoming dangerously corrupt. The scandal of the Banca Romana divided the Crispi régime into two periods; he resigned in 1891, but returned to power in 1893 as dictatorial as ever. In Sicily, certain labourers' associations set up as relief organizations, known as *Fasci*, had declared strikes and organized demonstrations characterized, as contemporaries noted, by the presence of red flags, portraits of Garibaldi and images of the Virgin Mary. Faced with these demonstrations and other similar ones that broke out in Lunigiana, Crispi not only called in the army; he even disbanded the Socialist Party, in spite of the fact that it was not in any way responsible, indeed was much embarrassed by what had occurred. Like Bismarck, Crispi strove to curb the development of the workers' movement and to retain the government's administrative bias in favour of the upper classes; for five years more he was to succeed.

Italy's unsuccessful exercise in colonialism: the occupation of Cassala in July 1894. This drawing is by an Abyssinian soldier present at the battle. The subsequent errors of the commanding general, Oreste Baratieri, caused the government to decide to replace him; in an effort to retrieve his reputation he provoked a full-scale battle at Aduwa in March 1896, but was defeated with the loss of 6,000 men. The army was withdrawn from Abyssinia to Eritrea and Cassala ceded to Great Britain.

In March 1896 the worst fears of the Socialist opposition were realized. In the course of Italy's colonial expansion in Eritrea – pursued with the ultimate aim of gaining a protectorate over Abyssinia – an army of 6,000 men was completely routed at Aduwa with heavy losses. Crispi's efforts to extend and strengthen the weak colonial centres in Africa were revealed as hopelessly inadequate.

The Crispi régime and its end confronted the Italian ruling class with a complex of problems. The workers' movement continued to make its presence felt, but it was the Rightist leader Marchese di Rudinì who took over as prime minister. The situation at home was by now as dramatic as that abroad. At the beginning of 1898 the outbreak of the Spanish-American war and the consequent reduction of grain imports from the United States created a famine. Rioting was widespread, leading to an attempted *coup de'état* which was bloodily repressed. The conservatives' solution was to strengthen the powers of the government by curbing those of Parliament. The opposition of the Socialists and the formation of a large security front prevented this from succeeding, but a dramatic end of the century was inevitable. On 29 July 1900, in Monza, the anarchist Gaetano Bresci assassinated King Umberto.

The new king, Victor Emmanuel III, was living proof that the Right had failed, and that a change of political direction was not only timely but was also what a large part of the country wanted. With the first year of the new century the Zanardelli-Giolitti government was formed and the so-called 'Giolitti era' began.

It was a relatively prosperous period, in which the process of industrialization reached its peak; in which foreign policy became less fanatically pro-German and it was possible even to flirt with France and England; and in which there was an attempt – partially fulfilled – to expand the bases of the State.

The process of building up a solid industrial base had already begun at the end of the 19th century, relying mainly on the electrical, chemical and mechanical sectors. At first one finds features common to the whole of European industry at this time: rising prices that had followed the end of the agricultural depression; a consequent increase in industrial investments in place of those that had been merely speculative; and the growth of joint stock companies and industrial firms. The production of electricity, which had risen during the years 1895–8 from 1,243 to 2,264 plants and from 36,021 to 86,175 kW. total power installed, was to increase continuously at an annual rate of about 20 per cent until the First World War. The electrification of the country gave an enormous push to increased productivity in every sector and in particular to engineering and the chemical industry, which already had proved themselves to be the fields destined to prosper. Engineering concentrated upon factory and agricultural machinery, railways and cars (Fiat was founded in 1899). The chemical industry scored a spectacular success with the production of tyres, mainly because of the incredibly fast growth of Pirelli, and also played a primary part in modernizing the agricultural system through the production of artificial fertilizers. One drawback of electrification, however, was that all the great hydro-electric schemes were in the North; thus North and South were driven even further apart.

During the first years of the century life in Italy was better than it had been twenty years before, and all the participants in this progress – from the active middle-class entrepreneurs and the lower middle class of the cities to the factory workers of the North and the day labourers of the Po Valley – were ready to taste the fruits of the *belle époque*. Fashions were changing and the tranquil decorum of the Umbertian era had given place to *cafés chantants* and *tabarins* – even the language was showing French influence again. The young Gabriele d'Annunzio was beginning to thrill the public with his poems, novels and flamboyant lifestyle. As elsewhere in

Futurism was a movement in modern art begun in 1909 by Marinetti who declared that for the modern age true beauty was inherent in machinery alone. This caricature by one of the movement's leading artists, Boccioni, shows a Futurist evening – one of the many public performances involving manifesto reading, poetry declamation and theatrical interludes. Futurist paintings are displayed behind gesticulating artists, while the bourgeois public swoon with horror. Such performances provoked audience outrage to a gratifying degree; the performers often ensured that all the seats were double booked to create a suitable mood of furious pandemonium.

Europe, the cultural avant-garde was busy rejecting the past, proclaiming the worthlessness of traditions and worshipping speed, machinery and violence. Marinetti, the poet and novelist, called the movement 'Futurism' when he wrote its manifesto in 1909. The motor-car, he proclaimed, was more beautiful than the *Winged Victory of Samothrace*. Although its attraction lay partly in its ability to shock conventional taste, Futurism – at least in the best painting of Carlo Carrà, Giacomo Balla and Gino Severini – did for a few years brilliantly succeed in expressing the exhilaration of speed and mechanical power, the 20th century's mastery of nature. And nowhere in art is motion so uncannily conveyed in a static object as in some of Umberto Boccioni's works.

For all their emphasis on modernity, the Futurists were in many ways remote from ordinary life. Much closer to social reality, though less revolutionary as artists, were the Italian Impressionists, like Giovanni Segantini, and even more the Post-Impressionists such as Giovanni Pelizza de Volpedo, whose work provides a vivid picture of agricultural life in the 1890s. (At the other end of the scale one might mention the sensuous, self-absorbed world of Amedeo Modigliani; he is probably the most famous Italian painter of the years around the First World War, but it may be significant that in order to find his own style he had to leave Italy at the age of twenty-two and settle in Paris).

Truth to reality, the acceptance of modern life in all its aspects – *verismo* – was also the watchword of contemporary literature and music. In literature it produced one outstanding figure in the Sicilian Giovanni Verga, whose novels and stories present the harshness and suffering of peasant life without false sentimentality. The best known, *Cavelleria Rusticana* (1880), was put onto the stage as an opera with music by Pietro Mascagni. Indeed it is through opera that *verismo*

still lives today, though in the hands of its greatest exponent, Giacomo Puccini, its passion, violence and psychological perception run the risk of being submerged in a sea of lyrical melody. In all the arts, Italy seemed to be rediscovering itself in modern terms without sacrificing that sense of style that had always marked it in the past.

Pre-war to post-war: 1903–22

It was this developing country that Giolitti had to govern from 1903. The main lines of his policies were determined by the belief (shared by many old Liberals) that the capitalist system was capable of regulating itself. For this reason, instead of undertaking abstruse economic programmes, Giolitti aimed at encouraging private enterprise, convinced that by developing the free associations that represented specific group interests he could bring about an economic equilibrium. In Giolitti's eyes, the 'real' nation, the people of Italy, had become dangerously distinct from the 'legal' nation, the State. Democracy, for a number of reasons, was not working. For over a quarter of a century it had been undermined by Catholic abstention; it was threatened by a worker's movement which, however responsibly organized, never lost its tendency towards rebellion; and it was circumscribed by an electoral law that excluded, in law and in fact, the majority of the population from any political rights. His programme was intended to tackle the problem at all three levels: first by trying to get Italian Catholics to participate in political life (the electoral pact of 1912 represented the first significant change in the political configuration of the Italian ruling class); secondly, by showing in the fields of employment, union activities and workers' organizations, a truly Liberal attitude: the State was not to interfere in conflicts between capital and labour, and the right wing of the Socialist Party was to be wooed to participate in the national government, which it in fact did after the split of 1912; thirdly, by introducing a new electoral law, applied for the first time in 1913, which gave universal suffrage to adult males.

Such a policy at home could not help having consequences abroad, even if these consequences were to remain more programmes than actual accomplishments. Giolitti in fact accentuated the defensive character of the Triple Alliance and initiated a policy of rapprochement, first with France and then with Russia. The result was that Italian imperialist ambitions were rekindled, this time in the direction of Libya. In September 1911 Italy declared war on Ottoman Turkey (of whose ramshackle empire Libya was a part) and by November had gained the victory. But the conquest of Libya did not have the effects that Giolitti had expected. True, the nationalists and imperialists drew ideas and strength from the experience; the financiers and those with an economic interest in the war intensified their pressure. The workers, on the other hand, united in a gigantic movement against it. Hardly anybody wanted to go to live in 'the sandpit', as Libya was called, though mass emigration from Italy continued to the United States, Argentina and Australia. Moreover the cost of the Libyan war, caused not only by Turkish forces but also by the resistance of the Berber tribes of the interior, proved to be much greater than had been foreseen. threatening the precarious balance that the State budget had reached.

For Germany and Austria, Italy was certainly not a particularly welcome ally, and during the Libyan war there were even voices raised in Vienna in favour of attacking her. The Italians, for their part, were still waiting for Germany and Austria to promise the 'restoration' of Trieste, Gorizia and the Italian zones of Istria and Dalmatia if Italy took part in a successful war as a member of the Triple Alliance. These requests were ignored and this helped to push Italy into the arms of England and France in the first months of the world conflict.

War was being prepared in any case, not only in the war ministries of the central empires, but also in men's minds. The anti-Giolitti newspapers were demanding a bigger role for Italy and a revival of national pride. The early Italian film studios were turning out colossal epics glorifying heroic struggle (*Cabiria, Quo Vadis?*). 'Liberty, Equality and Fraternity' were openly derided. D'Annunzio's heady and image-laden prose called for war, a regenerating blood bath , a trial of courage as the only measure for judging men.

When war broke out in 1914, however, Italy did not join her allies in the Triple Alliance. For nearly a year she remained neutral, while domestic, foreign and even financial pressures mounted in favour of intervention on the other side. The most influential personality of Italian Socialism, Benito Mussolini, became so convinced of this policy that he renounced pacifism, left the

'*Guerra nell' Adriatico*' : a collage by Carlo Carrà (1881–1966), one of the original Futurists, made in Milan towards the end of 1914 to illustrate an anthology of his writings. In common with other artists of the movement, Carrà glorified war.

party and campaigned violently for war. In April 1915 Italy signed a treaty with Britain and France, which promised her all the territory that had been denied her by Germany and Austria; a week later she ended the Triple Alliance; and a fortnight after that she declared war on the side of the Allies. So there was a war, as the intellectuals had hoped and as the industrialists interested in military profits had asked. And it was a blood bath. But it did not have the regenerating effect that had been hoped for. Far from it.

The men who did the fighting could not feel that the war was their own. The generals and professional soldiers, almost all of whom had been influenced by imperialistic and nationalistic ideologies, found themselves commanding, in a long war with an uncertain outcome, a mass of unwilling conscripted soldiers who were being forced into heroism in spite of themselves. The war was a tragedy but – in the bloodiest and most dramatic way – it did what the politicians had failed to do: it united Italy. In the trenches of Carso, in the mud of Caporetto, all the different Italys finally got to know each other for the first time. Southern peasants torn away from their families, Emilian day-labourers, Tuscan share-croppers, farmers of all kinds and from every region were thrown into the battle, and as cannon fodder they were introduced to their communal fatherland. Cynical or courageous members of the lower middle class, adventurers and heroic fighters suffered side by side for three long years. They lost many battles, but they succeeded, with their allies, in winning the war.

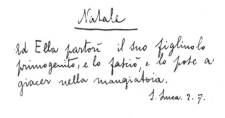

'The child of War': an anti-Fascist cartoon of 1920 by the Socialist Giuseppe Scalarini. In a grim parody of the Nativity, War gives birth to Fascism, which is nurtured in the manger of capitalism.

Victory, however, brought few satisfactions. At the peace conference only a few of the Italian demands were taken into consideration. The war, both in its course and in its outcome, had satisfied no one's hopes; it was not just a coincidence that Italy alone, among all the victorious nations, was immersed in an intensive wave of social battles that brought the old Liberal State to its knees. There was also something in the unimaginative management of the war and the muddle of the peace negotiations that contrasted with the sturdy and dignified behaviour of Giolitti's Italy. Men like the prime minister Vittorio Emmanuele Orlando or the foreign minister Sidney Sonnino seemed lacking in certainty. The crisis was not only economic and social, but moral as well.

Industry had difficulty settling back into the slower production rates of peacetime. Veterans returning from the war could not find work; peasants who in 1916 had been promised land if they won the war found that they had been deceived; the middle classes, realizing that they were losing their status both as a result of inflation and also because in the new post-war life they were no longer in command, tried, together with D'Annunzio, to prolong a nationalist war of their own with the occupation of Fiume. This was an extraordinary adventure in which D'Annunzio, buoyed up on a wave of popular patriotism, turned Fiume into an ultra-Italian city state, defying the government and the rest of Europe for over a year until in January 1921 he was forced to surrender.

Union membership increased dramatically. In the 1919 elections the Socialist Party became the leading party, while another 'mass' party, the first Catholic party in Italy's history, was also developing: the Partito Populare Italiano. Through the renewal of political conflicts, through strikes, through the occupation of factories and land, the masses were beginning to assert their presence. The Liberal State, unable to change its élitist structure, had reached a crisis. Social contrasts – or, as they were now seen to be, social conflicts – could not be reconciled within the old structure. Nobody wanted that structure any more – not the workers, who hoped to achieve power, nor the capitalists, who were being crippled by strikes, nor the landowners whose land had been occupied. Italy was ripe for civil war – and for the coming of Fascism.

The experience of Fascism

In the perspective of almost the whole 20th century, the experience of Fascism is a fairly brief historical chapter, but its cost in terms of arrested national development was very high.

Contrary to the opinion of Benedetto Croce, for whom Fascism was a sort of disease or a foreign body that attacked the life of the country from outside, it has now become clear that Fascism grew out of economic forces and political and social trends present throughout Italy's history. Mussolini was well aware of that history and was able to appeal to many facets of political feeling. His ideology was remarkably elastic, combining reactionary nationalism and populist demagogy, and moving from Republicanism to Monarchism without undue strain. Mussolini and his group of collaborators founded the first *'fasci de combattimento'* (combat groups) in 1919; slowly but steadily they gained supporters, and using every means, from active propaganda to terrorist violence, were able to strengthen their organization while at the same time destroying that of their adversaries.

It is often asked why the anti-Fascist forces, the Socialists, Liberals and Catholics, did not stop Mussolini in his rise to power. The answer lies partly in internal weakness and lack of will and partly in the fact that they were as bitterly opposed to each other as to the Fascists. The result was that no common strategy could be developed and no leader emerged as an alternative to Mussolini. The Socialists were reluctant to oppose violence with violence. The Liberals could not or would not apply normal police laws. And the Catholics actually supported Mussolini in Parliament and took part in the first Fascist government.

It is not, however, enough to explain the outcome of a battle simply by pointing to the shortcomings of the defeated. The Fascists, whose leader had been summoned by the king to form a new government near the end of October 1922 (after a ridiculous march on Rome that any competent régime could have checked with ease), had in reality gained the support of many

Badate, lavoratori, che vuole divorarvi!

'*Take care, workers, he wants to devour you!*' *Scalarini's cartoon of 1921 depicts the ravening jaws of Fascism, ready to batten on the discontents of Italy's workforce after the First World War.*

elements of society: industrialists, landowners, middle classes and, most important, the Crown itself.

Fascism was in fact the first real party of the Italian bourgeoisie, the first active political force that seemed able to cut through the tangle of shifting parliamentary alliances and Freemasonry and take charge with a programme of normalization of the State that satisfied all the different types of conservatives, from the king to Liberal Right, from the industrialists to the landowners of the North and South.

The 'normalization' plan that was actually put into effect went far beyond any of the conservatives' demands. Between 1922 and 1924 a ruthless campaign was fought against the opponents of Fascism of any sort, whether Catholic, Communist or Liberal. It was in effect a civil war, and one that often saw members of Fascist organizations and State police fighting side by side. Communists and Socialists were beaten to death, as well as Liberals and priests, whenever they opposed the assertion of Fascist power; even when the enemy was the parliamentary leader of a party, as in the case of the Socialist delegate Giacomo Matteotti, the Fascists did not hesitate to kill him too.

It was at the end of 1924, a few months after the Matteotti assassination, that Fascism seemed most isolated, both from the nation and from the other political parties; but it was also then that Mussolini, in a threatening speech in Parliament, explicitly asserted that he assumed total responsibility for what had happened, and dumbfounded the incredulous delegates

by threatening them with the occupation of Parliament by a squad of a thousand armed Fascists. From 1925 on, a radical change took place. The Fascists abandoned any pretence of legality. A year later, the parliamentary delegates who had declared themselves against Fascism – leaving the Chamber of Deputies and withdrawing to Aventino – were declared to have forfeited their seats. Many others, including the secretary-general of the PCI (Italian Communist Party), were illegally arrested. The so-called 'Fascist Laws' of November 1926 dissolved all other political parties and union organizations, while a new electoral law (prepared in 1923) entrenched Fascism more deeply than ever.

Whether or not the Italian people realized it, the régime was now dominating every aspect of life. To get a job one had to be a member of a Fascist organization; the Fascist unions were the only ones allowed, and they also settled questions of salary with Fascist employers. Young men were formed into Fascist youth organizations; so were young women and even children. Furthermore, everyone had to make a public affirmation of obedience to Mussolini. What was behind this inflexible regulation of the everyday lives of millions of people? Of what did it actually consist? In the words of one historian:

None of the signs that usually accompany periods of prosperity were missing: building speculation; a first modest boom in car production, with the manufacture of the first standard car, the Balilla; a widespread enthusiasm for sports, theatres and films, entertainment and popular songs. The beaches and holiday resorts in the mountains were crowded during the summer with middle-class families, while for those who could not afford that luxury there were trains organized by the National Institute for Recreation, thanks to which one could spend a pleasant weekend, or rather a 'Fascist Saturday', by the sea. . . . In this new wave of modest

LA VETTURETTA DEL LAVORO E DEL RISPARMIO

A poster of 1935 advertising the popular Fiat 500 – 'the car of those who work and those who save' – exploits the potent patriotic symbol of the ancient sculpture of the she-wolf suckling Romulus and Remus.

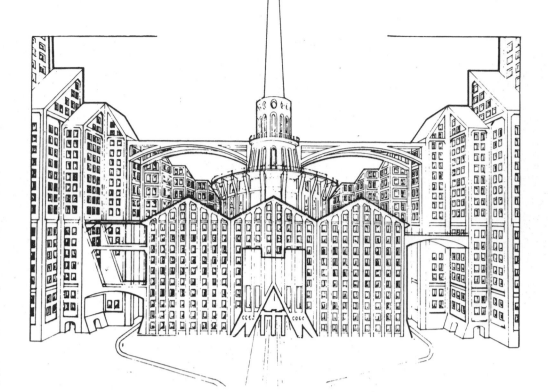

and limited prosperity there was something intensely different from the happy years of the *belle époque*: it was more vulgar, more insensitive to the very serious problems that still existed and, above all, more corrupt. The corruption increased slowly as the régime was strengthened almost to the point of becoming an institution. The 'new men' brought to power by Fascism – the so-called hierarchy – were for the most part parvenus and provincials, with rough tastes and superficial culture, completely unused to power and without that detachment towards it which is typical of a ruling class that is well tested and seasoned.

That summary says something, but not all. However 'untested' and 'unseasoned', the new ruling élite did in fact represent certain social levels well enough, from the landowning aristocracy to the lower middle class of the services and state administration, passing through the middle class of the professions and industrialists. But others it could not claim to represent, in particular the workers, whose wages were losing their buying power. They were not able to oppose it with force, nor did they want to lose their jobs, and therefore they obeyed. But they did not consider themselves represented by Fascism: their 'consent' was for the most part purely passive, and it would become dissent as soon as conditions were right. Before this happened many years had to pass, not only because the meshes of the Fascist net were very tight and no form of opposition was able to survive the severity of the police laws but also because Fascism, between 1929 and 1935, had succeeded in consolidating its base by a number of shrewd political initiatives. In 1929 it had been able to conclude an agreement with the Vatican which, by making considerable concessions to the Church, solved the 'Roman question'. Then in 1935 Mussolini found a

pretext for reopening the war with Abyssinia, and this time succeeded where all previous attempts had failed. After six months' fighting, Addis Ababa fell and Victor Emmanuel was proclaimed emperor. In spite (or perhaps because) of widespread world disapproval and economic sanctions against Italy, Mussolini's popularity increased. Last of all, the Fascist 'rural' campaign had met with several successes with the land reclamation of considerable areas of Central and Southern Italy.

This was also a period when, paradoxically as it now seems, the arts in Italy experienced an unexpected flowering. Much of it was marked by a sense of disillusion, a questioning of accepted values, that no doubt had its origin in the social and political context. In the case of Luigi Pirandello this questioning included even the sense of individual identity and his best known plays (such as *Six Characters in Search of an Author* and *Henry IV*) examine areas of the mind where reality and illusion overlap. Italo Svevo died in 1928, when Fascism had only just established its hold, but in his best novel, *The Confessions of Zeno*, the world is portrayed with wry irony as an unpredictable place where luck is more important than merit or morals.

Giorgio de Chirico's paintings are in some ways the visual equivalents of Pirandello's literary landscapes. Both explore the subconscious and both men were drawn to themes deriving from Italian tradition. De Chirico belonged to the Surrealists until 1925 and his most interesting work was done before and during the First World War. But the dream-like architecture that features in so many of them looks forward to the austere, pared-down classicism of the Fascist years. Here one should also mention the visionary architect

Antonio Sant'Elia, who was killed in action in 1916 but whose bold schemes for cities of the future exerted a compelling influence on the planners of Mussolini's Italy. The merits of that planning, the railway stations and public buildings with their plain functional lines and travertine surfaces, are only now being given the benefit of unbiased appreciation.

In music a great operatic era ended in 1926 with the posthumous performance of Puccini's unfinished *Turandot*, the last Italian opera to keep a place in the world's repertoire. Ferruccio Busoni and Ottarino Respighi continued to produce highly original works that were still part of the old tradition. It was left to Luigi Dallapiccola to lead Italian music along the path of serialism, though he preserved many traditional elements. In general, the Fascists failed to exercise a cultural tyranny to match their political one and the undercurrent of free expression among intellectuals was never entirely stopped.

After 1935, in fact, it grew stronger. Until then the political forces of anti-Fascism in exile had acted independently and sometimes against one another. Now, galvanized by the Nazi victory in Germany and the accentuation of the Fascists' aggressive foreign policy, a policy that was to bring Italy into war, they were able to regroup and to some extent unite.

Already during the Spanish Civil War, in which once again Italian Fascist volunteers were fighting against Italian volunteers of the international brigades, groups of young intellectuals who had experienced the contradictions of 'Leftist Fascism' had deviated from the régime. Many joined the ranks of one or other of the anti-Fascist parties and in particular the Communists, the only anti-Fascist party which had a web of clandestine organization throughout the country. It was also the only party to include a writer of genius among its apologists – Antonio Gramsci, whose letters and commentaries from prison are now recognized as one of the few really creative additions to Marxist theory.

Mussolini's alliance with Nazi Germany and the adoption of an anti-semitic legislation that was neither felt nor shared by the majority of the country also played a part in weakening the support for Fascism. But there is no doubt that the decisive element which made the régime lose those classes and sectors that had hitherto upheld it was Italy's participation in the Second World War and the course of its military operations.

There is no need to follow these in detail. From September 1939 to June 1940 Italy remained neutral. When Germany invaded France, encountering only weak resistance, and a rapid end to the war seemed in sight, Mussolini too invaded France from the south. But he had miscalculated. The failure of the German air offensive against England later that year, Italy's rash invasion of Greece in 1941 followed by the almost complete destruction of her fleet at Taranto, the war

against the British in North Africa, participation in Hitler's aggression against Russia and finally the entry of the United States into the war against her – all these highlighted Italy's dramatic state of unpreparedness and gave increasingly lurid glimpses of the possibility of defeat.

By the beginning of 1943 the country's situation was becoming critical and its 'home front' was beginning to show large cracks. The first protestors to make themselves heard were the workers of the big factories in the North, who succeeded in evading the Fascist police net and organized a powerful and extensive series of strikes. Not far behind, however, were the Fascists themselves – and with them the king, the court and wide sectors of the industrial world – all desperately searching for a way out. They found it by making Mussolini the scapegoat for the country's tragic situation. Fascism's highest body, the Great Council, withdrew its confidence from him and he was forced to resign. But the king went even further: he had him arrested, disbanded the Fascist party and began preparations in secret for negotiations towards an armistice with the Allies.

Birth pangs of a new Italy

These were among the darkest days of Italian history. Once the armistice had been settled and made public, the king and the new government fled to the zones already occupied by the Allies. Mussolini, rescued on Hitler's orders from the mountain retreat where he was imprisoned, resumed nominal rule over a puppet state in the north under the Nazis, the Italian Social Republic, known as the Republic of Salò. Here and in Central Italy, still controlled by the Germans, began the Resistance movement of the partisans.

Whether the Resistance could have liberated the country without Allied help is a question that is still debated, and if we confine ourselves to the level of 'war games' the answer is surely no. But the Resistance meant more than military action. It involved a radical rethinking at the social and political level. Between 1943 and 1945 traditions of struggle and attitudes of insubordination and rebellion which had been typical of the Italian people up to the 1920s revived and came back to life. These traditions had now to be reconciled with the strong political motivations of all the anti-Fascist groups – Socialists, Liberals, Catholics, but especially the Communists – which tended to offer themselves as the new ruling nuclei of Italy once it was liberated from Fascism. The lower classes experienced a new raising of their political consciousness, much as they had during the decades immediately following unification. Two entire generations – the one born during the Giolitti era and the one, born immediately following the First World War, which had grown up under Fascism – were called upon to make quick, important decisions.

Some of these decisions were absolutely crucial to the

From 1943 Italy was divided between Mussolini, by now a German puppet, and the allies, backed by partisan fighters. The struggle between the two was in part a civil war. This drawing of two partisan soldiers in 1945 is by Lorenzo Vespignani.

individuals involved. When an eighteen-year-old in North Italy was called up to fight for the Republic of Salò he had to choose whether to die on the Germans' side or to join the partisans. Most of them chose the second course. This was just one way in which the experience of war changed peoples' lives. It was a tragedy that hit the entire civilian population without distinction. A virtual civil war was going on parallel with the campaigns of the opposing armies, mass deportation, bombardments and German occupation followed by Allied occupation. As for the country's economic resources, either they did not exist at all or they were cut to the bone. It is not by chance that a great part of the attention of Italian film-makers after the Second World War was directed at the war and the Resistance: it was in just those years that the dominant personalities of the new Italy were being formed and it was then that the great political problems of Italy after Fascism began to take shape.

The historical origins of the Italian Communist Party, no matter how far back in time one traces them, find their turning point in the fight against Fascism, and especially in the Resistance. Among the wide range of anti-Fascist forces, for the most part scattered and disorganized, the Communists had been and continued to be the only ones able to present a programme that was in any way farsighted and with a solid organizational base. They did not ask for a society on the Soviet model, merely promising to liberate Italy from the Nazis and Fascists; they carried forward a policy of national unity and opened their doors not only to indoctrinated Marxists, but also to the young Demo-

crats, Catholics and Monarchists – anybody who had fought or was fighting against Fascism. In this way the Communist Party gathered prestige, fame, and a link with the popular elements of society that would last for a long time and that forms, even today, one of the aspects of Italian society. In the rank and file of the party whose ideology had been defined by Gramsci and Togliatti, workers of the industrial triangle found themselves side by side with agricultural workers of the Po valley, Tuscan farm workers and many young intellectuals, some of whom – from Amendola and Sereni to Visconti and Bianchi Bandinelli – came from important upper-class families and even from the aristocracy.

In reality, it was during the Resistance and the years immediately following that the foundations of the two great – and opposing – mass parties in recent Italian history were laid: the Italian Communist Party and the Christian Democratic Party (Democrazia Cristiana). The latter inherited the anti-Fascist mantle of the supressed Partito Popolare. During the years of reconstruction it became recognized as the leading political organ of the Catholics. But who exactly were 'Catholics' in a country where 99 per cent of the population were baptized in church? In fact, the party's members were by no means all closely concerned with religion. The groups which had the strongest tradition of religious organization – small landowners and farmers – formed the original core; but along with these must be mentioned the urban middle class of merchants and civil servants, who saw the party as a party of law and order, and also wide sectors of the entrepreneurial and financial world.

The fact is that from the beginning of the Resistance until 1947, despite the difference in programmes, social representation and political style, Christian Democrats and Communists – and along with them Socialists, Liberals, etc. – worked together first in the Committee of National Liberation (Comitato di Liberazione Nazionale) and later in the preparation of a republican constitution (the monarchy had been abolished in the referendum of 2 June 1946). Soon after this, international anti-Fascist unity was broken and the beginning of the Cold War opened an unbridgeable gap between the two Italian mass parties. What was being decided in the elections of 18 April 1948 was not only the balance between the Italian political forces, but also the ways and means by which the country was to be reconstructed. This reconstruction was in fact to take place under the guidance of the Christian Democrats and with the aid of the Marshall Plan. It called for a massive effort; but the sacrifices made by the workers and the consistent economic policy of the government yielded results, so that by the mid-1950s a large part of the war damage had been repaired. The first signs were already apparent of the economic development that would reach significantly high levels by the end of the decade.

Meanwhile the automobile industry (particularly Fiat) threw itself into the mass production of the Topolino and later of the 500, discovering in the *Mille Miglia* (thousand mile) motor race a great chance for publicity. These were also the years when an extensive system of motorways (the *autostrade*) was beginning to change the face of Italy with feats of engineering that evoked comparison with classical Rome; the years of the so-called 'economic miracle' which, in the Winter Olympics in Cortina d'Ampezzo and the Olympic Games in Rome, would show the new Italy to the world in all its modernity and ambition.

While, after years of political oppression and economic difficulties, the middle and lower classes began to taste the first fruits of economic success, the upper middle classes were tasting fruits that were sweeter and riper: Via Veneto and the '*Dolce Vita*' which Fellini immortalized in his film were replacing the myths and models of Hollywood as images of sophistication. Italy was assuming its place as one of the most important centres of the international film industry. The earlier post-war commitment to extreme realism and concern for individual values (explored in a masterly way by Rosselini and De Sica) gave way to a more mannered, polished and sometimes puzzling brilliance in the work of Antonioni, Visconti and Fellini. It is their heirs (Pasolini, Bertolucci and others) who have continued to keep Italian films in the forefront of critical attention.

Nothing that Italy has produced in the fine arts, literature or music has had the same universal impact as the Italian film, although there have been outstanding figures in all these fields. Giorgio Morandi, whose quiet still-lifes had been painted mostly in the 1930s, won belated acclaim at the end of the '40s. Among writers the best known is doubtless Alberto Moravia; his novels and stories, dwelling upon personal and sexual themes and predominantly pessimistic in tone, have been widely translated. In music one can point to Luciano Berio who has experimented creatively with serialism and with new electronic techniques.

It is in architecture and design, however, that modern Italy has impressed itself most successfully on the world's consciousness. Qualities that have been characteristic of her art at so many of her greatest periods – functional elegance, a flair for using materials in new ways, fine craftsmanship, boldness of invention and a lively sense of enjoyment in physical objects – have surfaced again in the design of buildings, furniture, household appliances, clothes and even advertising. The greatest name is the architect Pier Luigi Nervi, whose vast exhibition halls, sports stadia and high-rise commercial buildings are as remarkable for their engineering skill as for their beauty of line. All these products have been the outward and visible sign of Italy's 'economic miracle'.

But, no matter how 'miraculous', economic development alone could not overcome the dramatic problem of the poverty and backwardness of the South. Indeed, it was becoming worse, because of the ever growing emigration from the South to the North or abroad. The governments of the centre which followed each other from 1948 on seemed deaf to the requests for social reforms in such fields as housing, health care and transport. In 1960 there was even an attempt to move further to the right. This was resisted both by the country at large and within the principal political forces. Conditions were then established for a government coalition between the Christian Democrats and the Socialist Party which, with a few intervals, has lasted now for almost twenty years.

The energy crisis and the social disruption of 1968 have changed the face of Italy since the years of the 'miracle', but they have not modified the constant tendency towards government instability (forty governments since 1945, with an average duration of no more than two months) combined with stability in political alliances. Nor have they changed Italy's role on the world market, where in a computer era she continues to be famous for the products of her extraordinarily high-quality craftsmanship.

Italy today, marked like the rest of the Western world by the contradictions of development and the decline of prosperity, seems characterized more than anything else by her age-old ability to adapt, to resist and to survive.

The emblem of Milan's Borsa del lavoro, from a pamphlet of 1890. This trade union organization was designed to aid workers in finding jobs.

Select Bibliography

I Rome and the Empire

Italy before the Romans has been exhaustively covered in the eight volumes edited by G. Mansuelli, *Popoli e Civiltà dell'Italia antica* (Rome 1976–8); M. Pallottino, *Genti e culture dell'Italia preromana* (Rome 1981) looks at the same field more concisely. For prehistoric Italy see A. M. Radmilli, ed., *Guida della Preistoria italiana* (Florence 1975). More specialized studies on the Greek, Phoenician and Etruscan contribution include the following: J. Boardman, *The Greeks Overseas*, 2nd ed. (London 1980); A. Parrot, M. H. Chéhab and S. Moscati, *Les Phéniciens: L'expansion phénicienne, Carthage* (Paris 1975); R. Bianchi-Bandinelli and A. Giuliano, *Etrusker und Italiker vor der römischen Herrschaft* (Munich 1974).

There are a number of authoritative works on the Roman Republic, of which the following may be recommended: E. Badian, *Foreign Clientelae (264–70 BC)* (Oxford 1958); R. Bloch, *The Origins of Rome* (London 1960); P. A. Brunt, *Italian Manpower 225 BC–AD 14* (Oxford 1971); K. Christ, *Krise und Untergang der Römischen Republik* (Darmstadt 1979); M. Crawford, *The Roman Republic* (Glasgow 1978); E. T. Salmon, *Roman Colonization under the Republic* (London 1969); A. N. Sherwin-White, *The Roman Citizenship*, 2nd ed. (Oxford 1973); R. Syme, *The Roman Revolution* (Oxford 1939); A. J. Toynbee, *Hannibal's Legacy*, 2 vols (London 1965); J. Vogt, *Die Römische Republik*, 6th ed. (Munich 1979).

Books on the *Imperium Romanum* may conveniently be divided into general historical surveys and studies of particular topics. In the first category are the following: K. Christ, *The Romans* (London 1983) and *Römische Geschichte*, 3rd ed. (Darmstadt 1980); A. H. M. Jones, *The Roman Economy. Studies in Ancient Economic and Administrative History* (Oxford 1974); M. Rostovtzeff, *Social and Economic History of the Roman Empire*, 2nd ed. (Oxford 1957); L. P. Wilkinson, *The Roman Experience* (London 1975). On Roman society see: G. Alföldy, *Römische Sozialgeschichte*, 2nd ed. (Wiesbaden 1979); J. P. V. D. Balsdon, *Life and Leisure in Ancient Rome* (London 1969); J. A. Crook, *Law and Life of Rome* (London 1967); M. I. Finley, *Ancient Society and Modern Ideology* (London 1980); R. MacMullen, *Roman Social Relations 50 BC to AD 284* (New Haven 1974); F. Millar, *The Emperor in the Roman World (31 BC–AD 337)* (London 1977); G. R. Watson, *The Roman Soldier* (London 1969). On Roman religion: R. M. Ogilvie, *The Romans and their Gods* (London 1969); J. M. C. Toynbee, *Death and Burial in the Roman World* (London 1971). On engineering, architecture and art: J. G. Landels, *Engineering in the Ancient World* (London 1978); A. G. McKay, *Houses, Villas and Palaces in the Roman World* (London 1975); J. M. C. Toynbee, *The Art of the Romans* (London 1965).

During the last two decades much attention has been paid to the period of crisis and decline. Particularly valuable are: A. Alföldi, *Studien zur Geschichte der Weltkrise des 3. Jahrhunderts nach Christus* (Darmstadt 1967); M. Grant, *The Climax of Rome* (London 1968); A. H. M. Jones, *The Later Roman Empire 284–602. A social, economic and administrative survey*, 2 vols (Oxford 1964); R. MacMullen, *Roman Government's Response to Crisis AD 235–337* (New Haven 1967); J. Vogt, *The Decline of Rome* (London 1967).

Finally, one should add a list of books dealing with the influence of classical culture on subsequent history, and with the evolution of our knowledge about the classical world. Among the most notable are: R. R. Bolgar, ed., *Classical Influences on European Culture, AD 500–1500* (Cambridge 1971), *Classical Influences on European Culture, AD 1500–1700* (Cambridge 1976) and *Classical Influences on Western Thought, AD 1650–1870* (Cambridge 1979); K. Büchner, ed., *Latein und Europa. Traditionen und Renaissancen* (Stuttgart 1978); K. Christ, *Römische Geschichte und deutsche Geschichtswissenschaft* (Munich 1982) and *Von Gibbon zu Rostovtzeff*, 2nd ed. (Darmstadt 1979); E. Curtius, *European Literature and the Latin Middle Ages* (Bern 1948; London 1953); W. Goez, *Translatio imperii* (Tübingen 1958); R. Koebner, *Empire* (Cambridge 1961); A. Momigliano, *Contributi alla storia degli studi classici e del mondo antico*, 6 vols (Rome 1955–80); H. T. Parker, *The Cult of Antiquity and the French Revolutionaries* (Chicago 1937); F. Schneider, *Rom und Romgedanke im Mittelalter* (Munich 1926).

II The Medieval Centuries

There are a number of good and recent works of synthesis in Italian that cover most of the areas dealt with in this chapter: the volumes of *Storia d'Italia*, edited by G. Galasso and of the *Annali*, both published by Einaudi (Turin), of the *Storia d'Italia*, and the series

Società e Costumi both published by UTET. Inevitably the contributions to these vast series are mixed in quality, though many are very thorough and very interesting.

Coverage in English is more patchy, but often excellent. On the general history of Italy, C. Wickham, *Early Medieval Italy* (London 1981) and J. K. Hyde, *Society and Politics in Medieval Italy: the Evolution of Civil Life, 1000–1350* (London 1973) cover the earlier and later periods very well and are full of interest, though mainly for the North and Centre of the peninsula. J. J. Norwich, *The Normans in the South* and *The Kingdom in the Sun* (London 1967 and 1970) provide more detail on the Norman South and Sicily, and D. Bullough in D. Talbot Rice, ed., *The Dark Ages* (London 1965) has a good text and illustrations for the Ostrogoths and Lombards. For the economic life of the Peninsula there is an introductory study in G. Luzzatto, *An Economic History of Italy* (London 1961) and a more detailed analysis of later mercantile achievements in R. S. Lopez, *The Commercial Revolution of the Middle Ages, 950–1350* (Cambridge 1976). The city-states are treated in Hyde (cited above) and in D. Waley, *The Italian City Republics* (London 1978). There is no good general survey in English of the religious life of Italy; but the papacy has attracted a number of studies: G. Barraclough, *The Medieval Papacy* (London 1968) and W. Ullmann, *A Short History of the Papacy in the Middle Ages* (London 1972) are introductions to the whole period; J. Richards, *Consul of God* (London 1980) provides a biography of Gregory the Great.

The best books in English on the visual arts and written culture of Italy in this period deal with particular areas. A more general picture for art and architecture can always be formed from the relevant volumes of the Pelican History of Art: P. Lasko, *Ars Sacra* (Harmondsworth 1972); R. Krautheimer, *Early Christian and Byzantine Architecture* (Harmondsworth 1970); K. J. Conant, *Carolingian and Romanesque Architecture* (Harmondsworth 1959); P. Frankl, *Gothic Architecture* (Harmondsworth 1962); and C. R. Dodwell, *Painting in Europe 800–1200* (Harmondsworth 1971). R. Krautheimer, *Rome: Profile of a City* (Princeton 1980) is a fascinating study of the politics and art of the medieval city; J. Larner, *Culture and Society in Italy 1290–1420* (London 1971) is an excellent book on the culture of the late medieval city-states in its political and social context; D. Haynes, *The Italian Renaissance in its Historical Background* (Cambridge 1977), though mainly relevant to the period after 1350, has much that is of interest on the Middle Ages.

III Humanism and Renaissance

As a general introduction to the whole background of Renaissance Italy, Jacob Burckhardt's *Civilization of the Renaissance in Italy*, first published in 1860, is probably still the best. It has been reprinted and translated many times and is available in illustrated editions. More recent works covering the same field are Peter Burke, *Culture and Society in Renaissance Italy 1420–1540* (London 1972; also published as *Tradition and Innovation in Renaissance Italy*, London 1974); Denys Hay, *The Renaissance in its Historical Background* (Cambridge 1961); and Lauro Martines, *Power and Imagination; city-states in Renaissance Italy* (London 1980). John Larner, *Italy in the Age of Dante and Petrarch 1216–1380* (London 1980) is a useful survey of what I have called 'pre-Renaissance'.

For intellectual history, the development of humanism and the rediscovery of classical learning, see W. K. Ferguson, *The Renaissance in Historical Thought* (Boston 1948), the classic account of the development of thinking about the Renaissance; B. Kohl and Ronald C. Witt, eds, *The Earthly Paradise: Italian humanists on government and society* (Manchester 1978) – texts in translation with a useful introduction; P. O. Kristeller, *The Classics and Renaissance Thought* (Cambridge, Mass. 1955) and Roberto Weiss, *The Renaissance Discovery of Classical Antiquity* (Oxford 1969), the best account of the cult of ancient objects and ideas.

The major artists have all been the subject of specialized studies. On art in general, Michael Baxandall's *Painting and Experience in fifteenth century Italy* (Oxford 1972) raises fundamental issues in a short compass. Ernst Gombrich's *Norm and Form* (London 1966) and *Symbolic Images* (London 1972) are collections of essays on iconographical subjects, exemplifying – with illustrations – the fusion of thought into art. Three volumes of the Penguin series 'Style and Civilization' also offer guidance in relating art to ideas: Michael Levey, *The Early Renaissance* (Harmondsworth 1967) and *The High Renaissance* (Harmondsworth 1975); and John Shearman, *Mannerism* (Harmondsworth 1967). F. Starn and L. Partridge, *A Renaissance Likeness. Art and Culture in Raphael's Julius II* (California 1980) explores the depth of meaning that can be found in a single work. On sculpture the standard works are John Pope-Hennessy, *Italian Renaissance Sculpture* (London 1958) and *Italian High Renaissance and Baroque Sculpture* (London 1963); on architecture Peter Murray, *The Architecture of the Italian Renaissance* (London 1963); and on music H. M. Brown, *Music in the Renaissance* (Englewood Cliffs and London 1976).

Turning to individual cities, Florence has inevitably stimulated the greatest amount of discussion. The histories of Machiavelli and Guicciardini are still highly readable and easily accessible in translation. Felix Gilbert, *Machiavelli and Guicciardini: politics and history in sixteenth century Florence* (Princeton 1965) places them in their context. To this should be added George Holmes, *The Florentine Enlightenment 1400–1450* (London 1969) and Gene Brucker, *Renaissance Florence* (California 1969). On Venice the most accessible book is D. S. Chambers, *The Imperial Age of Venice 1380–1580*

(London 1970) attractive and heavily illustrated; on Rome, Peter Partner, *Renaissance Rome 1500–1559* (California 1976); and on Ferrara, W. Gundersheimer, *Ferrara: the style of a Renaissance despotism* (Princeton 1972) an elegant demonstration of the why and how of princely rule.

Of Castiglione's *Courtier* there is a fine Elizabethan translation by Sir Thomas Hoby (1561) and a modern one by G. Bull (1967). For critical comment see J. R. Woodhouse, *Baldesar Castiglione: a reassessment of 'The Courtier'* (Edinburgh 1978).

Fuller bibliographies, as well as brief entries on all personalities and topics touched upon in this chapter, may be found in J. R. Hale, ed., *A Concise Encyclopaedia of the Italian Renaissance* (London 1981). It covers history, art and manners and is intended to lead to further study.

IV Disaster and Recovery

Among the many works covering the history of the various states that made up Italy in this period, the most important include the series *Storia d'Italia*, edited by G. Galasso and published by Einaudi (Turin). Volumes now published relevant to my chapter are: Vol. 9, Claudio Costantini, *La Repubblica di Genoa* (1978); Vol. 13¹, Furio Diaz, *Il Granducato di Toscana, I Medici* (1976); Vol. 14, Mario Caravale and Alberto Caracciole, *Lo Stato Pontificio* (1978); Vol. 17, Lino Martini et al., *I ducati padani, Trento e Trieste* (1979). For states not yet covered in this series, see: Guido d'Agostino and Giuseppe Coniglio, *Storia di Napoli*, Società Editrice 'Storia di Napoli', (Naples) Vol. 5; Federico Chabod, *Storia di Milano nell'epoca di Carlo V* (Turin 1961); Giuseppe Giarizzo, *La Sicilia dal viceregno al regno*, (Naples 1978); Francesco Caracciolo, *Il Regno di Napoli nei secoli XVI e XVII* (Rome 1966); Helmut Koenigsberger, *The Government of Sicily under Philip II* (London 1951); Jean Delumeau, *Rome au XVIe siècle* (Paris 1975); Paolo Prodi, *Il sovrano pontefice* (Bologna 1982).

Books dealing with individual cities in the period 1527–1750 include: Francesco Cognasso, *Storia di Torino* (Milan 1961); J. R. Hale, ed., *Renaissance Venice* (London 1973); Gaetano Cozzi, *Repubblica di Venezia e Stati italiani* (Turin 1982); John Julius Norwich, *A History of Venice* (London and New York 1982), Part 4; Eric Cochrane, *Florence in the Forgotten Centuries* (Chicago 1973); Peter Partner, *Renaissance Rome, 1500–1559* (Berkeley and London 1976); Marino Berengo, *Nobili e mercanti nella Lucca del Cinquecento* (Turin 1965).

Among the many studies of High Renaissance and Mannerist culture, the following are particularly relevant to my account: *Storia dell'arte italiana*, ed. Giovanni Previtali and Federico Zeri (Turin 1979); *Storia della cultura veneta*, Vol. 3 (Venice 1980–81); *Omaggio a Tiziano, La cultura artistica milanese nell'età di Carlo V* (Milan 1977); *Ricerche sulla cultura dell'Italia moderna*, ed.

Paola Zambelli (Bari 1973); Riccardo Scrivano, *Il manierismo nella letteratura del Cinquecento* (Padua 1959); Peter Murray, *The Architecture of the Italian Renaissance* (London 1963); Marco Ariani, *Tra classicismo e manierismo* (Florence 1974); Paul Renucci, 'La cultura', in Vol. 2² of *Storia d'Italia* (1974); Carlo Dionisotti, *Geografia e storia della letteratura italiana* (Turin 1967); *La Rinascenza a Firenze: Il Cinquecento* (Rome 1981); Bernard Weinberg, *A History of Literary Criticism in the Italian Renaissance* (Chicago 1981); Eric Cochrane, *Historians and Historiography in the Italian Renaissance* (Chicago 1981).

Important examinations of the significant role of religion and the Church in the Cinquecento include: *Problemi di vita religiosa in Italia nel Cinquecento* (Padua 1960); *Il Concilio di Trento e la riforma tridentina* (Rome and Freibourg 1962); *Storia della Compagnia di Gesù in Italia*, Vol. 4: Mario Scaduto, *L'epoca di Giacomo Lainez* (Rome 1974); Carlo Ginzburg, *Il Nicodemismo* (Turin 1970); Antonio Rotondò, *Studi e ricerche di storia ereticale italiana del Cinquecento* (Turin 1974); Delio Cantimori, *Eretici italiani del Cinquecento* (Florence 1967); Paolo Prodi, *Il cardinale Gabriele Paleotti* (Rome 1959).

Various aspects of the social and economic conditions prevailing in Italy during the period 1527–1750 are dealt with in the following books: Carlo Cipolla, *Before the Industrial Revolution: European Society and Economy, 1000–1700* (New York 1976); Cipolla has also written several monographs on the plague; Giuseppe Galasso, *Economia e società nella Calabria del Cinquecento* (Naples 1967); Domenico Gioffrè, *Gênes et les foires de change* (Paris 1960); Ottavia Niccoli, *I sacerdoti, i guerrieri, i contadini* (Turin 1979); Marco Spallanzani, ed., *La lana come materia prima* (Florence 1974); Renzo Paci, *La scala di Spalato e il commercio fra Cinque e Seicento* (Venice 1971); Domenico Sella, *Crisis and Continuity: The economy of Spanish Lombardy in the Seventeenth Century* (Cambridge, Mass. 1979); Guaro Coppola, *Il mais nell'economia agricola lombarda* (Bologna 1979); Paolo Malanima, *La Decadenza di un'economia cittadina* (Bologna 1982).

More information about the arts and sciences of 17th-century Italy can be found in: Paul Lawrence Rose, *The Italian Renaissance of Mathematics* (Geneva 1975); Riccardo Scrivano, *La norma e lo scarto* (Rome 1980); Edoardo Taddeo, *Il manierismo letterario e i lirici veneziani* (Rome 1974); James Mirollo, *The Poet of the Marvellous: Giambattista Marino* (Columbia 1963); Michael Murrin, *The Allegorical Epic* (Chicago 1980); Paolo Cherchi, *Enciclopedismo e politica della riscrittura: Tommaso Garzoni* (Pisa 1980); Cesare Vasoli, *L'enciclopedismo del Seicento* (Naples 1978); Ernan McMullin, ed., *Galileo, Man of Science* (New York and London 1967); Paolo Galluzzi, *Momento: Studi Galileiani* (Rome 1979); Giovanni Papuli, *Girolamo Balduino: Ricerche sulla logica della scuola di Padova* (Manduria 1967).

Finally, the age of the Baroque and its aftermath – 'Arcadia' – have been analysed in numerous studies, the most important of which include: Rudolf Wittkower, *Art and Architecture in Italy, 1600–1750* (Harmondsworth 1958); Francis Haskell, *Patrons and Painters* (London 1963); Paolo Portoghesi, *The Rome of Borromini* (New York 1968); *L'effimero barocco: Strutture della festa nella Roma del '600* (Rome 1978); Salvatore Boscarino, *Sicilia barocca* (Rome 1978); Marco Fantuzzi, *Meccanismi narrative nel romanzo barocco* (Padua 1975); Ezio Raimondi, *Poesia come retorica* (Florence 1980); Maria Teresa Muraro, ed., *Venezia e il melodramma del Seicento* (Florence 1980); Franco Croce, *Tre momenti del barocco letterario italiano* (Florence 1966); Vittor Ivo Comparato, *Uffici e società a Napoli (1600–1647)* (Florence 1974), Rosario Villari, *Ribelli e riformatori* (Rome 1970); Maurizio Torrini, *Dopo Galileo: Una polemica scientifica* (Florence 1979); Paolo Rossi, *I segni del tempo* (Milan 1979); Raffaele Ajello, ed., *Pietro Giannone e il suo tempo* (Naples 1980).

V The Age of Romanticism

The most recent history in English of Italy during this period is Stuart Woolf, *A History of Italy 1700–1860* (London 1979). It contains an extensive bibliography. An earlier version of this appeared in *Dal primo settecento all'Unità*, vol. 3 (1973) of the *Storia d'Italia*, edited by G. Galasso and published by Einaudi (Turin), which also contains an important essay by Franco Venturi, the leading historian of Italy in the 18th century. A selection of his essays has been translated and published in England under the title *Italy and the Enlightenment* (London 1972). Denis Mack Smith has published a number of important studies of the Risorgimento, including *Cavour and Garibaldi in 1860* (London 1954) and *Garibaldi* (London 1957), as well as a general history of Italy in the 19th century. Pastor's *Lives of the Popes* (English translation, London, from 1891) remains indispensable, but deals with only the first part of the period covered in this chapter. Owen Chadwick's *The Popes and European Revolution* (Oxford 1981) is of the highest interest and importance. Volumes XII, XIII and XIV of the seventeen volumes of the *Storia di Milano* (Fondazione Treccani, 1953–66) constitute the best available study of every aspect of Milanese history in the 18th and first half of the 19th centuries. For an introduction to Caserta and Naples in the 18th century see the catalogue in two volumes of *The Golden Age of Naples* (Detroit and Chicago 1981). The fuller Italian catalogues of the parent version of this exhibition were published in 1979 (*Civiltà del '700 a Napoli*). Many of the articles in the Italian Encyclopaedia are of great value, and although the *Dizionario Biografico degli Italiani* has only reached the letter C, it should be consulted wherever possible.

The background to archaeological excavations and museums in 18th-century Rome is discussed in Francis Haskell and Nicholas Penny, *Taste and the Antique* (New Haven and London 1981), which has an extensive bibliography.

A number of specialized studies of Neoclassical and Romantic architecture have been published in Italy in recent years. There is a useful general survey in English by Carroll L. Meeks: *Italian architecture, 1750–1914* (New Haven 1966), and a valuable study of the situation in Milan during the revolutionary years by Carroll William Westfall ('Antolini's Foro Bonaparte in Milan' in the *Journal of the Warburg and Courtauld Institutes*, 1969).

For painting, see the catalogue *Painting in Italy in the Eighteenth Century: Rococo to Romanticism* (Chicago, Minneapolis and Toledo 1970). The period after 1800 has not been seriously discussed in English, and even Italian surveys are patchy.

The literature on Piranesi is now vast. Important books have been written in English by Jonathan Scott (1975), John Wilton-Ely (1978) and Nicholas Penny (1978).

English and American historians of Italian literature tend to get rather bored after the Renaissance and none known to me can be recommended whole-heartedly as far as the later period is concerned. An early 19th-century English translation of Alfieri's memoirs has been edited by E. R. Vincent (Cambridge 1953), who has also written an account of Foscolo's life in England: *Ugo Foscolo: an Italian in Regency England* (London 1961). There is an excellent biography of Leopardi by Iris Origo (London 1953) and Manzoni's *I Promessi Sposi* has been translated by Archibald Colquhoun. Belli has aroused some interest in England and America in recent years, but his poems are not easily translatable, and the essential literature on him is in Italian.

There are basic studies of individual composers and of music as a whole in the new edition (London 1981) of *Grove's Dictionary of Music and Musicians*. Stendhal's *Vie de Rossini* (which exists in various French editions) remains indispensable for conveying the atmosphere of the time; there is an English translation by Richard N. Coe (London 1956).

Neo-Classicism (Harmondsworth 1968) and *Romanticism* (London 1980) by Hugh Honour (who has written a number of fundamental articles on Canova) set the Italian achievement within the wider European context.

VI Modern Italy

Useful general studies with the most complete and up-to-date information are: the *Storia d'Italia* edited by G. Galasso and published by Einaudi (Turin) and in particular the three parts of vol. 4, V. Castronovo, *La storia economica* (Turin 1975); A. Asor Rosa, *La cultura* (Turin 1975); E. Ragionieri, *La storia politica e sociale* (Turin 1976); G. Candeloro, *Storia dell'Italia moderna*, 9 vols (Milan 1956–81); the series published by Il Mulino *Storia d'Italia dall'Unità alla Repubblica* of which only three volumes have been published: R. Romanelli, *L'Italia liberale 1861–1900* (Bologna 1979), A. Aquarone, *L'Italia giolittiana 1896–1915*, I, *Le premesse politiche ed economiche* (Bologna 1981), and D. Veneruso, *L'Italia fascista 1922–1945* (Bologna 1981); finally, see also G. Carocci, *Storia d'Italia dall' Unità ad oggi* (Milan 1975).

Other extremely helpful works are: D. Mack Smith, *Italy, A modern history* (Ann Arbor 1959); Christopher Seton-Watson, *Italy from liberalism to Fascism, 1870–1925* (London 1967); and the second volume of G. Procacci's *Storia degli italiani* (Bari 1968).

Under the title *Il mondo contemporaneo. Storia d'Italia*, 3 vols, F. Levi, U. Levra and N. Tranfaglia have put together a group of subjects in the style of an encyclopaedia, each containing a useful bibliography (Florance 1978).

Concerning individual events and separate aspects of the history of modern Italy, excellent anthologies of documents are available such as those dealing with the 'Mezzogiorno' problem: R. Villari, *Il Sud nella storia d'Italia* (Bari 1966); economic development: L. Cafagna, *Il Nord nella storia d'Italia* (Bari 1972); Socialism: G. Manacorda, *Il socialismo nella storia d'Italia* (Bari 1970); the Parliament: G. Carocci, *Il Parlamento nella storia d'Italia* (Bari 1964); the Italian image abroad: E. Ragionieri, *Italia giudicata 1861–1945* (Bari 1969); and the Church: P. Scoppola, *Chiesa e Stato nella storia d'Italia* (Bari 1967).

On economic history see the *Breve storia della grande industria in Italia* by R. Romeo (Bologna 1965) and the essays edited by G. Fuà, *Lo sviluppo economico in Italia. Storia della economia italiana negli ultimi cento anni* (Milan 1969) and by G. Toniolo, *Lo sviluppo economico italiano 1861–1940* (Bari 1973).

On the subject of foreign policy, there is F. Chabod's classic work *Storia della politica estera italiana dal 1870 al 1896*, vol. 1, *Le Premesse* (Bari 1951); see also C. Morandi, *La politica estera dell'Italia. Da Porta Pia all'età giolittiana* (Florence 1972) and G. Carocci, *La politica estera dell'Italia fascista 1925–1928* (Bari 1969).

Extremely useful works concerning Fascism are: L. Salvatorelli and G. Mira, *Storia d'Italia nel periodo fascista* (Turin 1956); E. Santarelli, *Storia del movimento e del regime fascista*, 2 vols (Rome 1967); the monumental political biography of Mussolini by R. De Felice of which the first 5 volumes have appeared (Turin 1965–81); the excellent work of P. Spriano, *Storia del Partito comunista italiano*, 5 vols (Turin 1967–75).

On the Second World War and the Resistance one can still profitably consult R. Battaglia *La Seconda guerra mondiale* (Rome 1960) and *Storia della Resistenza italiana* (Turin 1953).

Finally, of the few historical works which exist dealing with the most recent period, we should note N. Kogan, *L'Italia del dopoguerra* (Bari 1968); G. Mammarella, *L'Italia dalla caduta del fascismo ad oggi* (Bologna 1974); the essays collected by V. Castronovo, *L'Italia contemporanea 1945–1975* (Turin 1976) and the fundamental study by P. Sylos Labini, *Saggio sulle classi sociali* (Bari 1974).

Sources of Illustrations

Sources of Illustrations

Index